The White House's
Unruly Neighborhood

The White House's Unruly Neighborhood

*Crime, Scandal and Intrigue
in the History of Lafayette Square*

EDWARD P. MOSER

McFarland & Company, Inc., Publishers
Jefferson, North Carolina

ISBN (print) 978-1-4766-7486-5
ISBN (ebook) 978-1-4766-3693-1

LIBRARY OF CONGRESS AND BRITISH LIBRARY
CATALOGUING DATA ARE AVAILABLE

© 2020 Edward P. Moser. All rights reserved

*No part of this book may be reproduced or transmitted in any form
or by any means, electronic or mechanical, including photocopying
or recording, or by any information storage and retrieval system,
without permission in writing from the publisher.*

Front cover image: Postcard of the White House, Washington, D.C., ca. 1930–1945
(The Tichnor Brothers Collection / Boston Public Library / Digital Commonwealth)

Printed in the United States of America

*McFarland & Company, Inc., Publishers
Box 611, Jefferson, North Carolina 28640
www.mcfarlandpub.com*

To lovers of history, the study of everything
until the moment that just passed.

It's been a long time, but some things you never forget.
—Marion Barry

Table of Contents

Acknowledgments — ix
Preface — 1

1. The Secretary of State Is Nearly Stabbed to Death — 3
2. The Unsung Slave Whose Family Sparked a Civil Rights Revolution — 7
3. The Perilous Life of America's Greatest Foreign Friend — 10
4. The Craziest Inaugural Party of Them All — 17
5. The Biggest Slave Escape in American History — 21
6. The "Big Cheese" Receives a Mammoth Gift — 26
7. Mrs. Lincoln's Sad Search for Her Deceased Son — 30
8. The Plantation Owner's Startling Army of Diversity — 35
9. The Burning of the White House and the Rescue of Its Riches — 40
10. A White House Surgery That Echoed Bullets and Brawls — 44
11. The Populist Politics of Pennsylvania Avenue's Park — 49
12. The Biggest Sex Scandal in Washington's History — 52
13. The Tragic Wife of America's Premier Thinker — 57
14. The Secret Life of the Intrepid Explorer — 62
15. The Cunning Craft of a Deadly Spy — 68
16. The Backstory of the American Revolution's Martinet — 73
17. The Violent End of America's Bravest Sailor — 80
18. A Duel Between the Oddest and Most Famous of Congress — 88
19. The King of the Camel Corps — 91
20. The Enslaved Woman Who Sued the Head of the State Department — 98
21. The War-Hero Womanizer Who Slayed the Son of Francis Scott Key — 103
22. The Accursed Life of the Man Who Tried to Save the President — 107
23. A Shocking Seedling from the Victory at Yorktown — 111
24. The Bloody Assassination Attempt on President Truman — 117

25.	Lincoln Makes Lee an Offer He Could Refuse	120
26.	The Wretched Life Behind the Gaudiest Place	127
27.	How a Personal Vendetta and Patriotic Passion Led to America's Most Honored Place	134
28.	The Spook Who Spied on the President and Inspired the Formation of the NSA	144
29.	The Most Criminally Inept Family in Military History	149
30.	A Peerless Singer Lays the Groundwork for "I Have a Dream"	155
31.	The Miracle Manse	160
32.	The Lost Barracks of the National Mall	164
33.	George Washington, the Flinty Scot, the Powerful Mayor, and the Children's Angel	169
34.	The Near Drowning of the President in the Potomac	177
35.	The Forgotten Terror Attack	180
36.	A President's Brush with Death After a Deadly Navy Accident	184
37.	The Poetess Behind America's Most Inspiring Song	191
38.	Hamilton! The Tour!!: A White House Area Itinerary	198
39.	Murder Bay and Hooker's Division	209
40.	A Wartime Tavern Keeper's Unwanted Guests	215
41.	A Humble Cleaning Lady Gulls a Mighty Invader	218
42.	The Entrepreneur and the Ingénue: A Match Made in Heaven Gone to Hell	222
43.	The Black Businessman Whose Workplace Birthed Jim Crow	227
44.	The Financial Wizard Who Helped Stave Off a Civil War	233
45.	The Crooked Bank for the Former Slaves	238

Index   245

Acknowledgments

The many institutions and publications providing information on the rich history of Washington, D.C., Lafayette Square, and the White House and Treasury Department environs were a boon to the author. Sources included the Library of Congress, the National Archives, the White House Historical Association, the Smithsonian, the Ghosts of DC blog, Cultural Tourism DC, the Architect of the Capitol, and the Guild of Professional Tour Guides of Washington, D.C., as well as writers Claudia Swain, James L. Swanson, Robert V. Remini, and John DeFerrari (of the Streets of Washington blog), to mention a few chroniclers of the place.

This book is largely based on stories researched for, and described in, the author's "Lafayette Square Tour of Scandal, Assassination, and Spies" (https://www.meetup.com/Lafayette-Sq-Tours-of-Scandal-Assassination-Spies-Meetup/).

The author would like to thank his middle school instructor, Father John Shelley, and his own parents, Rose and Ed, lovers of books and periodicals, for inspiring the love of history threaded through this book. The study of history is a noble and far-reaching pursuit, for it is the study of all things, right up to the moment that just passed.

Preface

The great bulk of the millions of tourists who visit the White House area each year briefly view the front entrance of the presidential mansion and take a few photographs and selfies before moving on. A small percentage of the visitors do the standard, hour-long tour of the White House or take a stroll through Lafayette Square, or walk along the adjacent 17th or 15th streets to and from the museums and memorials of the National Mall.

But a careful look at the neighborhood's buildings, byways, and famous and forgotten personalities reveals two centuries of drama. Lafayette Square has borne witness to high-profile murders, slave escapes, assassination attempts, infamous spies, lascivious Lotharios, femme fatales, and a throng of heroes and heroines both celebrated and unsung.

This book reveals the wild, hidden history of one of the most historic, if often overlooked, locales in the world. Enjoy the thrilling saga of a neighborhood that is America's story in brief.

1

The Secretary of State Is Nearly Stabbed to Death

U.S. Court of Appeals for the Federal Circuit, 717 Madison Place, the Former Site of the William Seward and Commodore Rodgers Mansion

On the evening of April 14, 1865, the Secretary of State could hardly believe his bad luck. It seemed as though everyone in Washington was celebrating the victory of the Union in the Civil War—except him. Just the week before, the Confederate capital of Richmond, Virginia, had fallen, and General Lee had surrendered. Each day and night in the federal city, excited crowds celebrated to the toot and stomp of marching bands. But on April 5, the 63-year-old William Seward had been thrown from his carriage. He had broken his jaw, smashed up his ribs, and dislocated a shoulder. Since then he'd been confined to a bedroom on the third floor of his house on Lafayette Square. His neck was in a metal brace, his shoulder in a sling.

Seward was one of President Lincoln's top advisors. He had persuaded the powers of Europe to stay neutral during the war. Now he was an injured man confined to his home. If anyone should have gotten to celebrate, it should have been him. But at least Seward had his magnificent house. It was spacious and so convenient: just a stroll across Pennsylvania Avenue from his boss, the President. Seward resided in a mansion built by a Navy hero of the early republic, John Rodgers.

Commodore Rodgers had been a legend of the sea service. Once, during a voyage in the North Sea under arctic conditions, his men feared Rodgers was leading them to their deaths. In protest, they refused to work. Rodgers could have ordered them hanged. Instead, he led by example. Stripping to the waist, he climbed a mast and in freezing gusts made repairs to the riggings himself. Ashamed, his crewmen ended their mini-mutiny and aided their captain in his work, helping him complete a safe return to port.

During the War of 1812, Rodgers captured more than 20 British ships. This was an unheard-of feat against the invincible Royal Navy and its merchant marine. In revenge, when an English fleet in 1813 raided towns and harbors throughout Chesapeake Bay, its Admiral, George Cockburn, singled out Rodgers. Royal Marines were dispatched to burn down Rodgers' Maryland home.

Like the valiant Commodore, Seward and Lincoln endured much to achieve victory. The injured Secretary of State had that as solace—and the comfort of his family. In the house that night were three of his sons: Frederick Seward, an Assistant Secretary of State; Augustus Seward, a Union Army Major; and his youngest son, William Seward, Jr., also a

Union officer. His daughter, the slight, 19-year-old Frances "Fanny" Seward, was watching over him. Also in his bedroom were a male nurse as well as a bodyguard, Sergeant George Robinson. Not that a bodyguard seemed needed in the heart of a Union capital defended by thousands of troops, in a home right across from the White House and the War and Navy Departments, during a war that was all but over, run by a President who waved aside pleas that he move about with an armed escort.

An Unwelcome Visitor

Around 10 p.m. that cool, damp night, as Seward lay resting in his house, a sharp knock was heard on the front door. The African-American butler, the youthful William Bell, answered it. On the doorstep he spied a tall, well-dressed, and very muscular man whose accent betrayed a Georgia and Florida upbringing. The hulking, 20-year-old, former soldier carried a package. He said it contained medicine that Seward's doctor had ordered him to deliver personally to the Secretary of State. The butler answered that no one could see Seward and that he would take the medicine to him. But the visitor was insistent on delivering the package himself. He added angrily he would never take orders from "a nigger." With Bell in tow, the man rushed up the stairs of the house.

On the third floor he was met by Frederick Seward, who adamantly refused to let the man see his father. Frederick figured the visitor was too dimwitted to realize strangers couldn't be allowed in the house. The intruder, named Lewis Powell, pulled out a revolver. He pointed it at Frederick Seward. He pulled the trigger. The gun misfired. He then beat Seward over the head with the butt of the gun. The Assistant Secretary of State crashed to the floor with a fractured skull.

A horrified Bell ran down the stairs, screaming, "Murder! Murder!"

Seward's daughter, Fanny, then made an understandable mistake. Hearing the ruckus in the hall, she opened the door to Seward's bedroom, giving away its location. Powell rushed toward it. In the corridor he ran into Seward's son Augustus and stabbed him. Powell, a Confederate veteran of Gettysburg, pushed his way into Seward's bedroom. In the dim light he stabbed the nurse in the lungs, knifed Sergeant Robinson, and injured Fanny as well.

Lewis Powell leapt onto the cot of the Secretary of State and slashed away as Fanny screamed. With his dagger he cut Seward's chest and ripped open his face from ear to chin, leaving a great chunk of flesh hanging from the cheek. He literally went for the jugular, slashing at the neck, but the metal brace Seward had worn since the carriage accident kept his throat from being slit. In desperation, Seward rolled over, crashed onto the floor, and crawled under the protective cover of the bedframe. In falling down, he broke his shoulder again. Bleeding and in shock, he fell into unconsciousness.

Meanwhile, Sergeant Robinson and the nurse jumped on top of Powell. Despite their own wounds, they managed to wrestle him out of the room. In the hall, another of the Secretary's sons, William Seward, Jr., confronted the marauder. Powell knifed him in the abdomen. Certain he'd killed Secretary Seward, Powell hurried back toward the stairs. He bumped into a State Department messenger named Emerick Hansell and left him with a paralyzing knife wound in the back.

The Confederate veteran was like a "Terminator"—in minutes, and without a working gun, he injured eight persons. Powell bounded down the stairs, left the house, and walked back into Lafayette Square. He mounted his horse, trotted up to H Street, and headed east.

An Atrocity's Aftermath

In the bedroom, Fanny was also certain her father had died. But Seward opened his eyes. He said, "I'm not dead. Send for a doctor. Send for the police. Close the house."

Word then filtered into Lafayette Square of Lincoln's assassination at Ford's Theater. Rumors flew among residents that assassins had killed Cabinet members, that a Confederate army had entered the city. In the meantime, Powell, possessed with considerable nerve but a lousy sense of direction, botched his getaway. Instead of fleeing into Maryland and meeting up with Lincoln's killer, John Wilkes Booth, he got lost in the city. He may have hidden out for some time in Congressional Cemetery, perhaps by the gravestones of the family of Mary Surratt, in whose boardinghouse the members of the Lincoln conspiracy had met.

Three days after his assault on Seward, Powell showed up at Surrat's lodging (which is today the Wok and Roll Restaurant in D.C.'s Chinatown). He hoped to reconnect with his fellow conspirators. Policemen arrested him there.

Powell was tried, convicted, and sentenced to hang with his accused fellow plotters. These were Mary Surrat, Powell accomplice David Herold, and George Atzerodt, the would-be killer of Vice President Andrew Johnson. While in prison aboard a Union Navy gunship, Powell tried to kill himself by banging his head against a metal wall. He lived and was made to wear a padded hood.

The conspirators were executed that July at the Washington Arsenal, today's Fort McNair across from the Jefferson Memorial and Hains Point. Yet Powell cheated death—for a while. When the hangman dropped his body from the scaffold, Powell was strong enough to pull his knees up to his chest, preventing his neck from breaking.

Photographer Alexander Gardner took pictures of Lewis Powell in prison after his arrest for the attempted assassination of Secretary of State William Seward (Library of Congress, photograph by Alexander Gardner).

He dangled and kicked in the air for five minutes before his body finally went slack. He may have suffocated from the hood on his head.

Secretary Seward survived his knife wounds. A week after the attack, he gazed from the window of his home out onto Pennsylvania Avenue. There he saw the horse-drawn coach bearing the body of Abraham Lincoln en route to Philadelphia, and then New York, and then westward across the nation to its final resting place in Springfield, Illinois.

Lafayette Square, seemingly an oasis of calm in a bustling city, could be a wild and bloody place.

Sources

Bishop, Jim. *The Day Lincoln Was Shot*. New York: Harper Perennial, 2013 (originally published in 1955).

Greenspan, Jesse. "The Other Targets of Booth's Murder Conspiracy." *History*, April 15, 2015. https://www.history.com/news/the-other-targets-of-booths-murder-conspiracy.

History Engine. "The Attempted Assassination of Secretary Seward." University of Richmond, 2008–2009.

Linder, Douglas O. "Trial of the Lincoln Assassination Conspirators: Lewis Powell." *Famous Trials*. University of Missouri–Kansas City School of Law, 2012.

Morgan, David. "Lincoln Assassination: The Other Murder Attempt." CBS News. *Sunday Morning*, May 10, 2015. https://www.cbsnews.com/news/lincoln-assassination-the-other-murder-attempt/.

Paullin, Charles Oscar. *Commodore John Rodgers: Captain*. Cleveland: Arthur H. Clark, 1910.

Stahr, Walter. *Seward: Lincoln's Indispensable Man*. New York: Simon & Schuster, 2012. 1st ed. https://www.amazon.com/Seward-Lincolns-Indispensable-Walter-Stahr/dp/1439121168/ref=tmm_hrd_swatch_0?_encoding=UTF8&qid=&sr=.

Swain, Claudia. WETA. *Boundary Stones*. "Even More Little Known Victims of the Lincoln Assassination Plot," March 28, 2013. https://blogs.weta.org/boundarystones/2013/03/28/even-more-little-known-victims-lincoln-assassination-plot.

Swanson, James. *Manhunt: The 12-Day Chase for Lincoln's Killer*. New York: Harper Collins, 2006.

2

The Unsung Slave Whose Family Sparked a Civil Rights Revolution

Southeast Side of the Square, Near Madison Place and Pennsylvania Avenue

In the early years of the capital, a visitor might have seen the President of the United States, Thomas Jefferson, dismount near this spot. Jefferson was a noted equestrian and took a daily two-hour ride through the then-rustic federal village. In fact, the low white colonnade connecting the White House to today's West Wing was originally a stable built by Presidents Jefferson and John Adams for the horses of the Chief Magistrate.

Even more than horses, Jefferson loved food, particularly fresh fruits and vegetables of the kind he and his servants grew at his Monticello gardens and of the type served at his White House dinners. In fact, the Library of Congress has a handwritten produce chart of Jefferson's from that time. On one side it lists the 37 vegetables and fruits then sold in the Washington region, and on the other side when each was in season.

The young city had several produce markets. The biggest was Center Market, founded by Jefferson, on Pennsylvania Avenue and 7th Street. With the construction in 1997 of the Capital One sports and music arena near the long-vanished market, the area has again become a center of the city's commercial life. Jefferson also founded the original Eastern Market, for the benefit of the nearby Congress. It's said he shopped at those markets himself, sometimes running into his rival politico, Supreme Court Chief Justice John Marshall.

An Enslaved Entrepreneur

Right outside the White House was another food market. It was smaller but of high quality. President Jefferson and his French chef shopped there. Its exact location is unclear, but the then-busy intersection of Pennsylvania Avenue and Madison Place would have been a logical place for it. The enterprise was run by a remarkable woman who would have a remarkable impact across two centuries on the nation's capital and the nation generally.

The lady was Alethia Browning Tanner. A slave, she was owned by the mother of the Maryland Governor Thomas Pratt. Alethia was the daughter of a British man and a woman of African descent. She lived in Anacostia, on the east side of town. She had a lovely name, Alethia, and lovely nicknames: Lethe and Lithe. In Greek, Alethia means an obvious or self-evident truth. Jefferson, who knew Greek, used that phrase in the opening sentence of his Declaration of Independence. Perhaps he thought of it when he shopped at Alethia's store.

Like many slaves in the old Tidewater tobacco region of Maryland, Virginia, and the new capital city, Alethia was hired out for money. Many owners, their tobacco lands worn out and no longer profitable, rented out their slaves. Sometimes they kept their slaves' wages; other times the slaves kept a part of what they earned. Indeed, some slaves were paid 75 cents a day in laboring to help build the White House and the Capitol Building. Others worked for wages in hotels, stables, and other businesses in town.

Alethia Browning Tanner didn't only earn wages, she also ran her own business—a very successful one that catered to the President, diplomats, and Cabinet members, as well as less-famous folk. Alethia may have worked in Jefferson's White House for a time. A letter of his notes a payment to a physician for treating a woman named "Lithe."

The business of Lethe, or Lithe, was so successful she saved enough money to buy her freedom. She did so when she was just 25 years old, on July 10, 1810. The price of her freedom was $1,400, paid in installments of $277. This amounts to about $28,000 today. But Alethia Browning Tanner didn't stop there. As a free woman, she continued to run her grocery and kept pulling in money. She used the profits to buy the liberty of her sister Laura Browning Cook. And of Laura's 10 children. And of Laura's seven grandchildren! She also bought the freedom of seven friends, according to author Tom Lewis.

Alethia was aided in her work by another of her sisters, Sophia Browning Beall, and by their husbands. In fact, as a for-hire gardener, Sophia Beall made enough money to free her own husband.

Long-Term Impacts

Over time, Alethia's actions had a very beneficial impact on the city's African-American community. She and her relatives helped found the Metropolitan African Methodist Episcopal (AME) Church, the oldest continuously operated black church in Washington.

Further, Alethia and three men set up the first school for free blacks in the city. Moreover, one of the nephews she freed, John Cook, Sr., became an influential minister, educator, and civil rights advocate. Cook founded—three blocks north of the White House—the First Colored Presbyterian Church. It in turn gave birth to the nation's first black high school—the Preparatory School for Colored Youth. In 1916, already a noted local institution, it was renamed Dunbar High School, after the black poet Paul Lawrence Dunbar.

In the 20th century, one of Dunbar's graduates, Charles Hamilton Houston, built up the influential law department of Howard University, the predominantly black college named for Civil War General and abolitionist Oliver Otis Howard. As a crusading attorney, Hamilton formulated a clever, and counterintuitive, strategy for overturning the "separate but equal" laws requiring distinct schools, restrooms, and other public facilities for blacks and whites. Hamilton and his legal team sued to make towns operating under such directives build separate facilities that were in fact equal in quality. This placed considerable financial stress on such communities, spurring them to end segregation.

In 1954, Charles Hamilton Houston won an epochal case. That was *Brown vs. Board of Education*, the Supreme Court ruling that overturned public school segregation in the United States. A fellow attorney in the suit was Hamilton's protégée, Thurgood Marshall, later the first black Supreme Court Justice.

Thus the enslaved businesswoman Alethia Tanner Browning, the grocer to the President—by gaining the freedom of herself and her relations and by helping found influential churches and schools—set off a chain of events that 150 years later sparked a civil rights revolution.

And she operated her enterprise right from Lafayette Square.

Sources

Baltimore Sun. "Thurgood Marshall, Civil Rights Lawyer," February 26, 2007. http://www.baltimoresun.com/features/black-history-month/bal-blackhistory-thurgood-story.html.

Beckert, Sven. *Empire of Cotton: A Global History.* New York: Vintage, 2015.

Cultural Tourism DC. "Fifteenth Street Presbyterian Church, African American Heritage Trail." https://www.culturaltourismdc.org/portal/fifteenth-street-presbyterian-church-african-american-heritage-trail.

Gatewood, Willard B., Jr. "John Francis Cook: Antebellum Black Presbyterian." *American Presbyterians* 67 (Fall 1989).

Harbster, Jennifer. Library of Congress. "The President and the Parsnip: Thomas Jefferson's Vegetable Market Chart (1801–1808)," April 15, 2015. https://blogs.loc.gov/inside_adams/2015/04/the-president-and-the-parsnip-thomas-jeffersons-vegetable-market-chart-1801–1808/.

Lewis, Tom. *Washington: A History of Our National City.* New York: Basic Books, 2015.

National Archives. *Founders Online.* "Statement of Account with Edward Gantt, 20 November 1802." https://founders.archives.gov/documents/Jefferson/01-39-02-0033.

Sharp, John G. "Alethia 'Lethe' Browning Tanner." *Washington, D.C., Genealogy Trails.* http://genealogytrails.com/washdc/biographies/bio6.html.

Smith, Jesse Carney, ed. *Notable Black American Women.* Book 2. Farmington Hills, MI, 1995.

University of Virginia. "Opportunity: Race in Anacostia through the Civil War." *American Studies.* http://xroads.virginia.edu/~cap/anacostia/early.html.

White House Historical Association. "Self-emancipation in Lafayette Park," April 15, 2015. https://www.whitehousehistory.org/self-emancipation-in-lafayette-park.

3

The Perilous Life of America's Greatest Foreign Friend

Lafayette Statue, Southeast Part of the Square

The former President's Park is justly named for Marie Joseph Paul Yves Roche Gilbert du Motier—Marquis de Lafayette.

Without France, its critical ally, America likely would have lost its war of independence. Lafayette, France's most important representative to the fledgling United States, gets a good share of the credit. Lafayette was only 19 years old when the Continental Congress appointed him a Major General. He joined George Washington's remarkable, and youthful, staff. It included 19-year-old Lt. Colonel Alexander Hamilton as well as Hamilton's friend and fellow aide-de-camp to Washington, 22-year-old John Laurens.

Along with his precocious nature, Lafayette was a visionary, far ahead of his time. He was in favor of democracy and democratic republics before any of any size, in the U.S., and much later France, had been established. He was an abolitionist almost a century before America abolished slavery and two generations before the British Empire did. He was a prominent advocate of the French Revolution's ban on it before Napoleon brought it back. Lafayette was ever nudging his friends among the Virginian leadership of the American Revolution—Washington, Jefferson, Madison, Monroe, and others—to do more about restricting slavery. And the Marquis practiced what he preached. In 1785, he set up a spice plantation in French Guiana, which over time freed and educated over 60 enslaved workers there. It was an experiment in manumission, giving liberty to slaves. Unfortunately, when the French government imprisoned Lafayette during the French Revolution, his plantation, Le Belle Gabrielle, was confiscated and its laborers sold off.

The Marquis could be a pain in the side. Along with hectoring American leaders about slavery, he goaded General Washington into letting him fight in the Revolution. Washington was reluctant: Lafayette might die in battle, robbing the Americans of their liaison to France. In 1777 however, Washington allowed Lafayette to fight in the Battle of Brandywine, in Pennsylvania. Yet, as Washington feared, Lafayette was badly wounded, taking a bullet in the calf. Fortunately, a young Virginia sharpshooter, James Monroe, the future President, came upon the Frenchman and tended to him until Washington's own surgeon, James Craik, administered medical aid. Lafayette and Monroe became friends for life.

3. The Perilous Life of America's Greatest Foreign Friend

The Best of Times and the Worst

This 1834 portrait depicts Lafayette in 1791, two years after the start of the French Revolution (Portrait by Joseph Desire Court at the Palace of Versailles).

Lafayette's statue occupies a corner of Lafayette Square, not the center of the park named for him, because the figure of Andrew Jackson preceded it there. Jackson's statue dates from 1853, a full 38 years before Lafayette's image was sculpted. Congress discussed swapping Jackson and Lafayette, but congressmen from Old Hickory's home state of Tennessee objected.

The sculptors, Alexandre Falguière and Antonin Mercié, put a figure of Lafayette at the top of the monument. The French admirals and counts, the Comte d'Estaing and the Comte de Grasse, are on the east side, on the viewer's right and left, respectively. Ironically, in the American Revolution D'Estaing was largely a failure. Later, in the French Revolution, he made the mistake of defending Queen Marie Antoinette. Just as she had been, D'Estaing was put to death. De Grasse was more successful. His defeat of a British fleet in the run-up to the Battle of Yorktown allowed Lafayette, Alexander Hamilton, and the rest to perform their derring-do at that climactic fight of America's Revolution.

According to National Park Service records on the construction of the statue, its west side is supposed to feature General Rochambeau, to the viewer's left, and General Louis Duportail, to the right. Rochambeau was the commander of the French land forces in America, and Duportail was Washington's chief of military engineers. But some wonder if they are the actual figures there.

"Duportail" rather resembles Lafayette. Further, "Rochambeau" looks little like his portraits. He seems a dead ringer for a Founding Father who served as U.S. Minister to France at the start of the French Revolution in 1789, when Lafayette was commander of the French National Guard and a leader of the Revolution's early, moderate phase. Assuming the figure to the right is Lafayette, the fellow clasping his right hand to the right hand of Lafayette's is Thomas Jefferson.

This makes some sense, as at the time Jefferson, with his "happy talent for composition," cowrote—some say ghostwrote—France's "Declaration of the Rights of Man." That is, France's own influential equivalent of the Declaration of Independence, penned by Jefferson, and of the U.S. Bill of Rights, largely formulated by Jefferson's friend George Mason, and the Constitution, largely crafted by Jefferson's colleague James Madison. Did sculptor Falguière change the original plans and pair an American with the Marquis? One wonders.

In any case, when the French Revolution sank into an orgy of blood, things went badly for Lafayette. The Marquis was a "moderate" revolutionary. He wished to keep Louis XVI as the king but as a constitutional monarch, with an elected parliament holding much of the power. To the regicidal radicals in power, his stance amounted to counterrevolution. Crowds even called for the blood of his wife, Marie Adrienne Françoise de Noailles, Marquise de Lafayette. When Lafayette ordered troops to fire on a mob wanting to oust the King, his status became untenable.

In summer 1792, General Lafayette was leading a French army near the Netherlands against Austrian and Prussian forces seeking to crush the French Revolution. But in Paris, the Ministry of Justice put out a warrant for his arrest. This would have meant imprisonment and death by the guillotine, that novel, "humane" means of execution. Lafayette crossed the border into Holland, then an Austrian province, to escape arrest.

Minister to France Jefferson, in the meantime, had returned to the United States to serve as Secretary of State in President Washington's new federal government. He was succeeded as ambassador by Gouverneur Morris of New York, the author of the Constitution's "We the People" preamble. Morris was in turn succeeded by Jefferson's protégé James Monroe—the very man who had helped save Lafayette's life at the Battle of Brandywine. Monroe then proceeded to save the life of Lafayette's wife.

In the fall of 1792 the French radicals, after failing to arrest Lafayette, imprisoned the Marquise Adrienne and much of her family in Paris. They guillotined her mother, her grandmother, and her aunt. Adrienne herself was slated for execution via the blade.

Minister Monroe and his valiant wife, Elizabeth Kortwright Monroe, schemed to save Adrienne. James Monroe was in a delicate position, as President Washington and his envoys were trying to remain above the fray of France's increasingly tumultuous revolution. So Elizabeth Monroe acted as a kind of stand-in for her husband. She made a big show of visiting Adrienne during her detention at La Force Prison. Mrs. Monroe journeyed there, past the baying mobs of Paris, in a regal diplomatic carriage, complete with liveried coachmen. She met Adrienne, greeted her warmly, and upon leaving announced she'd soon visit Adrienne again. The message was clear: The United States would look unkindly on the execution of the wife of a hero of America's own revolution. The prison authorities backed down and released Adrienne.

Her own life spared, Adrienne's concern became her son, the 13-year-old George Washington Lafayette, the godson of the U.S. President. His life was in peril as long as he remained in France during its Reign of Terror. The Monroes came to the rescue again. They regularly hosted dinners at their Paris home with Adrienne and with a visiting Boston merchant, Tom Perkins. Perkins was struck by Adrienne's predicament. He noted, "She is much worn down by her misfortunes, which she says ... will know no end but in the grave. Poor woman."

The group hatched a plan of escape. Minister Monroe issued an American passport for the son under the name Motier, Lafayette's little-known family name. The credential ignored his aristocratic title, which might have alerted the militants. In the meantime, Perkins obtained the required French travel documents and arranged for a ship. The teen slipped onboard at the port of Le Havre. Several months later George Washington Lafayette arrived safely in New England. He remained for a time in New York, in the care of Alexander Hamilton. Later, he resided with George Washington at the presidential mansion in Philadelphia, and later still at Mt. Vernon.

Yet, Adrienne's life was still at risk. James Monroe got hold of passports for her family from, of all places, the State of Connecticut, as Connecticut had granted American citizenship to the Lafayette family. Adrienne Lafayette was able to leave France with her daughters Anastasie and Virginie. Monroe's securing of documents for Adrienne, her daughters, and her son seems like a scene out of the movie *Casablanca*, where the Humphrey Bogart character provides "letters of transit" to allow the Ingrid Bergman character and her paramour to escape imprisonment and death in Nazi-controlled Morocco.

Imprisonment and a Daring Try at Escape

Meanwhile, Lafayette, after crossing into the Netherlands to escape France's revolutionaries, was arrested by the Prussians—as a revolutionary! The King of Prussia clapped Lafayette into jail. Two years later the Marquis was transferred to a prison in distant Olmütz, a town of Prussian ally Austria in today's Czech Republic.

His plight put President Washington in a bind. Washington had a fatherly affection for Lafayette. But with his new government fragile and his new nation weak, the President wanted to avoid entanglement in Europe's wars. Helping Lafayette could mean taking sides against the coalition of monarchies, including Austria, arrayed against revolutionary France. In any event, the U.S. had no diplomatic relations with Vienna. Moreover, Washington, Hamilton, and Supreme Court Chief Justice John Jay were then hammering out a U.S. policy of neutrality toward France and its chief enemy, Britain. Washington did send James Marshall—the brother of future Supreme Court Chief Justice John Marshall—to Austria for unofficial talks to try to gain Lafayette's release. But the discussions failed.

Still, Washington's men helped the Lafayette family financially while the Marquis languished in jail. Jefferson discovered an obscure legal provision that let the federal government pay Lafayette, with interest, for his half-dozen years of U.S. military service. Washington and Hamilton contributed money of their own, and Gouverneur Morris advanced a hefty sum to Adrienne.

While the American government could do little, friends of Lafayette, including close acquaintances of Hamilton and Jefferson, hatched an astonishing plot in 1794 to rescue the Marquis from prison. The conspirators were Angelica Schuyler Church and her husband

The sister-in-law of Alexander Hamilton, Angelica Schuyler Church, devised a daring plan with her English husband to free Lafayette from prison (Richard Cosway, artist, circa 1790).

John Barker Church. Angelica was the sister of Hamilton's wife, Elizabeth, as well as a friend of Jefferson's. John Church was a pro–French member of the British Parliament. While residing in the U.S. during the American Revolution, he'd supplied arms to American and French soldiers. The Churches decided Lafayette must be freed.

According to documents at Cornell University, the couple hired as their secret agent an Anglo-German physician, Justus Bollman. Dr. Bollman in turn recruited Francis Huger, a South Carolinian attending medical school in Austria. Back in 1777, Huger's family had hosted Lafayette after his arrival in America. On the Continent, Bollman learned of tight security at the Olmütz prison, an indication that a VIP was detained there. He lodged at a tavern nearby and confirmed Lafayette's whereabouts. Next, he befriended the head of the prison's hospital. He persuaded the man to smuggle into Lafayette's hands documents supposedly from the Marquis' relatives. But scrawled on the papers was invisible ink, which when heated revealed plans for a daring escape.

Lafayette was permitted to take occasional carriage rides near the prison under military guard. One afternoon, he and his conveyance, guarded by a corporal, were rolling along in the countryside. Suddenly, Bollman and his fellow agent Huger charged up on their horses. In a wild fracas, they detained the soldier but not before he nearly bit through Lafayette's hand. The two rescuers hoisted the bleeding Marquis up on a horse. Bollman and Huger yelled at Lafayette in English to head to the nearby town of Hof. There another horse-drawn carriage, with a hidden compartment, would whisk him out of Austrian territory and to freedom.

However, Lafayette misheard the command "Go to Hof" as "Get off," as in "Get away from here!" He sprinted ahead on his mount, took a wrong turn, and got lost in the surrounding hills. Betrayed by a workman, he was ambushed by an armed posse of a royal magistrate. The authorities threw him back into the prison and placed him in solitary confinement. The great escape attempt had failed.

Lafayette's woeful situation was alleviated the following year, however, by his courageous wife, Adrienne. After fleeing France, she wangled an interview with the Austrian Emperor by pretending to be someone other than the spouse of a notorious revolutionary. After speaking with Adrienne, the Emperor agreed to allow her and her daughters to join the Marquis in prison. Lafayette's spirits soared with the family reunion. However, Adrienne took sick from the jail's dank conditions and suffered for years from welts and sores. She would die in 1807 at age 48.

In 1797, after five years of confinement for Lafayette, General Napoleon Bonaparte arranged for his release. But for the rest of a long life, Lafayette was a pariah in his own homeland. Due to his calls for democracy Napoleon shunned him. So did Louis XVIII, Louis XVI's grandson, who regained power when Napoleon met his Waterloo in 1815. Until his death in 1834, Lafayette was largely barred from politics.

A Grand Reunion

Yet one nation put out a welcome mat. In 1824 the Marquis, at age 66, made a 16-month tour of the United States, by then an established and rapidly growing democratic republic. With his son, George Washington Lafayette, he traveled by horse and steamship through all 24 U.S. states. Throughout his journey wild crowds greeted him, feted him, named streets for him. Elderly veterans of the Revolutionary War met him with tearful shouts of "Yorktown!" and "Monmouth!" and other battles.

In Tennessee his steamboat sank, but his son saved him. He met, and was charmed by, Andrew Jackson. In Virginia he journeyed to Mt. Vernon and wept at Washington's grave. At Monticello he reconnected with the 81-year-old Jefferson and remained 13 days, his longest stay on the trip, conversing in French and drinking French wine. He was joined there by another ex-President, 73-year-old James Madison. In Massachusetts he supped with another former Chief Executive, John Adams, then 88 years old. (Adams' son John Quincy Adams was elected President that year over Jackson.)

While Lafayette was in the Boston region, its roads packed with 200,000 spectators, he laid the cornerstone to the Bunker Hill Monument, a memorial obelisk to the Revolutionary War battle. The ceremony's keynote speaker, Senator Daniel Webster, said of Lafayette, "Heaven saw fit to ordain the electric spark of liberty should be conducted, through you, from the New World to the Old." To the puzzlement of some, Lafayette arranged to send canvas bags filled with soil from Bunker Hill back to France.

In Washington City, Lafayette was the White House guest of honor of the President—the friend who had fought with him at Brandywine: James Monroe. The Marquis' aide, Auguste Levasseur, was astonished at the simple attire of the President of a republic. He noted the Cabinet room's absence of pomp, instead of "those puerile ornaments which so many ninnies wear in the ante-chambers of the palaces of Europe." At this time, Monroe renamed President's Park "Lafayette Square."

On Capitol Hill the Marquis was the first foreigner to address a joint session of Congress. At a congressional dinner, he seemed to presage the two world wars and America's salvation of France and other nations. He toasted the "perpetual union of the United States. It has always saved us in times of storm; one day it will save the world." Congress awarded him a fortune of $20,000, and over 20,000 acres of Florida land. Lafayette was whisked back to Europe aboard the warship USS *Brandywine*, named for the battle where he fell wounded.

When Lafayette died in 1834, his family buried him at Picpus Cemetery in Paris. There, attendees performed a highly unusual ceremony. They lowered his coffin into a grave. They brought out canvas bags of soil. Then Lafayette's son—George Washington Lafayette—poured the earth onto the casket. The soil was from Bunker Hill, collected during the Marquis' visit there a decade before.

Thus Lafayette, blocked throughout his life from bringing freedom to his own nation, rests for all eternity under the soil of a free people.

Sources

Adams, Anne. "Elizabeth Monroe: Elegance in the White House." *History's Women*. http://www.historyswomen.com/1stWomen/elizabethmonroe.html.
Auricchio, Laura. *The Marquis: Lafayette Reconsidered*. New York: Knopf, 2014.
Bailey, Ronald. "Hail, Lafayette." *American History*, December 3, 2010. http://www.historynet.com/hail-lafayette.htm.
Baker, James Wesley. "The Imprisonment of Lafayette." *American Heritage* 28, no. 4 (June 1977). https://www.americanheritage.com/content/imprisonment-lafayette.
Cornell University. *Lafayette: Citizen of Two Worlds*. 2006 exhibit. http://rmc.library.cornell.edu/lafayette/exhibition/english/introduction/index.html.
Grubiak, Margaret. "The History of the General Marquis de Lafayette Statue, Lafayette Park, Washington, D.C." National Park Service, 2001.

History Things. "The Life of Revolutionary Marquis de Lafayette." October 18, 2016. http://historythings.com/life-revolutionary-marquis-de-lafayette-part-three/.

National Archives and Records Administration. *Records of the Office of Public Buildings and Public Parks of the National Capital*. Record Group 42 and 46 (Lafayette statue). Washington, D.C.

Schiller Institute. "Lafayette Gains His Freedom from the Prison of Olmutz," September 2012. http://schillerinstitute.org/educ/hist/eiw_this_week/v4n37_sep9_1797.html.

Seaburg, Carl, and Stanley Paterson. *Merchant Prince of Boston: Colonel T.H. Perkins, 1764–1854*. Cambridge, MA: Harvard University Press, 1971 (originally published 1832). Digital ed. es://archive.org/stream/merchantprinceof00carl/merchantprinceof00carl_djvu.txt.

Spalding, Professor Paul. "Sites of Lafayette's German Captivity, 1792–97." *The Arthur H. and Mary Marden Dean Lafayette Collection, 1520–1849*. Cornell University, 2006. http://rmc.library.cornell.edu/lafayette/collection/prison/.

Unger, Harlow Giles. *The Last Founding Father: James Monroe and a Nation's Call to Greatness*. Boston: Da Capo, 2009.

4

The Craziest Inaugural Party of Them All

Lafayette Square, Southeast Corner, Off Pennsylvania Avenue Facing the White House

It was the wildest inauguration event in presidential history. It could have killed the President. It almost wrecked the President's House. It forced the new President to find a hotel for the night.

Andy Jackson was elected in 1828 as the first true "populist" President. He was a man of the people and of his time. Raised dirt poor, he was born on the border of North Carolina and South Carolina in a place so remote we don't know in which state he was born. He'd risen by ambition and grit to be a wealthy Tennessee plantation owner and a fabulously successful general.

He prospered in politics during the "Jacksonian Era," where the vote was extended from a small number of rich property holders to almost universal white male suffrage. A clear majority of the American people wanted him to be President. They saw him as one of them and proof that most anyone in the new republic could become the head of the land. Jackson ran for, and won, the popular vote for President in 1824, but lost in the Electoral College. This only increased the ardor of his supporters for the next election. In 1828, Jackson handily beat incumbent President John Quincy Adams in the Electoral College as well as in raw voter appeal.

For his inauguration, on March 4, 1829, his supporters—many of them of modest means, many from the rustic, western frontier—wanted to be there, to touch his coat. Thousands traveled to the capital to watch him take the oath of office. After his inaugural address on the east portico of the Capitol, a boisterous crowd surged forward, snapped a protective ship's cable, and jostled about the new President. Officials hustled the 61-year-old Jackson inside the sanctuary of the Capitol. On its west side, he climbed on a white horse for a one-and-a-half-mile ride along Pennsylvania Avenue to the Executive Mansion. More masses of humanity, on horseback, carriage, and foot, accompanied him along the route.

The celebration didn't stop there. That afternoon, the new administration held a White House gala. As befitting a populist President, the party was open to all.

Crashing the Party

Even before the President's arrival, a throng had gathered about Lafayette Square opposite the White House entrance. Some had been drinking throughout that warm March day.

All were in a festive mood. They pushed against the fence surrounding the mansion. They knocked it to the ground. The jolly Jacksonians swarmed to the front door.

Then there was no Secret Service. There wouldn't be one until the Lincoln presidency, and then it would be used to go after counterfeiters, not to protect the President. There were no formal guards for the nation's chieftain at all. Later, when Old Hickory went about the capital city, he had a sturdy hickory cane to protect himself. But he hadn't expected trouble that day. The door to the White House was opened and some of the windows, and the people went pushing and climbing inside. Within, unwashed frontiersmen climbed atop satiny chairs and did victory dances. Plain folk cupped dirty paws into barrels and bowls of liquor and orange punch and slopped the liquor down their throats. Drunken revelers broke costly porcelain bowls and plates of china.

Cheek by jowl with the plebes was the city's elite: finely dressed diplomats, judges, members of Congress, and merchants. On hand was a horrified Supreme Court Justice, Joseph Story, a staunch member of the more highfalutin' Federalist faction opposed to Jackson's populist Democrats. He'd recall seeing the "most vulgar and gross in the nation" mixing with "the highest and most polished." Story added, "The reign of KING MOB seemed triumphant!"

A senator was agog and aghast at the numbers, and base culture, of the guests: "Spirits black, yellow, and grey poured in in one uninterrupted stream of mud and filth," he recalled, "among the throngs many fit subjects for the penitentiary." The town's erudite chronicler,

Crowds lined up outside the White House for President Andrew Jackson's first inaugural in 1829. Inside the mansion, attendees ignited a near-riot (Library of Congress, illustration by Robert Cruickshank, 1841).

Mrs. Margaret Bayard Smith, echoed his sentiment. "*The Majesty of the People* had disappeared," wrote Smith, "and a rabble, a mob, of boys, negros, women, children, scrambling, fighting, romping. What a pity." Jackson's aides and servants were horrified—at the damage to the mansion but far more at the risk posed to the President's frail health. Due to bullets lodged in his body from dueling and brawls, Jackson suffered from internal bleeding, inflamed lungs, and toxins of lead.

That late-winter day was unusually hot, and the air inside the packed mansion was oppressive. As the people pushed near him, wishing to shake his hand, Jackson, his back to a wall, started to feel faint. Smith reported the President was almost "pressed to death and nearly suffocated and torn to pieces."

A Flight to Safety

Friends and staffers, perhaps with help from enslaved servants, locked arms in a human chain to keep the sea of supporters at bay. Aides hustled the President to a side exit. According to one story, they took him to the second floor, where they fashioned a makeshift rope from bedsheets and passed it through a window to the ground. The President grabbed hold of the line and was lowered to the White House lawn.

Once outside, Old Hickory clambered atop a horse and fled back along Pennsylvania Avenue to the National Hotel. That 6th Street emporium was where he'd lodged the night before the inauguration. (The place was owned by John Gadsby, later an owner of the Decatur House and then the owner of the still-existing Gadsby's Tavern in Alexandria, Virginia.) Jackson glumly spent the first evening of his presidency there. A rail-thin man of little appetite, he sampled bits of ox steak with his Vice President, John C. Calhoun of South Carolina (with whom he would have a bitter falling-out the following year). All in all, his Inauguration Day seemed ill-omened. Jackson retired early, far from the madding crowd.

After Andy Jackson's departure from the White House that day, staff and servants remained in crisis mode. Their quick thinking may have stopped the President's own supporters from crushing him to death, but his hard-drinking backers still ran rampant over his residence. Then someone, perhaps White House steward Antoine Michel Giusta, had a brainstorm. Four years before, Giusta had saved President John Quincy Adams from drowning in the Potomac (see Chapter 34, "The Near Drowning of the President in the Potomac"). Now, Giusta's colleagues saved the White House. The President's men opened up the windows of the mansion to provide extra exits, and hoisted up the buckets of drink that had spurred the crowd into a drunken craze. They carried the pails of potables through the front entrance or handed them out through the windows. Then they conveyed the liquor over the trampled-down fence and into Lafayette Square. They also lugged over heaps of a then-rare treat: ice cream. After putting the potions and sweets in the park, they saw their scheme was working. The inebriated throng swarmed out of the President's House and into the Square. The tubs of refreshments served as the perfect lure, and the mansion was saved from ruin.

"It was the People's day," summarized Smith, "and the People's President, and the People would rule."

Sources

Bomboy, Scott. National Constitution Center. "The Story of the Wildest Party in White House History." *Constitution Daily*, March 4, 2013. https://constitutioncenter.org/blog/the-story-of-the-wildest-party-in-white-house-history/.

Eyewitness to History. "The Inauguration of President Andrew Jackson, 1829." http://www.eyewitnesstohistory.com/jacksoninauguration.htm.

Heidler, David S., and Jeanne T. Hiedler. The White House Historical Association. "Not a Ragged Mob: The Inauguration of 1829." https://www.whitehousehistory.org/not-a-ragged-mob-the-inauguration-of-1829.

Remini, Robert V. *The Life of Andrew Jackson.* Newton, CT: American Political Biography Press, 2003.

Smith, Margaret Bayard. *The First Forty Years of Washington Society.* New York: Scribner's, 1906.

5

The Biggest Slave Escape in American History

Outside St. John's Church, Between the Chamber of Commerce Building at 1615 H Street, Site of the Former William Corcoran Mansion and the Senator Daniel Webster Residence, and the Dolley Madison House at 1520 H Street

In spring 1848 freedom was in the air, as democratic revolts erupted throughout Europe. From Ireland through the German-speaking countries to Russia, the people rose up against princes and kings. In Lafayette Square orators such as Senator Henry Foote of Mississippi hailed the spread of liberty overseas. Foote, pro–Union yet a lawyer who represented slave-owning interests, lauded the prospect "to the whole family of man … the universal establishment of civil and religious liberty … the age of tyrants and of slavery was rapidly drawing to a close."

Down by the Waterside

The irony of lauding democracy abroad while tolerating servitude at home was not lost among some members of Washington's African-American community. Aided by white abolitionists, they were determined to act. On the night of Saturday, April 15, 1848, scores of blacks quietly walked or rode by horse or carriage through the darkened streets of Washington. They moved out from houses and work places near the White House, Georgetown, and about Capitol Hill. Traveling individually or in very small groups under cloudy skies, they moved fast, as they had to beat the 10 p.m. city curfew on travel by African Americans.

In Lafayette Square, some of them went near the residence of a skeptic of slavery and fervent supporter of national unity: Massachusetts Senator Daniel Webster. In 1830, during a Senate debate on whether states could void federal law, Webster had declared, "Liberty and Union, Now and Forever, One and Inseparable!" Yet in 1850, to head off civil war, Webster backed a compromise that empowered slave owners to recapture escaped slaves. In the Square some of the blacks passed near the Dolley Madison House, half a block from Webster's home. In the years before her death in 1849, the former First Lady lived in abject poverty. Webster had asked Paul Jennings, a former slave who'd been President Madison's body servant, to care for Mrs. Madison. If you've seen the television series *Downton Abbey* you'd recognize that the body servant is a domestic who washes and dresses the Earl of

Grantham. That had been Jennings' role with President Madison. In 1847 Paul Jennings had been able to buy his freedom through a $120 loan given him by Daniel Webster. From time to time Jennings took the impoverished Mrs. Madison groceries. The former slave even lent his former owner cash.

In the darkness of that April 15 night, the blacks, probably 77 people in all, kept walking or riding along. They wanted to be invisible. They welcomed the evening gloom, made gloomier by the overcast sky and by the fact the city had few whale-oil street lamps. The African Americans—men and women, adults, teenagers, and children—headed to the south part of town. A light rain fell as some went across the National Mall. Some crept by the Smithsonian Castle under construction or past the half-built Washington Monument. Their destination was the 7th Street wharf on the Anacostia River, about a mile south of the Mall at today's rebuilt Waterfront.

The 77 souls made up the largest attempted slave escape in American history.

Awaiting them was a 54-ton schooner, the *Pearl*. On board were two white men who were ship captains and abolitionists: Captain Edward Sayres and Captain Daniel Drayton. The weather-beaten, 56-year-old Drayton had spent years sailing the Chesapeake, where he'd encountered slaves fleeing bondage. He wondered, "Why had not these black people, so anxious to escape from their masters, as good a light to their liberty as I had to mine?"

The passengers boarded the *Pearl*. Sayres and Drayton slipped the ship out of dockside. They piloted the schooner quietly down the Anacostia River then southward on the Potomac toward the Chesapeake Bay. They fretted when the *Pearl* encountered a calm, and also met a contrary tide. Then the wind picked up, and the tide reversed. Their strategy was to head all the way up the Chesapeake to Delaware, not far from the borders of Pennsylvania and New Jersey, where slavery was banned. The route was about 225 miles long. Once the slaves reached the soil of a free state, they'd be free.

The daring escape took a lot of planning, especially in requisitioning a ship and pilots and in coordinating the simultaneous movement of many slaves. Usually, in traveling north via the Underground Railroad of safe houses, fleeing slaves would journey alone or in small groups to avoid attention. The escape was likely planned in large part by William Chaplain, a New York abolitionist, and was largely financed by a wealthy Empire State abolitionist, Gerrit Smith. (In 1859, Smith would secretly back John Brown's attempted slave insurrection starting from the federal arsenal in Harpers Ferry, in today's West Virginia.) Chaplain and Smith thought the odds for a successful escape were slim. However, they figured the endeavor would spotlight the issue of slavery in the nation's capital. The two main plotters got help from local members of the Underground Railroad. One was blacksmith Daniel Bell, a free man of color whose enslaved family members boarded the *Pearl*. Another was Samuel Edmonson, who got onto the schooner with five of his sisters and brothers.

A Getaway Foiled

When dawn broke on April 16, many slave owners in Washington, Georgetown, and the town of Alexandria woke up expecting to see their slaves cooking breakfast, tending the garden, or preparing to go to work at a hotel or boardinghouse. But their servants had vanished. Word of the absences spread. And word spread even quicker because of a betrayal by an African-American carriage driver, Judson Diggs. After driving an enslaved woman to the *Pearl*'s dock, Diggs was riled when the woman told him she lacked money for the fare. He was also angry at another passenger, Samuel Edmonson's sister Emily, who had previously declined Diggs' offer of marriage. He would even the score.

That morning, word of the escape reached Georgetown's Francis Dodge, Jr. His family owned a large tobacco warehouse on the Georgetown waterfront at Water Street and Wisconsin Avenue. The stone structure is still there, at today's K Street. Dodge owned three of the *Pearl* escapees. As fire alarms signaling the escape rang out throughout town, Dodge formed an armed posse of several dozen men. They pressed aboard his steam-powered boat, the *Salem*, reputedly the river's fastest vessel. In the meantime, Diggs, the embittered hack driver, told others in the region-wide manhunt of the escape.

Dodge and his posse steamed rapidly down the Potomac. They neared the Chesapeake without sighting the fugitive ship and almost gave up the chase. On the *Pearl*, according to author Mary Kay Ricks, the passengers sang hymns and recited Bible verses. However, at Point Lookout, where the Potomac flows into the mighty Chesapeake Bay, a squall forced the *Pearl* to lay anchor. This allowed the *Salem* to catch up. Spotting its prey, it pulled alongside. The slaves, their hopes of liberty dashed and having no weapons, surrendered. The *Salem* towed the *Pearl* and its human cargo back to Washington City.

In town, thousands of whites gathered in anger. They cursed the captured blacks, who were then taken in shackles to a slave pen near the southwestern foot of the Capitol. The white captains were taken in chains toward the city jail on the other side of the Capitol, at today's Judiciary Square. On the way, a white mob accused the pair of inciting a slave revolt. A man slashed at Captain Drayton, cutting his ear. Fearing a lynching, police hustled the two into a horse-drawn cab that carried them to their cells.

During the ensuing Washington Riot of 1848, the mob turned its fury on the press. On April 18 a crowd nearly destroyed the offices of an abolitionist newspaper, the *New Era*, located near the old Patent Office Building, today's National Portrait Gallery. Its stalwart editor, Gamaliel Bailey, told the teeming throngs he would not "surrender a great constitutional right" of free speech. Around the building, President James K. Polk stationed additional guards, totaling over 75 in number. After a few days of turmoil, the riot fizzled out.

Meanwhile, the owners of the captured slaves—now deemed untrustworthy—didn't want their charges back. They quickly sold them off at the Bruin and Hill slave trading firm in Alexandria. People in Louisiana and Georgia purchased them.

Washington's District Attorney, Philip Barton Key II—the son of Francis Scott Key—led the prosecution of Captains Sayres and Drayton. The court convicted them of 77 counts of "illegal transportation." Their defense attorney was Massachusetts educator Horace Mann. Seven years earlier, Mann had defended, with former President John Quincy Adams, 53 slaves who'd escaped the Spanish ship *Amistad*. (There is a riveting Steven Spielberg movie about it, with Anthony Hopkins in the Adams role.) The court sentenced both captains to prison. In 1852 President Millard Fillmore of New York pardoned them.

The *Pearl* saga became a political football. In the Capitol, northern and southern congressmen traded invective until an Illinois lawmaker, Abraham Lincoln, moved to shut down debate. The following year Lincoln proposed buying and freeing all the slaves in Washington. The next year the Senate fiercely debated its Compromise of 1850 over slavery. During a rancorous session, Senator Foote, the pro-democracy orator, pulled a gun on fellow Senator Philip Hart Benton—even though both men were for the Compromise! The law that resulted strengthened the Fugitive Slave Act, the Senator Webster–backed measure giving owners more clout to recapture escaped slaves. The same legislative deal, however, outlawed much of the slave trade in Washington, D.C.

Giving Birth to a Bestseller

The saga of the *Pearl* continued. Two of the women who were sold off became icons of abolition. These were teenaged sisters: 15-year-old Mary Edmonson and 13-year-old Emily Edmonson. It was Emily who'd spurned Diggs, and it was their brother Samuel who'd helped plan the escape. A statue of the Edmonson sisters stands outside the former Alexandria slave pen from which they were sold. Today the operators of the building buy and sell houses.

An abolitionist minister in Brooklyn, New York, took up the torch of the Edmonson sisters. He raised enough money from his congregation, from abolitionists, and from the Edmonsons' father, Paul, a free black man, to purchase their freedom. The name of the minister was Henry Ward Beecher. The name of Beecher's sister was Harriet Beecher Stowe.

The enslaved Edmonson sisters became a cause célèbre among abolitionists such as Harriet Beecher Stowe after their capture aboard the escape ship *Pearl* (Sculpture by Erik Blome, 2010; photograph by "Bronzecastman," 2010).

Harriet was fascinated by the story of the *Pearl*. It inspired her to write a novel indicting slavery, a book that became a mammoth bestseller. The book was *Uncle Tom's Cabin*. It was serialized by Gamaliel Bailey, the man whose newspaper the mob had threatened. Greatly popular in the North and banned in the South, *Uncle Tom's Cabin* presaged the Civil War. It also coined the term "Uncle Tom," as in a subservient black—rather like Judson Diggs.

After the fact, the identities of some of the other plotters in America's largest slave escape came to light. Senator Daniel Webster might have been involved—the Senator who'd agreed to the law leading to the capture of more fugitive slaves after helping the massive escape! Another plotter was Paul Jennings, the former slave Webster had asked to watch over Dolley Madison and who had labored for the Madisons for decades! The largest escape of them all failed, but it had quite an impact.

A postscript: At the end of the Civil War, and after his three sons had fought in the Union Army, Jennings published a memoir about James Madison. He harbored no ill will. He wrote, "Mr. Madison, I think, was one of the best men that ever lived. I never saw him in a passion, and never knew him to strike a slave, although he had over one hundred; neither would he allow an overseer to do it. Whenever any slaves were reported to him as stealing or 'cutting up' badly, he would send for them and admonish them privately, and never mortify them by doing it before others."

From the perspective of the 21st century, the city's antebellum era seems a weird and wild one indeed.

Sources

Blakemore, Erin. "The Largest Attempted Slave Escape in American History." *History*, August 23, 2017. https://www.history.com/news/the-largest-attempted-slave-escape-in-american-history.

Fishman, Susan Hoffman. "The Escape of the Pearl: Teaching about Slavery with Primary Source Documents." https://www.questia.com/library/journal/1G1–108048792/the-escape-of-the-pearl-teaching-about-slavery-with.

Jennings, Paul. *A Colored Man's Reminiscences of James Madison*. Brooklyn: George C. Beadle, 1865. Electronic ed. University of North Carolina at Chapel Hill. https://docsouth.unc.edu/neh/jennings/jennings.html.

NPR. "Failed Escape Sheds New Light on D.C. Slavery," May 9, 2007. https://www.npr.org/templates/story/story.php?storyId=10103500.

Paynter, John H. "The Fugitives of the Pearl (excerpt)." *Journal of Negro History,* July 1, 1916. From HU ArchivesNet, Howard University.

Ricks, Mary Kay. *Escape on the Pearl*. New York: HarperCollins, 2009.

_____. "Escape on the Pearl." *Washington Post*, August 12, 1998, p. H01. https://www.washingtonpost.com/wp-srv/national/horizon/aug98/pearl.htm.

6

The "Big Cheese" Receives a Mammoth Gift

1600 Pennsylvania Avenue, East Room of the White House

Starting on New Year's Day 1802 and continuing through 1804, the spacious East Room of the White House played host to the most unusual, and largest, snack in the city's history. The sharp-tasting and sharp-smelling treat in question involved scientific explorations, fundamental disputes over religion, political brawls, and, perhaps, a war against pirates.

It started with the desire of a dissident cleric, Baptist preacher John Leland of Cheshire, Massachusetts, to thank President Thomas Jefferson, who had been newly elected in autumn 1800. The Baptists of New England were the victims of religious bias by the sect that had been the official religion there since the Plymouth colony—namely the Puritans, also known as Congregationalists.

In the 1800 race between challenger Jefferson and incumbent President John Adams, religion was an issue. Some in the Federalist Party of Adams and Alexander Hamilton desired an official state religion, like that of the Church of England in colonial days. Jefferson's Anti-Federalist party, on the other hand, wanted what we would call freedom of religion, with no special treatment for, or repression of, any denominations. Jefferson's critics, pointing to his "deist" skepticism toward religious miracles and his sympathy toward the French Revolution—whose radicals strove to erase the Christian faith entirely—viewed him as an apostle of atheism and social chaos. After his election, some devout Federalists buried their family Bibles in their gardens for fear the new administration would confiscate them.

Giants from the Past and Pasture

Reverend Leland had lived for 16 years in Virginia, where he and Jefferson had become friends. In New England, Leland's Cheshire County had voted overwhelmingly, unanimously in fact, for Jefferson in the election, with the lone Federalist ballot tossed out. Leland's flock decided to express their support for the new President's tolerant stance—and in the oddest way. In summer 1801 the farmers of Cheshire, led by engineer Darius Brown, built the world's largest cheese press. Adapted from an apple "cyder press," it measured six feet across and sported an extra-strong hoop. It was put to work with the product of the county's farmers and milkmaids, who'd suckled the milk out of 900 cows. The result was the world's largest cheese, weighing in at 1,235 pounds. That winter the Baptists sent the cheese off as a giant gift to Jefferson. Handlers transported it more than 400 miles by sleigh over snowy roads to New York, then by ship to Baltimore, and finally by horse-drawn wagon to Washington City.

Not long before this, amateur scientists had unearthed near Newburgh, New York, the fossilized remains of a very large, extinct mammal with matted hair and curved, protruding tusks. Due to its size, the animal, an extinct species of elephant, was dubbed a "mammoth." It was actually a mastodon, scientifically speaking. The big dig was managed by Philadelphia portraitist and naturalist Charles Wilson Peale. As a friend of Peale, Jefferson had backed the expedition. Along with being the U.S. President, Jefferson was president of the American Philosophical Society, a kind of early Smithsonian Institution, and had an interest in such things.

The excavation got tangled in a scientific dispute between two continents. The world's leading naturalist, Frenchman Comte de Buffon, wrote in his widely read "theory of American degeneracy" that animals in North America, compared to Europe, were puny. Patriots like Jefferson and Peale were displeased. When the former journeyed off as Minister to France, he took with him the skins of an American moose and a big mountain lion. According to *Smithsonian* magazine, he met Buffon and to prove his point wagged the specimens at the Euro chauvinist. Comte Buffon's buffoonish-sounding beliefs spurred Beale to find examples, like the giant mammoth, to refute him.

The detection of the mammoth critter was big, big news. Soon after, so was the big cheese. Thus, it naturally got nicknamed the "Mammoth Cheese." Indeed, doing things in gargantuan fashion turned into a national craze. In Washington City, for instance, a man with a giant appetite swallowed 40 eggs in 10 minutes. He billed himself the "Mammoth Eater."

During its journey to Washington by land and sea, the Mammoth Cheese gave Jefferson's critics heartburn. Federalist newspapers chided it as an example of anti–Federalist pretention and excess. Scribes sarcastically suggested fermenting a giant batch of apple cider and baking a gigantic loaf of bread to accompany the protean protein.

On New Year's Day 1802, Baptist teamsters drove a six-horse wagon laden with their gift along Pennsylvania Avenue and up to the White House. Jefferson's aides, adept at political outreach and propaganda, had made up a sign: "Greatest Man Greatest Cheese." The President, garbed in his usual plain black suit to underline republican simplicity, greeted the arrivals with open arms at the front entrance to the President's House. The Baptists presented the Mammoth Cheese, which was inscribed with a Jefferson maxim: "Rebellion to tyrants is obedience to God." Leland stressed to the President the cheese "was produced by the personal labor of *Freeborn Farmers*, with the voluntary and cheerful aid of their wives and daughters, without the assistance of a single slave." The preacher further noted that no cow owned by a Federalist had contributed milk.

Thomas Jefferson, known to be charming in private but reticent in public, pulled out prepared remarks and gave a rare public talk. He lauded the Cheshire farmers for "extraordinary proof of the skill with which those domestic arts which contribute so much to our daily comfort are practiced." The President further characterized the mammoth product as "an ebullition of the passion of republicanism in a state where it has been under heavy persekkcution [*sic*]." It was Jefferson's practice to refuse gifts, so he gave Leland $200 for the cheese and a chunk of it as keepsake.

A Whey Forward to Religious Freedom

It's no coincidence that on the very same day, President Jefferson crafted his famous statement about "separation of church and state." This took the form of a declaration to a Baptist group in Connecticut that referenced the First Amendment. The letter stated the following: "Believing with you that religion is a matter which lies solely between Man & his God, that he owes account to none other for his faith or his worship, that the legitimate powers of government reach actions only, & not opinions, I contemplate with sovereign reverence that act of the whole American people which declared that *their* legislature should 'make no law respecting an establishment of religion, or prohibiting the free exercise thereof,' thus building a *wall of separation between Church & State* [emphasis added]."

Jefferson's meaning can be misinterpreted today. He did not intend to banish religion or Christianity from American life. In fact, he invoked Providence in his public pronouncements, and regularly attended church services at the Capitol. He wanted to—and in time he and others succeeded in doing so—quash the establishment of an official religion in America. Given the nation's tradition of religious pluralism and the violent disputes over religion today in the Middle East, South Asia, and central Africa, most view his approach as a wise one.

The Mammoth Cheese, however, posed a practical difficulty. Where to put and keep the thing? The East Room, then as now a place of banquets, was a natural choice. For several years, congressmen, out-of-town visitors, or people off the street would treat themselves to chunks of cheese or take them as souvenirs. There was then no Secret Service and no White House fence, and Jefferson in his slippers and robe would sometimes greet those knocking on the front door for nibbles. Some sources, possibly apocryphal, assert the Big Cheese was employed to help fight pirates. In 1801 the Jefferson administration began to wage America's first foreign war—against the Barbary Pirates of the Mediterranean. However, Treasury Secretary Albert Gallatin was pushing tax cuts. The question arose: How to pay for the war? One modest solution was to sell off or give away leftovers from the Mammoth Cheese at political gatherings and fundraisers. Such affairs may have been held at the White House and the Capitol. For one such event the Navy apparently baked a Mammoth Loaf to go with the oversized rind. Large amounts of alcohol were on hand. At its start, an official, possibly the President, wielded a pen knife to cut off chunks for the guests. The President then quietly departed, as the event, mobbed by congressmen and commoners, descended into a session of binge drinking and eating.

One giant food led to another. In 1835 President Andrew Jackson was the recipient of a More Mammoth Cheese. Dairy farmers in Oswego, New York, created a 1,400-pound dairy product. It took 24 horses to haul it from the Empire State to Lafayette Square. Its creator, Colonel Thomas S. Meacham, presented the big block to Jackson at the Executive Mansion. (Coincidentally, one of Jackson's biographers is a Meachem, bestselling author Jon Meacham.) A somewhat lesser Big Cheese, Vice President Martin Van Buren, got an 800-pound cheese. (Van Buren was apparently OK with that: hailing from Kinderhook, New York, he was nicknamed "Old Kinderhook," which allegedly birthed the term "OK.")

After two years, the More Mammoth Cheese was less large but still taking up valuable White House space in the East Room. Thus, Old Hickory invited the public, on George Washington's birthday, to a big cheese party. By then the dairy product had ripened. Its fumes overcame the weaker-kneed, namely the "dandies and lackadaisical ladies," observed a writer for a Rhode Island journal. Van Buren noted that even after most of the cheese had been eaten and its maggot-infested remnants tossed into the Potomac, the smell of it permeated the mansion for months.

Sources

American Philosophical Society. "An American Behemoth: Peale's Mastodon," 2006. https://www.amphilsoc.org/exhibits/treasures/mastodon.htm.

Conniff, Richard. "Mammoths and Mastodons: All American Monsters." *Smithsonian*, April 2010. https://www.smithsonianmag.com/science-nature/mammoths-and-mastodons-all-american-monsters-8898672/.

Dresibach, Daniel L. "Thomas Jefferson and the Mammoth Cheese." Acton Institute, July 20, 2010. https://acton.org/pub/religion-liberty/volume-12-number-3/thomas-jefferson-and-mammoth-cheese.

National Archives. "Editorial Note: Presentation of the 'Mammoth Cheese.'" *Founders*, June 13, 2018. http://founders.archives.gov/documents/Jefferson/01-36-02-0151-0001.

PBS. WETA. "People and Ideas: John Leland." http://www.pbs.org/godinamerica/people/john-leland.html.

Petito, Jackie. National Portrait Gallery. "The Big Cheese: Presidential Gifts of Mammoth Proportions," January 17, 2017. http://npg.si.edu/blog/big-cheese-presidential-gifts-mammoth-proportions.

Pohl, Robert. "Presidents on Capitol Hill." *HillRag*, November 5, 2013. http://www.capitalcommunitynews.com/content/presidents-capitol-hill-0.

Rupp, Rebecca. "What's More Presidential Than a Gift of Big Cheese?" *National Geographic*, February 23, 2015. https://www.nationalgeographic.com/people-and-culture/food/the-plate/2015/02/23/whats-more-presidential-than-a-gift-of-a-big-cheese/.

Thomas Jefferson's Monticello. "Mammoth Cheese." https://www.monticello.org/site/research-and-collections/mammoth-cheese.

7

Mrs. Lincoln's Sad Search for Her Deceased Son

1600 Pennsylvania Avenue. Mr. Lincoln's bedroom was in the rear, southwest corner of the mansion on the second floor. The grand East Room is on the east side of the first floor. The Red Room is on the first floor to the west of the entrance.

The Civil War was by far the bloodiest of America's conflicts. As scholars conduct more research, the body count grows. Perhaps 700,000 soldiers, Union and Confederate, died from battle or disease. The population of the United States at the time was 30 million. Prorate the number of fatalities to today's population of over 300 million, and you'd have over seven million dead—a veritable holocaust.

From 1861 to 1865 almost every American had a father, brother, nephew, cousin or son who died in the war. Many among the heart-struck longed to see a deceased loved one again. A surprising proportion of Americans tried to do just that, as a weird social trend of the war was séances.

The fascination with spiritualist-led gatherings seeking to connect the bereaved with the deceased dated to the late 1840s. Leah, Maggie, and Kate Fox, sisters living near Rochester, New York, were mediums who claimed supernatural powers. Famous figures later linked to the Union cause were intrigued by them, including abolitionists William Lloyd Garrison and Sojourner Truth and newspaper publisher Horace Greeley. In the second half of the 19th century, many educated people adhered to spiritualism. One of the best-known was British writer Sir Arthur Conan Doyle, creator of Sherlock Holmes.

During the War Between the States, the most famous participant in these assemblies was the First Lady herself, Mary Todd Lincoln. Although in Mrs. Lincoln's case, she didn't try to get in touch with a family member who had died in battle. Her concern was her deceased son, William Wallace Lincoln, or Willie. He had died in the White House in 1862, at age 11, probably from typhoid, possibly from tainted water, as the city then had no reliable water or sewer systems.

The death of Willie devastated the Lincolns. The President was said to have locked himself in a "weeping room" in the White House to privately grieve. The First Lady never again set foot in the room where Willie died or the place in the mansion where he'd been embalmed. Willie's passing came at a time when she and her husband were already under tremendous stress from the war and from the many people they knew who had died in it. Mrs. Lincoln cast about the cottage industry of seers, mediums, and hucksters who sprang up to offer hope to those gripped by sorrow. She attended the otherworldly sessions of a "witch of Georgetown," Margaret Laurie.

An Ignoble Imposter

But Mary Todd Lincoln was truly taken with a spiritualist who went by the name of Lord Charles J. Colchester. He claimed, falsely, to be the illegitimate son of a British duke. (The actor John Wilkes Booth, later Lincoln's murderer, befriended him.) During his séances, attendees heard strange metallic rumblings that seemed to shoot out of the ether. Lord Colchester claimed they were the dead mumbling aloud or tapping transparent hands on hard surfaces. The First Lady attended a number of these sessions. In one, at the city's Soldier's Home for wounded war veterans, Colchester claimed to connect with the ghost of Willie (today the place, near Catholic University, is the Old Soldier's Home and cemetery).

Abraham Lincoln fretted about these bizarre gatherings. The President asked his friend Joseph Henry to look into Colchester. Henry, the head of the Smithsonian, was a noted scientist and the inventor of the electrical relay, a device that generates the buzzing noise when you push a door bell and the switch that enabled long-distance phone calls. No fool, Henry invited the medium to a room at the Smithsonian Castle on the National Mall. There he asked Colchester for a demonstration of his powers.

While great numbers of soldiers perished in the Civil War, Mary Todd Lincoln was swept up in a fad of connecting with the spirits of the dead through mediums and séances (Library of Congress, Brady-Handy Collection).

During their sitting Henry became convinced Colchester produced his sounds of the dead through some hidden, mechanical trick. He couldn't prove it, though, without a body search, and Colchester declined to disrobe. Henry informed Lincoln of his suspicions. The President turned to a reporter friend, Noah Brooks of Boston's *Atlantic Monthly* magazine. Lincoln asked him to sit in on a Colchester "reading." Brooks did and wrote a detailed account of it. It reads like a scene out of a Hollywood potboiler.

One night, Brooks and a friend travelled to the Washington home of a man who was a devotee of Colchester. The fellow was hosting a séance, with the British seer and Mrs. Lincoln herself in attendance. With the gas lighting kept low, Brooks sat around a table with his friend and Colchester, Mrs. Lincoln, and the other guests. On the table were laid out a banjo, bells, and a ball. Everyone fell silent, expectantly waiting. Colchester led the séance, calling on the spirits of the dead to make their presence known. Mary Todd hoped Willie Lincoln would be among the ghostly arrivals.

To the amazement of some, the banjo twanged and the bells rang. A knocking sound was heard. The medium attributed this to Willie signalling Mary Todd from beyond the grave. Brooks doubted this and reached under the table toward a drumming sound. As the reporter recalled, he "grabbed a very solid and fleshy hand in which was held a bell that was being thumped on a drum-head." Brooks cried out, "Strike a light!" What was struck was his forehead, as Colchester smacked him with the drum, injuring him slightly. Brooks' friend then struck a match. With the room illuminated, the surprised guests spied Brooks, his head bleeding, with a firm grip on the supposed seer. Brooks was enraged at the deceit, and Colchester irate at his unmasking. The session broke up in disorder; the spiritualist made a hasty exit.

Although Mrs. Lincoln's faith in Lord Colchester was shaken, she continued to attend gatherings run by other spiritualists. The most noted was 21-year-old Belle Miller, the daughter of a post office official from Georgetown. In December 1862 Mrs. Lincoln invited Mrs. Miller to the Executive Mansion. A group gathered in its well-appointed yet cozy Red Room—or Red Parlour, as it was then called. The Lincolns employed it as their living room as well as a place to entertain guests. However skeptical one might be about spiritualism, Miller appears to have been a talented and insightful woman. During her visit, she played a grand piano near a portrait of Sen. Daniel Webster, the apostle of perpetual federal union. Suddenly Abe Lincoln himself, the President of the Union, surprised everyone by entering the room.

After a brief give-and-take between Lincoln and Miller, the young lady fell into a reverie, as if she was at a séance. Seemingly in an unconscious state, she commented at length, in words directed to Mr. Lincoln, about the immense pressure he was under. She urged him to stick to his ideals despite the pushback he was getting from foes. At that time, the President was moving to enact his Emancipation Proclamation freeing the slaves, even as many tried to block the measure and even as the Union Army was suffering a major defeat at the Battle of Fredericksburg, Virginia.

Miller later recalled she told Lincoln "he was assured [Emancipation] was to be the crowning event of his administration and his life, and that while he was being counseled by strong parties to defer the enforcement of it … he must in no wise heed such counsel, but stand firm to his convictions and fearlessly perform the work and [fulfill] the mission for which he had been raised up by an overruling Providence." The President was evidently impressed with the young lady's knowledge of events and also, seemingly, of his own internal thinking. He reportedly replied to Miller, "It is taking all my nerve and strength to withstand such pressure." Of course, the woman might have picked up much of what she said from the newspapers, which were full of speculation about the President's plans for abolition.

Phony Photography

In addition to séances, another strange cottage industry sprang up from spiritualism, one that drew upon an emerging technology: photography. An unscrupulous man would take a picture of a dead person and in a photographic lab pair an image of the deceased with a photo of a loved one. In the doctored image, it would appear the deceased was paying a ghostly visit to a live relative. The con artist would then present the phony photo to a grieving relation or friend—for a price. One such image, developed after President's Lincoln murder, drew on an image of Mrs. Lincoln herself. In that "spirit photograph," the ghostly visage of Abe Lincoln appeared behind his widow! The spirit photographer in that case was the notorious William Mumler, a jewelry engraver from Boston. He concocted many such pictures with a secret chemical process that no photographic expert of the time could ascertain. (He also created a bona fide technique for the mass reproduction of photographs in newspapers.)

None other than Phineas Taylor "P.T." Barnum, of circus fame, looked into Mumler's work. Barnum was famously linked to the lines "there's a sucker born every minute" and "no one ever lost a dollar by underestimating the intelligence of the American public." He thought Mumler took such nostrums too far by playing on the grieving. Indeed, Mumler was accused of breaking into houses to steal the photos of the dead relatives of people he scammed. Mumler was eventually brought to trial for fraud, and Barnum testified against him. To illustrate how a hoax might be executed, Barnum had a fake photo made of himself with the deceased President Lincoln.

The spirit photographer was acquitted, but Mumler's business took a hit from negative trial publicity, and he died in poverty in 1884. Surprisingly, many people who bought images from Mumler and other hucksters suspected they were fake. But so great was their anguish about a death in the family that despite themselves they were willing to do almost anything, including buying an evidently phony image, to imagine they and their beloved ones were together again.

The incidents with Lord Colchester showed that Mary Todd Lincoln was a troubled woman. She was pushed practically over the edge when she witnessed the assassination of her husband on April 14, 1865. Things only got worse for her state of mind after that. In 1875 she became so unstable that her surviving son, Robert Todd Lincoln, had her briefly committed to a lunatic asylum. Enraged at what she saw as her son's betrayal, she tried killing herself with an overdose of opiates. In her old age, Mary Todd, who died in 1882, suffered from failing eyesight as well as spinal injuries from falls. She was never able to overcome the awful deaths of her son and her husband and her many personal demons.

A Presidential Prophecy

Although President Lincoln was dubious about mediums, he was a somewhat superstitious man, to which a well-known anecdote attests. In March or April 1865, not long before his murder, Lincoln told his former law partner and sometime bodyguard, the hulking Ward Hill Lamon, about a strange dream he'd had in the White House. Lincoln began by remarking how the Bible has many incidents involving dreams. "If we believe the Bible," Lincoln informed Lamon, "we must accept the fact that in the old days God and His angels came to men in their sleep and made themselves known in dreams."

In his vision, Lincoln said he awoke to "a death-like stillness about me." He heard noises coming from the East Room in the floor below where he slept. He went downstairs, and the noises got louder. Lincoln entered the East Room and found soldiers as well as mourners in distress. They were directing their grief toward a deceased person lying in a catafalque, or raised coffin, with the body covered. Lincoln continued recalling his dream to Lamon. "Who is dead in the White House?" he demanded of one of the soldiers. "The President," came the answer. "He was killed by an assassin!"

It's said the dream was the President's premonition of his own death. However, Lamon's account contradicts itself on exactly when Lincoln had this vision. And before his assassination Lincoln insisted, regarding the dream, that the man in the catafalque was not him but another President. Yet, after Lincoln was murdered, his embalmed body was placed in a coffin and onto a canopied catafalque. Thousands of visitors paid their respects to the slain leader before the transfer of his remains to the Capitol. The viewing took place in the East Room.

Sources

Alford, Terry. "The Spiritualist Who Warned Lincoln Was Also Booth's Drinking Buddy." *Smithsonian*, March 2015. https://www.smithsonianmag.com/history/the-spiritualist-who-warned-lincoln-was-also-booths-drinking-buddy-180954317/.
Goodwin, Doris Kearns. *Team of Rivals: The Political Genius of Abraham Lincoln*. New York: Simon & Schuster, 2005.
Kaplan, Louis. *The Strange Case of William Mumler, Spirit Photographer*. University of Minnesota Press, 2008.
Manseau, Peter. *The Apparitionists: A Tale of Phantoms, Fraud, Photography, and the Man Who Captured Lincoln's Ghost*. Boston: Houghton Mifflin Harcourt, 2017.
———. "Meet Mr. Mumler, the Man Who 'Captured' Lincoln's Ghost on Camera." *Smithsonian*, October 10, 2017. https://www.smithsonianmag.com/smithsonian-institution/meet-mr-mumler-man-who-captured-lincolns-ghost-camera-180965090/.
Mr. Lincoln's White House. "Mary's Charlatans: Charles J. Colchester." http://www.mrlincolnswhitehouse.org/residents-visitors/marys-charlatans/marys-charlatans-charles-j-colchester.

8

The Plantation Owner's Startling Army of Diversity

Andrew Jackson Statue, Center of Lafayette Square

Jackson had a wild and event-filled life. Slashed and scarred by a British officer during the American Revolution, he watched much of his family perish at the hands of the Brits. He nearly died in a duel with the most skilled gunman of the western states and engaged in countless other duels. He almost died in a hotel brawl during the War of 1812, when the brother of a colleague shot him in the back. After the war, he staged a raid into Spanish Florida, where he captured and hanged British agents suspected of instigating raids into American territory, while enraging both London and the U.S. Secretary of War, John C. Calhoun.

Some misinformed tourists, when they learn of the "Jackson" statue, believe it refers to "Stonewall" Jackson. But an image of the Confederate general would be unlikely in the center of the federal capital. Along with Andy Jackson's decisive moves to preserve the Union during his presidency, this equestrian monument honors his crushing, and extremely unlikely, victory over the British on January 8, 1815, at the Battle of New Orleans.

When sculptor Clark Mills created the Andrew Jackson statue in 1853, millions of Americans could still recall the War of 1812. They also recalled Jackson's triumph, which nailed the coffin on British hopes to overthrow the results of the American Revolution: America's independence and the relentless push westward across North America.

In 1815 Old Hickory's win shocked for two reasons. One was that his smallish army of U.S. regulars and irregulars beat the world's most powerful military. The second was that his force was the original Motley Crew. Made up of disparate ethnic groups of Americans and noncitizens, they, in today's parlance, were remarkable for their "diversity." It was a testament to Old Hickory's will and to the skill of the assorted units that the U.S. overcame such a mighty foe.

Before New Orleans, President James Madison and his party's Democrat-Republican Congress had suffered many setbacks after declaring war on Britain in July 1812. The losses surprised many, for when the conflict broke out Britain and its allies seemed close to defeat on the main battleground of Europe. Their nemesis, Napoleon, had conquered almost the whole continent. That summer he invaded Russia to make his rule in Europe complete. Then he could finish off the lone remaining obstacle to his supremacy, the island of Britain.

With London reeling, many Americans thought winning the war would be easy. The stretched British forces in British Canada would be readily overcome. Madison's friend, retired President Jefferson, wrote in August 1812 that the "acquisition of Canada this year, as far as the neighborhood of Quebec, will be a mere matter of marching; & will give us experience for final expulsion of England from the American continent."

But by winter 1814, things had turned around completely. Napoleon's *Grand Armée* of a half million men had dissolved amid the snows of Russia. Bonaparte, his conquests and throne lost, was in exile. An experienced British army and its huge, unrivaled navy, both vital to unhorsing Napoleon, now could turn their undivided attention on America to teach those Yankees a lesson for daring to take on their Empire again. Early in the war, multiple American invasions of Canada collapsed. Then, in August 1814, Royal Marines under Rear Admiral George Cockburn invaded and burned Washington, D.C., before being checked at Baltimore (see Chapter 9, "The Burning of the White House and the Rescue of Its Riches").

But far to the South was a richer prize than the humble American capital of 20,000 souls. The city of New Orleans lay at the mouth of three great rivers washing down the Mississippi Basin: the Missouri, the Ohio, and the Father of Rivers himself, the Mississippi. New Orleans was the chokepoint to the continent. If the British could seize it, they could block much of America's products—timber, cotton, metals, corn—from reaching the outside world. Its economy could collapse. Britain might even pry away the Louisiana Purchase and make London, not Washington, supreme again in the American West and in North America generally. Indeed, the Prime Minister, the Earl of Liverpool, thought his military should keep taking American territory until and unless it was stopped.

To grab the prize, the British sent to Louisiana a large and well-trained force made up of veterans of the Napoleonic Wars and commanded by Major General Sir Edward Pakenham—the brother-in-law of the conqueror of Napoleon himself, the Duke of Wellington. New Orleans, American turf for just 11 years, since the Louisiana Purchase, was panicked. Its citizenry was largely French, Spanish, Afro-Caribbean, and mixed-blood Creole. Loyalty to their new country seemed tentative, and the city was practically undefended. Some spoke of cutting a deal with the advancing Brits.

Mix and Match

However, bringing order out of chaos was the willful Jackson, then 47 years old, rail thin, with steel-gray hair. After arriving in the Crescent City in early December 1814, he acted fast. He imposed martial law and a curfew to brace morale and to stop information about his force leaking to the British. He forced his rough-hewn soldiers to abide by local standards and Army rules: stop using the city boulevards as open-air latrines, and refrain from deserting sentry posts to visit the city's houses of prostitution.

He picked as his aide-de-camp the head of the city's defense council, the brilliant attorney Edward Livingstone. At social gatherings, Jackson charmed the town's elegant belles, who had envisioned the Tennessean as an uncouth rustic. Still, General Jackson was woefully undermanned. He had only about a thousand troops and a few gunboats. In contrast, the British were readying 8,000 troops backed by about 50 ships. In mid-December their fleet routed armed American schooners at Lake Borgne just east of the city. Desperate for manpower, Jackson became the most unusual recruiter in American military history.

8. The Plantation Owner's Startling Army of Diversity

Jackson was a slave-owning planter and a states-rights southerner. Yet he accepted Louisiana Governor William Claiborne's request that New Orleans' "free men of colour" join his army. Informed the blacks were eager to prove their courage and patriotism, Jackson replied, "Our country has been invaded and threatened with destruction. The free men of colour ... would make excellent soldiers. They will not remain quiet spectators of the coming contest." The blacks, paid as regular army soldiers, formed two battalions, numbering about 600 men. One was from Crescent City and a resurrection of an old unit from the days of Spanish rule. The other was made up of refugees from Santo Domingo, today's Haiti, in chaos since a bloody slave revolt and a brutal French suppression. An Army paymaster, fearful of rebellion from armed blacks, objected to the recruits. According to historian Robert Remini, Jackson retorted, "Be pleased to keep to yourself the policy of making payments to the troops ... without inquiring whether the troops are white, black or tea."

Andy Jackson was a renowned Indian fighter. As President he would infamously begin to expel the "civilized tribes," who had adopted American culture, from the American Southeast. Yet he had adopted an orphaned Native American boy. He'd employed Indian tribes as military allies. The previous year, Choctaw Indians had fought as U.S. soldiers during a major Jackson victory over the British-backed Creek Indians. Joining him at New Orleans, therefore, was a squad of Choctaws, about 50 in number.

Adding to the jambalaya of Jackson's army were the citizen soldiers of New Orleans, including the Creoles, of French, Spanish and mixed Caribbean stock. Further, pouring down from the frontier state of Tennessee and adjacent Kentucky to join in the fight were thousands of mostly uneducated but frontier-tough volunteers. Many were of Scotch-Irish descent. Most were Protestant, unlike the residents of New Orleans, most of whom were Catholic. Many of the frontiersmen carried the accurate Tennessee long rifle, good for hunting bear and British alike. Some Frenchmen who'd fought with Napoleon and fled to the New World joined the Americans as well, as did American cavalrymen from militias in Mississippi.

Still, Jackson needed more fighters, and a stronger presence in Louisiana's vast expanse of bayous. Livingstone's council urged him to parley with a band of French pirates operating from a bay 60 miles south of New Orleans. For years their smuggling had sparked clashes with American authorities. Just three months earlier, a clutch of American ships had defeated the pirates in

Among the disparate forces General Andrew Jackson recruited for his army in New Orleans were the pirates of Frenchman Jean Lafitte (courtesy Rosenberg Library, Galveston, Texas, 81.086).

battle. Jackson himself had proclaimed them "hellish banditti." Still, some admired the spunk of these buccaneers, led by a charismatic Frenchman, Jean Lafitte. For his part, Lafitte reasoned smuggling would be easier under an American administration than under a British rule backed by the Royal Navy. He pleaded, bleated, to Governor Claiborne: "I am the stray sheep, wishing to return to the sheepfold." Besides, he was French, the mortal enemy of the British and thus a natural ally.

Livingstone persuaded General Jackson to pardon Lafitte's men for their brigandage. In return, the freebooters joined Jackson's variegated force as sailors and infantrymen. Their experience with ship cannons also made them good artillerymen, and their expertise with smuggling made them good provisioners. (Some readers may have seen the 1958 Hollywood potboiler *The Buccaneer*, starring Yul Brynner as Lafitte and costarring as Andrew Jackson an actor known for playing larger-than-life figures: Charlton Heston. Though its accuracy is shaky, the film entertains.)

Jackson and his motley band threw together a veritable fortress to block the main land route leading to New Orleans. Behind the Rodriguez Canal, they shoveled up a five-foot-high, thousand-yard-long rampart. Laborers deepened the channel's ditch, disputes breaking out over whether whites should perform the same laborious tasks as blacks. Anchored by the Mississippi to the west and a swamp to the east, the rampart canal made for a sturdy defense.

Leadership Matters

Given Jackson's various recruitments, the American force rose from 1,000 to about 4,000. The Americans were still outnumbered about two to one. However, Jackson was aided by the blunders of his adversary, General Pakenham. In the weeks before the fight, the British commander might have marched on a weakly defended New Orleans before Jackson built up his strength. But the cautious Pakenham waited for his own reinforcements. Moreover, instead of using a vastly superior navy to outflank the Americans, he determined on a frontal assault by land, against Jackson's fortified wall.

On the day of battle, Pakenham's army got a late start. Thus the delta fog was clearing when the Brits, with their bright red coats and loud marching bands, finally strode toward the Americans. Marching on open ground, they made inviting targets. A bombardment preceded their assault. But the "red glare" of their normally fear-inspiring rockets whizzed without effect over the American positions. Jackson calmed his men: "Don't mind these rockets, they're mere toys to amuse children." Incredibly, the British soldiers marched forward without bringing up sugarcane bundles to fill the canal ditch, and without ladders to scale the rampart. Neglectful officers had left both vital items behind in camp.

General Jackson had carefully marshaled his men. Near the center of the rampart were 350 soldiers of the U.S. Army 44th Infantry Regiment. On their right were the black battalions. Farther to the right was the citizen militia of New Orleans, and the flank was anchored by the U.S. 7th Army Regiment. Left of the 44th Regiment were the Tennessee and Kentucky sharpshooters. The left flank was anchored by horsemen commanded by Jackson's friend and fellow Tennessean, the able General John Coffee. To the rear were the cannons, some manned by pirate crews.

The British came within range. From the parapets and behind bales of cotton, the Americans poured out a storm of bullets and grapeshot from muskets and cannons and Tennessee long rifles. Each of three lines of soldiers would fire their muskets or rifles in turn, then duck and reload. A frontier informality marked their deadly work. The Americans handed each other bullets and powder, bantered and joked, and fired continuously. The troopers took skillful aim. The British leader, General Pakenham, was shot off his horse and killed. A general leading one of the two British columns was mortally wounded. The head of the other column was put out of action with a bullet in the groin. The attacking host turned into a writhing mass of red, some of it coats, most of it blood.

Valiant Britishers, though wounded, continued to crawl forward toward the rampart and ditch. "Shoot low, boys! Shoot low!" shouted a U.S. officer. "Rake them, rake them, they're comin' on all their fours!" Scottish troops rushed in to try to save their stricken comrades. Yet some 500 of the Highlanders fell. A British unit from the West Indies attempted to outflank Jackson through the swamp. There the Choctaw Indian scouts were waiting and shot up the attack. Some of the wounded drowned in the bogs.

In Napoleonic warfare, when things went south, a strategic reserve would be sent into the fray. However, the British reserves never entered the battle, in part because their bugler, in charge of sounding the advance, was shot in his playing arm. Another British force managed to cross the Mississippi, storm the positions west of the river, and turn captured American cannons against Jackson. However, they were ordered to withdraw when the main attack collapsed.

The death tally revealed one of the most lop-sided battles in military history, comparable to Cortez against the Aztecs or Pizarro versus the Incas. When the dust settled late that morning, Jackson had lost 13 men killed and 58 wounded. In contrast, the British suffered 2,042 casualties, with about 775 killed, captured, or missing in action.

It is well known that the brawl took place weeks after a peace treaty worked out in the Austrian Netherlands formally ended the war. Word of the accord reached New Orleans too late. Under the Treaty of Ghent, the British pledged to no longer hinder or harass American expansion westward. The battle guaranteed they'd keep their word. The Louisiana Territory, and in time all of the West clear to the Pacific, would be America's for keeps—due to Jackson and his motley men.

Sources

Kanon, Tom. *Tennesseans at War, 1812–1815*. Tuscaloosa, AL: University of Alabama Press, 2014.
Louisiana State Exhibit Museum. *Battle of New Orleans*. French Soldiers. http://laexhibitmuseum.org/historic-objects/battle-of-new-orleans/.
Moser, Edward P. "A Rebound from Wartime Devastation." (President Madison). In *The Two-Term Jinx: How Most Second-Term Presidents Stumble and Why Some Succeed*. Book 1. CreateSpace/Amazon (self-published), 2016.
_____. "Victory at New Orleans: Old Hickory's Motley Crew." In *A Patriot's A to Z of America*. Nashville: Turner, 2011.
National Park Service. "The Acquisition of Canada This Year Will Be a Mere Matter of Marching." https://www.nps.gov/articles/a-mere-matter-of-marching.htm.
O'Brien, Greg. National Park Service. "Choctaw Recruits Fight with the U.S. Army." https://www.nps.gov/articles/choctaw-indians-and-the-battle-of-new-orleans.htm.
Ramsay, Jack C. *Jean Laffite: Prince of Pirates*. Burnet, TX: Eakin, 1996.
Remini, Robert V. *The Life of Andrew Jackson*. New York: HarperPerennial, 1988.

9

The Burning of the White House and the Rescue of Its Riches

1600 Pennsylvania Avenue

It was supposed to be a joyous day. The First Lady had laid out a White House feast in the first floor's well-appointed dining room. With the help of her French chef and servants, she'd prepared dinner for forty people. Her husband, James Madison, was personally directing a battle that day, August 24, 1814. He was the first, and last, President to command a U.S. force in the field against a foreign foe. At Bladensburg, Maryland, just seven miles to the northeast, against an invading force of British Royal Marines during "Mr. Madison's War," the War of 1812. American soldiers, sailors, Marines, and militia had squared off against the British, who'd marched toward Washington from their fleet in the Chesapeake Bay.

The previous day, Dorothea Dandridge Payne Todd "Dolley" Madison had gotten a scribbled noted from her husband on campaign. He'd urged her, if things went badly, to deny vital government documents to the enemy. Putting on a brave face, Dolley had organized a White House dinner party, but no one in the panicked city had RSVP'd. Now, Dolley Madison eagerly awaited news of the battle's outcome. On the roof of the White House, she peered through a spyglass in the direction of the fight, searching for a sign. In the distance she heard the rumblings of cannon fire.

News came, disturbing news, first in a trickle then in a torrent. Two horsemen from Bladensburg rushed up to the White House. They informed the First Lady she'd be wise to flee. Dolley stayed. But shockingly, her personal guard of 100 militiamen stationed on the White House lawn—and led by a U.S. Army colonel—took flight. Also leaving Washington was the cowardly, incompetent Secretary of War, John Armstrong of New York. Defeated militiamen and U.S. Army soldiers began moving through the city—not in an orderly retreat but in panic. Major Charles Carroll of Georgetown arrived to urge Dolley to leave.

Rising to the Occasion

Most women faced with such peril would have taken fright. Most men would have too. But Dolley Madison, and her staff and servants, got busy. It was a group effort, involving those of French, Irish, African, Dutch, and English descent. White House steward Jean Pierre Sioussat, gardener Thomas McGraw, and the President's enslaved body servant, Paul

9. The Burning of the White House and the Rescue of Its Riches   41

Jennings, pitched in. So did two friends of Dolley's from New York, Robert Peyster and shipping merchant Jacob Barker. With the threat dire, they focused on important stuff. They saved an original copy of the U.S. Constitution. They put the White House silver service in a cart. Dolley eyed the famed Gilbert Stuart portrait of President Washington. "Save that picture if possible!" she shouted. "Under no circumstances allow it to fall into the hands of the British!" Servants tried unscrewing the painting, too slowly. They tried freeing the image by breaking its frame. Finally, according to some sources, Sioussat cut the likeness out with a pocketknife. Careful not to roll up the picture up lest he crack the paint, the steward stowed it in a wagon.

Today, the Washington portrait marks the grand entrance to the presidential portraits section of the Smithsonian's National Portrait Gallery. The National Archives displays in its atrium the Constitution and other founding documents. Americans have Dolley and her helpers to thank.

During the hubbub, another horseman raced up to the mansion. It was Jim Smith, a free man of color and servant of the President's. He cried, "Clear out, clear out!" The British were coming and were within an hour's march of President's Park.

Dolley Madison and her assistants in August 1814 saved invaluable items from the invading British, including a copy of the Constitution and a Gilbert Stuart portrait of George Washington (National Portrait Gallery, painting by Gilbert Stuart [Lansdowne], 1796, acquired through the Donald W. Reynolds Foundation).

The Washington portrait, the Constitution, and other valuables were packed into horse-drawn carts in front of the mansion. Peyster and Barker drove the wagons to the countryside and entrusted them to a patriotic farmer. Dolley and Carroll departed for Georgetown. Two days later the First Lady reunited with her husband in Virginia. Though the actions of Dolley Madison and even servant Paul Jennings are fairly well known, the work of another man is not. During the chaos, the Secretary of State, James Monroe, then also the acting Secretary of War in lieu of Armstrong, directed several State Department workers to salvage valuable documents from the federal buildings nearby.

The 38-year-old accounting clerk Stephen Pleasonton, belying his last name, had a dour and rather unpleasant countenance. But he and two other clerks, John Graham and Josias King, scrambled to grab original copies of the Declaration of Independence and the Bill of Rights, as well as the letters of General Washington and the official papers of the first sessions of Congress. They stashed the artifacts in linen bags and stuffed them in getaway carts.

The priceless articles were secreted at a grist mill a few miles up the Potomac, near Chain Bridge, Virginia. However, the mill was right across the river and its chain-bridge ferry from the Foxhall Foundry—the U.S. Army's largest munitions maker. Pleasonton worried the British would "detach a force for the purpose of destroying a foundry for canon and shot in its neighbor hood, and would be led by some evil disposed person to destroy the Mill and papers." So, on August 25, he and the two other clerks rode out to Chain Bridge, transferred the items to borrowed wagons, and took them out to an abandoned home in Leesburg, Virginia, a secure 35 miles from the capital.

The British Burning

After the frenzy of evacuation, the British arrived, only to find a strangely quiet White House. However, others had gotten there first. Looters had pulled open cabinets and scattered clothes about the place. The British took what they saw as just revenge. In 1813 an invading American force had captured the capital of British Upper Canada, the town of York, today's Toronto. U.S. troops had burned the parliament building and private residences and farms. York's Reverend Rector wrote former President Jefferson that the sack of Washington

Accountant Stephen Pleasanton played a vital role in spiriting historic artifacts away from the rampaging British (Library of Congress).

was a "small retaliation after redress had been refused for burnings and depredations, not only of public but private property, committed by them in Canada."

Commanding Admiral George Cockburn, Major General Robert Ross, and other Royal officers and men entered the mansion to find a treat—the banquet Dolley Madison had prepared for her husband and his men. Filthy, famished, and bone-dry thirsty from long hours of marching, fighting, and burning down buildings in the August heat, the Brits sat down and dined like kings. Or presidents. They savored the wine from glass decanters, toasting "Peace with America" but "Down with President Jemmy." Crowed Lieutenant James Scott, "Never was nectar more grateful to the palates of the gods than the crystal goblets of Madeira I quaffed at Mr. Madison's expense."

The invaders grabbed souvenirs. A soldier stuck the President's tri-cornered hats on his bayonet. Another grabbed the First Lady's portrait—stating he would "keep Dolley safe … in London." An infantry officer appropriated the President's ceremonial sword. One trooper carried off Madison's book of receipts and expenditures and another the President's medicine chest. (In 1939, the latter was returned, to President Franklin Roosevelt, by the grandson of the looter, Cockburn's paymaster.) The British were pleased to take back portraits of King George III and his wife, Queen Charlotte, that the Americans had captured. Today the paintings watch over Bermuda's parliament.

9. The Burning of the White House and the Rescue of Its Riches

After quick refreshment and looting, it was back to burning. The Royal Marines, 150 strong, shattered the windows of the mansion. Into rooms on the first floor they piled books, furniture, and government papers. They made a big pile in the oval-shaped drawing room, which presaged the West Wing's Oval Office of a century later. Added to the kindling were dozens of gilded couches, settees, and tables Jefferson had handed down to Madison. There was also a piano and a stringed instrument, according to historian Anthony Pitch.

A handful of sailors scampered up to the second floor, fired the curtains and beds, and scrambled outside. There 50 British Marines gathered around the White House, mostly on the southern side near today's garden and South Lawn. They stood with javelins wrapped with rags and soaked in oil. They lit the spears. At the officers' command, they hurled the missiles through the windows, igniting an inferno. The White House was burned to a shell. Still, its superstructure, built by master architect James Hoban, stood up to the flames.

Just north of the White House, hiding in the woods of that still-rustic village, refugees from the Brits watched the flames in horror and fear. They, like their government, had been put to flight, and their capital to the torch. It was one of the worst days in American history.

In 1941, when British Prime Minister Winston Churchill stayed at the White House for wartime planning, he was astonished to find the mansion's sandstone foundations scarred in blackened smoke, a token from the British fire of 1814.

Sources

BBC. "The Odd Objects Looted from Washington DC in 1814," August 29, 2014. https://www.bbc.com/news/blogs-magazine-monitor-28833238.

Costello, Matthew. "Paul Jennings: Slave, Freeman, and White House Memoirist." White House Historical Association, February 1, 2017. https://www.whitehousehistory.org/paul-jennings.

Fleming, Thomas. "When Dolley Madison Took Command of the White House." *Smithsonian*, March 2010. Adapted from *The Intimate Lives of the Founding Fathers*, by Thomas Fleming. https://www.smithsonianmag.com/history/how-dolley-madison-saved-the-day-7465218/.

Kratz, Jesse. "Rescue of the Papers of State During the Burning of Washington." White House Historical Association. *White House History* 35 (Summer 2014). https://www.whitehousehistory.org/rescue-of-the-papers-of-state-during-the-burning-of-washington.

Miles, Ellen. "Gilbert Stuart Paints George Washington." National Portrait Gallery, February 19, 2016. http://npg.si.edu/blog/gilbert-stuart-paints-george-washington.

Pitch, Anthony S. "The Burning of Washington." White House Historical Association. *White House History* 4 (Fall 1998). https://www.whitehousehistory.org/the-burning-of-washington.

Shaw, Benjamin. "Fire and Rain: The Storm That Changed D.C. History." WETA, *Boundary Stones*, July 30, 2015. https://blogs.weta.org/boundarystones/2015/07/30/fire-and-rain-storm-changed-dc-history.

10

A White House Surgery That Echoed Bullets and Brawls

1600 Pennsylvania Avenue

Even Old Hickory had had enough. For 19 years, Andrew Jackson had suffered excruciating pain from a lead slug and bullet ball that had shattered his left shoulder, and left the bullet lodged in his arm. From time to time the wound would fester and open up. While riding off to defend the city of New Orleans during the War of 1812, a large piece of flesh had sloughed off the affected limb. He'd sent it to his wife Rachel Donelson Jackson as a grimly humorous token.

That January of 1832, President Jackson was also pained by a bullet from an 1806 duel. The projectile was lodged permanently near his heart. All that lead in his body, along with medicines he took regularly—lead acetate and mercury-laced calomel—was likely poisoning him, and perhaps triggering his sometimes-rash behavior. Adding to his medical woes were dysentery, constipation and stomach cramps, headaches, toothaches, and inflammation of the kidneys. The worst were the bullet wounds, never healing, giving off pus and blood, internally as well as externally. The pellet in his chest caused severe inflammation of the lungs, hemorrhages, and violent coughing fits, at times pushing him close to death.

For his chest wound, Jackson consulted the aptly named Dr. Philip Physick, the "father of American surgery," from Philadelphia. Physick was physician to Dolley Madison. He'd recently removed gallstone fragments from Supreme Court Chief Justice John Marshall. But Physick realized the piece of lead was too close to Jackson's heart to risk surgery. He advised the President to improve his health by giving up smoking. But tobacco and coffee were two of the vices Jackson couldn't quit. However, the bullet stuck near his shoulder had over time shifted position and could now be discerned below the skin. It was, perhaps, ready for picking. So the President welcomed to his working office in the White House a Dr. Thomas Harris of Pennsylvania, for decades the Navy's foremost surgeon. Harris was the son of a Revolutionary War officer, and his younger brother would become Commandant of the Marine Corps.

The Gangs of Nashville

As the doctor prepared to cut Jackson open, the long-suffering yet frontier-tough President likely thought back to the Nashville, Tennessee, fracas that had brought him so much misery. The incident had occurred one year into the War of 1812 and one year before the great battle in New Orleans that would bring Jackson lasting fame. Ironically, it involved a man who had been, and would become again, one of his closest colleagues and friends.

At the start of the war, Thomas Hart Benton, a 30-year-old officer in the Tennessee militia, served as the chief recruiter for Jackson, a general of Tennessee's militia. But Jesse Benton, Thomas's younger brother, had a duel with William Carroll, later a Tennessee governor and then a major in Jackson's force. At the duel, Jackson stood in as Carroll's second, or assistant. It was one of the 103 duels in which Jackson participated as a gunman or a second. One needed a lot of guns for all that feuding, and it is thought Jackson had 37 duelling pistols in his collection. The confrontation itself was comic opera. Due to Carroll's nearsightedness, the two men stood just paces apart, backs turned, then turned to fire at the count of three. Perhaps to reduce the chances of being shot, Jesse Benton squatted and swivelled around to shoot. But Carroll fired low, low enough to strike Benton in his buttocks. Neither man was seriously wounded, though Jesse's affliction was painful and highly embarrassing.

Jesse's elder brother Thomas was livid at Jackson, his commanding officer, for taking part in a duel against his brother. He exchanged letters with Jackson, branding the duel "savage, unequal, unfair, and base." Them was fightin' words, but no duel followed. There was instead something worse than a duel that often resulted in no one being killed or badly hurt. Jackson swore to horsewhip Philip Hart Benton the very next time he saw him. That time came on September 4, 1813, during a pause in Jackson's wartime command.

He and two hulking friends, Colonel John Coffee and Stackley Hays, were staying at the Nashville Inn, in the city Jackson helped found. Coffee, later a hero at New Orleans, was a ranking officer in Jackson's army. Hays had been involved in Vice President Aaron Burr's 1804–1807 conspiracy to make himself ruler of Mexico and Louisiana. Nashville's City Hotel lodged Thomas Hart Benton and Jesse Benton, along with some toughs of their own. Both parties were armed with pistols and dirks—long Scottish knives. They also sported that violent era's "sword canes"—walking sticks of sharpened metal rods. The Bentons had taken a different hotel than Jackson's gang, they said later, to avoid trouble. This was unlikely, as their hostel was across the street from Jackson's gang.

In full daylight Jackson caught sight of Thomas Benton in front of the City Hotel. Impulsively, he strode across the dirt street, horse whip in hand. He shouted to his former friend: "Now defend yourself, you damn rascal!" Thomas, like his brother Jesse, packing two smoothbore pistols, started to pull one out. But Jackson, quicker on the draw, came at him with his own gun and took out a second. Aiming the pistols at Thomas's chest, Jackson walked him backwards down a hallway toward the rear porch of the hotel. All hell, and then some, broke loose.

As he backpedalled, Thomas glanced up to see his brother Jesse slip out from a doorway and step behind Jackson. Jesse fired his two pistols at Jackson's back, as Jackson fired at and missed Thomas. The bullets from Jesse's guns ripped into Jackson's left arm, smashing his shoulder. Jackson collapsed. The Bentons might have finished him off but for a bystander who blocked their way. Then mammoth John Coffee came swarming into the hall, intent on saving his friend. He fired both guns at Thomas Benton. Both guns misfired, the powder blasts burning a hole in Thomas' shirt. Joining Coffee was an accomplice, Alexander Donelson, the brother of Jackson's wife. The two slashed their knives at Thomas Benton and sent him tumbling down a flight of stairs. Turning to Jesse Benton, Coffee almost impaled him with his sword cane, but a large button on Jesse's shirt broke the weapon's tip. Coffee kept up the assault with his dirk. An accomplice of Jesse's aimed to blast away at Coffee with his own pistols, but those guns also misfired!

Fortunately for all, the single-shot pistols of the day were notoriously unreliable and not the six-shooters that dominated a later frontier. Astonishingly, as the smoke cleared, just one man was grievously hurt—Jackson, and desperately so. His shoulder and arm ran blood. He was placed on a mattress, and his blood soaked it through. His attendants put him on another mattress, and the blood from his stricken arm and shoulder soaked through that as well. It's said that every doctor in Nashville tried saving him. Jackson was carried to a hotel bed, and doctors urged amputation of the afflicted limb. Otherwise, sepsis could spread to the rest of his body, almost surely killing him. But as he passed out from the shock of blood loss, Old Hickory muttered, "I'll keep the arm." He did, and his life.

The Benton gang outside the hotel celebrated his destruction. An elated Thomas, his brother's duelling wound avenged, broke Jackson's sword over his knee. Andy Jackson was transferred to his estate, the Hermitage, and was bedridden for the next month. But a war was on, and a visit from Nashville's town fathers told of a massacre of 250 settlers in Mississippi not far from the Tennessee border. The Creek Indians, allies of the British, had committed the atrocity. Jackson promised his visitors he'd lead a punitive force within days. "The general is ready," he told his astonished listeners. Within a week, arm in sling, Jackson rode off with 5,000 men. In one half-day he covered over 30 miles. Old Hickory crushed the tribes responsible, wiping out two villages. The following year he vanquished the main Creek army at the Alabama Battle of Horseshoe Bend. "I was born for a storm," said Jackson, "and a calm does not suit me."

The next year, he conquered the seemingly unconquerable British at New Orleans. On the edge of death in 1813, from 1815 on Jackson seemed to many indestructible. But he hardly felt that way in the White House, from the shooting pains from the lead in his arm, thus the surgery of Dr. Harris. Antiseptics were as yet undiscovered, making any operation a risk from infection's spread. Anesthetics such as laudanum, an opiate, were known but rarely used. Jackson refused even the common painkiller of whiskey. With the doctor ready, Jackson stood up in his White House office, his arm and shoulder bared. The President readied himself. Harris felt for the pellet and cut into the arm, his patient uncomplaining. Luck was with the long-suffering man that day. The bullet ball quickly popped out. Andy Jackson felt almost immediate and major relief. For one of his serious maladies at least, the White House surgery was a success.

The Most Amazing Duel

However, to the end of his long life, Andrew Jackson suffered from a far worse injury. In 1806 he had rashly exchanged insults through the newspapers with attorney Charles Dickinson of Kentucky. The two men were plantation owners and rival horse breeders. Dickinson accused Jackson of reneging on a horse bet of $2,000, a huge sum at the time. Worse, he insulted Jackson's beloved wife, Rachel. The Tennessean fought dozens of duels

10. A White House Surgery That Echoed Bullets and Brawls

over slights to his spouse. Dickinson and Jackson agreed to settle things with pistols. Jackson may have quickly realized that, in accepting the gunfight, he'd made an awful mistake.

Dickinson was reputedly the best shot in Kentucky. The 26 year old had quick hands, unerring aim, and a fearlessness equal to Jackson's. Dickinson was a gunslinger not of the Wild West of the late 1800s but of the Southwest frontier of the early 1800s. If Dickinson had kept notches on his belt for every killing, he would have had 26—the number of men he'd sent to their graves. In contrast Jackson, although terrific in most military matters, had unusually poor aim. Yet unless he wanted to be viewed as a coward, he could not back out of the fight. But he was no coward. And he had a ferocious sense of honor. If Las Vegas had then existed, touts would have made the Tennessean a hopeless underdog. But Jackson and his friends determined on an outrageous strategy to try to steal a win in this fight to the death.

The killing grounds were near the shore of the Red River in Kentucky. Dueling was illegal in Jackson's home state, which seems odd given its brawling culture. Dickinson and Jackson stood 24 steps from each other, the former confidently, the latter grimly. Jackson wore a long, loose coat, like that of a future Tennessean, Johnny Cash. The coat somewhat blurred his body as a target. Andrew Jackson was tall and very thin; he presented a narrower bull's-eye than most duelists. Also, he stood obliquely, at an angle to Dickinson, further narrowing the target presented. Onlookers watched intently as a judge presiding over the affair told the duelists to begin. The two aimed their single-shot flintlocks at each other. Dickinson, hands rock steady, took accurate aim, and fired. Jackson, amazingly, just stood—and took the first shot! Without firing back, he took a bullet in the chest, which lodged within an inch of his heart.

THE DUEL.

Andrew Jackson was determined on a highly unusual stratagem to survive a duel against notorious gunman Charles Dickinson (Library of Congress).

Jackson staggered from the grievous blow, nearly collapsing. Blood poured from his chest. A stream of red dripped down into his boots, so much so his boots overflowed with blood. Dickinson was thunderstruck. As the gun smoke cleared and he saw that Jackson was standing, he cried, "My God! Have I missed him?" Then, with the iron will Old Hickory was known for, Jackson pulled himself together. In agonizing pain, he straightened himself out. He raised his gun at the horrified Dickinson, aimed, and pulled the trigger. The gun misfired! Now it was Dickinson who seemed to have dodged certain death.

But Jackson adjusted the hammer of his flintlock pistol. He aimed again at his petrified foe, and pulled the trigger. This time the gun fired. The bullet struck Dickinson in the abdomen, and he fell to the ground, mortally wounded. That night, as he lay on his deathbed, Dickinson's friends tried consoling him by assuring that Jackson's wound was also fatal. He hadn't really lost the duel, it was more of a tie. But they were wrong—barely so. Jackson's doctor informed him, "I don't see how you stayed on your feet after that wound." Jackson replied, "I would have stood up long enough to kill him if he had put a bullet in my brain."

After the Dickinson duel, some accused Jackson of breaking the rules of the "code duello" that governed such battles. Technically, his misfiring constituted the first shot. Dickinson's partisans, and others, claimed he should have let Dickinson reload and fire as Jackson fired his "second," and deadly, shot. But Jackson's backers figured anyone taking a bullet in the chest had a right to fire back. Jackson was later plagued by charges he'd murdered Dickinson. In the 1828 presidential election foes distributed the "Coffin Handbills," a false list of persons Jackson allegedly killed. President Jackson has a deserved reputation of having lived the bloodiest life of any Chief Executive.

One final, somewhat related, tale, involves St. John's Church across H Street from the Jackson statue, a story of the "six ghostly figures." These are distinguished men, clothed in the style of the American Revolution or the early Federal period, who are said to materialize at night in the church. Some believe they appear only at times of great moment. For instance, it's said they were spotted after Pearl Harbor and on 9/11. It's thought they are the first six Presidents, who from time to time check in on America to see how it's doing and to show their concern. Those six Presidents are Washington, John Adams, Jefferson, Madison, Monroe, and John Quincy Adams. Moreover, it's thought that soon after they appear, a seventh ghostly figure appears next to them—the spirit of the seventh President, Andrew Jackson. At that point, the terrified ghosts of the first six Presidents fly off into the night!

Sources

Doctor Zebra. "Health and Medical History of President Andrew Jackson." http://www.doctorzebra.com/prez/.
Hauck, Dennis. *Haunted Places: The National Directory*. 2nd ed. New York: Penguin, 2002.
MacMahon, Edward B., and Leonard Curry. *Medical Cover-Ups in the White House*. Washington, D.C.: Farragut, 1987.
Marx, Rudolph, MD. "The Health of the President: Andrew Jackson." *HealthGuidance*. https://www.healthguidance.org/entry/8908/1/the-health-of-the-president-andrew-jackson.html.
Remini, Robert V. *The Life of Andrew Jackson*. New York: HarperPerennial, 1988.
Washington Times. "Ghostly Washington," October 28, 2006. https://www.washingtontimes.com/news/2006/oct/28/20061028-085348-1209r/.

11

The Populist Politics of Pennsylvania Avenue's Park

Pennsylvania Avenue Between 17th and 15th Streets, the Pedestrian Boulevard North of the White House

When the White House was built in 1799 there was no street north of the mansion. Pennsylvania Avenue ended at 17th Street and picked up again at 15th Street, then ran eastward, as it does today, over to and around the Capitol. The future concourse was then the southern end of President's Park, and part of the land allotted to the Executive Mansion. What we know was Lafayette Square belonged to the President as his private preserve.

Extreme Electioneering

The Park, and its section of Pennsylvania Avenue, came about, not surprisingly, from politics—a politics of a very contemporary kind. Populist politics. In March 1801 Thomas Jefferson became President, by a whisker, after the bizarre 1800 election. It entailed 36 deadlocked ballots in the Electoral College between him and his own vice-presidential running mate, Aaron Burr. Alexander Hamilton, who held Jefferson in contempt but hated Burr more, threw his opposition party support to Jefferson, thus assuring his election. (Given its importance, then, and in the razor-close elections of 2000 and 2016, perhaps the Electoral College should be upgraded to the Electoral *University*.) During the campaign, Jefferson had run, among other things, on a populist platform, that is, taking the side of the common people against the wealthy "elites" of the time.

His Anti-Federalist Party had a base of support among the pioneers, farmers, and small businesses of the South and West, as well as the rural, western regions of the northern states. It was in counterpoint to the bankers and large merchant houses of the Northeast, and some of the more prominent businessmen and planters in the South. The fact that Jefferson was quintessential Virginia gentry, educated at William and Mary and possessing hundreds of slaves and thousands of acres of land, did not get in the way of his political rhetoric. He often termed the Federalists of John Adams and Alexander Hamilton as "monocrats" desiring to monopolize privilege and power.

Jefferson's supporters were mostly on the populist side of a burgeoning issue: whether to expand the franchise beyond men of property, the only voting bloc that counted in the earliest federal elections. Eventually, his followers, such as Andrew Jackson, would get their way and suffrage would become universal (by 1825 or so) for all white male voters. This would include all black male voters by 1870, in theory at least, after the Civil War and the 15th Amendment to the Constitution, and female voters by 1920 with the ratification of the 19th Amendment. In practice, it would include all hues by the 1950s and 1960s with the civil rights revolution.

Jefferson's party painted Adams and Hamilton's party as British royalists in disguise who wished to retain a British-style Bank of England in the guise of Hamilton's Bank of the United States and his Treasury Department. And who chipped away at freedom of expression under Adams' Alien and Sedition Acts of 1798, through which some federal judges jailed some men critical of federal officials. The Federalist backers of Hamilton and Adams hit back with gusto. During the 1800 campaign, Jefferson was accused of being in the pockets of the French. The sometimes "deist" Virginian, a person of Christian inclination skeptical of biblical miracles, was cast as an atheist and advocate of the French revolutionaries who'd consigned parish priests to the guillotine and stripped religious holidays from the public calendar—a backer of the unrestrained mob that would sweep away all tradition, the good along with the bad, the baby with the bath water. After his election, Jefferson was eager to make anti–Federalist and populist gestures. And he did from the start.

Symbolic Signaling

In the weeks before his inauguration, instead of staying at the mansion of a local grandee, he stayed at a boardinghouse for congressmen. This was Conrad and McMunn's Hotel, just 200 steps from the south end of the Capitol. On Inauguration Day, instead of being driven to the Capitol in a fancy carriage or even riding over, Jefferson walked. This drew a deliberate contrast with a Federalist predecessor, President Washington. As Chief Executive, George Washington traveled in a grand carriage with half a dozen matching horses and footmen garbed in luminous orange and red. It was one of the ways Washington strengthened the prestige of the new presidential office.

On March 4, 1801, Jefferson's inauguration day arrived. Yet, despite his soaring rhetoric and though charming in person, the Virginian was uncomfortable speaking in public in his thin, high-pitched voice. At the Senate chamber, he gave an inaugural address in a voice so muted that few could hear him. It was rather like the Monty Python *Life of Brian* scene where the Apostles are unclear about what Jesus is saying in his Beatitudes sermon. Jefferson's message of national unity after a divisive election, however, rang clear enough: that all Americans were "republicans" and "Federalists," the then-current terms for the two political parties. After receiving well-wishers at the Capitol for several hours, there was more populist symbolism, as he walked back to his boardinghouse. There he had supper at his usual chair at the foot of the table. An inaugural couldn't have been more low-key. Moreover, Jefferson didn't then head straight over to the White House, as every President has since and as he did after winning a second term in 1805. In 1801 the new President stayed at Conrad and McMunn's a full 15 days after the inaugural, until March 19, the day he finally moved into the President's House.

After arriving at the White House grounds, Jefferson was no doubt reminded of the aristocratic appearance of President's Park, a personal preserve, next to the home of the

11. The Populist Politics of Pennsylvania Avenue's Park

Jefferson at the White House in 1801, the year he became President. He holds his Declaration of Independence near a statue of Benjamin Franklin (Library of Congress).

Chief Magistrate of a democratic republic. This surely smacked of European aristocracy, many of whose noblemen had their own forestland and hunting grounds next to their manors.

As an architect, Jefferson also knew that the large amount of land about the White House, some 88 acres, undermined the symmetry of the mansion and its surroundings. The house got lost in the expanse of land around it. Lopping off seven acres of parkland would make the setting more balanced—just as an Enlightenment philosopher in the Age of Reason would want it. And so, during his first term in office, President Jefferson directed that Pennsylvania Avenue be extended though the north end of the park, from 15th Street to 17th Street, thus creating a public park out of the President's private woodland.

In 1805, after his second inaugural, Jefferson struck another and enduring theme, a populist one. He began the tradition, after taking the oath of office, of traveling from the Capitol down Pennsylvania Avenue to the White House. And he didn't ride down the boulevard, but walked. And he was accompanied by everyday laborers, so-called mechanics, to the astonishment of British onlookers used to the royal pageantry that marks the start of a kingly reign.

Populist politics has long been with us, and it unlikely to disappear soon.

Sources

Costello, Matthew. "The Revolutionary Inauguration of Thomas Jefferson." White House Historical Association, December 21, 2016. https://www.whitehousehistory.org/the-revolutionary-inauguration-of-thomas-jefferson.
Ellis, Joseph J. *Founding Brothers*. New York: Knopf, 2000.
Library of Congress. "U.S. Presidential Inaugurations: Thomas Jefferson." *Web Guides*, January 17, 2017. https://www.loc.gov/rr/program/bib/inaugurations/jefferson/index.html.
Moser, Edward P. "Surprising Trouble After a Sterling Start." (President Jefferson). In *The Two-Term Jinx: How Most Second-Term Presidents Stumble and Why Some Succeed*. Book 1. CreateSpace/Amazon (self-published), 2016.
Pohl, Robert. "Presidents on Capitol Hill," *HillRag*, November 5, 2013. http://www.capitalcommunitynews.com/content/presidents-capitol-hill-0.
White House Historical Association. "Carriages of the Presidents." https://www.whitehousehistory.org/white-house-horses/carriages-of-the-presidents.

12

The Biggest Sex Scandal in Washington's History

Center of Lafayette Square, Andrew Jackson Statue, West Side of Its Base

The center of Lafayette Square has an iconic equestrian statue of Andrew Jackson. The General and future President is mounted on a rearing horse, commemorating his smashing victory at the Battle of New Orleans in January 1815 (see Chapter 8, "The Plantation Owner's Startling Army of Diversity").

The statue was not constructed, however, right after the War of 1812. It was sculpted in 1853 as the Civil War loomed, at a nearby foundry on the south side of the Treasury building. It was meant to symbolize, along with Old Hickory's military skill, his role as a fierce protector of national unity. Visitors often miss the faint quotation inscribed on the west side of the statue's base: "Our federal Union. It must be preserved." The statement harks back to 1830, the year after Jackson entered the White House. It involved a sex scandal, the biggest sex scandal in D.C.'s history—which is saying a lot. The affair toppled most of Jackson's Cabinet and led to a serious crisis over secession—the desire of some southerners to leave the United States—until President Jackson took decisive action to preserve the Union.

A Petticoat Affair

The scandal's main character was a femme fatale, Margaret "Peggy" O'Neale. Born in 1799, she was the lovely and irrepressible daughter of a Georgetown innkeeper. According to biographer John Marszalek, Peggy had "since her teenaged days ... openly consorted with males in a confined place where alcohol was served, inhibitions were loosened." Recalled Peggy herself, "While I was still in pantalets and rolling hoops with other girls, I had the attention of men, young and old, enough to turn a girl's head." Peggy lacked inhibitions and was also a natural beauty. She was described as having "a well-rounded, voluptuous figure, peach-pink complexion ... large, active dark eyes ... full sensuous lips ready to break into an engaging smile." But the young lady had more than good looks. Her parents sent her to a fine school, and she could speak French, dance and sew, talk politics, and was an excellent pianist.

At ages 15 and 16, she attempted to elope with a military officer and, failing that, with another. It's thought her father foiled one late-night departure by hauling her back inside a window of his inn. At age 17, precocious Peggy seemed to settle down, as she married a 39-year-old navy purser, or accountant. This was the hard-drinking John Timberlake (Dupont Circle once had a Timberlake's bar named for the tippler). The couple had three children together.

Peggy and John Timberlake were then friends with a widowed senator from Tennessee, John Henry Eaton. Senator Eaton was a bosom friend of fellow Tennessean and former U.S. Senator Andrew Jackson. Both Eaton and Jackson had lodged at the tavern Peggy's father owned and where Peggy worked. At the pub, Peggy charmed Jackson with her piano playing and Eaton with her looks. With Timberlake often overseas with the Navy, blue-eyed Peggy and the handsome Senator deepened their friendship. They rode about town in a carriage and attended social events together. Rumors swirled they were intimate. The capital, then as now, placed a premium on appearance. Many among the city's movers and shakers distrusted Peggy's low-born status and viewed her as an amoral social climber.

In spring 1828, Timberlake died of a heart attack while serving aboard the USS *Constitution*. Some said he died of a broken heart, from the rumors swirling about his wife. Others attributed his death to suicide and worry over bills that Peggy had piled up. Senator Eaton had tried, and failed, to coax Congress into picking up Timberlake's debts.

The mourning for Mr. Timberlake was brief. On New Year's Day 1829, Peggy, then 29, and Senator Eaton, aged 38, were wed. Their marriage took place just eight months after Timberlake's death and two months before Jackson's inauguration as President. Andrew Jackson's future Secretary of State and Treasury Secretary, Maryland's Louis McLane, joked

A period cigar box bearing the image of Peggy Eaton, the alluring wife of President Jackson's Secretary of War. She brought down a Cabinet and nearly brought on a civil war.

Eaton "has just married his mistress—and the mistress of a dozen others!" After taking office, Old Hickory appointed his pal Eaton to the key post of Secretary of War. His choice guaranteed that Peggy O'Neale Timberlake Eaton would stay at the center of Washington City's salacious rumor mills.

The President's Cabinet was cool to Peggy Eaton—"that hussy," as she was deemed. Colder still were the wives of the Cabinet members. During an era when any woman of standing would immediately return a social call from another lady, Peggy was shunned. Department heads and their wives declined to show up for soirees that she and Secretary Eaton attended. The Cabinet member's spouse who disliked Peggy the most was Floride Bonneau Calhoun, the wife of Jackson's Vice President—John C. Calhoun of South Carolina. Jackson began to view the "Petticoat Affair," as the rumors spread about Peggy were called, as a conspiracy among his political rivals, led by Calhoun and by Kentucky's Henry Clay, the formerly Secretary of State and Speaker of the House. Yet even the President's personal secretary and adopted son, Andrew Jackson Donelson, and his wife, Emily Donelson, avoided Peggy. In response, the widower Jackson dismissed Emily, his surrogate First Lady, and put another relative in her stead. The President seemed the most upset over Peggy's female foes. "I [would] rather have live vermin on my back," he declared, "than the tongue of one of these Washington women on my reputation."

The President's psyche came into play as well. Peggy reminded Jackson of his late, beloved wife, Rachel Donelson Jackson. Rachel had died of a coronary a few days before Christmas in 1828. During the bitter presidential campaign of 1828, Jackson's enemies had accused Rachel of bigamy. Her first husband had sought a divorce back in 1790, but it wasn't formally granted until 1794, after she had married again, this time to Jackson. The campaign attacks had enraged the brittle Tennessean. Jackson grew bitter after Rachel died, convinced the verbal assaults had poisoned her health. At his wife's funeral, he stated, "May God forgive her murderers, as I know she forgave them. I never can." He viewed Peggy Eaton as he did his own spouse, as a victim of slander.

Yet President Jackson took his defense of Peggy Eaton to an extreme. He proclaimed to two clergymen that the twice-married mother of three was "as chaste as a virgin." Henry Clay answered sarcastically: "Age cannot wither, nor can time stale, her infinite virginity." The Jackson Administration became a laughingstock, and it was difficult to hold a productive Cabinet meeting because of the "elephant in the room." One newspaper opined the "interests of the nation were tied to [Peggy's] apron string."

One Cabinet officer who liked Peggy was, not coincidentally, one of the few unattached men among Jackson's advisors. This was his smooth Secretary of State, widower Martin Van Buren of New York. Van Buren, and the ambassadors of Britain and Russia, who were bachelors, all enjoyed Peggy's company at parties. After a full two years of the "Eaton malaria," as the press termed it, Van Buren had a brainstorm. The diminutive Secretary of State was a cunning and subtle man nicknamed the "Little Magician." He saw the Eaton crisis as a chance to undermine the career of Calhoun, his rival to succeed Jackson in the White House. He made a startling proposal to save Old Hickory's political hide, and made the following pitch to the President: "As the senior Cabinet member, I will submit my resignation. This will allow you to request the resignations of all the other Cabinet members, including the Vice President. That will give you a clean slate to appoint a new set of advisors, men much more to your liking."

In April 1831 this is exactly what happened. Except for the Postmaster General, the whole Cabinet was forced out. Jackson packed War Secretary Eaton, and his lightning-rod wife, Peggy, off to the distant Florida Territory, where Eaton served as Governor. Later he exiled the couple further by making Eaton Minister to Spain. Jackson appointed a second Cabinet more in his favor. The President would sweep to reelection in 1832, thrashing Henry Clay by 219–49 in the Electoral College. Calhoun tried to get revenge by blocking Van Buren's nomination as Minister to Britain. But the New Yorker got the last laugh, as he succeeded Calhoun as Vice President and Jackson as President after winning the election of 1836.

Van Buren's Peggy ploy came just in time, as the Eaton crisis bordered on bloodshed. Secretary Eaton, as he prepared to quit the Cabinet, challenged a Calhoun ally, Treasury Secretary Samuel Ingram, to a duel. Ingram declined, and Eaton branded him a coward. Then, with several colleagues, Eaton lurked threateningly about Ingram's Washington home. The Treasury Secretary hired a bodyguard and fled Washington. Jackson grilled Eaton about this threat to a fellow Cabinet member, then let it pass.

Civil Discord

After resigning, Calhoun and his wife, Floride, left in a huff for South Carolina. Calhoun's national career and ambitions to be President had vanished. But in the Palmetto State he became leader of a growing movement for nullification. That's the notion that a state, if it dislikes a federal law, can nullify it, that is, render it void. President Jackson was a slave-owning planter and a states-rights southerner. Yet he was even more a ferocious backer of the Union. As a teenager during the American Revolution, he'd been literally scarred for life by a British Major named Coffin. The officer slashed his face with a sword after Jackson refused to shine his boots. During the Revolution, one of Jackson's brothers died from heatstroke from fighting the British, and the other brother expired from smallpox in a British prison. Further, his mother died of cholera while tending to wounded American soldiers. For the rest of his life, Jackson burned with hatred against the British crown or anything else threatening American unity or strength.

South Carolina had threatened nullification and secession in 1830, the year before Vice President Calhoun's resignation. That April, Jackson and Calhoun, the latter already partial to nullification, both attended the annual Jefferson Day dinner of the Democrat Party that Old Hickory founded. Today, it's called Jefferson-Jackson Day, and party fundraisers are still held on that day. At the banquet, at the Indian Queen Hotel on Pennsylvania Avenue, many attendees gave toasts backing nullification. Jackson sat quietly steaming. Finally, the President rose, raised his glass, and with Calhoun sitting next to him, pointedly declared, "Our Federal Union: It must be preserved." Those are the words on the Jackson statue. At the dinner, Calhoun also gave a toast, in response to Jackson's. The Vice President stated, "The Union, next to our Liberty, the most dear."

Afterwards Jackson pledged that if South Carolina violently broke the federal compact, he'd lead an army into its capital of Charleston. "I will hang the first man I can lay my hand on engaged in such treasonable conduct," stated Old Hickory, "upon the first tree I can reach." Calhoun must have shuddered. Still, at the same time, Jackson engaged in quiet dealmaking with South Carolina's leaders. The issue of the moment was not slavery but tariffs, the tax on foreign goods that was despised throughout the South, which had to import most of its products. Tariffs then made up most of the federal revenues, and the South paid more than its share of them. The second part of Calhoun's toast at the Jefferson Day event had reflected this: "May we all remember that [Liberty] can only be preserved by respecting the rights of the States, and distributing equally the benefit and burden of the Union." In the end, Jackson and Calhoun, with Clay's support, agreed to sharply lower the "Tariff of Abominations." Through a combination of threats and give-and-take, President Jackson avoided civil war for a generation.

And what became of Peggy Eaton, the woman behind all that infighting? She outlived John Eaton and inherited his wealth. Her two daughters married "respectable" men. But at age 59 Peggy seemed to justify the view of those who long before had viewed her as a fallen woman. She wed Anthony Gabriele Buchignani, a twenty-something Italian dance and music teacher. He was a tutor to Peggy's 17-year-old granddaughter Emily. But Anthony tired of Peggy—and took off with her money, and with Emily! Later Peggy consented to a divorce with Anthony—if he married her granddaughter.

In 1879, a destitute Peggy, aged 80, passed away in a home for impoverished women. But she is remembered as the "gorgeous hussy" who brought down a Cabinet, nearly brought on a civil war—and late in life tried to make a respectable man of a gigolo.

Sources

Clark, Allen C. "Margaret Eaton (Peggy O'Neal)." *Records of the Columbia Historical Society* 44/45 (1942/1943), Washington, D.C.
Marszalek, John F. *The Petticoat Affair*. Baton Rouge: Louisiana State University Press, 1997.
Meacham, Jon. *American Lion: Andrew Jackson in the White House*. New York: Random House, 2008.
Oman, Anne H. "Passion on the Potomac." *Washington Post*, February 12, 1982.
Pierce, J. Kingston. "Andrew Jackson: The Petticoat Affair—Scandal in Jackson's White House." *American History*, June 12, 2006. http://www.historynet.com/andrew-jackson-the-petticoat-affair-scandal-in-jacksons-white-house.htm/4.
Remini, Robert V. *Andrew Jackson and the Course of American Freedom, 1822–1832*. New York: Harper & Row, 1981.
_____. *The Life of Andrew Jackson*. New York: HarperPerennial, 2010 (Reprint. ed).
Snelling, William Joseph. *A Brief and Impartial History of the Life and Actions of Andrew Jackson*. Boston: Stimpson & Clapp, 1831.
Swain, Claudia. WETA. "The Petticoat War." *Boundary Stones*, July 30, 2013. https://blogs.weta.org/boundarystones/2013/07/30/petticoat-war.
Yardley, Jonathan. "Just Say Wench." *Washington Post*, February 25, 1998 (Review of *The Petticoat Affair*).

13

The Tragic Wife of America's Premier Thinker

800 16th Street, North Side of H Street Between 15th and 16th Streets, Across from the Square

The Hay-Adams Hotel is named for two prominent men from turn-of-the-20th-century Washington: John Hay and Henry Adams. They lived across the street from Lafayette Square in side-by-side mansions.

Distinguished Denizens

John Milton Hay was one of the most noted public servants and diplomats in American history. He started out humbly yet notably as the campaign gopher for Abe Lincoln—during the Lincoln-Douglas debates of 1858. When Lincoln was running that year for the U.S. Senate from Illinois against incumbent Stephen Douglas, he would speak for many hours before large crowds. Yet even a peerless orator like Honest Abe ran out of things to say. The young John Hay would supply him with newspaper articles, speeches from other men, and famous quotations that Lincoln would slip into his own rhetoric.

When Lincoln was elected President, Hay became, along with John Nicolay, one of his private secretaries, and retained that position throughout Lincoln's presidency. Hay spent a very long time in and out of the federal government. He eventually became Secretary of State for President William McKinley during that little matter of the 1898 Spanish-American War. The U.S. gained much territory, from Puerto Rico to the Philippines, with relatively few casualties. Hay thus famously dubbed the conflict "a splendid little war."

When McKinley was assassinated in 1901 the new President, Teddy Roosevelt, insisted Hay remain at State. From offices at the War, Navy, and State Department building, he negotiated treaties that led to Roosevelt's construction of the Panama Canal. In between government jobs, he worked as a journalist. It was Hay who first fingered Mrs. O'Leary's cow as a cause of the Great Chicago Fire.

Hay's next-door neighbor, Henry Brooks Adams, was the scion of perhaps America's greatest political family. Adams was the great-grandson of the first First Family to live at the White House, John and Abigail Adams. Thus he was the grandson of President John Quincy Adams, John and Abigail's erudite son.

Henry Adams himself was the son of Charles Francis Adams, the chief Union diplomat to England during the Civil War. Henry Adams became a noted historian: he posthumously won the Pulitzer Prize for his book *The Education of Henry Adams*. It traced the transformation of America during his lifetime from a mostly rural country to a largely urban, industrialized land. For years a Harvard professor on the Middle Ages, he penned an exquisite "travelogue" through medieval civilization, *Mont Saint Michel and Chartres*.

Talented Yet Troubled

Indeed, Henry Adams had exquisite tastes, including in women. He was wed to Marian Hooper "Clover" Adams, the daughter of a noted, idealistic Boston surgeon who refused payment for most of his operations. Her mother, Ellen Sturgis Hooper, was a poet of the Transcendentalist School (think Thoreau's *Walden*) and an acquaintance of writers such Nathaniel Hawthorne (*The Scarlet Letter*) and Henry Wadsworth Longfellow ("Paul Revere's Ride").

In the Civil War Clover worked for Frederick Law Olmstead's Sanitary Commission, charged with supplying the vast Union army with fresh food and adequate medical supplies (Olmstead was the fellow who designed Central Park). Clover was one of the first female photographers. In her darkroom off Lafayette Square she became expert at using chemicals for bringing her sharply observed images to life.

The great-grandson of John and Abigail Adams, Henry Adams was a leading man of letters wed to an accomplished yet troubled wife (Harvard University Archives, photography by William Notman, 1885).

But Clover was also greatly troubled. A suicide gene legitimately ran in her family. Her mother's sister took her own life while she was pregnant. Clover's own sister would kill herself by leaping in front of a train. Her brother tried to kill himself by jumping out of a window, dying soon afterward. When Henry's brother Charles learned he was marrying Clover Hooper, he exclaimed, "Heavens, no! They're all crazy as coots. She'll kill herself, just like her aunt." Henry informed another brother, "I know better than anyone the risks I run. But I have weighed them carefully and accept them."

Henry Adams met Clover Hooper in Britain, when he was personal secretary to his ambassador father. After living for years in Boston's Back Bay, among the Boston Brahmans who dominated the city's cultural scene, they moved to Washington in 1877. They rented, from banker-philanthropist William Corcoran, the former John Slidell House at 1501 H Street. The irony of their residence was obvious to Henry Adams. Slidell had been one of the two Confederate diplomats—the other was James Mason, the grandson of George Mason—sent to Europe to enlist the help of France and Britain for the Confederacy. Adams had worked with his father to thwart their aims.

On the east side of Lafayette Square, in the old Cutts-Madison, or Dolley Madison,

13. The Tragic Wife of America's Premier Thinker

House, had lived Commodore Charles Wilkes. His 1861 seizure of Slidell and Mason off of a British ship in the Caribbean had nearly brought on war between Britain and the Union, which might have won the war for the Confederacy. All this was proof that, back in the day in D.C., everybody who was anybody knew everybody and often lived cheek by jowl.

In 1880, Henry and Clover moved into larger quarters at another Corcoran house, at 1607 H Street, across the street from the Square's northern end. Henry and Clover turned the place into the capital's intellectual center. They formed close friendships with John Hay, and his wife, Clara Louise Stone Hay. The fifth member of their Five of Hearts, as they wryly dubbed their pseudo-secret society, was Clarence King. King was then a world-famous geologist and explorer of the American West. It was rumored that any of the five might have had a hand in writing the best-selling *Democracy: An American Novel*. It was a critical look at the capital city's corruption in the Gilded Age of all-powerful business magnates. It was a template for many Washington novels to come. (*Democracy* was published anonymously, and later attributed to Henry Adams.)

The circle of friends hosted the cream of Washington society. Guests included future Supreme Court justice Oliver Wendall Holmes, Jr., and novelist and psychologist Henry James—whose novel *Daisy Miller* may have been based on Clover. The Hays and the Adamses could afford to entertain. Clara Hay was the daughter of banking and railroad magnate Amasa Stone. The Adamses had sizeable inheritances. Clover decorated their home with Japanese sculptures and masterworks of European painting. The two couples subsidized King's scientific expeditions. They made plans to expand their salon into lavish quarters. Adams hired his fellow Harvard alum Henry Hobson Richardson to design facing mansions for himself and Hay at the corner of 16th and H. At that time America's ranking architect, Richardson had designed Trinity Church in Boston's Copley Square and the imposing City Hall in Albany, New York. He put together plans for thick-walled, kitty-corner homes, made from his characteristic brown sandstone, in a Romanesque style that appealed to the medieval scholar in Adams. The two couples aimed to move into their new abodes in 1886.

But in April 1885, after years of seeming happiness with Henry, Clover Adams fell into a deep depression after her beloved physician father, Dr. Robert Hooper, passed away. Her melancholy may have been worsened by the fact that, at age 41, she and Henry had no children, even as their friends the Hays had four. Clover told a relative, "If any woman ever says to you that she doesn't want children, it isn't true. All women want children."

On Sunday, December 6, of that year, Henry left their home to visit a dentist. While leaving he ran into a woman coming over to meet Clover, and he took her back to the house. By the fireplace, Henry found his wife sprawled on the floor. She had swallowed potassium cyanide, one of the chemicals from her photography lab, a fatal poison. A doctor rushed over and confirmed the worst.

Now it was Henry Adams' turn to be depressed. To a friend of his deceased wife, he wrote, "I have not had the good luck to attend my own funeral, but with that exception I have buried pretty nearly everything I lived for." John Hay wrote of Clover: "Is it any consolation to remember her as she was? That bright, intrepid spirit, that keen, fine intellect, that lofty scorn for all that was mean, that social charm which made your house such a one as Washington never knew before and made hundreds of people love her as much as they admired her."

A devastated Henry Adams went on a trip to Asia, to forget. He spent a lot of time in Japan and studied Buddhism, believing it might provide solace. It didn't.

Tragedy's Tribute

Returning to America, he decided to honor his departed wife with a funeral sculpture. He approached America's preeminent sculptor, Augustus Saint-Gaudens. You may know his work from the movie *Glory*, the Denzel Washington and Morgan Freeman film about the Massachusetts 54th, the African-American regiment that fought in the Civil War. The movie shows a striking sculpture of Gaudens that depicts the black soldiers on the march with their white officer (played by Matthew Broderick in the film). For Clover Adams, Gaudens created a remarkable bronze figure of a shrouded person in seated repose. To frame the sculpture with a granite setting, Adams approached architect Stanford White, creator of New York's Washington Square Arch in Greenwich Village. (White would meet his own tragedy in 1906 when, after an affair with the married theatrical ingenue Evelyn Nesbit, he was shot to death by Nesbit's husband.)

Henry Adams claimed the Gaudens statue was not supposed to convey deep emotion, but was meant to suggest contemplation. But the people of Washington knew better. They gave the work a nickname that stuck. Art history books use it: *Grief*.

This 1891 sculpture is considered a masterpiece and is titled, *Grief,* **in memory of Clover Adams (Library of Congress, sculpture by Augustus St. Gaudens, 1891; photograph by Camilo J. Vergara, 1984).**

In 1927 the Hay-Adams mansions were torn down by real estate mogul Harry Wardman and replaced by today's Hay-Adams Hotel. It's said that the ghost of Clover Adams inhabits the place. She is supposedly an amicable, not angry, spirit, if a rather sad one, as she was in life.

Sources

Adams, Henry. *The Education of Henry Adams*. Bethesda, MD: Modern Library, 1995 (originally published in 1918).

_____. *Mont-Saint-Michel and Chartres: A Study of Thirteenth-Century Unity*. Princeton: Princeton University Press, 1982 (originally published in 1904).

Conroy, Sarah Booth. "The Lives of the Lafayette Square Literati." *Washington Post*, June 10, 1990. https://www.washingtonpost.com/archive/lifestyle/1990/06/10/the-lives-of-the-lafayette-square-literati/2610e166-d1f0-40e7-a055-6e9852f67ab6/.

Dykstra, Natalie. *Clover Adams: A Gilded and Heartbreaking Life*. Boston: Houghton Mifflin Harcourt, 2012.

Lewis, Tom. *Washington: A History of Our National City*. New York: Basic Books, 2015.

Richard, Paul. "Cloaked in Mystery." *Washington Post*, November 25, 2001.

Wilmerding John. "A Grave Marker Both Singular and Universal." *Wall Street Journal*, December 1, 2017. https://www.wsj.com/articles/a-grave-marker-both-singular-and-universal-1512164365.

14

The Secret Life of the Intrepid Explorer

800 16th Street, North Side of H Street Between 15th and 16th Streets, Across from Lafayette Square

Today we see the leading lights of the "Five of Hearts" circle of friends and intellectuals associated with the old Hay-Adams mansions off Lafayette Square as two colleagues. One was the Secretary of State and private secretary of President Lincoln, John Hay. The other was the historian and writer Henry Adams. But during their lives, both men thought themselves outdone by the "fifth wheel" of their group, Clarence Rivers King. Almost forgotten today, Clarence King was the most famed American explorer and geologist of the 1870s, when much of the Wild West was explored and surveyed for the first time, much of it by King. But unbeknownst to the brilliant Hay and Adams and their cultured wives, King lived a second, secret life that wasn't revealed until his death in 1901.

A Sherlock of the Mountains

Born in 1842, Clarence King was the descendent of Mayflower Pilgrims and of English nobility who had signed the Magna Carta, the distant precursor to the Bill of Rights. Raised in New England, the future "King of Diamonds" was much influenced by a Yale College instructor, James Dwight Dana. Dana had been the geologist for Commodore Charles Wilkes, the longtime resident of the Dolley Madison House on Lafayette Square, during Wilkes' epic 1838–1842 exploration of the South Seas.

In 1864 President Lincoln set aside a tract in the California wilderness known as Yosemite—a precedent for the national parks to follow. It was King who mapped out the boundaries of the place, not long after he co-discovered Mt. Whitney, the tallest American summit south of Alaska. From 1867 to 1872, he was the inspiration behind, and leader of, the government's path-breaking 40th Parallel Survey. Its 36-strong team of geologists, botanists, and zoologists explored and surveyed a vast expanse north and south of the 40th line of latitude. The tract stretched 80,000 square miles through the Sierra Nevada Mountains, from Wyoming to California. King's men gathered thousands of rock and mining samples, set up hundreds of weather measurement stations—and hunted for dinosaur fossils. King was just 25 years old when he led the survey. On finishing it, he authored a bestselling book on the outdoors, *Mountaineering in the Sierra Nevada*, which is still in print.

In 1872, while on his survey, King won worldwide acclaim for exposing the Great Diamond Hoax. The previous year, two Mexican-American war veterans, the slick-talking Philip Arnold and his listless cousin, the aptly named John Slack, made a startling pronouncement. They claimed to have found, in remote, southwest Wyoming, near Black Buttes, a fabulous vein of diamonds, rubies, sapphires, and emeralds. The stones were said to exceed the value of Nevada's legendary Comstock Lode, which had made millionaires of many silver prospectors.

As proof, the two cousins and business partners showed off bags of precious stones, allegedly from the vein, to investors in San Francisco and New York. Interested parties set up a stock company to exploit the find. They made up a who's who of America's financial and military elite. Speculators included the commanding General of the U.S. Army, General William Tecumseh Sherman; Horace Greeley, editor of the *New York Tribune*, whose injunction to "go West, young man," led many to mine metal in the Western mountains; Bank of California founder William Ralston, a bankroller of the transcontinental railroad and the Comstock Lode; and former Union Army commanding General and former Democratic Party presidential nominee George McClellan. None other than Charles Tiffany, the founder of the namesake jewelry firm, pronounced the gems had extraordinary value.

However, on hearing of the claim, Clarence King was doubtful. In his survey he had examined much of the territory near the jewels without finding many. He worried news of the discovery would damage his scientific reputation. In autumn 1872, he led out a cartographer and a rock expert in freezing weather to check out Arnold and Slack's find. After examining the Black Butte site and drawing on his expert knowledge of mineralogy, King deduced the diamonds at the site were mixed with other gems not normally found together in nature. More prosaically, he and his men saw footprints scattered around the diamonds and rubies they found near the surface of the soil. King concluded the alleged lode had been "salted" with precious stones from outside the region. Indeed, Arnold had made two trips to London, where he had bought up uncut jewels, many mined in South Africa. He then returned to America and, in between meetings with gullible investors, scattered the stones at Black Butte with Slack's help.

His detective work done, an alarmed King rushed back to San Francisco. At a hurriedly convened meeting, he convinced Ralston and other investors they'd been had. One investor suggested King "sit" on his revelations for a while and make a bundle by shorting the holding company's stock. King replied, "There is not enough money in the Bank of California to make me delay the publication [of the findings for] a single hour."

Word soon emerged of the swindle. The *San Francisco Chronicle* screamed the headlines "MAMMOTH FRAUD EXPOSED" and "Astounding Revelations." It added, "We have escaped, thanks to GOD and CLARENCE KING, a great financial calamity." The stock company was disbanded. Some of the investors sued Arnold, who settled out of court with one for $150,000. He kept the others at bay, partly because some feared publicity for having been such suckers. Arnold threatened to shoot people setting foot on the Kentucky farm he bought with his loot. He ended up pocketing perhaps $250,000 from the scam. He went into banking in the Bluegrass State, but during a violent argument with a fellow financier he received shotgun wounds to an arm. Within a year he was dead, at age 49, of pneumonia. His former partner Slack also fell into hard times. He ended up as a maker of coffins in White Oaks, New Mexico. Today the place is a ghost town better known for having hosted

Billy the Kid. King's reputation soared from all this sleuthing and surveying. In 1879 he was made the first head of the U.S. Geological Survey. Part of the Interior Department, the agency is still charged with classifying the nation's immense land and water resources.

Back in the civilized quarters of Lafayette Square, Adams and Hay marveled at their friend's exploits and high principles. Hay termed King "the best and brightest man of his generation, with talents immeasurably beyond any of his contemporaries." Adams wrote of King that "men worshiped not so much their friend, as the ideal American they all wanted to be." They also noted his quirks, such as a love of creature comforts in the wild, according to author Patricia O'Toole. On a Western trip, Adams encountered King on one of his expeditions. He recalled: "In the evening, after a long, gritty day in the field, [King] donned silk hose, gleaming shoes, and a suit freshly pressed by his valet. Materializing at the campfire, he looked … 'like a bird of paradise rising in the sagebrush.'"

A Secret Second Life

But Adams and Hay would have been astonished at an outlandish scenario that, beginning in 1887 or 1888, played itself out in New York for many years. Numerous times, a stocky, richly dressed man would leave a business meeting in Manhattan, then walk warily but with anticipation across the Brooklyn Bridge. At some point, after looking about to ensure he wasn't being watched, he'd seek out an alleyway or a tavern, perhaps—a place where he could change his clothes. There he'd take off his expensive duds, meant to impress investors about some new mining enterprise of his. He'd slip his tie and wool coat into a travel bag. Then he would pull out another, far humbler set of clothes and slip into the guise of a railway porter.

The long walk from Manhattan was nothing to the robust, athletic fellow, who went by the name of James Todd. After all, he was accustomed to daily hikes of 15 miles or more up steep mountain ridges. Eventually he arrived at his destination: 48 North Prince Street. There a smiling African-American woman named Ada, with their four small, mixed-raced children at her side, would greet her husband and usher Todd inside their house.

The father of this brood, James Todd, was, in fact—Clarence King! King was in a secret, common-law marriage with Miss Ada Copeland. Clarence King *was* James Todd, his alter ego, his secret persona.

As a young girl, Ada Copeland had been a slave. Ada was born in 1860, in West Point, Georgia, and in her mid-twenties moved to Brooklyn and found work as a nursemaid. As it was socially impossible in 1888 for a famous white explorer to admit to a relationship with a black woman, and one of humble social standing, King assumed a new identity. He told Ada he was from the Caribbean, of mixed white-and-black heritage, and that his name was James Todd. It's not uncommon for a "black" person to have "white" features, such as King's blue eyes and tawny skin, and of course the reverse can be true.

When they met, "James Todd" told Ada he had one of the best jobs an African-American man could hold at that time—the work of a Pullman porter, one of the force of black stevedores serving the luxury cars of the nation's richest industry, the railroads. As a Pullman employee, he'd be entitled to unusually high pay and unusually high status for a black laborer. And his job, he'd explain to Ada Copeland, took him faraway for extended periods.

14. The Secret Life of the Intrepid Explorer

The ruse allowed him, when he wasn't in Brooklyn, to continue his other, famous life in exploration and prospecting. Meanwhile, King's friends and relatives knew he was often away on expeditions, so his absences in New York weren't questioned. Some assumed he was a restless bachelor, a man of the world who couldn't settle down. If Ada Copeland doubted Todd's story, she didn't let on. She loved him and their children, as he loved them. Her common-law marriage to King, a "Pullman porter" with a solid income, raised her status in Brooklyn's black community. If she did have her suspicions, it was perhaps—in a time of much racial prejudice—a matter of not looking a gift horse in the mouth.

King and Copeland had five children together. Four survived to adulthood. The two sons would identify as mulatto, mixed race, according to census records. They served in the African-American regiments of the First World War. The two daughters would identify as white and married Caucasian men. Apart from his love for Ada and their children, there was another unusual, and philosophical, reason for King's secret relationship. He'd tell friends like Hay and Adams that racial mixing was a good thing. That the interbreeding of the various races in America, including blacks and whites, would lead to a uniquely superior American hybrid. This went completely against both the highbrow and lowbrow thinking of the era. The late 1800s was the time of the "white man's burden," in poet Rudyard Kipling's phrase, for the European powers to benevolently rule over their colonial subjects. It was also the time of the separate but "unequal" public facilities for blacks in much of America.

Throughout their 13-year relationship, King kept cloaked his life with Ada Copeland—until he lay dying from tuberculosis in late 1901. From his Phoenix, Arizona, deathbed he wrote Ada a tell-all letter that revealed his actual identity and career. Once she got over her shock, if she was shocked, Ada grew proud of the heroic figure with whom she'd raised a family. She formally changed her name, from Ada Copeland to Ada King.

At Clarence King's death, John Hay and Henry Adams also learned the truth of their friend's astonishing second life. Their reaction was one of true friends. They arranged to buy a house for Ada King. Through Hay's auspices, a fund was set up to support her and her children. In 1901 they ranged in age from four to nine. Hay's very wealthy daughter, Helen Hay Whitney (think Manhattan's Whitney Museum), also contributed money to Ada.

Ada Copeland King would wage a 30-year legal fight over a trust fund that King had left for her. However, a court finally determined Clarence King had been penniless at death and Ada got nothing. But due to Hay and Adams, she and her children weren't left destitute.

Hidden Hearts

The wild hidden story of the Five of Hearts doesn't end there. Scholars have discovered that John Hay had his own secret affair while married to Clara Louise Stone Hay, the mother of his four children. While Secretary of State he was intimately involved with Nanny Mills Davis Lodge—the wife of the congressman who had the most say over his State Department. That was the chairman of the Senate Committee on Foreign Relations, the powerful Boston Brahman Senator Henry Cabot Lodge. According to historian Warren Zimmermann, Nanny Lodge was to Hay everything his wife, Clara, was not. Nanny was "pretty and witty, small and slim with dark hair and eyes [of] 'unforgettable blue.'" In contrast, a portrait of Clara by Swedish artist Anders Zorn reveals a woman with rather blunt, heavyset features.

Henry Cabot Lodge would impede Hay's attempt to secure an American-owned passage from the Caribbean through to the Pacific, which later took form as the Panama Canal. He'd also obstruct Hay's famous "Open Door Policy" of free trade with, and fair play for, China. The two men were pillars of the Republican Party and supposedly of like minds on most issues. But Lodge may have learned of Hay's affair with his wife. If so, that may have shaped his views, both public and private, about the Secretary of State.

Astonishingly, Henry Adams had his own infatuation with another woman, although in his case, it was not at all a secret. The lady was the beguiling, dazzlingly dressed Elizabeth "Lizzy" Sherman, a niece of General Sherman. She was also the niece of the General's brother, the powerful Ohio Senator John Sherman, author of the Sherman Anti-Trust Act. In 1878, an impecunious Miss Sherman came to Washington on a distasteful task: to arrange her marital match with a wealthy but colorless and heavy-drinking former Secretary of War. This was Pennsylvania Senator James Donald Cameron. Miss Sherman and Senator Cameron consented to a marriage of convenience. The 20-year-old Lizzy wrangled a financial premarital agreement from the 45-year-old lawmaker. It guaranteed her $160,000 in bonds, worth about $3.6 million today. A cold and loveless union resulted, with the couple residing at the old Benjamin Ogle Tayloe townhouse at 25 Madison Place, on the east side of Lafayette Square. Burning far brighter was Henry Adams' unabashed affection for Lizzy, evident to all, at least from the time of Clover Adams' death.

In one of his love letters to her, Henry Adams described himself as, "In the grip of sex no man has ever thought." Scandalizing Washington, he would proclaim his love for the married woman in public settings. Yet their 40-year relationship may have stayed platonic. Lizzy, though captured by Henry's intellect and wit, found the bald, aging writer physically unappealing. Noted writer-philosopher Henry James of Lizzy and Henry, "Women have been hanged for less; and yet men have been, too, I judge, rewarded with more." Still, the mutual affection endured until Adams' death in 1918.

As for Ada Copeland King, she lived an extremely long time, until 1964—the year after Martin Luther King, Jr., made his "I Have a Dream" speech and the year of the federal Civil Rights Act. Passing on at age 103, Ada was one of the longest-surviving former slaves in America. She survived to witness the formal end of Jim Crow, generations after her bearing of forbidden fruit in a forbidding time. She was the heartfelt lover of the most unusual romancer in the Five of Hearts, Clarence Rivers King, mostly known for his scientific exploits.

But he and his friends are known also for their wild tangle of loves, for passions both apparent and secreted from view.

Sources

Adams, Charles Francis. "The Trent Affair: A Historical Retrospect." *American Historical Review* 17, no. 3 (April 1912). Oxford University Press on behalf of the American Historical Association. http://www.jstor.org/stable/1834388. Accessed: 09-05-2018 14:44 UTC.

Morris, Sylvia Jukes. "The Historian and the Hostess." *Washington Post*, December 25, 1983. https://www.washingtonpost.com/archive/entertainment/books/1983/12/25/the-historian-and-the-hostess/54dc2677-0641-4d52-be95-6b8943abf5b8/?utm_term=.46dadbabdeb9.

O'Toole, Patricia. *Five of Hearts: An Intimate Portrait of Henry Adams and His Friends*. New York: Harmony/Crown, 1990.

Sandweiss, Martha A. *Passing Strange: A Gilded Age Tale of Love and Deception Across the Color Line*. New York: Penguin, 2009.

Wilson, Robert. *The Explorer King: Adventure, Science, and the Great Diamond Hoax; Clarence King in the Old West*. New York: Scribner, 2006.

Zorn, Anders. "Portrait of Mrs. John Hay Née Clara Stone, 1883." *Artnet*. http://www.artnet.com/artists/anders-zorn/portrait-of-mrs-john-hay-n%C3%A9e-clara-stone-ewHtMpoi5aN8WNoS2giBBA2.

15

The Cunning Craft of a Deadly Spy

Park Benches, Facing the White House and the Eisenhower Executive Office Building, Southwest Section of Lafayette Square

In the spring of 1861, at the start of the Civil War, one could loll near this spot on the park side of today's General Rochambeau statue. There one might find Rose O'Neale Greenough. She was an affluent widow of a State Department linguist and a doyenne of the city's social scene. Born in 1813, she was the daughter of a Montgomery County, Maryland, plantation owner whose enslaved manservant had murdered him. Orphaned, she went to live with her aunt, who managed a boardinghouse on Capitol Hill catering to congressmen. There Rose made acquaintance with the power brokers of the federal city. She admired the thinking of boarder John C. Calhoun, the architect of secession. Rose idolized the aged Dolley Madison and befriended James Buchanan, the President who dawdled as the Civil War approached. Rose's sister married Dolley's nephew, and her own niece wed Illinois Senator Stephen Douglas, Abraham Lincoln's rival for the presidency.

Signals Intelligence

Rose had connections and smarts and an excellent memory. After the war's outbreak, she'd sit in Lafayette Square and observe the parade of Union Army officers entering the Executive Mansion or the War Department offices to meet with President Lincoln and ranking generals. Often she'd head over to the other side of the White House complex, to the Washington Monument, still under construction—a poignant symbol of a nation divided and incomplete. As crowds bustled about, she might chat with acquaintances, asking questions, making mental notes. She might take a carriage over to Capitol Hill and converse with her friends in Congress and among the congressional staff working on the funding and organization of the war. Later in the day, she might wind up back at the park benches: watching, conversing, thinking. Finally, she'd get up and stroll the two blocks up 16th Street to her townhouse, the site of today's St. Regis Washington hotel. There, she did an unusual thing.

She would rearrange, with precision, the shutters on her home. Rose then went inside and did another peculiar thing. She rearranged, with precision, the blinds to her windows. A careful observer might note this had little to do with the position of the sun, to let in more light or less. She also placed candles in various positions on the windowsills. Rose was employing her windows to compose a secret code that contained vital messages. Confederate agents stepping by her house took note of the intelligence in the panes. According to local lore, rebels across the Potomac on nearby Arlington Heights trained powerful spyglasses and binoculars on her house to collect this information.

Rose was a Confederate spy. The coded messages, composed in this unusual way, told of the strength and position of Union troops and the strategy of Union officials that she'd gleaned from her contacts. A key source was Massachusetts Senator Henry Wilson, later Grant's Vice President and a writer of steamy love letters to Rose. Along with window blinds and candles, Rose used couriers. To carry written messages, she employed fellow spy Betty Duvall, who hid the intel in a silken hair piece. (Duvall was an ancestor of actor Robert Duvall, who coincidentally played Confederate General Robert E. Lee in the movie *Gods and Generals*.) Rose took orders from her spy "handler," Confederate Captain Thomas Jordan. He and she built up an espionage network of 50 agents.

In July 1861, the Union Army marched out to confront Confederate troops at Manassas, Virginia, 30 miles west of the capital. This was the Battle of Bull Run, or Manassas, the first big fight of the war. Famously, many civilians in Washington rode out to the battlefield with picnic baskets. They expected to dine while watching an easy Union victory and the rebellion's swift end. However, in part due to the intel Rose had provided on the composition and intent of the Union forces, the rebels, led by commanders such as P.G.T. Beauregard and Thomas "Stonewall" Jackson, were primed for action. The federal assault was crushed. Union troops hastily retreated toward Washington, accompanied by hordes of civilians, their picnic turned to panic.

In gratitude to the information Rose had supplied, her handler wrote her: "Our President [Jefferson Davis] and our General [Beauregard] direct me to thank you.... The Confederacy owes you a debt." Later on, the head of Union Army security for Washington City acknowledged Rose's "masterly skill" and "her knowledge of all the forces which reigned at the Capitol."

A Spy Catcher to the Spy

Union commanders suspected intelligence leaks had led to the Bull Run debacle, and the head of the federal spy-catching operation was the founder of what became the Secret Service, one Allan Pinkerton. In the Chicago area, Pinkerton had become a famous detective and a participant in the Underground Railroad that sheltered escaped slaves. He also established what became Pinkerton's armored car service (though in his day they were armored carriages). There's a wonderful photograph, taken by Matthew Brady associate Alexander Gardner, of a conspiratorial-looking Pinkerton standing with a stove-pipe-hatted President Lincoln after the bloody 1862 Battle of Antietam.

In his spy catcher role, Pinkerton suspected that Rose, a vocal Southern sympathizer, worked for the other side. For this reason, he kept a close eye on her house. On August 22, 1861, he and a pair of agents observed a Union Army supply officer enter Rose's home. Eager to learn what was up, Pinkerton took off his boots and climbed onto the shoulders of his men. They boosted their boss up to a window, allowing Pinkerton to peer within and listen in on the chitchat (the incident popularized the term "to eaves drop").

According to Pinkerton's account, he heard the soldier tell Rose the location of Union troops. Rose and the officer entered a room together, and when they emerged their hair and clothes were in disarray. Evidently the man had whispered sweet nothings into Rose's ear as well as vital intelligence. When the officer left the house, it was raining. He strode down 16th Street in the summer squall back to Lafayette Square. Pinkerton hurried after him, still in his bare feet, splashing mud. The two men entered the Square, passed close to the benches where Rose staked out the area, and headed toward a Union Army quartermasters office. The man with the wet, muddy feet tailing a Union officer came under suspicion. Pinkerton was arrested—as a suspected Confederate agent! Pinkerton cleared himself, and had the suspicious officer arrested. The fellow was imprisoned at Fort McHenry, Baltimore.

Pinkerton put Rose Greenough under house arrest and had a female agent strip-search her. His men discovered incriminating evidence from scraps of documents Rose had burned. Her staked-out home was nicknamed "Fort Greenough." But the wily

Allan Pinkerton, left, looking for all the world like an intelligence agent, stands with a stovepipe-hatted President Lincoln after the 1862 Battle of Antietam (Library of Congress).

spy found other ways to get information to the Confederacy. Visiting relatives "bootlegged" out information in their socks. Rose had a maidservant put sealed missives in her undergarments and leave the house past guards who declined to inspect the intimate clothing of a woman. (Talk about an undercover agent!) Rose also employed her eight-year-old daughter, "Little Rose," to convey messages.

In January 1862 Pinkerton's patience ran out. He had Rose clamped in the Old Capitol Prison, at the site of today's Supreme Court building. The converted jail had been the very hostelry that Rose's aunt had run. Conditions were dire—Rose's bed sheets were infested with vermin, and Little Rose, who stayed with her mother, got the measles. Still, it's suspected Rose sent out more coded messages by arranging the blinds to her cell's window and by placing candles in certain sections of the sill. A photograph of Rose and Little Rose in prison shows the windows boarded up, possibly to stop such shenanigans.

After a few months Rose was released, supposedly to stop spying. She didn't. Rose

15. The Cunning Craft of a Deadly Spy

Rose Greenough with her daughter "Rebel Rose" in her boarded-up jail cell at the Old Capitol Prison (Library of Congress).

Greenough went off to the rebel capital of Richmond, Virginia. Confederate President Jefferson Davis granted her $2,500 and thanked her for "the valuable patriotic service rendered by you to our cause." In 1863, evading the Union Navy's blockade, she sailed off to Europe, where she lobbied for the South. Rose met Queen Victoria and became engaged to the 2nd Earl of Grenville. In France she was received by Emperor Louis Napoleon III, Bonaparte's nephew. She published a bestselling memoir on her acts of espionage, titled *My Imprisonment and the First Year of Abolition Rule at Washington*. She took her book royalties and sailed back to America in autumn 1864. But her ship approached the coast near North Carolina's Cape Fear, an appropriately named place of many shipwrecks. On October 1 a storm came up, and the ship stuck on a reef.

Rose had secreted $2,000 in gold inside her clothes. Intent on getting ashore to avoid an approaching Union warship and ignoring the ship captain's pleas, she climbed into a rowboat. But the storm-tossed waters overturned her dinghy. Weighted down by the precious metals, she drowned, dragged to the sea bottom. Afterwards, a rebel soldier patrolling the shoreline found her body. In Wilmington, North Carolina, the Confederacy accorded Greenough a military burial. Admirers still place flowers on her tomb.

"Rebel Rose" Greenough is perhaps the most famous spy of the Civil War—and one of the most effective. And she operated right out of Lafayette Square.

Sources

Blackman, Ann. *Wild Rose: Rose O'Neale Greenhow, Civil War Spy*. New York: Random House, 2005.

Brooks, Rebecca Beatrice. "Rose O'Neal Greenhow: Confederate Spy." *Civil War Saga*, October 3, 2012. http://civilwarsaga.com/rose-oneal-greenhow/.

Duke University. *Rose O'Neal Greenhow Papers: An On-line Archival Collection*. May 1996. https://library.duke.edu/rubenstein/scriptorium/greenhow/roseindex.html.

Greenhow, Rose O'Neal. *My Imprisonment and the First Year of Abolition Rule at Washington*. Whitefish, MT: Kessinger, 2007 (originally published in 1863).

Lineberry, Cate. "The Wild Rose of Washington." *New York Times*, August 22, 2011. https://opinionator.blogs.nytimes.com/2011/08/22/the-wild-rose-of-washington/.

National Archives (1817–1864). "People Description."

Pinkerton, Allen. *A Spy of the Rebellion: Being a True History of the Spy System of the United States Army*. Whitefish, MT: Kessinger, 2010 (originally published in 1883).

"Rose Greenhow." *Civil War Female Spies*, April 14, 2015. https://civilwarfemalespies.wordpress.com/female-spies/rose-greenhow-2/.

16

The Backstory of the American Revolution's Martinet

Northwest Corner of Lafayette Square

The towering, caped statue across from the Decatur House mansion honors Baron von Steuben: Friedrich Wilhelm August Heinrich Ferdinand Steuben. German names, like strung-together German nouns, tend to be long. A key to America's Revolutionary War victory, the Baron hailed from Prussia, the militarily powerful, German-speaking kingdom of the 18th century. His is one of four statues at each corner of the park, all dedicated to European officers who helped the United States win its independence. If the Marquis de Lafayette was the most valuable of the four—being integral to the alliance with France, America's crucial wartime ally—von Steuben might be a strong second. His military impact is legend. The statue—with its symbols and hidden meanings that suggest a secret life of the Baron's—is less so.

At birth, he was simply Friedrich Steuben, not yet a noble "von." Born in 1730, he was the son of a military engineer who served with both Russia and Prussia. Steuben himself fought skillfully under a famed soldier, Prussian Emperor Frederick the Great. The tens of thousands of German-speaking immigrants flooding into the Mid-Atlantic in the 1700s sometimes named their towns after Frederick's family dynasty. This was true of the two large towns north and south, respectively, of Washington City: Frederick, Maryland, and Fredericksburg, Virginia.

Emperor Frederick got his "Great" nickname during the Seven Years' War, called the French and Indian War in America. Through brilliant maneuvering and tight discipline, he led his outnumbered army to triumph over a mighty coalition of the day's Great Powers: France, Russia, and Austria. Steuben served as the Emperor's aide-de-camp, part of an elite team trained by Frederick himself in the art of war. Wounded several times in battle, Steuben rose to the rank of captain.

Masterful Martinet

Von Steuben arrived in America during the second of the two low points of the Revolution. The first was in December of 1776, when General Washington was confiding his gloom over the war's outcome due to dwindling enlistments. "I think the game is pretty near up," he wrote to his brother Samuel. Then came his men's remarkable crossing of the

During a freezing Valley Forge winter of scarcity, Prussian officer Baron von Steuben skillfully trained the fledgling Revolutionary War American Army (National Archives).

half-frozen Delaware River on Christmas and the rout of the British and their German Hessian allies at Trenton and Princeton, New Jersey.

Things were as dire the following winter, at the rude encampment of Valley Forge, Pennsylvania, near the town of King of Prussia, Pennsylvania, itself named after Frederick the Great. Of the 12,000 American soldiers there, about 2,500 would die of disease, short rations, and cold. An army in desperate straits needs discipline to keep itself together. So when von Steuben arrived at Valley Forge in February 1778, Washington viewed him as a godsend. The American soldiers, though resilient and brave, lacked the skills of a regular army. They couldn't march, much less assemble, in formation. Their marksmanship was poor. The troops didn't even know how to use a bayonet, according to the New England Historical Society. Von Steuben wrote of this incompetence with the long blade: "The American soldier, never having used this arm, had no faith in it, and never used it but to roast his beefsteak, and indeed often left it at home." The Prussian was perplexed at the lack of uniformity among the American officers and men, noting, "Each colonel exercised his regiment according to his own ideas, or those of any military author that might have fallen into his hands ... [and] march and maneuvering step was as varied as the color of our uniforms."

At Valley Forge, von Steuben's arrival altered all that within days. With Germanic efficiency, he trained a "model" force of 100 recruits, then unleashed the instructors on the whole army. They became in effect the drill sergeants of a winter boot camp. Von Steuben and his team taught the Americans how to march quickly in compact columns, at up to 120 steps a minute, instead of meandering strung out along a road. Twenty years later Napoleon would use such formations to defeat the powers of Europe, including Prussia. The Baron also stressed the quick and accurate use of firearms, at a time when it took 15 different steps and intense training to properly load and fire a musket.

Swearing in German and French, his stout, six-foot-plus frame looming over the men, he brandished the "swagger stick" that marked the authority of a Prussian officer. Von Steuben forced the men to drill, and drill, in the frigid damp of Valley Forge. The Americans, though hungry and weary, respected the strange foreigner for molding them into professional fighters. Remarked a teenage private of his drill master, "He seemed to me the perfect personification of Mars. The trappings of his horse, the enormous holsters of his pistols, his large size, and his strikingly martial aspect." For his part, the European nobleman grew to appreciate the New World's fondness for liberty. He wrote a foreign friend: "The genius of this nation is not in the least to be compared with that of the Prussian, Austrians, or French. You say to your soldier 'Do this and he doeth it'; but I am obliged to say: 'This is the reason why you ought to do that: and then he does it.'"

While explaining the usefulness of the bayonet, von Steuben forced through a regulation that his soldiers keep bayonets fixed on their muskets at all times. After incessant drilling, the men became adept with the sharp blade. In fact, a daring nighttime attack to capture a British fort, Stoney Point in New York, was executed solely with the bayonet. In June 1778, at the battle of Monmouth Courthouse, in New Jersey, General Washington's von Steuben–trained force fought the British regulars to a draw. It was the first time Washington's army was able to stay in the field in a pitched battle against European professionals.

A British general leading a failed attack at Monmouth, Charles Cornwallis, would lose the war's climactic 1783 battle at Yorktown, Virginia. There the Americans, reflecting the approach of their Old World tutors, fought with their French allies in a European-style siege of Cornwallis' defenses. Further, a nighttime bayonet attack—led by Alexander Hamilton and the Marquis de Lafayette—seized two key British forts in a reprise of von Steuben's tactics at Stony Point.

Controversial Precedents

In contrast to his exploits with Washington's army, Von Steuben's personal history before the American Revolution is familiar to few. In fact, he came to America under a cloud. His military resume was suspect, and he was on the verge of being thrown into a French prison. The Prussian's service for Frederick the Great in the Seven Years' War had ended in 1763. Then, like many military men after a conflict, he was hit by "downsizing." After peace broke out, cash-strapped princes slashed the size of their armies. For years Steuben, as he was then known, was out of work, living as an itinerant soldier eager to sell his services. Finally, he wangled the position of chamberlain, or household manager, for a minuscule German principality, Hohenzollern-Hechingen, in the southwest of today's Germany (which didn't then exist as a nation but as a loose collection of independent lands ruled by counts and princes).

In 1769 the nearby principality of Baden granted Steuben membership in a chivalric society and the title of Free Lord. Steuben took it and styled himself Baron, or Baron von Steuben. It was a tough climb back to modest respectability for a proud and able man. Then the roof fell in. An unsigned letter from the court of Hohenzollern-Hechingen, Steuben's former employer, alleged the following: "It has come to me from different sources that M. de Steuben is accused of having taken familiarities with young boys which the laws forbid and punish severely. I have even been informed that that is the reason why M. de Steuben was obliged to leave Hechingen and that the clergy ... intend to prosecute him by law as soon as he may establish himself." It was a charge of pedophilia. The letter gave no actual evidence, but it had been rumored that Frederick the Great's court tolerated men who loved men and that von Steuben was one such man. Local authorities prepared to toss the soldier into jail.

His reputation blackened, his liberty at risk, von Steuben made his way to Paris, the capital of America's Revolutionary War ally. The two U.S. envoys in France were Silas Deane, a Connecticut businessman, and the venerable Benjamin Franklin. They were procuring arms and interviewing foreigners as potential recruits for the American Army. The two diplomats were impressed by von Steuben. They were swayed, too, by his French friend, playwright Pierre Beaumarchais, author of *The Marriage of Figaro*, later made into the Mozart opera. Beaumarchais had set up a front company to funnel weapons to the American forces. He vouched for von Steuben's martial abilities. Franklin and Deane, though aware of the sex accusations and despite knowing the French church was starting to investigate von Steuben, figured he'd be a plus for their hard-pressed cause.

In recommending the Baron to the Continental Congress, Franklin fudged his resume. He claimed von Steuben had been a two-star general, much higher than his captain's rank in Prussia. Franklin also kept mum about a French court that was considering charging him with sodomy. Congress agreed to hire the former Prussian officer. In autumn 1777 von Steuben sailed into Portsmouth, New Hampshire, on a munitions ship. He came cheap, deferring his pay until the American side won the war—if it did—and receiving the salary only if he performed his duties with skill.

In 1778, in frigid weather, General Washington rode off to greet von Steuben as the latter approached Valley Forge. The foreigner's appearance might have given credence to rumors that he was gay.

A Closeted Life?

Washington found the Baron perched on a regal sleigh drawn by beautiful French Percheron horses. Swaddled in a robe of silk and fur, von Steuben literally rang jingle bells: two dozen bells graced his sled. Accompanying him was a teenager who served as his private secretary. Also in tow was his cook from France and his servants from Africa. He almost seemed the Liberace of liberation. He also was accompanied by his handsome, 17-year-old aide-de-camp, Pierre-Étienne du Ponceau. That fellow's youth belied a formidable intellect. Du Ponceau would become one of America's first experts in the Native American and Asiatic languages. He and von Steuben would cowrite the U.S. Army's first training manual, *Regulations for the Order and Discipline of the Troops of the United States*. Some of its instructions for military ceremonies are still followed today.

In America, von Steuben would become a close friend of another young man, John Mulligan, Jr., the son of Hercules Mulligan, the landlord of young Alexander Hamilton. Early in the war Hercules Mulligan pushed the originally pro–British Hamilton into taking the side of America. Hercules was part of New York City's famed Culpeper ring of spies for General Washington.

After the Revolution, in the 1790s, the younger Mulligan became a bosom buddy of Charles Adams, a troubled son of John and Abigail Adams, later the President and First Lady. An alcoholic, Charles Adams would die of cirrhosis of the liver in 1800. Letters between John and Abigail from 1793 show them fretting about a close emotional relationship between Charles Adams and John Mulligan, Jr. That year, they pressured Charles to move out of the lodgings of his friend. Stricken, Charles Adams wrote to von Steuben of his heartache. A sympathetic von Steuben, given the missive by Alexander Hamilton, replied:

> Your letter ... was handed me yesterday by Mr. Hamilton. In vain, my dear child, should I undertake to explain to you the sensation which the letter created in my heart. Neither have I the courage to attempt to arrest the tears you have so great reason to shed. For a heart so feeling as yours this was the severest of trials, and nothing but time can bring consolation under circumstances so afflicting....
>
> Despite moral philosophy I weep with you, and glory in the human weakness of mingling my tears with those of a friend I so tenderly love....
>
> I repeat my entreaties, to hasten your journey to Philadelphia [where von Steuben was residing] as soon as your strength permits. My heart and my arms are open to receive you. In the midst of the attention and fetes which they have the goodness to give me, I enjoy not a moment's tranquility until I hold you in my arms ... if our friend could accompany you! Embrace him for me, with the same tender friendship I feel for you.

Charles Adams and John Mulligan, Jr., both moved in with von Steuben, Charles for a brief time and Mulligan for several years, until von Steuben's death in 1794. Mulligan later became a top U.S. diplomat in Greece.

On the other side of the Baron's statue in Lafayette Square are images of two other young men and friends of his: William North and Benjamin Walker. The Baron legally adopted both of them. North, who was 23 years old at Valley Forge, was an extremely able administrator who helped propagate von Steuben's training techniques among Washington's soldiers. During the Revolution, North fought at Monmouth, the battle that showcased the success of von Steuben's discipline. North would also serve as the Speaker of the New York State Assembly and as a U.S. Senator. President John Adams would make him the chief administrative officer of the U.S. Army. Captain Ben Walker, who was 26 years old in 1778, was another of von Steuben's aides-de-camp. At Valley Forge he played a critical role, for the Baron knew almost no English, except for the "Goddamn!" he screamed out on the training grounds. Walker translated his drilling regulations into the Americans' tongue. The Baron fondly called him his "angel." Like North, Walker would serve as a congressman.

As adopted sons, Walker and North became von Steuben's heirs. Some authors have speculated there were romantic liaisons between Walker and North, and between von Steuben and either of these assistants. To sum up, von Steuben had four well-known young and winsome associates: Du Ponceau, Mulligan, Jr., North, and Walker. They became, respectively, a linguistics expert, a ranking diplomat, the army's chief administrator, and a congressman. There's no doubt von Steuben knew how to pick talented staffers.

Yet, was von Steuben involved, as rumored, in a romantic relationship with any of these men? First, there is some indirect evidence, involving marriage and children. John Mulligan, Jr., married a Kentucky woman and had six daughters and three sons with her. William North married Mary Duane, the daughter of a New York City Mayor, and had six children with her. Charles Adams married the sister of Williams Stephens Smith, a staffer for Lafayette. Adams and his wife had two children: Abigail Smith and Susanna Boylston. (Abigail as in Abigail Adams, Charles Adams' mother; and Boylston, as in his mother's maiden name, and a famous street in Boston, the Adams hometown.) It is unclear if Benjamin Walker ever married or had children.

Of course, a man can be gay or bisexual and still marry a woman and have children. Such behavior was more common in past eras, when homosexuals were likely to "stay in the closet." However, incontrovertible evidence seems absent on a physical relationship between Steuben and any of the officers of his retinue. Researchers have differing opinions on the topic. Given this speculation, it's interesting to observe, on the northeast side of the larger-than-life statue of the Baron, an image some believe is homoerotic—and a suggestion from the sculptor, Albert Jaegers, of the Baron's secret life. It shows a soldier of an ancient Roman legion teaching a naked young man how to wield a sword. Some interpret this as a reference to von Steuben's alleged amorous affection for his young aides. Others see it simply as a nod to the Baron's role of teaching the art of war to novice soldiers.

Sculptor Jaegers, by the way, got the commission for his work based on the recommendation of Augustus Saint-Gaudens, the renowned sculptor of the Clover Adams sculpture, "Grief" (see Chapter 13, "The Tragic Wife of America's Premier Thinker"). Given his ancestry, Jaegers got some grief of his own during the First World War. Having Teutonic ancestry was unpopular in a nation taking on the armies of the German Kaiser. Jaegers' statue of Germany as a maritime power, on New York's Alexander Hamilton U.S. Custom House, was changed, over his objections, to a statue of Belgium, a country Germany invaded in the war! In the Second World War, Jaegers' statue of Francis Daniel Pastorius, the founder of Germantown, Pennsylvania, and a progenitor of the "Pennsylvania Dutch" German-American communities, was cloaked from public viewing. Officials feared it might somehow bolster sympathy for Nazi Germany.

Whatever the significance of Jaegers' Roman soldier and boy, observers can indeed view a hidden meaning in the statue if they stand about 20 yards northeast of it and gaze at the top of it. The legionary is wearing a helmet that, at its apex, from every angle of sight except for one, appears to be a crest. But from the exact place mentioned, it appears as a spike atop the helmet. A spiked helmet—*pickelhaube*, or pointed hat, in German. The Romans never wore them, but they were notably worn by German soldiers and police from the 1840s into the Second World War.

The statue was unveiled in 1910, four years before the First World War began. The spiked helmet appears to be a sculptor's trick, a reference to the admiration at that time for Germany's military, a military that was then esteemed, before the First World War. After the world wars, and especially after the Second, the admiration turned to loathing.

Today the spiked headgear seems a subtle tribute to von Steuben's enduring military repute—whatever the truth of his private life.

Sources

Benemann, William E. *Male-Male Intimacy in Early America: Beyond Romantic Friendships*. London: Routledge, 2016.
Ferreiro, Larrie. *Brothers at Arms: American Independence and the Men of France and Spain Who Saved It*. New York: Knopf, 2016.
Fleming, Thomas. *Washington's Secret War: The Hidden History of Valley Forge*. Washington, D.C.: Smithsonian, 2005.
Lockhart, Paul. *The Drillmaster of Valley Forge: The Baron de Steuben and the Making of the American Army*. Washington, D.C.: Smithsonian, 2008.

National Park Service. Valley Forge. "General von Steuben." https://www.nps.gov/vafo/learn/historyculture/vonsteuben.htm.

New England Historical Society. "Baron von Steuben Shows the Army a Bayonet Is Not a Grilling Tool," 2018. http://www.newenglandhistoricalsociety.com/baron-von-steuben-shows-the-army-a-bayonet-is-not-a-grilling-tool/.

Park View, D.C. "Washington's Original Monument to Baron von Steuben." Retrieved June 2018. https://parkviewdc.com/2014/01/14/washingtons-original-monument-to-baron-von-steuben/.

Sheppard, Nicholas. "The Gay Man Who Saved the American Revolution." *Huffington Post*, July 23, 2016, updated. https://www.huffingtonpost.com/nicholas-sheppard/the-gay-man-who-saved-the_b_7838506.html.

Shilts, Randy. *Conduct Unbecoming: Gays and Lesbians in the U.S. Military*. New York: St. Martin's, 1993.

Trickey, Erick. "The Prussian Nobleman Who Helped Save the American Revolution." *Smithsonian*, April 26, 2017. http://www.smithsonianmag.com/history/baron-von-steuben-180963048/?utm_source=smithsoniandaily&utm_medium=email&utm_campaign=20170426-daily-responsive&spMailingID=28815659&spUserID=NzQwNDUzNDA5NjIS1&spJobID=1023833918&spReportId=MTAyMzgzMzkxOAS2.

U.S. Army. Headquarters Department. *The Soldier's Blue Book*. 2017.

17

The Violent End of America's Bravest Sailor

Decatur House, 748 Jackson Place, at the Corner of Jackson Place and H Street

On March 22, 1820, a horse-drawn carriage pulled up to the glittering Decatur House. The carriage doors opened, and somber Navy officers carried the broken body of America's great naval hero into a first-floor room of his red brick home.

As the 41-year-old Stephen Decatur lay dying, he cried out, "I did not know that any man could suffer such pain!" He called out a final request—that his friends shut the door to the room so his beloved wife, Susan, could not see him in his death agony. He left his $75,000 fortune to her. Thus the previously charmed life of Commodore Decatur came to an end.

Earlier that day, Decatur and a fellow Navy Commodore and bitter enemy, 51-year-old James Barron, had ridden out to the dueling grounds in Bladensburg, Maryland, seven miles to the northeast. Barron harbored a longstanding grudge, stretching back to the naval wars, both declared and undeclared, of the early Republic.

The Shores of Tripoli

From his earliest age Decatur had dreamed of sailing and fighting at sea. His father, Stephen Decatur, Sr., was a merchant mariner turned U.S. Navy captain in the American Revolution. The younger Decatur's first command was of a ship with a name that would become legend, the USS *Enterprise*, an armed schooner. Decatur had gained renown in 1804 as a hero of the war against the Barbary Pirates. For generations those cutthroats from today's Libya, Algeria, Tunisia, and Morocco had ravaged the Mediterranean, kidnapping, enslaving, and holding for ransom European and American passengers and crews. The early U.S. envoys to Europe, including John Adams, James Madison, and Thomas Jefferson, met with the pirates' representatives. They were aghast at their ideology, akin to the Islamic State (ISIS) of today, which justified through their holy book, the Koran, the enslavement or killing of Christians.

When Jefferson became President in 1801 he decided to end the tribute, or bribes, the U.S. government had been paying the Barbary Pirates. He ordered the fledgling U.S. Navy fleet created under the George Washington and John Adams administrations—whose construction many Jefferson backers had opposed—into the Mediterranean to take on the corsairs of Tripoli. The war took some wrong turns. In October 1803 the Barbary Pirates captured, near Tripoli, the 36-gun frigate USS *Philadelphia*, along with its captain, William Bainbridge, and its consignment of Marines. The pirates hauled the ship into the harbor of Tripoli city and imprisoned the crew belowdecks. Lieutenant Stephen Decatur, Jr., volunteered for the seemingly impossible mission of freeing them. He and his men devised a daring scheme.

A few months earlier he'd captured in battle a Tripolitan ketch, a small, two-masted ship. Decatur disguised the vessel, rechristened the *Intrepid*, as a merchant ship from the island of Malta. He ran British colors from it, as Britain had bribed the pirates into leaving its ships alone. He and 60 U.S. Marine volunteers got onboard, along with an Arabic-speaking Sicilian pilot, Salvador Catalano. For fire support, the 16-gun warship *Syren* sailed with them. On the night of February 16, 1804, under a crescent moon, the *Intrepid* slowly sailed into Tripoli harbor and approached the *Philadelphia*. Decatur and the Marines hid belowdecks. Catalano told the harbor guards his ship had been damaged in a storm and had lost its anchor. He asked if he could make repairs, perhaps berthing his ship near the captured American one. The unsuspecting pirates agreed.

Decatur ordered his Marines to draw swords, pikes, and knives and to use their guns only if necessary. Silence and stealth were essential. The American raiders slipped onto the captured ship. The detained Marines heard what was happening, burst from their prison, and joined their comrades. They rushed to the buccaneers onboard, killing some and

In 1804 the U.S. Navy's Stephen Decatur and his Marines engaged in wild melees with the pirates of the Barbary Coast (Department of the Navy—Naval Historical Center, painting in the U.S. Naval Academy Museum Collection, gift of Chester Dale, 1942, official U.S. Navy photograph).

forcing others to dive into the water to escape. Decatur was knocked to the deck and almost slain, but he and his fighters took back the ship without losing a man. Decatur realized the *Philadelphia* itself was unsalvageable, so his men set it ablaze, denying it to the enemy. About the seaport, Tripolitans realized what has happening and fired at the Americans. The support ship, *Syren*, shot back cannonades of covering fire. Decatur and his Marines rowed out of Tripoli harbor unharmed.

British Vice Admiral Horatio Nelson, the conqueror of Napoleon's fleet at Trafalgar, and the world's most famous sailor, dubbed the *Philadelphia* action "the most bold and daring act of the age."

Even more of a feat personally for Decatur was his hand-to-hand combat with a pirate during a subsequent assault on Tripoli. He learned that the captain of an enemy ship had mortally wounded his brother, James Decatur, by luring him on board after faking surrender. Irate but intent, Decatur gathered nine volunteer Marines. According to historian Charles Lee Lewis, they boarded the Tripolitan ship and hacked and shot their way through 50 pirates. In a scene out of a war movie, Decatur and the captain found themselves face-to-face. His hulking foe thrust forward a pike that busted the hilt of Decatur's sword. Another attacker almost killed him, but a Marine who threw himself onto Decatur absorbed the blow. The Barbary commander stabbed at Decatur with a knife, but Decatur shot him dead with a pistol. He had swiftly avenged his brother. In recognition of his heroism, the Navy made Decatur, at age 25, the youngest captain in U.S. naval history, until that time or since. The battles in and around Tripoli were the origin of the "to the shores of Tripoli" phrase of the Marines Corps anthem.

Back home, the dashing sailor was hailed a hero and feted at the White House. In 1806 Decatur also won the hand of a woman. This was the brainy, girlish-looking Susan Wheeler, daughter of the mayor of Norfolk, Virginia. Decatur had met his future wife at a ball put on by the ambassador of Tunis, part of the pirate alliance Decatur helped check. Based on the evidence, Susan had been the most eligible woman in Washington. She declined a marriage proposal from Jerome Bonaparte, Napoleon's brother, and also turned down the Vice President of the United States—Aaron Burr, later the slayer of Alexander Hamilton. Instead she married the most eligible bachelor in Washington: Captain Decatur.

At the Decatur House, she and her husband were the focus of the capital's social scene, entertaining such luminaries as President James Monroe and Speaker of the House Henry Clay. It was at an 1816 Washington banquet that Decatur proffered a famous toast: "Our country—in her intercourse with foreign nations may she always be in the right, and always successful, right or wrong." His statement was boiled down to the pithy, "My country, right or wrong."

Decatur also became a legend of the next war, the War of 1812. As that conflict grew near, the Navy ordered him to refit for action one of the nation's first frigates, the 32-gun USS *United States*. Captain Decatur readied his three-masted vessel in the harbor of Norfolk, hometown of his father-in-law and then as now a U.S. naval base. (Serving under Decatur was a Lieutenant Ichabod Crane, whose name author Washington Irving borrowed for his *Legend of Sleepy Hollow*.) While work on the *United States* proceeded, a British man-of-war, the HMS *Macedonian*, sailed into port. Its captain, John Carden, met Decatur, and the two skippers compared notes on their ships. It's believed each man good-naturedly boasted that if war came and their crews clashed his own ship would win out. They placed a bet on the outcome—the winner would get the most prized commodity of the day—a beaver pelt hat, worn by frontiersmen like Davy Crockett and European gentry alike.

When war erupted in July 1812, Decatur took the *United States* out on a hunt for British ships. In the Atlantic, well south of the Azores and by great coincidence, lookouts on the American ship spied the familiar lines of the *Macedonian*. The *United States* had more cannons and guns of greater range. Decatur skillfully ran rings around the *Macedonian*, pummeling it with broadsides and forcing its surrender. Then, for weeks on the open seas, Decatur and his men repaired the captured ship. Next, they towed it clear across the Atlantic and into port. It was the first time a U.S. vessel had brought in a mighty British warship as a prize of war. At the news, America's seaports erupted in patriotic celebrations.

Decatur employed prize money from capturing the *Macedonian* to build a home. For designing the Decatur House mansion, he turned to the best: Benjamin Latrobe, the architect, with William Thornton and George Hatfield, of the original Capitol building. It remains the largest home in Lafayette Square other than the White House itself.

An Affair of Dishonor

The incident that brought on the 1820 blood match between Commodore Decatur and Commodore Barron occurred a full 13 years before the fatal firefight. Back in 1807 the United States was officially at peace but already, if unofficially, embroiled in a maritime war with Great Britain. The British was seizing hundreds of American commercial ships and "impressing," or kidnapping, thousands of American sailors to labor on Britain's manpower-starved ships. England, in a wartime death grip with Emperor Napoleon, was willing to use any means possible to bolster his naval crews. Some of the men seized were British citizens who had jumped ship for the less harsh conditions aboard American vessels. From 1800 to 1810, astonishingly, Britain seized perhaps 10,000 U.S. citizens and Britons who had switched to American ships. These were acts of war, and war nearly came on June 22, 1807, off Norfolk.

James Barron was then captain of the 38-gun frigate USS *Chesapeake*. He had stuffed the decks of his vessel with naval stores to take to the Mediterranean Squadron, the U.S. fleet patrolling the Mediterranean during a lull in the Barbary Pirate wars. The British had information that four deserters had joined the *Chesapeake*. The British contacted Decatur, who informed them that the recruitment of crews was outside his jurisdiction. They then contacted Barron, who after examining his crew determined they were all U.S. citizens. Nevertheless, the British ordered their ships in the region to stop and search the *Chesapeake*. The warship HMS *Leopard* spotted the *Chesapeake* soon after it left Norfolk. Its commander, Captain Salusbury Pryce Humphreys, demanded Barron give up the four sailors. Barron refused. His ship was unprepared for a fight. Indeed, preparing for a battle would have been difficult, as the decks of his ship were crammed with supplies.

Captain Humphreys then did something unheard of. The British and French often fired on merchant ships they suspected of carrying contraband or deserters but never on a combatant ship of a foreign nation, which could directly lead to war. Humphreys had his ship fire its cannons on the *Chesapeake,* then again—and again: three broadsides of 50 guns against the unprepared ship from a distance of just 20 yards. Three Americans were killed and 18 wounded. After his ship got off just a single shot a shocked Barron raised a white flag of surrender. The British then boarded, seized four of Barron's crew, several of them African-American, and later hanged one of those taken.

The incident screamed from the front pages of newspapers throughout the United States. Fed up with the constant British depredations, outraged citizens cried for revenge. President Jefferson, however, against the advice of his Cabinet, including his adept Treasury Secretary Albert Gallatin, decided to try to hurt Britain's economy while avoiding a war with the military superpower. Instead, Jefferson placed a trade embargo on Britain—and, indeed, on every other country! It was America's first comprehensive set of economic sanctions, the first of many to come up to the present day. However, the embargo wound up hurting the American economy more than it did Britain's, and after triggering a stiff recession it was repealed.

In the meantime, the Navy Department, dismayed by Barron's failure to put up a stiffer fight, court-martialed him. Barron, as his vessel was acting essentially as a supply ship and the British assault was unprecedented, thought the trial unfair. The *Chesapeake*'s other officers, thinking otherwise, petitioned the Navy to discipline him. The Navy court dismissed the more serious charge of cowardice. However, it convicted Barron of failing to clear his ship for a battle. Among the judges on the court was none other than Stephen Decatur. Barron was suspended without pay for five years. Despised by a public seized by war fever, he went into exile in Europe. When the War of 1812 came, he claimed he wanted to go back to America to fight but that financial woes prevented it. When he finally returned to the U.S., he rejoined the Navy.

For years, James Barron could not forget or forgive Decatur's role in his court-martial. Decatur deepened Barron's anger by publicly berating him. He stated, probably falsely, that Barron had avoided the War of 1812 due to cowardice. In 1820, according to author C.S. Forester, Decatur joked that Barron would have been better off battling the British in 1812 than taking on Decatur at the present time. Barron made his own negative comments about Decatur. He once claimed that around the time of Decatur's wedding to Susan Wheeler his rival "had a woman in another port."

A 19th-century portrait of Navy Commodore James Barron, the fatal foil of Commodore Stephen Decatur (Department of the Navy—Naval Historical Center, 19th-century engraved portrait; photography received from the Commandant of the Philadelphia Navy Yard, Pennsylvania, 1925).

A Deadly Challenge

In early 1820 Barron challenged his fellow Commodore to a

duel. Decatur accepted. Just two years earlier Decatur had been the "second," or assistant in a duel, to a commander as famous as he, Commodore Oliver Hazard Perry, noted for his victory in the pivotal War of 1812 Battle of Lake Erie. He was famed also for informing Major General and future President William Henry Harrison after that fight, "We have met the enemy, and they are ours," as well as his battle ensign: "Don't Give Up the Ship." During another conflict, the Second Barbary Pirate War of 1815, Perry had chided and slapped an ill-behaving Marine officer named John Heath. Captain Heath demanded a duel, and in 1818 the two men met at Weehawken, New Jersey. This was the same killing field where Aaron Burr in 1804 had slain Alexander Hamilton. Before the gunfight Perry wrote that he had no intent of firing at Heath. At the duel Heath shot and missed, while Perry, true to his word, held his fire. Decatur then rushed over to Heath, showed him Perry's letter of intent, and urged he end the duel. Heath agreed.

In contrast, for their own duel both Decatur and Barron had seconds who egged on their dispute. A second was supposed to be a close friend with the best interests of the duelist at heart, namely to avoid, if possible, the potentially fatal fight. Yet the seconds to Decatur and Barron both disliked Decatur and likely wanted, and may have abetted, the death match. Decatur's second was Commodore William Bainbridge, the very commander he'd rescued at Tripoli. Yet a jealous Bainbridge had long been irked that Decatur had blocked his promotion during the Barbary Pirate wars. He reconciled with Decatur not long before the duel. Some scholars believe his rapprochement was fake, allowing Bainbridge to act in effect as an enemy in Decatur's camp. Barron's second was Captain Jesse Duncan Elliott. He had long hated Decatur's friend Commodore Perry due to Perry's view of his alleged tardiness during the Battle of Lake Erie. Elliott believed Decatur had documents from Perry that chided his role at Lake Erie. Elliott in the meantime stoked Barron's ire by relating some of Decatur's disparaging remarks about him.

In 1820, dueling was frowned upon in the District of Columbia. So the two Commodores, their seconds, doctors, and other high-ranking Navy officers rode out to the killing grounds at Bladensburg, Maryland, where duels were legal. On hand were Navy royalty. Commodore John Rodgers, Decatur's friend, fellow War of 1812 hero, and fellow owner of a Lafayette Square mansion, was there. Also in attendance was Commodore David Porter, the father of David Dixon Porter, who later was an Admiral in the Civil War captured the key Mississippi river port of Vicksburg (the elder Porter was also the adoptive father of Union Admiral David Farragut, of "Damn the Torpedoes!" fame). As senior officers, Rodgers and Porter might have moved to resolve the dispute. They did not.

Often a duelist would "throw away his fire," that is, fire into the air. But Commodore Barron intended to shoot Decatur if Decatur didn't renounce his view that Barron had been a coward. Barron probably intended to fire a wounding shot, not a kill shot, at Decatur. For his part, Decatur also intended to try to disable, not kill, Barron. Remarkably, this echoed a duel he'd had a full 11 years before. Back in 1809, Decatur had a confrontation in Philadelphia with a recruiter of sailors. The recruiter, in Decatur's presence, had insulted the Navy and its crews. Decatur, then 21 years old and a Lieutenant, had laughed the matter off. However, his father, Stephen Decatur, Sr., insisted his son uphold the honor of his family and the fleet with a duel. For the ensuing firefight, the younger Decatur decided not to kill his antagonist. An expert shot, he shot the man near the hip, disabling and wounding him but sparing his life.

Whatever their intents at Bladensburg, there was no love lost between Barron and Decatur, and their seconds didn't help. This was clear when the two men lined up for battle. Their associates positioned them not the usual 10 paces from each other but just eight paces. The stated reason for the short distance was that Barron was myopic, and he and his second wanted him to be close enough to Decatur so that he couldn't miss. The duelists stood obliquely from one another, presenting smaller targets for the vital areas of the heart and lungs. But such a stance presented their hips as big and inviting targets. As they faced off, Barron told Decatur he was wrong in thinking Barron had deliberately avoided fighting in the War of 1812. The remark offered an opening for the seconds to get the two foes to reconcile. Such an effort often ended a duel before it began. But neither second, Bainbridge nor Elliott, took any action.

Bainbridge called out the rules of the encounter: "I shall give the word quickly—'Present, one, two, three.' You are neither to fire before the word 'one,' nor after the word 'three.'" Other attendees stood to the sides of the duelists, watching expectantly. Decatur and Barron raised their pistols at each other. They cocked their weapons. They tried to keep their breathing, and thus their shooting hands, steady. The spectators held their own breaths. Bainbridge called out, "Present" then an instant later, "One…." Both duelists fired, almost at the same moment. As he intended, Decatur struck Barron in the abdomen near the hip. The bullet ricocheted down into the thigh. Barron fell to the ground hurt, but the leg wound wasn't fatal. Barron in turn shot Decatur in his pelvis. However, the bullet tracked into his groin, slashing into arteries. Decatur collapsed, and knew the wound was mortal. "Oh, Lord!" he cried out, "I am a dead man." From the ground, Barron told Decatur he forgave him "from the bottom of his heart."

Barron's second seemed to panic. Elliott raced away from the grounds in Barron's carriage, though it was urgently required to take Barron back to Washington City for medical care. Elliott might have thought he'd get the blame for the bloody encounter, which he made no attempt to stop. Commodore Porter raced after him on a horse and eventually browbeat him into returning to the capital with Barron. Decatur's colleagues put the bleeding Commodore in his carriage. In great pain, Decatur offered to take Barron back to the city with him, but Rodgers and his doctor vetoed the notion. After exchanging their bloody shots, both men were apologetic. Barron shouted out to his foe, "God bless you, Decatur." Decatur murmured in return, "Farewell, Barron, farewell." If only they had spoken to each other in such a way before the gun blasts.

Decatur was taken on an agonizing carriage ride along bumpy roads back to Decatur House. He died that night. A public funeral for America's naval hero followed. It seemed all of Washington was there for it. President Monroe, much of Congress, Supreme Court justices, and Decatur's fellow Commodores: Rodgers, Porter, Thomas Tingey, the Commander of the Washington Navy Yard during the 1814 British invasion, and Thomas MacDonough, a victor at the key War of 1812 Battle of Plattsburgh, New York. In all, 10,000 people watched the procession. At the funeral, an aggrieved sailor cried out, "He was the friend of the flag, the sailor's friend. The Navy has lost its mainmast!"

The widowed Susan Wheeler Decatur was enraged that her spouse had died at the hand of a fellow Commodore, and that the seconds had possibly aided his demise. She abandoned Decatur House, now filled with the dark memory of her husband's death, and moved to a townhouse, which still stands in east Georgetown. The couple had no children, and

Susan donated much of her inheritance to Georgetown College, today's Georgetown University. She lived until 1860, dying at the age of 83. James Barron recovered from his wound to live long enough to become the Navy's senior officer. He died in 1851, at age 82.

One positive thing came out of the Stephen Decatur tragedy: the Navy blocked gunfights among its top commanders. For the sea service, the Decatur-Barron duel was the last of its kind.

Sources

Clark, Allen C. "Commodore James Barron, Commodore Stephen Decatur: The Barron-Decatur Duel." *Records of the Columbia Historical Society, Washington, D.C.* 42/43 (1940/1941).

DeFerrari, John. "Triumph and Tragedy at Decatur House." *Streets of Washington*, December 27, 2010. http://www.streetsofwashington.com/2010/12/triumph-and-tragedy-at-decatur-house.html

Forester, C.S. "Bloodshed at Dawn." *American Heritage* 15, no. 6 (October 1964). http://www.americanheritage.com/content/bloodshed-dawn.

Hickman, Kennedy. "War of 1812: Commodore Stephen Decatur," November 7, 2017. Thoughtco.com. http://military-history.about.com/od/naval/p/sdecatur.htm.

Lewis, Charles Lee. *Famous American Naval Officers*. Boston: L.C. Page, 1924.

Long, David F. "William Bainbridge and the Barron-Decatur Duel: Mere Participant or Active Plotter?" *Pennsylvania Magazine of History and Biography* 103 (1979).

Mackenzie, Alexander Slidell. *Life of Stephen Decatur: A Commodore in the Navy of the United States*. Boston: C.C. Little and J. Brown, 1846.

Melero, Julius. "The Burning of the USS *Philadelphia*," February 18, 2015. U.S. Naval Institute. Naval History Blog. https://www.navalhistory.org/2015/02/18/the-burning-of-the-uss-philadelphia.

Tucker, Spencer. *Stephen Decatur: A Life Most Bold and Daring*. Annapolis, MD: Naval Institute Press, 2004.

18

A Duel Between the Oddest and Most Famous of Congress

Decatur House, 748 Jackson Place and H Street

In his long career, losing three runs for the presidency and being targeted in court by a female slave weren't the only headaches for Secretary of State Henry Clay of Kentucky (see Chapter 20, "The Enslaved Woman Who Sued the Head of the State Department"). In 1826, the most famous resident of Decatur House faced a blood match with one of the most cantankerous congressman in Washington's history.

A Congressional Eccentric

In some ways, Representative John Randolph of Roanoke, Virginia, seemed a stereotypical southerner. A radical proponent of states' rights, he had broken with Thomas Jefferson, a Virginia states' righter himself, for being too soft on the federal government. Randolph formed his own split-off group, called Tertium Quids, roughly translated, the Third Way. He and his followers wanted the authorities in Washington to have almost no authority at all.

On slavery, for instance, Randolph thought the federals should not regulate or restrict involuntary servitude in any way—nor encourage or expand it for that matter. For him, slavery—like every issue—was up to the individual. Randolph owned a group of 383 slaves, and with views like his you would have thought he'd keep them all and maybe buy some more. In fact, in his will he freed each and every one. Moreover, as a wealthy man, he set aside money to pay for their education. George Washington did the same for the 123 slaves he owned. But Randolph did Washington one better. He bought an expanse of land in the Ohio Territory, where slavery was forbidden, so that his former slaves could settle there on free soil, without the bane of servitude around them.

In his personal life as well as his public actions, John Randolph was known for extreme eccentricity. As a youth he contracted tuberculosis, which prevented him from going through puberty. As a result, throughout his adulthood he had little facial hair, fair skin like that of a woman, and a high-pitched voice. Perhaps this made him try to prove his manhood through very aggressive behavior. His health suffered as well from regular use of laudanum, or opium.

Randolph lived across town from Henry Clay near Capitol Hill. At his boardinghouse,

Randolph got into a brawl with a fellow congressman and boarder, Representative Willis Alston. During the melee, the two hurled forks and knives at each other but without serious injury. Later on, in the House chamber, Randolph beat Alston with a cane for complaining about the hunting dogs he brought to debates there. Congress socked Randolph with a fine. Indeed, in Congress, Randolph would arrive garbed like a country gentleman on a hunt, with riding boots, riding crop, and dogs. Clay, when he was House Speaker, strived to bring decorum to the unruly chamber. He ordered Randolph, to the Virginian's chagrin, to leave the riding regalia at home.

Opposites Detract

Representative Randolph got into shouting matches with other congressmen and government officers. He branded John Quincy Adams a "traitor" and Senator Daniel Webster a "vile slanderer." But his biggest foil was Clay. The two men's differences in style were widened by their politics. While Randolph was what we might today call a libertarian, Clay led a political philosophy that was a direct hand-me-down from Alexander Hamilton. The Secretary of State, much like the first Secretary of the Treasury, stood for an "American System" where the federal government would foster domestic commerce through tariffs on imported goods and by bankrolling canals and roads. This was anathema to Randolph, the apostle of state privileges and the "sovereign individual."

Naturally, the two men were on the opposite sides of presidential elections, particularly the very contentious one of 1824. That year, Randolph's candidate, Andrew Jackson, won the popular vote but lost in the Electoral College to John Quincy Adams, that turncoat in Randolph's mind. According to one historian, Randolph may have had a mild romantic affection for the loser, Old Hickory. Adams won after gaining the Electoral College support of the powerful Clay, whom Adams later made Secretary of State.

In 1826, on the floor of the House, Randolph bitterly ripped Clay over this so-called "Corrupt Bargain" whereby Clay had become head of the State Department, which was then the steppingstone to the presidency. Randolph blistered Adams and Clay together as the "Puritan with the blackleg." The former referred to the founding religion in Adams' state of Massachusetts, the latter to an ugly animal disease. The Virginian accused Secretary Clay of "crucifying the Constitution" and, worse, of cheating at cards—a cardinal sin among the gamblers and backslapping politicos of Clay's frontier Kentucky. The Secretary of State demanded an explanation, got none, and demanded a duel. Randolph accepted.

Henry Clay had experience with dueling. In 1808 he'd fought things out against a fellow Kentucky congressman, Humphrey Marshall, the brother-in-law and cousin of Supreme Court Chief Justice John Marshall. At a time when the U.S. had imposed a strict embargo on imports of British clothes, and Clay wore American homespun to Congress, Humphrey Marshall pointedly wore British broadcloth. The political turned pugilistic. At their duel, the two fired at each other three times and slightly wounded each other twice before ending the firefight.

In 1826 dueling was illegal in Virginia. Yet it was allowed in Maryland and was held at the dueling grounds in Bladensburg. In fact, Clay wound up living in Decatur House because of Bladensburg's killing field. There in 1820 Navy Commodore Stephen Barron had mortally wounded Commodore Stephen Decatur. Decatur's widow vacated the house, and Clay later moved in (see Chapter 17, "The Violent End of America's Bravest Sailor").

Bladensburg beckoned again. But Randolph, that exemplar of states' rights, insisted, "If I am to spill my blood, let it be onto the soil of my 'home country.'" He meant his Old Dominion of Virginia. So the two prominent statesmen rode out to Great Falls, Virginia, 12 miles from the District, to fight an illegal duel.

Randolph evidently did not want to harm the Secretary of State. He reportedly told friends he had an "entire unwillingness" to "make a widow of Mrs. Clay." Clay's intentions going into the duel were less clear. He was no murderer, but he was piqued at Randolph's verbal assaults. At a dueling ground, men sometimes waited until the last moment before deciding whether to shoot to kill or even to shoot at all. Still, most duels did not result in death. Sometimes duelists aimed at, then deliberately missed, their foe. Sometimes, after firing past each other or slightly wounding one another, the duelists would shake hands and wish each other well, the matter settled. Just showing up for a duel was frequently enough to retain one's reputation.

On April 8, the two congressmen faced off at Great Falls, just west of Virginia's Chain Bridge. Once a long metal chain for guiding ferries across the Potomac, today it's a steel-and-concrete bridge that links the Old Dominion to Maryland. At the slaughter field, Randolph and Clay played by the standard rules. According to most accounts, they stood at 10 paces from each other. Each was to fire one round after a count. Friends and helpers looked on nervously. When the moment came to shoot, Randolph "threw away his fire," sparing the Secretary of State. At that very moment Clay's intent became clearer. He seemed to want to teach Randolph a lesson by scaring him but not harming him. He fired at Randolph, who wore a long dark coat that hung loosely about him. Clay's bullet passed through the cape-like apparel and tore the fabric, but did not hit Randolph.

As frequently happened with a duel, after all the pre-fight trash talking, both men were relieved neither had been hurt. They rushed over to each other. "I trust in God, sir," said Clay to Randolph, "that you are untouched. After what has occurred, I would not have harmed you for a thousand words." Randolph was pithier. He wryly told the Secretary, "You owe me a new coat, Mr. Clay." The onlookers, relieved, broke out in laughter. The Secretary of State and the Congressman walked off the dueling ground together. In a sign of friendlier relations, they soon exchanged business cards.

In their case, a duel did what it was usually supposed to do: allow two adversaries to blow off steam and uphold their honor without inflicting injury or death.

Sources

Bruce, William Cabell. *John Randolph of Roanoke, 1773–1833*. New York: G.P. Putnam's Sons, 1922.
Heidler, David S., and Jeanne T. Heidler. *Henry Clay: The Essential American*. New York: Random House, 2010.
Madigan, Andrew. "The Pair of American Politicians Who Fought the 19th Century's Silliest Duel." *AtlasObscura*. January 8, 2016. https://www.atlasobscura.com/articles/the-pair-of-american-politicians-who-fought-the-19th-centurys-silliest-duel.
Sawyer, Lemuel. *A Biography of John Randolph, of Roanoke*. New York: Burgess, Stringer, 1844.

19

The King of the Camel Corps

Decatur House, 748 Jackson Place and H Street

For most of two centuries, intriguing personalities resided at the Decatur House: Congressional potentate Henry Clay, whose 1850 legislative Compromise restricted the slave trade in the District; Clay's enslaved servant, Charlotte Dupuy, who took Clay to court to try to obtain her freedom; Secretary of State and future President Martin Van Buren, who flashed secret messages to his boss, President Andrew Jackson, from a lantern in a window of the House; another Vice President, George Dallas, for whom Dallas, Texas, might be named; Senator Judah Benjamin, later the Confederacy's Secretary of State, Treasury, and War; the war hero and doomed duelist Commodore Decatur himself—and others. Yet, the most colorful owner of the place might have been the explorer, soldier, rancher, and spy who bought Decatur House in 1874.

An appointee of five Presidents, he performed wartime heroics with fellow frontier legend Kit Carson. He was the first man, after a record-breaking, cross-continental trek, to bring news of the California Gold Rush to Washington. In the wild American Southwest of the 1850s, he crossed paths with many personalities later famous in the Civil War. President Grant would make him, as he was fluent in foreign languages, ambassador to the polyglot kingdoms of Austria-Hungary. Further, he was a friend to "Buffalo Bill" Cody. Most astonishingly, on several epic expeditions he used the strangest means of transportation in U.S. military history.

Sailor, Soldier, Spy

Edward "Ned" Fitzgerald Beale was born in 1822 in Georgetown, the son of Congressional Medal winner George Beale, who'd fought gallantly at the War of 1812 naval triumph on Lake Champlain. The younger Beale was the grandson on his mother's side of Commodore Thomas Truxtun, one of the first U.S. Navy captains. Truxtun had served with Stephen Decatur himself and with John Rodgers of the long-gone Rodgers mansion on the other side of Lafayette Square.

Appointed by President Andrew Jackson to Philadelphia's Naval School, a precursor to the U.S. Naval Academy at Annapolis, Beale rose, at age 23, to be master of the frigate USS *Congress*. In 1845 he served on it under Captain Samuel Dupont, who lent his name to D.C.'s elegant Dupont Circle and fountain. Also onboard was Commodore Robert Stockton, who'd captained the USS *Princeton* in 1844 when an explosion onboard killed the Secretary of State and the Secretary of the Navy (see Chapter 36, "A President's Brush with Death, After a Deadly Navy Accident"). The youthful Beale became Stockton's private secretary.

Under the aggressive President James Knox Polk, the United States was then verging on war with Britain over the Oregon Territory. Many Americans, referring to the northern latitude of that disputed land, cried, "Fifty-four forty or fight!" When the USS *Congress* came across a Danish ship heading for England, Captain Stockton, a confidante of President Polk, impulsively sent Fitzgerald to board it. He was ordered to journey to Britain and undertake a spy mission there on behalf of the President. The Danish ship had lost both its captain and its first officer, so the versatile Beale navigated it to its destination. Under cover in England, he gleaned information on British fleet movements and sized up London's willingness to go to war over Oregon. Beale sailed back to Washington and presented his findings to Polk and to Navy Secretary George Bancroft, founder of the Naval Academy. The following year, in 1846, Polk and Secretary of State James Buchanan reached a compromise with Britain that placed the American border of the territory at the 49th line of latitude, encompassing the future states of Oregon and Washington.

Also that eventful year, the U.S. verged on war with Mexico, with the Mexican province of California at issue. Beale sailed to Peru, where he reunited with Captain Stockton and the *Congress*. The ship went on to Monterey, California, where the crew learned war had broken out. Stockton again ordered Beale, now a Lieutenant, on a special mission. After remaking the ship's crew into infantry, in early December he led the unit east from San Diego to meet up with a small force headed by General Stephen W. Kearny. This was the uncle of Philip Kearny, Jr., later the first American soldier to enter Mexico City during the conflict, and later still a valiant Union commander of the Civil War.

After Beale and his men met up with Stephen Kearny, however, a superior Mexican force defeated the Americans in battle. Surrounded by the enemy and close to surrender, a wounded Kearney accepted Beale's offer to try to slip through the Mexican lines to obtain help. His fellow volunteers were his Indian servant and, remarkably, Kit Carson, the famed scout then teamed up with Kearny's men. The trio took off their boots, discarded their clanking canteens, and crawled through picket lines of enemy guards. After 36 hours of sleepless travel, with Beale's feet slashed open from cactus, they all covered the 28 miles back to San Diego. Alerted, Stockton dispatched to Kearny a 200-man rescue unit that forced the Mexicans to withdraw. In January 1847 the remaining Mexican forces in California surrendered.

In 1848 Beal was stationed in California with the flagship of the Pacific Squadron, under a Commodore named Thomas Catesby Jones. Years before, a rampaging sperm whale had nearly sunk Jones's ship, which inspired a passenger on board, Herman Melville, to write *Moby Dick*. The prickly Jones had consigned Beale to land duty after Beale had branded him a braggart. But Commodore Jones gave his upstart officer a chance to make amends. Gold had been discovered at Sutter's Mill, California, creating a sensation. Jones challenged Beale to be the first to make it to Washington with the news. His competitor was an army envoy sent out by California's Governor for the same purpose.

Beale took a schooner to Mexico's coast and headed inland. In the postwar chaos, robbers infested the countryside. Riding night and day, Beale again went undercover and, dressed in leather pantaloons, red flannel, and brimmed sombrero, posed as a south-of-the-border cowboy. During his journey he ran into a decorated soldier of the Mexican-American War, one Ulysses S. Grant. Beale paused in Mexico City to relay the news about the gold strike to the American embassy, then slogged onward, his thick dispatches about the gold find stashed in his saddlebags. On the way to Vera Cruz he galloped away from the gunfire of a thief. From the port city he boarded a sloop for Mobile Bay, Alabama, and from there he took a speedy stagecoach. His record-breaking, cross-continental trip of 47 days won the "Gold Dust Derby." Beale arrived in Washington to inform President Polk and the nation of the gold discovery. His story was front-page news, helping spark a rush of thousands from around the world to the Golden State.

P.T. Barnum, the circus impresario, offered big bucks for Beale's gold samples. Instead, Ned Beale gave much of the bullion to the Patent Office, which served, before the Smithsonian Institution, as a trove of historic items. He sold the rest to buy a wedding ring for childhood sweetheart Mary Edwards, daughter of a Pennsylvania congressman. Beale and Edwards would have three children, including Emily Beale, who married John McLean, later the owner of the *Washington Post*, and Truxtun Beale, who became a diplomat and owner of the Decatur House.

Beasts of Burden

With all the land from Texas to California now American, officials pondered the best way of hauling people and goods through the arid Southwest. To find out, the U.S. Army, with a U.S. Navy assist, conjured an incredible—and almost forgotten—scheme. As early as 1836 a U.S. Army officer had proffered the outside-the-box notion of using camels, the ships of the desert, to transport stuff across the continent's dry-bone wastelands. Army Lieutenant George H. Crosman reported, "For strength in carrying burdens, for patient endurance of labor, and privation of food, water & rest ... the camel and dromedary ... are unrivaled." In 1847 a colleague of Crosman's, Major Henry Wayne, urged the import of camels for army use. Mississippi Senator Jefferson Davis, a Mexican-American War hero, head of the Committee on Military Affairs and the future President of the Confederacy, was impressed. When President Franklin Pierce in 1853 selected Davis as his Secretary of War, Davis persuaded Congress to appropriate $30,000 to test the outlandish notion.

One of the oddest voyages ensued. Davis directed Lieutenant David Dixon Porter, skipper of the prosaically named transport the USS *Supply*, to sail across the Atlantic to the Mediterranean. There he was to acquire a consignment of camels and drivers and bring them to the American Southwest. (The irony was rich, as Porter would in the Civil War plague Confederate President Davis when he seized rebel New Orleans and the vital Mississippi River port of Vicksburg.) Porter took pains to prep the *Supply* with specially constructed camel cabins and sturdy hoists to move the thousand-pound creatures on and off the ship.

With Major Wayne onboard, Porter's vessel journeyed to Tunis, near where U.S. Marines 50 years before had fought to "the shores of Tripoli." From there he went on to Malta, Greece, Turkey, and Egypt. Obtaining hard-to-get export licenses from local officials, Wayne and Porter purchased 33 camels, 19 of them females—the bazaar price for the bizarre critters: about $250 each. The breeds were dromedaries (one-humped), Bactrian (two-humped), Arabian, an Arabian calf, Tunis beast of burden, and a "Tuili or Booghdee." Porter's team also hired eight men of Greek, Arab, and Turkish ancestry to return to America as breeders and drivers. These fellows, most of whom quickly acquired nicknames, were Hadji "Hi Jolly" Ali; Yiorgos "Greek George" Caralambo; Anastasio "Short Tom" Coralli; Michelo Georgios; Yanni Iliato; Giorgios Costi; Mimico "Mico" Teodora; and Hadjiatis "Long Tom" Yannaco.

In a related mission, Wayne traveled clear to the Crimea to learn from British Army officers on how camels fared in the Crimean War. He also dropped in on the newfangled institution of the zoo, in Paris and London, to glean from expert breeders the unique habits of the dromedary. Porter sailed across the Atlantic and the Gulf of Mexico to drop off his load in Texas. He then sailed right back to the Middle East to obtain another 40-odd camels, returning with them in early 1857. Major Wayne and his hirelings drove the animals 180 miles to a "camel corral," dubbed Camp Verde, northwest of San Antonio. He learned that the beasts, though normally docile, might stomp a man to death if they were riled—or spit oily, smelly cuds in their direction. He also discovered their strong body odor frightened horses. Yet in a 120-mile trial run to and from San Antonio, the camels carried twice as much weight as mules and made the distance in less than half the time.

As for Ned Beale, he'd left the Navy in 1851 and supervised properties in California for his old boss, Commodore Stockton. The next year, President Millard Fillmore picked Beale as Superintendent of Indian Affairs for California and Nevada. In this role he did much to improve the living conditions of the Native Americans and to protect more peaceful tribes against attack from the more bellicose. In 1856 California's Governor made Beale a general in the state militia after he scouted out a route for the planned transcontinental railroad.

When James Buchanan took over as President in 1857, Major Wayne was assigned back to the Army's Quartermaster agency in D.C., as Virginia Governor John Floyd replaced Jefferson Davis as War Secretary. Floyd was crooked and incompetent. Colleagues of his siphoned off federal contract funds from the Pony Express, and when the Civil War loomed Floyd, a Southern sympathizer, shipped federal weapons off to arms depots in the South to prepare for secession. (In the war Floyd, as a Confederate General, would surrender Fort Donelson, Tennessee, unconditionally to General Grant, thus lending the latter his nickname "Unconditional Surrender" Grant.)

However, as the prewar War Secretary, Floyd was just as keen for the novel beasts of burden as Jefferson

Decatur House resident Edward Fitzgerald "Ned" Beale had a thrilling life as a spy, soldier, trailblazer, businessman, and diplomat.

Davis had been. But he needed someone to put the camels to the acid test, all while finding the best route from west Texas to booming California. After a petition of some 60,000 citizens demanded such a path, Congress authorized money to survey and construct a wagon road stretching from Fort Defiance, Arizona, to the California border. The winner of the federal contract for this task was none other than Ned Beale. No one else was more familiar with the region's terrain or people. But Beale balked when he learned that camels came with the deal. He thought they'd only complicate an already daunting task. Still, Secretary Floyd insisted on seeing results from the large government investment in the animals.

So it was that in June 1857 Beale set off from Fort Verde, Texas, with 25 camels, several drivers, 12 wagons, mules, horses, and a company of soldiers. In just a month they made the 830 miles to Fort Defiance. Despite their 700-pound loads, the camels left the mules in the dust. A skeptical Beale was transformed into a zealot. He wrote to Floyd that the test subjects "are the most docile, patient and easily managed creatures in the world, and infinitely more easily worked than mules."

The head camel driver was Hadji "Hi Jolly" Ali. He was a poster child for mid–19th century "multiculturalism." Born in the Turkish Empire, his dad was Syrian and his mother Greek. Raised Christian, he converted to Islam. Before joining the U.S Army, he worked for the French Army in North Africa. In the U.S. he converted back to Christianity and Anglicized and Latinized his name to Philip Tedro—but not before his American companions nicknamed him Hi Jolly because they couldn't pronounce Hadji Ali.

On the next stage of the trek, to the Colorado River, Beale was wowed by the camels' capacity to go without water for a full 10 days while traveling up to 40 miles daily. When the expedition got lost and went without water or food for a day and a half, a scouting party on camels found a faraway stream and led the rest of the party to it. Beale enthused, "Certainly there never was anything so patient or enduring and so little troublesome as this noble animal ... I have subjected them to trials which no other animal could possibly have endured.... I may speak for every man ... [that] there is not one of them who would not prefer the most indifferent of our camels to four of our best mules."

The surveying mission was a success. The path Beale and his camels traced became the basis not only for a wagon road but, later on, for the famed Route 66. Ned Beale then took his "Oriental expedition" into the Golden State, ending, at Fort Tejon north of Los Angeles, its journey of 1,200 miles. Fortuitously, he left the camels at a business partner's ranch. When Mohave Indians attacked the hacienda, ranch hands repelled their assault by charging the enemy atop the beasts. It was Lawrence of Arabia in America. Two years later, in 1859, Beale led a second wagon route expedition westward out of Fort Smith, Arkansas. Once again his corps of camels, 25 strong, excelled. Beale wrote, "They pack water for days under a hot sun and never get a drop; they pack heavy burdens of corn and oats for months and never get a grain; and on the bitter greasewood and other worthless shrubs, not only subsist, but keep fat."

In 1860, after Beale left the project, the Army blundered. Under Captain Winfield Scott Hancock, later a hero of the Battle of Gettysburg, the camels were tested as a speed delivery service, along the lines of the Pony Express. In two brutal, 300-mile test routes near Camp Mohave in the New Mexico Territory, camels in the experiment died from exhaustion. At the same time, Hancock's future foil at Gettysburg, federal Army Colonel Robert E. Lee, had better luck with the dromedaries. In spring 1860, while in acting command of the Army's Department of Texas, Lee ordered a reconnaissance of the Pecos River region. A fort was needed to keep watch on the Comanche Indian tribe there. The expedition's soldiers tramped through unforgiving badlands and nearly died from lack of water. A trio of mules perished. All 20 camels survived. Lee wrote of the camels' "endurance, docility and sagacity ... but for whose reliable services the reconnaissance would have failed." The coming of the Civil War in 1861—and a change in the federal administration—ended the far-ranging experiment. Given wartime priorities, the Union Army's commanders were less enthused about the Camel Corps than their Confederate-to-be predecessors had been.

President Lincoln's Secretary of War, Edwin Stanton, was appointed to clean up waste in Union Army procurement. This might have colored his thumbs-down view. "I cannot ascertain that these [camels] have ever been so employed as to be of any advantage to the Military Service," Stanton stated, "and I do not think that it will be practical to make them useful." At war's end, the remaining 44 animals at Camp Verde were sold off for $32 each. The ships of the desert wound up on ranches, in mines hauling precious metals, and at circuses eager for a novelty act. The hardy camel can live into its eighties, and the last known member of the Camel Corps passed away in 1934 in Los Angeles's Griffith Park.

Hi Jolly, aka Hadji Ali, was honorably discharged from the Army in 1870. He parlayed his experience with epic expeditions into running a freight business. (In this he echoed explorer William Clark's freed slave York, who turned his service in the Lewis and Clark expedition into a transport service.) Hi Jolly also served as a military scout and mule driver for the fight against the skilled Apache chieftain Geronimo. Mr. Jolly obtained U.S. citizenship, married a lady from Tucson, and fathered two children. The family kept some of the camels for personal use. Hi Jolly's personality reflected some of the prickly, unjolly nature of his beasts. Once, insulted for being barred from a Los Angeles picnic, he disrupted the outing by charging it with a carriage drawn by a duo of camels. After his death in remote Quartzite, Arizona, in 1902, Jolly/Ali was buried, in a nod to his ancestry and lifelong occupation, under a stone pyramid topped by a copper camel.

Family Follow-Ups

Ned Beale did not neglect his private interests during his time as the king of camels. In the 1850s and 1860s he bought up old Mexican land grants near today's Bakersfield, California, and assembled the 40,000-acre Tejon Rancho. His cost was four cents an acre. This formed, and remains, the largest block of privately owned land in the Golden State. Today the ranch, with its cattle herds and crops, is the publicly traded Tejon Ranch Company.

Dividing his time between the mammoth hacienda and Washington City, Beale bought the Decatur House in 1874 for $60,000. There he'd often entertain the former soldier he had encountered in his Gold Dust Derby: President Grant. In fact, Grant appointed Beale "Envoy Extraordinaire and Minister Plenipotentiary" to the twin kingdom of Austria-Hungary. While in the Washington region, Beale spent time at a second estate in Ash Hill, Maryland, where he'd host Wild West acquaintances like Buffalo Bill Cody. (Beale seemed the Forest Gump of his time, running into and charming almost everyone who was anyone.) After Ned Beale died at the Decatur House in 1893, his son Truxtun Beale inherited the home. Wide-ranging like his ancestors, Truxtun served as U.S. Minister to exotic locales like Persia and Serbia. In 1894 he married Harriet Blaine, the daughter of Vice President James G. Blaine. After a difficult divorce, in 1902 he married again, to Marie Chase Oge. Truxtun and Marie Beale continued the home's tradition of holding grand social events for the city's elite.

Truxtun died in 1936. In 1944 his widow had the Decatur House restored it to its original spare but stately Federal style. In 1950 Marie turned the old servants annex and carriage house on H Street over to the Navy Historical Foundation. Under Admiral Ernest King, it became the Truxtun-Decatur Naval Museum. The space was too tiny, however, so in 1982 its artifacts were moved to the Washington Naval Yard's Navy Museum. At the same time, the National Trust for Historic Preservation acquired the Decatur House and transformed it back into the historic home of Commodore Decatur. Today it's also a center of presidential history operated by the White House Historical Association.

Yet a few still recall the protean life of resident Edward Beale and the strange saga of his Camel Corps.

Sources

Beale, Edward Fitzgerald, Laurence R. Cook, and Andrew F. Rolle. *Collection Related to Edward Fitzgerald Beale*. Huntington Library, Art Collections and Botanical Gardens, San Marino, California, 1940.

Bonsal, Stephen. *Edward Fitzgerald Beale: A Pioneer in the Path of Empire, 1822–1903*. New York: G.P. Putnam's Sons, 1912.

Carroll, Charles C. *The Government's Importation of Camels: A Historical Sketch*. Report of the Chief of the Bureau of Animal Industry. Vol. 20. United States Department of Agriculture, Washington, D.C., 1903.

Hawkins, Vince. "The U.S. Army's 'Camel Corps' Experiment." Army Historical Foundation, July 16, 2014. https://army-history.org/the-u-s-armys-camel-corps-experiment/.

Shapard, John. "The United States Army Camel Corps, 1856–66." *Military Review* (August 1975). https://www.armyupress.army.mil/Journals/Military-Review/Directors-Select-Articles/The-United-States-Army-Camel-Corps-1856-66/.

Woodbury, Chuck. "U.S. Camel Corps Remembered in Quartzsite, Arizona." *Out West* (2003). http://www.outwestnewspaper.com/camels.html.

20

The Enslaved Woman Who Sued the Head of the State Department

Decatur House Annex, on H Street, Around the Corner from the House's Front Entrance at 748 Jackson Place

Even more than Commodore Decatur, the most noted resident of the Decatur House was House Speaker and Secretary of State Henry Clay of Kentucky. Clay was the most influential member of Congress in the first half of the 19th century. A leader of the original "hawks" demanding war with Britain in 1812, he was the author of the American System of using federal carrots and sticks to bolster U.S. commerce. But he is best known as the "Great Compromiser" who forged two legislative deals over slavery that staved off the Civil War for 40 years.

Clay's Compromise of 1820 kept the political balance between South and North by bringing Missouri into the Union as a slave state and bringing in Maine—which had seceded from Massachusetts—as a free state. (Yes, a northern state seceded from another northern state, mostly because Massachusetts had poorly defended its region of Maine during the War of 1812.) However, over time the Compromise, by permitting slavery above the Mason-Dixon Line's boundary between North and South, heightened the regional differences.

In 1820 Thomas Jefferson made famous remarks, using the analogy of a fire engine company, that warned Clay's accord was "like a fire bell in the night, [that] awakened and filled me with terror. I considered it at once as the knell of the Union. [It] is hushed indeed for the moment. but this is a reprieve only...." The former President continued: "A geographical line, coinciding with a marked principle, moral and political, once concieved [sic] and held up to the angry passions of men, will never be obliterated; and every new irritation will mark it deeper and deeper."

Jefferson was right. Thirty years later, civil war was even more of a threat. So Clay, at age 72, reemerged to push through the Compromise of 1850, which brought in as a free state California, swelling with settlers from the '49ers Gold Rush. Yet it also strengthened the Fugitive Slave Act, which empowered slave owners to cross state boundaries to seize and return escaped slaves. The act enraged northerners who witnessed bounty hunters grab runaway slaves, and sometimes free blacks, off of streets and farms and hustle the human cargo back to the South. The blacks, runaway or not, weren't too pleased either.

Back in 1829, while living in the Decatur House and serving as Secretary of State, Clay

20. The Enslaved Woman Who Sued the Head of the State Department

himself had become embroiled in the "peculiar institution."

A Slave's Solicitation

Attached to the rear of the Decatur House is a light-colored brick building, greater in length than the mansion though lower in height. Nowadays it houses a gift shop. On the other side of the store is a spacious courtyard. This innocuous-looking annex to the main house was, in Clay's time, a slave house. It is one of the few surviving former slave dwellings in the United States. The slave annex was built, according to archaeological evidence, in the early 1820s. Up to 21 enslaved servants were kept there, living on the second floor and eating their meals on the first. The owner or leasers of the Decatur House would keep their slaves in the annex. Many of the

While holding the high office of Secretary of State, Henry Clay was caught up in a court case with one of his slaves, Charlotte Dupuy (Library of Congress).

enslaved persons worked in hotels downtown or as household servants. Even in the capital's early days, the ownership of slaves could be embarrassing. Therefore owners kept their servants out of sight in the courtyard. Penning them there also prevented their making an escape.

In 1829 Clay was one of the leaders of the Whig Party (the name referred not to the powdered hairpieces of the Founding Fathers but to a reform party in Britain). Although the Whigs represented northern interests, Clay was from a southern border state and owned slaves. Indeed, quite a few northerners still owned slaves at this time. One of Clay's slaves was a woman by the name of Charlotte Dupuy, who lived at the annex.

Charlotte, or Lottie for short, had been born around 1787 in Cambridge, Maryland, on the Eastern Shore of the Chesapeake. Both her parents were slaves who were paid wages. As such, they were able to save enough money to buy their freedom. This was a fairly common practice in Tidewater Maryland and Virginia during the early years of the republic. Unfortunately, before her parents obtained their liberty, a man purchased their daughter from their owner. Breaking up families was all too common a practice throughout the history of slavery. In 1805 slave buyer John Condon took Charlotte with him to Kentucky. She was then about 18 years old. Condon promised her manumission, that is, freedom, if she worked hard for an extended period. But the following year, an up-and-coming lawyer in Kentucky, one Henry Clay, bought her for $450. Condon thought one year of work had been too short a time for Charlotte to deserve her freedom.

In 1806 Charlotte met another slave, Aaron Dupuy. Charlotte and Aaron fell in love—at first sight, it's said. They asked Mr. Clay to buy Aaron to increase their chances of staying together as a family. Clay did so. After their marriage they had two children, Mary Ann and Charles. The family lived and worked at Clay's sprawling Ashland plantation in Lexington, Kentucky. Clay moved to Washington in 1809 to serve in the Senate—illegally. He was just 29 years old, and the Constitution mandates a Senator must be at least 30. However, there was little protest over it.

In 1825, after several terms as House Speaker, Clay became Secretary of State for President John Quincy Adams. In 1829, after Adams lost his try for reelection, Clay prepared to move back to his Ashland estate. During his time at the Decatur House, the Dupuys were his house servants. The prospect of returning to Kentucky disturbed Charlotte, for she thought she should be free. She knew it was not unheard of for a slave to petition for her freedom and even take her owner to court. So Charlotte brought suit against the Secretary of State, Henry Clay, to obtain freedom for herself and her two children! But Clay was determined to keep Charlotte. He thought political foes, to embarrass him, had urged Charlotte to sue. Condon, her previous owner, seemed to have that opinion. Writing to Clay, he speculated about "some evil disposed person operating upon the mind of Lotty improperly."

High-powered lawyers entered the fray. Clay's attorney in the matter was Philip Richard Fendall II, related to the powerful Lee family of Virginia. In fact, the Fendall family home in Alexandria, Virginia, then part of the District, was just down a cobblestoned street from the boyhood home of Robert E. Lee. Presiding over the case was a local attorney who had handled, or would handle, cases for Presidents Jefferson and Jackson and for future Republic of Texas President Sam Houston. This was none other than Francis Scott Key, author of "The Star-Spangled Banner." At Key's urgings, Clay and Fendall had to answer Dupuy's demands in court, at the U.S. Circuit Court of Appeals. Charlotte's lawyer was a persuasive man named Robert Beale. He got the court to stay her removal to Kentucky until her case was resolved. He told the judges that Charlotte and her daughter Mary Ann "are people of color who are entitled to their freedom and who are now held in a state of slavery by one Henry Clay (Secty of State) contrary to the law and your petitioners just rights."

Oddly, Clay, and Key, too, were seen as "moderates" on the issue of slavery, although both owned slaves. Like many slave owners of the time they averred that slavery was wrong, and should be gradually eliminated. They were both backers of the American Colonization Society, which set up the nation of Liberia in West Africa for free African Americans. Such views, however, mattered little to someone like Charlotte Dupuy.

While the federal court considered Charlotte's petition, Clay returned to Kentucky. He took Aaron Dupuy and the two Dupuy children with him. While the case was being adjudicated, Charlotte lived in the slave annex. She worked there for the then-resident of the Decatur House: President Andrew Jackson's Vice President—and later President—Martin Van Buren of New York. Van Buren paid Charlotte wages for her work. Two decades later, Van Buren would be the presidential nominee of America's first truly antislavery party, the Free Soil Party.

It took 18 months for the court to decide Charlotte's fate. The wheels of justice grind slowly, perhaps especially for slaves. Finally, late in 1830, Dupuy lost her case against Clay. The Circuit Court ruled Clay was not bound by any agreement Charlotte may have made with her previous owner. However, Charlotte Dupuy refused to give in. Though still a slave, she refused to return to Kentucky to join Clay. Henry Clay responded by moving to detain Charlotte in an Alexandria prison while he pondered what to do with her. He wrote his lawyer Fendall: "I approve entirely of your order to the Marshall to imprison Lotty. Her husband and children are here. Her refusal therefore to return home ... was unnatural towards them as it was disobedient to me.... How shall I now get her, is the question?... In the mean time, be pleased to let her remain in jail."

Eventually, Clay and his wife, Lucretia, had Charlotte sent to New Orleans to live with their daughter Ann and her husband. Clay wrote that Charlotte's "conduct has created insubordination among her relatives here, I think it high time to put a stop to it, which can best be done by her return to duty." In New Orleans, Charlotte cared for the couple's children. Ann and her spouse loved Charlotte's work. In 1832, Ann wrote to Lucretia Clay: "I cannot thank [you] enough for having spared Lotty to me, she is the best creature I ever saw and appears to be quite attached to the children."

In 1836 Martin Van Buren was elected President and prepared to move from the Decatur House to the White House. At that time, the most prominent hotel owner in Washington was John Gadsby of Alexandria. Gadsby purchased the Decatur House from Susan Decatur, Commodore Stephen Decatur's widow. Gadsby was owner of Gadsby's Tavern in Alexandria, Virginia. The tavern, which is still in operation as a museum and colonial-style restaurant, hosted inaugural balls for the first six Presidents, from Washington to John Quincy Adams. Gadsby also built and operated, from 1827, the grand National Hotel on Pennsylvania Avenue and 6th Street—on the site of the Newseum museum of the news. Many of the servants in Gadsby's businesses were slaves who worked in his hotels. As with other owners and residents of Decatur House, he kept his servants in the annex.

Back to Charlotte's plight. Overtime, Henry Clay apparently decided that Charlotte Dupuy had worked long and hard enough for her freedom. In 1840 Clay manumitted her as well as her daughter, Mary Ann. Her son, Charles, remained Clay's enslaved manservant for the next four years, accompanying the famous politician on speaking tours. Then Clay freed him as well. In 1852 Clay freed Aaron Dupuy. At last, Charlotte and Aaron and their children, Mary Ann and Charles, all got to live in liberty. The Dupuys obtained work with John Clay, Henry Clay's son, and a renowned breeder of race horses.

Banning Slavery

As mentioned, an elderly Henry Clay cobbled together the Compromise of 1850 to sidestep a civil war over slavery, in part by strengthening the hands of slave owners seeking to capture escaped slaves. But the Compromise contained another provision, one that may have been influenced by Clay's experience with the Dupuys. In a concession to northern abolitionists, his legislation banned the slave trade in Washington City—not slavery itself, but the buying and selling of human beings, which often entailed breaking up families like Dupuy's. Some think it was one of the Great Compromiser's greatest achievements.

For generations, slave markets had existed in Washington. Two of the most notorious slave pens and auction markets, Robey's and Yellow House, were located off of (ironically) today's Independence Avenue, just south and west of the Capitol, the legislature of the land of the free. But due to Clay and pressure from opponents of slavery, that baleful commerce ended in the capital. Four years earlier, in 1846, the city of Alexandria—part of the Washington City since its founding—had returned to the state of Virginia. This was partly due to the growing controversy over Washington's slave trade. Although a majority of blacks in Alexandria were free by that time, the town had a lucrative business in selling surplus slaves to the burgeoning cotton plantations of the Deep South. (Another, perhaps even bigger, reason was that Alexandrians, as long as they were part of Washington City, could not vote in federal elections. "Taxation Without Representation" still pertains to the District of Columbia today.)

It wasn't until the Civil War that slavery in Washington City was abolished outright. And this wasn't done, as many people think, through Lincoln's Emancipation Proclamation. That applied only to slaves in the Confederate states, not the federal capital. Dusting off an old idea of James Madison and a young congressman named Lincoln, President Lincoln ended slavery in Washington by buying out its slaveholders. Great Britain had pursued a similar approach in 1833 to end slavery in its empire. Lincoln's "DC Emancipation Act" freed 3,100 Washington City slaves via compensation to some 966 owners, authorizing the payment of $300 a slave to owners loyal to the Union. Some slaveholders submitted claims attesting their slaves were worth considerably more. The President signed the act into law on April 16, 1862. That was seven-and-a-half months before his Emancipation Proclamation of January 1, 1863. The District still celebrates every April 16 as Emancipation Day. It was the day on which many Charlotte Dupuys became free at last.

Sources

Heidler, David S., and Jeanne T. Heidler. *Henry Clay: The Essential American*. New York: Random House, 2010.

King, Gilbert. "The Day Henry Clay Refused to Compromise." *Smithsonian*, December 6, 2012. https://www.smithsonianmag.com/history/the-day-henry-clay-refused-to-compromise-153589853/.

Wheeler, Linda. "A Slave Gets Her Say." *Washington Post*, February 26, 2000. https://www.washingtonpost.com/archive/local/2000/02/26/a-slave-gets-her-say/b41e8257-e795-4dcf-bdf6-30bfbd9be5e1/?utm_term=.796d357d676c.

White House Historical Association. "Charlotte Dupuy: She Has Been Her Own Mistress." https://www.whitehousehistory.org/decatur-house-and-charlotte-dupuy.

21

The War-Hero Womanizer Who Slayed the Son of Francis Scott Key

722 Jackson Place

An elegant townhouse on Jackson Place was the home to one of the great scoundrels in the city's annals. He was a man who slaughtered a most prominent Washingtonian right in Lafayette Square, yet he might have been partly responsible for America's most important military victory. Congressman Daniel Sickles had an apt last name for someone with a violent temper. He was a man of wildest passions indeed.

Amorous Lawmaker

Like other powerful men in the capital's history, Sickles had a wandering eye, and his reputation preceded him to Washington. When he was a New York legislator, he was known for walking into the state capitol arm-in-arm with a prostitute, a Miss Fanny White. On a diplomatic mission to London he supposedly introduced the madam to Queen Victoria. His waywardness seemed strange, as he was married to the brilliant and beguiling Teresa Bagioli Sickles, the granddaughter by blood of Mozart's librettist. The gifted young woman was conversant in five languages.

In 1852 Dan and Teresa married when she was 15 or 16 and pregnant. After Sickles' election to Congress in 1856, with backing from the Tammany Hall political machine, they moved into Lafayette Square. In Washington Dan's dalliances continued. But wife Teresa decided that two people could two-time each other. In the spring of 1858 she began an intimate relationship with a friend of her husband.

Her spouse's pal wasn't just any man: he was the U.S. District Attorney for Washington. His last name, Key, betrayed quite a family tree. He was Philip Barton Key II, the son of Francis Scott Key, author of the National Anthem! He was also the nephew of the Chief Justice of the Supreme Court, Maryland's Roger Taney. Handsome, flirtatious, and a widower with children, Philip Barton Key II was the city's chief law enforcement officer. In that role, in 1857, he'd put down an election-day riot between rowdy Irish-Americans and anti-immigrant gangs of Baltimore "Yankees." To stop the mayhem, in which 10 people were killed, Key called in leathernecks from the Marine barracks near the Washington Navy Yard.

Both Key and Dan Sickles frequented the National Club, a lounge for gentlemen. It was where the federal Circuit Court of Appeals now stands, across Lafayette Square from the Sickles House. The building was the old residence of Commodore John Rodgers and would be the home of Secretary of State William Seward. During his affair in 1858 and 1859 with Teresa Sickles, Philip Barton Key rented a love nest in a seedy neighborhood on 14th Street between K and L streets. Key and his mistress worked out a most unusual means of meeting up for their dangerous liaisons. When Philip wanted to rendezvous with Teresa, he'd stand in the Square across from her home and wave a handkerchief in her direction. After seeing the signal, Mrs. Sickles would hurry out to meet him. However, word filtered back to the 39-year-old Sickles that he was being cuckolded. He received an unsigned note that stated, "I do assure you that [Key] has as much the use of your wife as you have."

On February 26, 1859, a shaken Sickles sat Teresa down in their bedroom and made her write out a confession to the affair as their five-year-old daughter, Laura, sat in the next room. In the confession Teresa wrote, "I did what is usual for a wicked woman to do. I undressed myself. Mr. Key undressed also." She added, "Mr. Key has kissed me in this house a number of times. I do not deny that we have had connection in this house—in the parlor, on the sofa." The following morning, Dan and Teresa Sickles were at home when the Congressman glanced out the second-floor window of their house and spied Key in the Square. Key was looking toward their house—and waving a handkerchief. It was like waving a red flag at a bull.

Sickles grabbed two derringers and a five-shot revolver. Loaded for bear, he rushed down the steps of the house and into the park. Moments later, he appeared before Key near the gentleman's club on Madison Place. Sickles pulled out one of the guns and aimed at his erstwhile friend. "Key, you scoundrel!" he cried. "You have dishonored my house. You must die!" Representative Sickles pulled the trigger. The bullet hit the District Attorney in the hand, slightly wounding him. A horrified Key threw his opera glasses at Sickles. Then the men grappled with each other on Madison Place. Sickles fired a second time, and the bullet smashed through Key's groin and into his leg. Key toppled into a tree in the park, yelling, "Don't shoot me!"

Onlookers, stunned at this bloody fight between two noted citizens, gathered about. Sickles again pulled the trigger, but the gun misfired. He fired again, and the bullet entered Key's chest near the heart. The Congressman then pointed his weapon at the head of the Attorney

In 1859 Representative Dan Sickles fatally shot Philip Barton Key II, the city's chief law officer. In the murder trial that ensued, Sickles was acquitted by reason of temporary insanity. He later fought at the Battle of Gettysburg (National Archives).

General. The gun again misfired. It didn't matter. Onlookers carried Key into 21 Madison Place, the Benjamin Taylor Ogle House, which belonged to a wealthy Tidewater family. Key died there later that day.

The "trial of the century" followed (at least it was until the trial six years later of the Lincoln assassination conspirators). Public attention was great due to the killing by a congressman of D.C.'s top law enforcement official and the son of the author of "The Star-Spangled Banner." It seemed an open-and-shut case. Sickles had, with intent, killed his romantic rival—and in front of witnesses. Sickles admitted, "Of course I killed him. He deserved it." The Congressman was imprisoned but treated liberally, according to author Maggie MacLean. He was permitted to have a gun and he used the warden's living quarters to meet visitors.

Sickles decided to fight the charges. A cunning man, he hired a squad of high-powered attorneys, led by Edwin Stanton of Ohio. Accustomed to the legal spotlight, Stanton had represented the U.S. government in California land cases. He had taken on Cyrus McCormick, the inventor of the mechanical reaper, in a patent case. A few years later, Stanton would ably administer the Union Army as Abraham Lincoln's Secretary of War.

In the three-week jury trial, Stanton's team argued that Sickles should not be held accountable for his actions. Upon seeing his wife's lover signaling for another illicit meeting, Sickles had been seized by blind rage. He should be acquitted, the defense argued, due to temporary insanity. After an hour of deliberation the jury agreed. It was the first successful use of the temporary insanity plea in America's courts.

To us, the verdict seems shocking. However, throughout the highly publicized trial most people sided with Sickles. In the Victorian Era, it was beyond the pale for a woman to be unfaithful to her husband. A husband might stray and might be forgiven, but a woman—never. Sickles benefited from the double standard, but then he threw away the public's regard. Instead of separating from Teresa, he announced that he forgave her, and was harshly criticized for this. Most people believed forgiving an adulteress was worse than killing her lover. Sickles responded, rather elegantly: "I can now see in the almost universal denunciation in which [Teresa] is followed … the misery and peril from which I have rescued the mother of my daughter. I shall strive to prove to all that an erring wife and mother may be forgiven and redeemed." The public was unmoved. And, naturally, some thought he'd gotten away with murder. With the fallout from the killing, the trial, and the reconciliation, Sickles' public career seemed over.

Wrong Man in the Wrong Place at the Right Time

How could a wealthy and prominent but disgraced man get his reputation back? The opportunity came two years later, in 1861, with the outbreak of the Civil War. Private citizens of means were allowed to recruit and outfit their own troops. Sickles did so, mustering regiments of New York troops. Plying his political connections, he was made a Major General. He and his men wound up in a fateful spot at a fateful time: the Peach Orchard on July 2, 1863, in Gettysburg, Pennsylvania. It was the second day of the Battle of Gettysburg and they were facing surging Confederate troops under General James Longstreet and General John Bell Hood, intent on rolling up the center of the Union line as well as capturing the high ground of Little Round Top. If the rebels could take that strategic summit, they might win the pivotal battle of the war. General Sickles, against the direct and repeated orders of the Union commander, General George Meade, ordered his entire corps of soldiers off a solid defensive position and onto the open terrain of the orchard. Longstreet's troops raked them with murderous fire from three sides, and Sickles' unit was all but destroyed.

Still, the action slowed down the Southerners' advance toward Little Round Top. The Confederates, exhausted from the day's marching and fighting in the July heat, were just barely beaten back at the summit by Union troops who had run out of ammunition and had to charge with bayonets under valiant commanders such as Maine Colonel Joshua Chamberlain. The next day the frustrated Confederate commander, Robert E. Lee, ordered an attack, Pickett's Charge, on the dug-in center of the Union line. The assault was crushed, and the shattered rebels retreated south. Through his blundering and disobedience, Sickles might have helped win the Civil War.

Not only was his unit mangled on that fateful summer day, but its leader was also mauled. A Confederate cannonball smashed up Sickles' right leg. Taken to a surgical tent to have it amputated, Sickles retained a sardonic sense of humor, telling a soldier to save his ruined leg as a souvenir. Sickles emerged from the conflict in the eyes of some as a valiant savior of the Republic. Some fellow officers, however, thought his insubordination could have lost them Gettysburg and the war. They were unhappy when the Army, largely due to Sickles' political clout, awarded him the Medal of Honor. In time, his severed souvenir became a keepsake of the National Museum of Health and Medicine. The preserved bone even has a nickname: "Pickled Sickles."

By becoming an unlikely war hero, Sickles regained a measure of public esteem, although his relationship with Teresa never fully recovered. In 1867 she died of tuberculosis. In 1869 President Ulysses S. Grant appointed Sickles U.S. ambassador to Spain. In Madrid, it's believed his behavior of old continued: he had an alleged affair with the deposed Queen, Isabella II. In Iberia he married the daughter of a Spanish nobleman. The couple had two children, then separated. Back in his home state of New York, Sickles was suspected of pilfering funds slated for Civil War monuments. The builders of his memorial at Gettysburg declined to place a statue of him there.

He may have felt he got the last laugh on all his critics, as he lived until 1914—a full 51 years after Gettysburg and 55 years after killing Key.

Sources

Brammer, Robert. "Love, Adultery, and Madness." Library of Congress. February 13, 2015. https://blogs.loc.gov/law/2015/02/love-adultery-and-madness/.

Flowers, R. Barri. *Murder of the U.S. Attorney: Congressman Sickles' Crime of Passion in 1859*. CreateSpace/Amazon (self-published), 2018.

Keneally, Thomas. *American Scoundrel: The Life of the Notorious Civil War General Dan Sickles*. New York: Doubleday, 2002.

MacLean, Maggie. "Teresa Sickles." *Civil War Women Blog*, August 19, 2009. https://www.civilwarwomenblog.com/teresa-sickles/.

Sickles, Daniel Edgar, and Felix Gregory De Fontaine. *Trial of the Hon. David [sic] E. Sickles for Shooting Philip Barton Key*. New York: R.M. De Witt, 1859.

22

The Accursed Life of the Man Who Tried to Save the President

712 Jackson Place

The Rathbone townhouse near the south end of Jackson Place is linked to a long chain of tragic events. It began on perhaps the most notorious day in American history—April 14, 1865, Good Friday—that year a very bad Friday. President Abraham Lincoln and First Lady Mary Todd Lincoln were planning for their evening at Ford's Theater downtown, to attend the comedy "Our American Cousin." The First Family, like most people in the federal capital, were in a joyous mood. After four years of carnage the Civil War was ending. On April 3, Union troops had taken the Confederate capital of Richmond, Virginia. On April 9, General Lee had surrendered his Confederate army at Appomattox, Virginia. Every night and day since then celebratory crowds and marching bands had swirled through the streets of Washington.

A Witness to Tragedy

But the Lincolns had a small concern. To unwind from the stress of the war they often went to see a play downtown, and it was their practice to take along another couple. But that day, no one would go with them. They invited the head of the Union Army, General Ulysses S. Grant, and his wife, Julia Dent Grant. But Mrs. Grant had borne the brunt of an anger fit from Mrs. Lincoln at a recent review of Union troops. So Julia Grant convinced her husband that day to travel to New Jersey to visit their children. The Lincolns then asked the Secretary of War, Edwin Stanton, and his wife. But she also had poor relations with Mary Todd Lincoln. The Speaker of the House of Representatives, Schuyler Colfax, declined, as he was preparing to go out of town. Attorney Adolphe de Chambrun, of the French embassy, was invited. But he deemed it bad taste to take in a comedy on Good Friday. The President's journalist friend Noah Brooks, who had exposed a fraudulent medium preying on the superstitious Mrs. Lincoln, also begged off (see Chapter 7, "Mrs. Lincoln's Sad Search for Her Deceased Son"). Even the President's eldest son, Robert Todd Lincoln, weary from service with General Grant, decided to spend the evening at the White House.

Finally, Mrs. Lincoln recalled a couple she knew from White House socials. The *engagées* were Major Henry Rathbone, 27, a veteran of the bloody battles of Antietam and Fredericksburg, and Clara Harris, 30, the daughter of New York Senator Ira Harris. After

THE ASSASSINATION OF PRESIDENT LINCOLN.

The illustration from 1908 depicts Major Henry Rathbone, on the left, reacting to John Wilkes Booth's shooting of President Lincoln. Booth badly injured Rathbone with a dagger (Library of Congress).

a lengthy luck of the draw, it was they who accepted the Lincoln invitation. At 8:20 that night the President and First Lady were taken in the presidential carriage to the Senator Harris home at 15th and H streets, one block from Lafayette Square. There they picked up Henry and Clara—the pair gratified to be so honored. Then the foursome rode off to Ford's Theater six blocks away. At about 10 p.m., John Wilkes Booth entered the President's theater box, slipped behind Lincoln, and shot him with a derringer in the back of the head.

Major Rathbone, sitting just feet away, rushed over to try to save the President, shouting, "Stop that man!" He grabbed the assassin. Booth attacked him with a dagger, loosening Rathbone's grip and piercing the soldier's left arm to the bone from shoulder to elbow. Still, Rathbone managed to grab Booth's coat as the actor leapt down to the stage, with Booth catching his riding spur on a banner. Clara shouted, "The President is shot!" Landing awkwardly on the stage, the assassin fractured his leg. After brandishing his weapons and shouting to the audience, he hurriedly limped to the theater's rear entrance, mounted a waiting horse, and galloped away. His broken leg hobbled him during 12 days of flight, aiding Union troops in cornering the killer and shooting him dead.

At Ford's Theater and then at the Petersen House, where the mortally stricken Lincoln was taken, the attending physicians focused on the President. Rathbone stood by and fainted from loss of blood. In fact, he almost bled to death. In a delirium, he cried out about the stricken President: "God in heaven, save him!" He was then taken back to Senator Harris' home. An Army doctor sewed up his wounds as Clara, steely-calm that terrible night, served as a nurse. When Rathbone recovered, the nation looked on him fondly as a war veteran who had tried to save the President's life. In 1867 he married Clara. The first of three children, Harry, was born three years later—on Lincoln's birthday. The family took up residence at 712 Jackson Place. They lived across Lafayette Square from where, on the night of Lincoln's slaying, Booth conspirator Lewis Powell almost killed Secretary of State William Seward (see Chapter 1, "The Secretary of State Is Nearly Stabbed to Death").

Henry and Clara Rathbone could afford their 22-room brownstone, for both were wealthy. They were also related, and in an unusual way. In 1848 Clara Harris' father, a widower, had remarried. Harris' new wife was a widow, Pauline Rathbone. From her previous marriage, she had two sons, including Henry, then 10 years old. So Henry and Clara, then 13, were step-brother and step-sister. Over time they fell in love.

Post-Traumatic Strains

Their marriage, however, was ever troubled by Henry's ill health. During the war Rathbone was ravaged by fevers and a form of malaria. In 1864 a doctor told him "these repeated attacks of a wasting and debilitating disease were likely to permanently injure your constitution." But the main problem was his mental health. In the years after Lincoln's murder, though he fully recovered from the knife wounds Booth had inflicted, Henry Rathbone became ever more depressed—and deranged. He was gripped by paranoid delusions of the type that when he looked up at someone's portrait he thought the person inside the picture frame was staring at him. He was fixated on the notion that Clara and the children would desert him.

In search of a cure, Rathbone often traveled with his family to Germany to visit spas and medical experts. In 1883 the Rathbones resided for seven months at an apartment in Hanover. But Henry's condition worsened. On the day before Christmas Eve that year, early in the morning, Henry wanted to enter the children's bedroom. Clara, fearing for the youngsters' safety, tried to detain her husband in their bedroom. Henry took a pistol—and shot her. He also stabbed her. Then he turned the dagger on himself, stabbing himself half a dozen times. It was almost as if Rathbone was reenacting the Lincoln assassination. As with Booth's knife attack, he was wounded but survived. As with Booth's shooting, the target, Clara, perished.

When the German authorities arrested Rathbone, they realized he was not a cold-blooded killer but schizophrenic and, in today's parlance, perhaps a victim of post-traumatic stress. After a U.S. diplomat had visited him, he reported that Rathbone was "hopelessly insane [and] suffering from the worst form of Melancholia and imagines that everyone is conspiring against him." Rathbone was committed to an asylum for life. His living arrangements in an old Benedictine monastery were comfortable. Still a wealthy man, he was permitted books and gentleman's clothes. But in 1891 a doctor examining him reported he still suffered from "delusions of persecution." Rathbone was convinced ghostlike figures in the halls were after him and that a device in the walls shot poison gases his way. Major Rathbone lived until 1911, dying 46 years after Lincoln's murder and stricken the whole time with paranoid fantasies. He was buried next to his wife in Hanover's ornate cemetery.

In a strange way, the Rathbone tragedy continued. By 1952 Germany had gone through the Second World War and its cemeteries had filled up with millions of war dead, those killed in battle, in concentration camps, aerial bombings, and the wounded and diseased who didn't recover after the war. The Hanover resting place thus sought to free up space for the recently departed. The graves of the two forgotten Americans were reclassified as abandoned, and the remains of Henry and Clara Rathbone were unearthed and disposed of. It's said that Major Rathbone, in death as in life, never found peace.

There is a more positive postscript. Rathbone's son, Henry Riggs Rathbone, had a successful life in public affairs. Elected to Congress in 1922, he was instrumental in turning the old Ford's Theater into a museum on President Lincoln. Further, a distant English cousin became famous in the mid–20th century for movie roles as macabre as the life of Major Rathbone. That actor was Basil Rathbone, perhaps the most famous screen version of Sherlock Holmes.

Sources

Ruane, Michael E. "A Tragedy's Second Act." *Washington Post*, April 5, 2009. http://www.washingtonpost.com/wp-dyn/content/article/2009/03/27/AR2009032701576.html?noredirect=on.

Smith, Gene. "The Haunted Major." *American Heritage* (February/March 1994). http://www.americanheritage.com/content/haunted-major.

Stephens, Caleb. *Worst Seat in the House: Henry Rathbone's Front Row View of the Lincoln Assassination*. Fredericksburg: Willow Manor, 2014. https://www.amazon.com/Worst-Seat-House-Rathbones-Assassination-ebook/dp/B00K08R1UO.

23

A Shocking Seedling from the Victory at Yorktown

General Rochambeau Statue, Southwest Corner of Lafayette Square

Lafayette Square's statue of the French warrior Rochambeau was completed in 1902, a fitting year for its unveiling. Theodore Roosevelt had become President the previous year, succeeding William McKinley. During his term McKinley had presided over the emergence of America on the world stage, via the 1898 Spanish-American War, which brought the United States possession of the Philippines, the Hawaiian Islands, and Puerto Rico. Roosevelt himself had won valor during the U.S. invasion of Spanish Cuba in the war's Battle of San Juan Hill and Kettle Hill. As the builder of the Panama Canal and of the Great White Fleet of Navy ships he sent around the world, Roosevelt was an archetype of American strength.

TR and his successor, William Howard Taft, supervised the construction of the West Wing and Oval Office, to give the Chief Executive of a powerful nation proper working quarters. The offices are separate from the White House residence where previous Presidents had labored. Also suggesting America's power and global reach in the early 1900s was this likeness of a general from a world superpower at the time of the American Revolution. A soldier from France who, by helping the U.S. secure its independence, helped set it on its own path to power.

Rochambeau's full name was Jean-Baptiste Donatien de Vimeur. A French aristocrat, his titled name was Comte, or Count, de Rochambeau. He was known too as Marshal Rochambeau, as in field marshal, as the Germans called it—a general of generals. Marshal Rochambeau commanded the 8,000 French soldiers at the American Revolution's climactic 1781 battle of Yorktown.

It was Rochambeau who had dissuaded General Washington from the folly of assaulting the heavily defended, British-occupied city of New York. Instead, he and Washington and their combined forces snuck a quick march down hundreds of miles of Eastern Seaboard to southern Virginia. There they surprised and besieged the forces of the unlucky British General Charles Cornwallis, thus forcing the surrender of his 7,500 soldiers. They were much aided by Rochambeau's fellow Count, the Comte de Grasse, François Joseph Paul de Grasse, who defeated a British fleet sent to resupply Cornwallis' army.

At the end of the American Revolution in 1783, Rochambeau's nephew—Louis François Bertrand Dupont d'Aubevoye, or the Comte de Lauberdière for short—wrote glowingly of America. He termed it "a vast country [that] raised itself up ... [and] acquired its independence from British power and monarchy with the help of the arms of France.... Liberty reigns here! Who can as yet say and predict what the consequences of this immense and glorious event will be??"

From Illegitimacy to High Command

From 1783 fast forward to 1844. In that year, just yards from where the Rochambeau statue would be placed 58 years later, the head of the U.S. Navy was often seen coming and going from his office at the old State, War, and Navy Department building. Friends knew him by his first name, Lewis. Lewis had enjoyed a high-flying Navy career, having risen from a most humble status. He was the bastard son of a Williamsburg, Virginia, woman of modest means named Rachel, and a father whose exact identity remains unknown. Luckily, his aunt Suzannah, though at first horrified at his illicit parentage, grew to love the lively, tousle-headed boy. She bequeathed him a large inheritance, with which Lewis acquired a proper education.

He began his maritime career in 1800 as a midshipman on the USS *Chesapeake*—the warship whose failed firefight in 1807 with the HMS *Leopard* and the latter's subsequent impressment of American sailors from the *Chesapeake* nearly touched off a war with Britain (see Chapter 17, "The Violent End of America's Bravest Sailor").

Later, Lewis and his crewmates fought against the pirates of the Caribbean—not the buccaneers of Johnny Depp, but actual pirates and privateers preying on American shipping. Lewis then served, and made Lieutenant, while fighting against an even more famous gang of cutthroats, the Barbary Pirates, along the shores of Tripoli in today's Libya on such warships as the USS *Enterprise*. He reached his greatest acclaim as a Master Commandant during the War of 1812 against the Royal Navy. While serving mostly on the armed sloop *Peacock*, he plotted three raiding voyages that took him from Cape Canaveral (today's Cape Kennedy in Florida) to the Shetland and Faroes islands, north of Scotland, and all the way to the Dutch East Indies (today's Indonesia). During these expeditions his ships bagged, respectively, 14, 14, and 4 British merchant vessels and fighting ships. It was an amazing tally against the seemingly invincible British fleets.

His last victory, in late June 1815, triggered an international row, as the treaty ending the War of 1812 had been signed a full seven months earlier. Communications with ships on the South Seas were slow. The *Peacock* came upon the British brig *Nautilus*, and Lewis ordered it to surrender. Its captain called over that the war was over. Believing this to be a ruse, Lewis called for an attack, which killed perhaps seven British sailors and brought on the surrender of the *Nautilus*. Upon boarding the brig, Lewis was presented with documents attesting that peace had indeed broken out. The British were irate, but a U.S. court of inquiry cleared the American officer.

For his many exploits, federal lawmakers awarded Lewis the Congressional Gold Medal, and Virginia officials presented him a gold sword. Given four decades of achievements, Lewis became a leading candidate to head the Navy in 1844 after an explosion aboard the USS *Princeton* killed Secretary of the Navy Thomas Gilmer. President John Tyler dubbed Lewis Acting Secretary of the Navy, with quarters just west of today's Rochambeau statue. It was an amazing climb up for a bastard son.

French Soldiers and Southern Belles

Also remarkable was that Lewis' birth stemmed from his mother's romance with French troops, led by Rochambeau, who went into winter quarters in Yorktown after the 1781 Franco-American victory. At Yorktown the Count de Lauberdière—the Rochambeau nephew who waxed eloquently on American independence—had critical views of Americans themselves. The eagle-nosed, 23-year-old Lauberdière had been a musketeer in the French King's court. He joined his uncle Rochambeau in America as his aide-de-camp and landed on American soil in Rhode Island, where he found the locals industrious but avaricious. Lauberdière saw himself "at the mercy of the usurer." A fellow French official wrote the New Englanders "overcharged us mercilessly. They treat us more like enemies than friends.... Their greed is unequalled."

Later, in tidewater Yorktown, Lauberdière viewed the Virginians as uncultured and lazy, spoiled by a reliance on slavery. In his journal he wrote "the attempts by Virginia planters to ape the manners of European courts only emphasized their lack of true culture." They were "used to from infancy to do nothing but give orders to their blacks. They live in idleness and indolence." Nor was he fond of General Washington's spouse. Martha Washington, he wrote, had "no intellectual faculties or appearance which responds to the supreme impression suggested today by the name of Washington. She enjoys a very great fortune which she could not have put to a better use than to share with a hero." Her husband though, in his mind, was exceptional. "His stature is very grand, his bearing is noble, his figure beautiful," he wrote of Washington. "[H]is personality is cool but at the same time pleasant and affable, his manner of receiving someone is easy and inspires trust, he often has an expression of troubling thoughts on his face."

Despite its failings, the Count felt Williamsburg had saving graces, in particular southern hospitality, as we would call it, and the region's alluring southern belles. In fact, the elegant and cultured French officers were a hit among the local women folk, and supremely confident of their abilities. Noted Lauberdière, with Gallic pride bordering on the hilarious: "The Frenchman is always the same. No other people has mastered better than he the charming art of making himself loved.... His nimbleness, his gallantry … always meets with an agreeable response" from womankind. "Compliments," he continued, "whether true or false, seduce them, are always in season with them. At first our manners astonished the Americans. Before long our courtesies, our politenesses conquered them, and they quickly recognized our superiority," according to author Robert A. Selig.

Lauberdière was friends with his cousin and fellow French officer Donatien-Marie-Joseph de Vimeur. The latter was the Vicomte, or Visicount, de Rochambeau, and Marshal Rochambeau's son. The Visicount was a handsome fellow with dark eyebrows that framed attentive eyes. In fact, both the Count of Lauberdière and the Visicount became romantically involved with Rachel—Lewis' mother—as well as with her sister Camilla. To the aristocratic Lauberdière, an affair with a low-born American woman was a lark. "As the chanson [song] says, 'Let us make love, let us make war,'" he wrote. "[T]hese two occupations are filled with attraction. In fact, we tried to combine the one with the other … [and] our desires were fulfilled."

Rachel had likely first encountered Frenchmen as wounded soldiers while she worked as a nurse in Williamsburg. Later she met the dashing foreigners in polite, and not so polite, society. Tidewater tongues began to wag about her and her sister. Two prominent scolds were Betsey Ambler and Mildred Smith. Betsey Ambler was a member of a prominent Virginia family; her father was part of Governor Thomas Jefferson's wartime brain trust. Betsey and Mildred Smith, her friend, savaged Rachel's behavior and the predicament that resulted. Betsey wrote of Rachel and Camilla that "their late conduct [h]as been So extraordinary that all eyes are fixed upon them ... [and] their heads seemed turnd [sic]." After Rachel's affair with a French officer became known, Mildred wrote that Rachel "is indeed lost to every thing that is dear to Woman," stating she should have "kept in View the dignity of her Sex." Jealousy seemed to play a role in all this. Mildred wrote that Rachel had "more bewitching talents for seducing a guileless heart then any human being I have ever known." The catty pair themselves found the Frenchmen exceedingly attractive. Wrote Mildred, echoing Lauberdière, "There is something so flattering in the [att]entions of these elegant french officers ... their style of entertaining and their devotion to the Ladies of Yk. [Yorktown] is so ... that almost any girl of 16 would be enchanted."

The product of Rachel's romantic attachment was child, a boy. The mother's full name was—Rachel Warrington, the mother of Lewis, whose full name was Lewis Warrington, the future head of the U.S. Navy! The father of Lewis Warrington never acknowledged the son. In 1786 Rachel Warrington, yielding up hope her French lover would return to America, wed a humble Virginia farmer. Her young boy, meanwhile, began charming those who had mocked his illicit origin. Betsey Ambler noted that the eyes of Lewis, as he grew, were "certainly ... the finest" and "his playful vivacity" a "delight." Her friend Mildred wrote he was "a lovely fellow." The records are sketchy, but Rachel probably died sometime during the War of 1812. She thus lived long enough to rejoice in the martial exploits of her son.

There is dispute over who the actual father was. Speculation has centered on either the Count of Lauberdière, Rochambeau's nephew, or the Visicount of Rochambeau, Rochambeau's son. No DNA tests have been performed to help resolve the matter. However, placing a sketch of Lewis Warrington side by side with a bust of Lauberdière reveals a resemblance between the two. Or, as Lauberdière was a Rochambeau, a resemblance between Warrington and the Rochambeaus generally.

Some have wondered if Marshal Rochambeau himself was the father. The General had married a wealthy Portuguese beauty, Jeanne Thérèse Tellez d'Acosta, in 1749. He had several children with Jeanne, including the Visicount. The French com-

The father of U.S. Navy chief Lewis Warrington may have been the Comte de Lauberdière, a nephew of Marshal Rochambeau, the commander of the French army in the United States during the American Revolution (Wikimedia Commons).

23. A Shocking Seedling from the Victory at Yorktown

Lewis Warrington, the bastard son of a ranking French officer, rose to command the U.S. Navy from an office just yards away from a future statue of a blood relation, French General Rochambeau (Minneapolis Institute of Art, William Hood Dunwoody Fund; photo: Minneapolis Institute of Art, portrait by Rembrandt Peale).

mander would have been 57 years old at the time Rachel had her son. However, no evidence supports a liaison between him and Rachel. Lauberdiere's journal, on the other hand, states that he and the Visicount had romantic relationships with Rachel and her sister Camilla. Which one was Lewis' father? A 1783 love letter from Lucy Randolph, of Virginia's aristocratic Randolph family, to a French regimental commander, the Comte Christian de Deux-Ponts, states that Rachel Warrington had given birth to "a son, whom she named Louis after his father Monsieur Lobidier [Lauberdière]." On the other hand, Rachel's nephew, a Mr. Philips, believed the father was the Visicount. He tried to contact the Visicount of Rochambeau via the French King's retainers to persuade him to marry Rachel, but to no avail.

With the American Revolution won, the Visicount left Williamsburg for France. He never owned up to a possible love child with Rachel. His attitude might have been: Why should a noble Count vouch for a boy sired with a vulgar foreigner? Whatever was the case, Lewis Warrington, as acting Navy Secretary of the United States, worked literally within a stone's throw of the future statue of his father's son if not his nephew—or the father himself! Truly, in the case of the Rochambeaus, the apple doesn't fall far from the tree.

The subsequent life of Lauberdière, the most likely father, may be instructive. Seven years after the end of the American Revolution, as the French Revolution was breaking out, he married an Irish woman, who was all of 17 years old. He fought for his own country's revolution, then the radicals of Robespierre almost guillotined him. Then he fought for Napoleon before deserting that cause. Lauberdière was a brave and vigorous man but not especially loyal to any one person, militarily or romantically.

In 1930 an American made a pilgrimage to the castle where Lauberdière had dwelled. The place was falling into ruin. But the visitor did come upon a thick tulip tree, the product of a seedling Lauberdière had taken back with him from America, symbolic, perhaps, of a secret and valorous seed he had spread in the New World.

Sources

Forester, C.S. *The Age of Fighting Sail*. New York: Doubleday, 2000.
Jamestown Settlement and American Revolution Museum at Yorktown. "Rachel Warrington: Her Encounter with Rochambeau Created Scandal in Williamsburg." https://www.historyisfun.org/learn/learning-center/colonial-america-

american-revolution-learning-resources/american-revolution-essays-timelines-images/people-of-the-revolution/rachel-warrington/.

Roosevelt, Theodore. *The Naval War of 1812; or, The History of the United States Navy During the Last War with Great Britain to Which Is Appended an Account of the Battle of New Orleans.* New York: Modern Library, 1882.

Selig, Robert A. "America the Ungrateful." *American Heritage* 48, no. 1 (February/March 1997). https://www.americanheritage.com/content/america-ungrateful.

———. *The Washington-Rochambeau Revolutionary Route in the State of New York, 1781–1782: An Historical and Architectural Survey.* Hudsonrivervalley.org., 2001.

Sullivan, Bill. "An Unconventional Woman of Williamsburg." *Making History Now.* Presented by Colonial Williamsburg, March 27, 2015. http://makinghistorynow.com/2015/03/an-unconventional-woman-of-williamsburg-2/.

"Peacock I." *Dictionary of American Naval Fighting Ships.* Department of the Navy, Naval Historical Center, January 29, 2004.

24

The Bloody Assassination Attempt on President Truman

Steps of the Blair-Lee House, Near the Awning, 1651 Pennsylvania Avenue, Half a Block West of Lafayette Square

Residing with President Harry Truman in the White House was his musically talented daughter, Margaret. She performed in public as a pianist and singer. Yet not all her performances were well received. *Washington Post* critic Paul Hume wrote, in a review, "Miss Truman ... cannot sing very well, is flat a good deal of the time ... has not improved in the years we have heard her." Truman was known for honesty and combativeness. His written reaction, which the *Post* published, was Trumanesque: "Mr. Hume: I've just read your lousy review of Margaret's concert. I've come to the conclusion that you are an eight ulcer man on four ulcer pay.... Some day I hope to meet you. When that happens you'll need a new nose, a lot of beefsteak for black eyes, and perhaps a supporter below!"

Margaret Truman practiced on a grand piano on the second floor of the Executive Mansion. One day in 1948 she found that her home's rickety old upper floor had cracked open and the legs of her piano were sticking through the gap. Clearly, the White House needed work. It hadn't had a major renovation since the early 20th century, under Presidents Teddy Roosevelt and William Howard Taft. The one before that was in 1814, after the British burnt it down. So engineers and workmen rebuilt the place. It was a massive project that lasted into 1953. Meanwhile, Truman and his family took up quarters at the Blair-Lee House, one block west across Pennsylvania Avenue.

After the Oklahoma City bombing by the vile Timothy McVeigh in 1995, the Secret Service feared a domestic or foreign terrorist might blow up a bomb near the White House. Officials closed off the once-busy section of Pennsylvania Avenue adjacent to, and just north of, the White House and the Eisenhower Executive Office Building. Today, the only vehicles near the stately Blair-Lee House are scooters and bikes. But in the fall of 1950 the Avenue bustled with buses, pedestrians, and cars.

Attackers and a Stalwart Defense

The afternoon of November 1, 1950, was unusually warm. After lunch, President Truman took a nap in a bedroom on the second floor, off a hallway facing Pennsylvania Avenue. A Secret Service agent, 41-year-old Donald Birdzell, stood near the railed entrance steps.

The South Portico of the White House in 1950 during the rebuilding of the Executive Mansion. President Harry Truman took up temporary quarters at the Blair-Lee House, where he was targeted by assassins (National Archives, photography by Abbie Rowe, 1950).

Two District of Columbia policemen were in sentry booths placed on the sidewalk on either side of the building. A third policeman was outside the ground-floor basement, and several other Secret Service agents were close by. It seems striking, the rather small amount of security to protect the head of the world's most powerful nation, even more so as the nation was at war, the Korean War having broken out that July.

Suddenly, at 2 p.m., two men strode from opposite directions along Pennsylvania Avenue's sidewalk and toward the President's temporary home. The two, Griselio Torresola and Oscar Collazo, had been keeping Blair-Lee under observation. Now, gripping pistols, they made their move. Slipping up to one of the sentry booths, Torresola shot the policeman inside it—40-year-old Leslie Coffelt—three times in the chest and torso, mortally wounding him. In the meantime Collazo approached the entrance of the house. There he'd crept behind Birdzell, aimed at his back—and found he'd forgotten to place a bullet in his gun's chamber! He quickly loaded, fired, and hit the Secret Service man in the knee. Another Secret Service man, Vincent Mroz, after hearing shots, emerged from the house's basement and, with two other officers, pumped bullets into Collazo, who crashed unconscious face first in front of the entrance steps. In the Avenue, cars swerved and screeched to a halt and bystanders screamed out in horror.

Torresola, moving toward the steps, shot policeman Joseph Downs in the neck, hip, and back. But with a mighty effort Downs crawled back into the house and locked the doors. The wounded Birdzell, shot a second time, did a valiant thing. The Secret Service agent limped into Pennsylvania Avenue, drawing attention toward him and away from the President. As Torresola arrived at the stairs and reloaded, an awakened President Truman stuck his head out the second-floor window, just 31 feet from the gunman, to see what was going on. A Secret Service man shouted and waved at Truman to duck back inside. He did so. Coffelt, the gravely wounded policeman, then crawled outside his sentry booth, leaned against it, and with his 38-caliber revolver shot Torresola in the head, killing him. Coffelt died hours later at a hospital.

Some 27 bullets were fired during about a minute of mayhem. It was the most serious presidential assassination attempt near the White House ever. The motive for the assault? The two assailants were Puerto Rican nationalists. Their attack took place two days after bloody fighting on Puerto Rico between insurgents demanding independence and police and National Guardsmen backing the Truman Administration's support of Puerto Rico as a U.S. Commonwealth. By killing the President, the attackers hoped to strike a blow for their cause. Collazo, having survived his wounds, was tried, convicted, and sentenced to death. President Truman commuted the sentence to life. Twenty-nine years later President Jimmy Carter paroled Collazo, who spent his remaining years in Puerto Rico.

Nearly as remarkable as the assassination attempt was Truman's behavior after the attack. He was scheduled to speak that afternoon at Arlington National Cemetery, where he planned to mark the unveiling of a statue of British Field Marshal John Dill, an ally from the Second World War. Naturally the Secret Service assumed Truman would cancel his talk. But the President, unintimidated, gave the speech after heading to the cemetery in a limousine with a squad of armed and alarmed Secret Servicemen, who held grimly and gamely to its running boards. In that age before the Internet and instant communications, many in the crowd listening to the President weren't aware of what had happened at the Blair-Lee House. It was only when a murmur went through the audience—passing word of the dramatic events earlier that afternoon—that everyone realized the President had narrowly escaped being shot.

The plucky President went back to his normal habit of taking strolls around downtown D.C. with a handful of aides and guards, waving at passersby and shaking hands with people in the street. Security around the President and his inner circle was very different in 1950. It would remain that way until November 22, 1963, when President Kennedy was assassinated. After that, a wall of security fell over the President and First Family. That was both good and bad. It much increased their security. But it also cut off spontaneous contact with the public. Ever since, the residents of the White House have lived in a bubble.

Sources

Ayton, Mel. *Hunting the President: Threats, Plots, and Assassination Attempts from FDR to Obama*. Washington, D.C.: Regnery History, 2014.
Bainbridge, John, and Stephen Hunter. *American Gunfight: The Plot to Kill Harry Truman*. New York: Simon & Schuster, 2005.
Healy, Paul. "Assassination Attempt on President Truman Fails in 1950." *New York Daily News*, November 2, 1950. http://www.nydailynews.com/news/national/assassination-attempt-president-truman-fails-1950-article-1.2412955#.
McCullough, David. *Truman*. New York: Simon & Schuster, 1992.

25

Lincoln Makes Lee an Offer He Could Refuse

Blair-Lee House, 1651 Pennsylvania Avenue, Washington, D.C.

It seemed a political and military masterstroke by the new President, Abraham Lincoln, this offer of a high-ranking military post. It had been a tumultuous week, the month after his March 4, 1861, inauguration. Rebel troops had fired on Fort Sumter in Charleston Harbor, South Carolina, on April 12, leading to the surrender of federal troops there. On April 15 Lincoln called for 75,000 volunteers to suppress the rebellion of seven Deep South states. At a secession conference on April 17, the pivotal state of Virginia, which had previously voted to stay in the Union yet fearing occupation by federal troops, voted to join the Confederacy.

New to the job, with hardly any military experience, the President faced a crucial decision on whom to pick to lead the Union Army in a time of war. True, the army's current Commanding General, Winfield Scott, was a legend, with 54 years of military service extending back before the War of 1812. In 1847 he was one of the two chief U.S. Commanders, with Zachary Taylor, of the Mexican-American War, at which time he captured Mexico City. Scott would give Lincoln sage advice on how to defeat the Southern rebels, namely his "Anaconda Plan," whereby the Union Navy, like a giant snake, would squeeze the Southern economy to death by seizing its sea and river ports. Thus blocking export of its cotton cash crop, wrecking its currency, and savaging its economy and war production.

Winfield Scott also had the advantage of being from Virginia, the most populous and the most influential Southern state, and the place of so many Founding Fathers who had striven for a more perfect Union. Quickly overcoming Southern resistance in the Old Dominion would strike the fledgling Confederacy a severe blow. But Scott was 74 years old, infirm—and obese. Soldiers had to work a hoist to lift him out of his office chair in the War Department building. Such a man couldn't take the field to lead an army in battle. As he met with his War Cabinet, Lincoln knew he needed someone younger and more vigorous.

A Leading Candidate

Secretary of War Simon Cameron of Pennsylvania suggested a soldier with much appeal—a man who had served as a personal aide to Scott during the Mexican-American conflict and had been Commandant of the U.S. Military Academy at West Point. As such, he had trained many of the officers now making up their minds whether to stand with the Union or the South. Moreover, he was a Virginian of Southern sympathy yet with an unmatched patriotic pedigree. His father had been a favorite cavalry general for George Washington during the American Revolution, and after Washington's death had written his eulogy of being "first in war, first in peace, and first in the hearts of his countrymen." Indeed, the father had been a staunch Federalist and Unionist who rode out with President Washington to quell the first revolt against Federal authority, the 1794 "Whiskey Rebellion" of tax-protesting farmers.

This soldier was actually married to the former Mary Anna Randolph Custis, the granddaughter of Martha Washington from Martha's first marriage. Mary was herself a descendant of the prominent Randolph family of Virginia, as well as of Lord Baltimore, a Governor of Virginia's sister Tidewater state of Maryland. Mary's father, and thus her husband's father-in-law, was the son of Martha Washington and the adopted son of George Washington: George Washington Parke Custis. After the latter's death in 1857, Mary's husband had taken over management of the Custis mansion estate, Arlington House, its lands visible across the Potomac from Washington City.

In March 1861 Lincoln, with this impressive background in mind, had appointed the skillful, 54-year-old soldier, one Robert Edward Lee of Alexandria, Virginia, to full Colonel.

So on April 18, the day after Virginia's vote to secede, War Secretary Cameron and President Lincoln instructed presidential advisor Francis Preston Blair to meet with Robert E. Lee. The tête-à-tête took place at Blair's townhouse, across from the War Department building and just down Pennsylvania Avenue from the White House. The emissary and the meeting place also seemed a masterstroke of Lincoln's. The high-powered Blair was a Southerner, originally from Kentucky. He had long been a leading citizen of the Washington Border-South region, having settled in what became Silver Spring, Maryland. His son Montgomery Blair was Lincoln's Postmaster General, then a key post for dealing out federal patronage. Francis Preston Blair had served as a top advisor to President Andrew Jackson when Old Hickory faced down a serious move toward secession in 1830 from South Carolina's John C. Calhoun.

Blair's house was next door to the Lee House. Today the two are combined as the Blair-Lee House. In 1859 Francis Preston

A handsome Robert E. Lee in 1838 as a 31-year-old Lieutenant in the Army Corps of Engineers (Washington-Custis-Lee Collection, Washington and Lee University, portrait by William Edward West).

Blair had built the Lee House, not for Robert E. Lee, but for the latter's cousin, Navy Commander Samuel Phillips Lee, after the latter married Blair's daughter, Elizabeth Blair. Samuel Phillips Lee, who bore a strong resemblance to Robert E. Lee, was thus Blair's son-in-law. It seemed the stage was perfectly set to entice Robert E. Lee into continued, high-level service for the Union.

An Uneasy Relationship with Servitude

But the matter was not as clear-cut as Blair, Cameron, and Lincoln might have hoped. For Lee, like many others from the near South and beyond, had conflicting loyalties. One part of him was strongly unionist. Earlier in 1861, as the nation verged on breakup, he wrote a relative: "I can anticipate no greater calamity for the country than a dissolution of the Union.... Secession is nothing but revolution." He continued with an elegant defense of one nation: "The framers of our Constitution never exhausted so much labor, wisdom, and forbearance in its formation, and surrounded it with so many guards and securities, if it was intended to be broken by every member of the Confederacy at will. It was intended for 'perpetual union' ... for the establishment of a government, not a compact, which can only be dissolved by revolution, or the consent of all the people in convention assembled." He also found "dictatorial" the rigid mindset of Southern firebrands demanding immediate secession. Further, unlike many Southerners, Lee believed that if war came it would be long and bloody.

But another part of him tilted strongly toward the South. He believed the Northern abolitionists, like the Deep South secessionists, were goading the nation into war. In the same letter, he wrote, "The South ... has been aggrieved by the acts of the North.... I feel the aggression, and am willing to take every proper step for redress.... As an American citizen, I take great pride in my country, her prosperity and institutions, and would defend any State if her rights were invaded." As for an overriding issue of the time, Lee thought slavery a wrong, and even more for whites than for blacks. In an 1856 letter to his wife, he stated, "Slavery as an institution, is a moral & political evil in any Country. It is useless to expatiate on its disadvantages. I think it however a greater evil to the white man than to the black race, & while my feelings are strongly enlisted in behalf of the latter, my sympathies are more strong for the former." He did not hold a modern view of civil rights. He continued: "The blacks are immeasurably better off here than in Africa, morally, socially & physically. The painful discipline they are undergoing, is necessary for their instruction as a race, & I hope will prepare & lead them to better things. How long their subjugation may be necessary is known & ordered by a wise Merciful Providence."

Moreover, he was against restricting slavery in the new territories, believing that doing so had led in the 1850s to bloodshed between pro-slavery and free-soil bands in Kansas and Nebraska. In 1861 he backed the Crittenden Compromise, an attempt by Kentucky Senator John Crittenden to avert war by guaranteeing the continuance of slavery without interference in the Southern territories and states. Another consideration influencing Lee was his own searing experience with slavery and insurrection. By 1857, he was managing his father-in-law's estates, including Arlington House, and its 200 or so slaves. According to Custis' will, the slaves were to be freed within five years and beforehand if practical. If practical—but Custis had mismanaged his estates and died in debt. His lands' finances had to be turned around. Lee was vexed at being unable to find a reliable supervisor to take over management of the Custis properties. Near the height of his federal army career, therefore, he took a two-year leave to supervise the estates himself. He proved an adept administrator and was able to turn them into moneymaking enterprises.

However, some of the Custis/Lee slaves were greatly upset at the delay in obtaining their liberty. They believed they were going to be freed right after Custis' death, and they blamed Lee for not freeing them immediately. They were further angered when Lee, to raise revenue, sent some of the slaves from Arlington House along with their families to work on distant properties. In 1858 a group of slaves surrounded Lee and threatened him. He later informed his son William Fitzhugh "Rooney" Lee, "I have had some trouble with some of the [enslaved] people. Reuben, Parks & Edward ... rebelled against my authority—refused to obey my orders, & said they were as free as I was, etc., etc.—I succeeded in capturing them & lodging them in jail. They resisted till overpowered & called upon the other people to rescue them."

In 1859 three slaves who had escaped from the Arlington estate were captured near Pennsylvania and returned to Lee. According to one of the escaped slaves, Wesley Norris, their master punished them with 50 lashes of the whip. Anonymous letters claimed Lee had personally performed the whipping. Of the alleged incident, which was reported in the *New York Herald Tribune*, Lee wrote his son Custis: "The *N.Y. Tribune* has attacked me for my treatment of your grandfather's slaves, but I shall not reply. He has left me an unpleasant legacy." Historians disagree on whether the whipping took place. In 1862, in the midst of the Civil War and according to the five-year deadline of the Custis will, Lee freed the Custis slaves, including Wesley Norris. In 1863 Lee freed his own slaves.

Also in 1859, Lee had been right in the middle of a major, precipitating incident of the war, one involving slavery. That October the abolitionist and insurrectionist John Brown, having cut his teeth in the Kansas-Nebraska bloodletting and supplied with weapons by abolitionists, seized the federal arsenal at Harpers Ferry, Virginia (now in West Virginia). Brown's force consisted of 18 other armed men, both white and black. President James Buchanan placed Lieutenant Colonel Robert E. Lee in charge of a force of militia, Army troops, and U.S. Marines to quash Brown's raid. Lee's aide-de-camp in the action was his future Confederate cavalry commander, Army Lieutenant James Ewell Brown "Jeb" Stuart. On October 18 Lee's force captured Brown and his men. Brown and six others were then tried and hanged for treason against the state of Virginia. In the aftermath, many residents of Virginia, which had the largest slave population of any state, feared both a widespread slave rebellion and the demand of northern abolitionists for slavery's swift end.

Before Fort Sumter, violence had nearly broken out between federal troops and Confederate forces in Texas, which seceded from the Union in February 1861. Lee, who'd served as military Governor of Texas, was then stationed in the Lone Star State. His Army commander there, General David Twiggs, surrendered his 4,000 federal troops to the rebels, along with many guns and horses at the federal arsenal—the Alamo. Although the soldiers were later released, Lee was angered at what he viewed as a shameful capitulation. It's intriguing to think how history might have changed if Twiggs' troops, including Lee, had resisted instead of giving up. Texas, not Fort Sumter, might have sparked the Civil War, Lee might have stayed with the Union, and he might have become a hero of the North!

But the incident as it occurred did not push the Virginian to the Union side. As he returned to Washington in a covered wagon, a trooper queried Lee about his sympathies, asking, "Colonel, do you intend to go South or remain North?" Lee responded: "I shall never bear arms against the United States—but it may be necessary for me to carry a musket in defence of my native State, Virginia, in which case I shall not prove recreant to my duty." Then came Lincoln's promotion of him to full Colonel, Fort Sumter's fall, and the President's call for volunteers.

Epochal Decisions

On April 17, the day Virginia seceded, Lee had dinner with his cousin Samuel Phillips Lee and his older brother, also a Navy Commander, Sydney Smith Lee, the former head of the U.S. Naval Academy. The Navy officers were in high spirits, but the Army Colonel was glum. Alarmed, Samuel Phillips Lee went across Pennsylvania Avenue to see General Scott, suggesting the War Department treat with Robert E. Lee lest it lose him to the Confederacy. But Lincoln's own gambit was being put into play.

At the Blair-Lee House meeting the following day, Francis Preston Blair made Colonel Lee a beguiling offer. He told him that President Lincoln and War Secretary Cameron wanted to promote him to a two-star major general, and place him in charge of the army defending Washington, D.C. This would make him in effect the head of a main Union force charged with quashing the rebellion. Lee replied to Blair: "I look upon secession as anarchy. If I owned the four millions of slaves in the South I would sacrifice them all to the Union; but how can I draw my sword upon Virginia, my native state?" According to Montgomery Blair, Lee stated, "I could take no part in an invasion of the Southern States." The meeting being concluded, Lee walked across Pennsylvania Avenue to the office of General Scott, who had earlier requested the two meet. Lee, normally very composed, was so distracted he walked right past Scott's secretary and into the Commanding General's office.

A conflicted Lee told Scott of his decision to turn down Lincoln's offer. Lee said he was considering not taking either side in the coming war. According to author Elizabeth Brown Pryor, Scott answered, "I have no place in my army for equivocal men." He told the younger officer, "Lee, you have made the greatest mistake of your life, but I feared it would be so." Colonel Lee got up to leave. The two men shook hands, their throats catching, neither able to utter a word. After Lee left, according to a journalist, Scott "laid on his sofa, refusing to see anyone and mourning, as if for the loss of a son. General Scott added, with great emotion, 'don't mention Robert Lee's name to me again, I cannot bear it.'" Indeed, the War Department building in those days was a place of much anguish. The Army's Quartermaster, or chief of supply, General Joseph E. Johnston of Georgia, collapsed after resigning and was carried from the building. He later became the Confederate commander of the Western theater.

After the meetings with Blair and Scott, Lee was unclear about his next step. Returning to Arlington House, he found a house divided. His wife and six of his children were pro-Union. Only daughter Mary was staunchly for secession. Lee's wife, Mary Anna, told her husband she would abide by his decision. Colonel Lee spent the next two days lost in thought. According to some accounts, he paced back and forth inside the mansion and prayed aloud. It seems more likely, according to an 1871 letter of daughter Mary, that he spent the time reflecting alone in his Arlington House office. According to an Arlington slave, Lee also walked around his garden distractedly. Recalled the servant, "He didn't cahr [sic] to go. No ... he didn't cahr to go." Knowing that Virginia, like the federal Army, would likely offer him high command, he weighed the alternatives. On April 20 he made up his mind. Lee wrote out a letter of resignation from the Army and gave it to a slave to deliver to General Scott. He informed his family of his decision, telling them, "I suppose you will all think I have done very wrong." Daughter Agnes remarked the estate seemed "as if there had been a death in it, for the army was to him home and country." On April 21 representatives of Virginia's secession convention requested Lee's presence in Richmond, the state capital. Upon his arrival he was offered command of the state's forces. As a token of his family history, officials gave him a sword that had belonged to George Washington.

The irrevocable decision had been made. Lee would go along with the 60 percent of federal officers from Virginia who joined the Confederacy. Among the other 40 percent was George Thomas, the future Union General and "Rock of Chickamauga" at a critical Tennessee battle. Thomas would be disowned by his pro–Confederate sisters. Robert E. Lee's nephew, Fitzhugh Lee, a future Confederate General and postwar Virginia Governor, would follow his uncle's lead. So would the Navy's Sydney Smith Lee, the ex-Naval Academy chief, but with much reluctance. He would later blame the Palmetto State for starting the war: "South Carolina be hanged.... How I did want to stay in the old navy!" Lee cousin Major John Fitzgerald Lee, the Judge Advocate of the U.S. Army, remained with the Union. So did the Navy's Samuel Phillips Lee, who rose to the rank of Rear Admiral and intercepted at sea Southern blockade runners, an integral part of Scott's Anaconda Plan. Asked about his cousin's decision to join the Southern states, he retorted, "When I find the word Virginia in my commission I will join the Confederacy." After Robert E. Lee resigned, his pro-Union sister Anne never spoke to him again. Indeed, it is said the Civil War was one of father against son and sister against brother. The Lincolns themselves were split: most of Mary Todd Lincoln's relations sided with the South. Lincoln's attempted masterstroke of appointing the noted Virginian to lead the North came to naught.

A postscript, and another "what if": What if Lee had instead decided to fight for the Union? Most historians believe this would have been a boon for the North. Instead of going through a succession of less-than-stellar commanding generals for the first two years of the war, President Lincoln would have had an able commander from the start. The war would have ended sooner and with far less bloodshed. Further, as General Grant became President Grant due to his battlefield success, it's possible that a postwar President of the United States would have been Robert E. Lee. An alternate view holds that Lee, given his sympathy for the South, would not have waged the war as aggressively for the North as he did for the South. Like General George McClellan and General George Meade, castigated by Lincoln for being insufficiently aggressive toward the Confederate Army, Lee might have fallen into the same category.

We'll never know. But we do know that rarely has Lafayette Square witnessed such high drama as during the opening weeks of the Civil War.

Sources

Davis, William C., and James I. Robertson, Jr., ed. *Virginia at War, 1861.* Virginia State Convention.
Encyclopedia Virginia. "Statement by Francis Preston Blair," April 14, 1871. https://www.encyclopediavirginia.org/Statement_by_Francis_Preston_Blair_April_14_1871.

Freeman, Douglas S. *R.E. Lee: A Biography*. New York: Charles Scribner's Sons, 1934.
Good, Cassandra. "George Washington Parke Custis." George Washington's Mt. Vernon. http://www.mountvernon.org/digital-encyclopedia/article/george-washington-parke-custis/.
Lee, Robert E. *Memoirs of Robert E. Lee: His Military and Personal History*. Edited by A.L. Long. New York, Philadelphia: J.M. Stoddart, 1897.
Linder, Prof. Douglas O. "Col. Robert E. Lee's Report Concerning the Attack at Harper's Ferry." University of Missouri—Kansas City School of Law. October 18, 1959. Archived from the original, July 22, 2010.
Naval History and Heritage Command. "Rear Admiral Samuel Phillips Lee, USN, (1812–1897)."
Poole, Robert M. "How Arlington National Cemetery Came to Be." *Smithsonian*, November 2009. https://www.smithsonianmag.com/history/how-arlington-national-cemetery-came-to-be-145147007/.
Pryor, Elizabeth Brown. "The General in His Study." *New York Times*, April 19, 2011.
_____. "Robert E. Lee's 'Severest Struggle.'" *American Heritage* 58, no. 3 (Winter 2008). https://www.americanheritage.com/content/robert-e-lee%E2%80%99s-%E2%80%9Cseverest-struggle%E2%80%9D.

26

The Wretched Life Behind the Gaudiest Place

Eisenhower Executive Office Building (EEOB), the Former State, War, and Navy Building, Pennsylvania Avenue and 17th Street

It is said by believers in the paranormal that Lafayette Square is among the most haunted places in America. The ghost of Philip Barton Key II—Francis Scott Key's son, killed by Congressman Dan Sickles in 1859—allegedly appears on the east side of the square. The spirit of Commodore Stephen Decatur, who after an 1820 duel expired in the Decatur House, is said to inhabit his former home. After Decatur's death, many swore they saw his ghost gazing forlornly out of the windows of his home. The windows in question have long been shuttered, supposedly to spare passersby the fright of seeing his bloodied apparition.

Yet, if the Square is haunted, the portion of Pennsylvania Avenue just southwest of the park may be the most promising place for ghost hunters. In 1950, near the steps of the Blair-Lee House, an assassin was shot to death trying to kill President Truman. Just feet away, a D.C. policeman gave his life helping to save Truman's. Only yards to the south, in 1846 a top-ranking Navy official took his own life after a deadly explosion aboard the USS *Princeton*.

Architectural Antecedents

Then there's the man who designed the large, ornate federal office building across Pennsylvania Avenue from Blair-Lee and the Renwick Gallery. Completed in 1888 and originally housing the State, War, and Navy Departments, and today hosting White House personnel, it's the Eisenhower Executive Office Building, or EEOB. Its architect, Alfred Bult Mullett, led one of the most troubled lives of any Washington public servant.

Born in 1834 and an immigrant from England, Alfred Mullet grew up in Ohio. Though a talented man, he was hotheaded and a control freak. After joining an architectural firm Mullet got into arguments with its head, Isiah Rogers, and left the firm in a huff. In Cincinnati he got into a street fight with a city official, assaulting the man when he questioned Mullet's honesty. After Civil War military service, Mullet joined the Treasury Department—only to find that his boss was his old supervisor and foe, Isiah Rogers. This time it was Rogers who left and Mullet who stayed—after the latter pulled political strings to undermine his present and past superior.

Mullet became the Treasury's Supervising Architect, which meant far more than managing the mammoth Treasury Building itself. He designed many revenue-producing custom houses and post offices around the nation as well as a lot of courthouses, more than three dozen buildings in all. Incapable of delegating work to other designers, he bit off more than he could chew. Still, in output and quality his creations impress the modern eye. Mullet was the architect, for instance, of the U.S. Custom House in the vital port of New Orleans, as well as the edifice responsible for those little S's on some of your pennies—the San Francisco Mint. He built the mint sturdy enough to withstand the 1906 earthquake. These buildings were elegant yet—compared to his opulent State, War, and Navy Building—spare.

One of his career highlights—until his work there was hit by tragedy—was New York's City Hall, Post Office and Courthouse complex. Mullet was selected as its designer by none other than James Renwick, the architect of the Square's Renwick Gallery, as well as New York's St. Patrick's Cathedral.

Mullet landed the contract after criticizing its original $500,000 cost, although he would complete the project for $8.5 million. Its resemblance to the State, War, and Navy Building is striking.

The Gaudiest of Creations

In 1871 Mullet was given the daunting task of designing what would become his most famous construct. Given his already full workload, he may have taken the job reluctantly. Also, he knew the locale had been unlucky from the beginnings of Washington, D.C. The original War and Navy offices there had been burned by the British in 1814. The successor building was much too small and quickly overflowed with officers and clerks. In the 1840s a plan was approved to replace the structures. Then the Mexican-American War intervened, and the scheme was nixed. In the 1850s architect Thomas Walter, the designer of the Capitol's mighty dome, offered up a blueprint for a new building. His scheme foundered. During the Civil War, with the military agencies critically short of offices, engineers simply slapped an extra floor atop the old building. Afterwards, President Grant's accomplished Secretary of State, Hamilton Fish, took charge. Fish gave Mullet the challenge of putting up new spaces for his State Department and for War and Navy—all in one place again.

Tourists today, in seeing what resulted, take note of it, partly out of surprise. Many have never heard of it. The place is barely known compared to the White House and the city's monuments. First-time observers are struck by its size and grandiosity, which can overwhelm the buildings around it—and was a criticism of it from the start. Four floors tall and containing over 560 rooms and two miles of hallways, it is topped by a massive French mansard roof inspired by the Louvre and spiked with strutting chimneys. In the 1880s, as the Washington Monument became the world's tallest man-made structure, the State, War, and Navy Building became the world's largest set of offices. That honor was apt, because when the War Department departed this locale with the advent of the Second World War, it moved to the world's largest office building of its time—the Pentagon. Even for Washington, that's a lot of largesse.

The building's mountain of Maine and Virginia granite had four wings, one each for the Navy Department and the State Department—the Navy Department on the Pennsyl-

26. The Wretched Life Behind the Gaudiest Place

The State, War, and Navy Building—known today as the Eisenhower Executive Office Building—was, like the Pentagon that followed it, the largest office building of its time (Library of Congress).

vania Avenue side and the State Department in the rear facing the Ellipse, the park south of the White House. Two wings were for the much bigger War Department, on the north side facing Pennsylvania Avenue and to the west facing 17th Street. The four wings together are bigger than the White House, even though the Executive Mansion was—from its construction in 1799 and well into the 19th century—the largest residence in the United States.

Mullet made an astute move in selecting Austrian immigrant Richard von Ezdorf to design the interior. Though as opulent as the exterior, the inside is more refined. Von Ezdorf's masterwork is a library in the Navy wing called the Indian Treaty Room. Crafted from onyx, marble, wrought iron, and bronze, it was never really a library but a reception area. And, despite its name, treaties with Native American tribes weren't signed there. Perhaps someone thought, correctly or not, that Indian treaties were stored there. It was much later the locale of the signing of the United Nations charter. In any event, for a cost of $56,000, it became one of the city's grandest creations. The seahorses in the railings and the stars for celestial navigation on the walls mark its origins as the Navy Department's headquarters.

Still, many of Mullet's contemporaries mocked his lavish vision. Visitors weren't sure what to make of the giant stone pile, with its jumble of cornices, columns, chimneys, window pediments, and grand stairways. It's hard to know where the entrances are amid the clutter of the design elements. Henry Adams, the dean of D.C. intellectuals operating from his Lafayette Square salon, termed it a "squashed wedding cake" and "an architectural infant asylum." More charitable observers said the place, by adopting Renaissance and French-

The Indian Treaty Room of the old Navy Department has nothing to do with Indian treaties, but is a masterpiece of interior design (Library of Congress, Carol M. Highsmith, photographer).

Empire styles on the grandest scale, outdid its European predecessors. It applied Old World techniques to suggest the New World's power and size.

Another criticism, odd given the building's extent, was that it was too small. Its military and diplomatic quarters, like their predecessors, soon filled to overflowing. This was a bit surprising, as the Army and Navy had been drastically cut after the Civil War. Perhaps due to the so-called Iron Law of Bureaucracy the space demands for the military just kept growing.

Architect in Agony

A critique of Alfred Mullet himself was that he overspent. This irritated people more than it might have because Mullet worked during the Grant Administration scandals. More than a few of Grant's colleagues were caught lining their pockets with taxpayer funds. Mullet, hard-working and honest albeit lacking in charm and temperament, became a sort of whipping boy for the profligacy of others. His boss, reformist Treasury Secretary Benjamin Bristow, had blown the whistle on Grant scandals like the Whisky Ring, a scam to deny the Treasury its excises on liquor. Closer to home was the Seneca quarry affair, where owners of the Maryland digging site that supplied much of the material for the city's public buildings went broke after the owners sold cut-rate shares of the company to President Grant and friends (see Chapter 45, "The Crooked Bank for the Former Slaves"). In that era of scandalous exposé, investigators launched five separate inquiries into Mullet's handling of federal construction projects. He wasn't found guilty of any crime but, as with President Grant, he was tarred with the malfeasance of others.

Meanwhile, by 1874, three years into the project, Mullet had yet to finish any of the planned four wings of his State, Navy, and War structure. That same year, he got into heated arguments with Treasury boss Bristow. Around the same time, former Treasury Secretary and then-Supreme Court Chief Justice Salmon P. Chase chastised Mullet as "the little fellow from Cincinnati who explodes at the lowest pressure of any man now living." In seeming proof of Chase's view, Mullet suddenly quit his architectural perch, just as he had stormed out of his Cincinnati firm years before.

Washington's "Mr. Fixit," General Thomas Lincoln Casey, was brought in to complete Mullet's creation. Casey's dad had been valiant during the Mexican-American War's key battle, the seizing of Chapultepec Castle in Mexico City. The younger Casey, long the Army Corps of Engineers' chief engineer, would go on in 1884 to finally finish the Washington Monument, originally envisioned in 1788. Casey would do this by ruthlessly stripping the monument of any adornment, keeping to a plain if soaring obelisk, and doing away with Robert Mill's original plan for a temple at the base. Still later, Casey almost finished building the Thomas Jefferson building, with its exquisite reading room, for the Library of Congress. When he died in 1896 his son Edward Pearce Casey quickly completed the project. (Another son might have bonded with Mr. Jefferson. Both were naturalists, with the former a world authority on the classification of insects.) Despite his efficiency and no-nonsense approach, it took General Thomas Casey 10 more years to finish the massive State, War, and Navy Building. And it ended up costing taxpayers $10 million (over a quarter of a billion in 2018 dollars). An expensive item, though a work of art like the Indian Treaty Room, was the Secretary of War Suite, the department's gilded meeting place from 1888 to 1939. Its designer was Stephen Decatur Hatch, named of course after the Commodore of the nearby Decatur House.

Mullet, after leaving his project and departing Washington, formed an architectural firm in New York City. Perhaps the name of his partner, Hugo Kafka, as in Kafkaesque, signaled what was to come. Mullet, financially strapped, often wasn't compensated for his contracts. Worse, calamity befell one of his proudest creations, the old New York City Post Office and Courthouse in City Hall Park. His Post Office was eye-catching, but the site was so cramped its noisy loading docks were plopped next to City Hall. Then, in May 1877, its

French Empire–style roof collapsed, killing three laborers. A grand jury was convened, and it found that the rooftop hadn't been bolted down properly. Mullet was blamed, probably without cause. Another of his partners, William Steinmetz, a competent architect who served on the board of the Brooklyn Bridge, had been replaced before the tragedy. Taking his place as the building's head of construction was a man ignorant of architectural engineering. Nonetheless, Mullet was pilloried for the fatal accident. Further, his Post Office's gaudy design was derided as "Mullet's Monstrosity." The *New York Times* huffed, "The Mullett Post Office has always been an architectural eyesore, and has, from the first, been unsatisfactory to the Postal Service and the Federal Courts beneath its roof." Less elegantly than the Grey Lady, a New York tabloid branded Mullet "the most arrogant, pretentious, and preposterous little humbug in the United States."

Mullet's misfortunes piled up. He made unwise investments in real estate. To boost his income, he moved back to Washington and worked on residential and commercial properties. Still cash-starved, in 1889 he sued the federal government for his design work a quarter century before on the State, War, and Navy Building. He claimed that, overburdened with other tasks, he had labored on his own time, and dime, and deserved $158,441 in compensation. The court ruled against him.

As with the talented but troubled wife of Henry Adams, Clover Adams, depression ran in Mullet's family. According to the blog *Streets of Washington*, Mullet's brother Thomas, a captain in the Coast Guard, suffered from "melancholia." In 1887 Thomas Mullet killed himself.

Habitually short-tempered, and now often depressed, Alfred Mullet seemed unusually chipper on October 20, 1890. He had apparently made his mind up about something. Returning home from work late that afternoon, he asked his wife to make him some beef tea, the beverage popularized by African-American hotelier James Wormley. Then he went to his room, shut the door, and placed a pistol to his head. His troubled life then came to a sudden and tragic end. From its offices a few blocks east of the Treasury, the *Evening Star* newspaper commented: "Weary of a financial struggle that promised to end disastrously and lacking the mental elasticity which keeps mankind in something like an equitable condition, A.B. Mullett, ex-supervising architect of the Treasury, yesterday evening took it upon himself to put an end to his earthly career. For several months he had suffered from fits of depression and, being naturally an extremely nervous man, his ordinarily irritable temperament was not soothed or amended by these later-appearing periods of melancholy."

Postmortems

Even after his sad end, Mullet's State, War, and Navy Building made him a whipping boy for generations. Mark Twain called his handiwork "the ugliest building in America." Charles Follen McKim, the designer of New York's imposing Morgan Library, said of Mullet's structure, "If I only had a rake!" In the 1940s President Truman called it the "greatest monstrosity in America."

Congress moved, slowly, to either demolish or remodel the place. High-powered builders tried pushing the lawmakers along. John Russell Pope, designer of the National Archives and the Jefferson Memorial, proposed remaking it into a matching companion of the Treasury building. Echoing his notion was Treasury Secretary Andrew Mellon, art collector par excellence and endower of the National Gallery of Art. Capitol Hill set aside $3 million to make it happen. But the building was saved by the Great Depression. With millions of Americans out of work, Congress deemed it unseemly to spend millions of dollars on a "beautification project." After the Second World War, the city's cultural elite again tried to consign the place to the dustbin. In the late 1950s a presidential commission counseled demolition and replacement. "Mullet's Monstrosity" dodged more bullets than Andrew Jackson in his duels.

Then opinions changed. Critics began to like his "squashed wedding cake" as an arresting, if over-the-top, example of the Renaissance Revival style and of the optimistic spirit of the late 1800s. Around 1960 the preservation movement, aided by Jacqueline Bouvier Kennedy, began saving historic buildings in Lafayette Square. Finally, in 1971, the Secretary of the Interior made Mullet's masterpiece a national historic landmark, lending it protected status. After teetering on the chopping block for generations, the structure was saved.

So, if you're an adherent of the paranormal, you might spy the stricken ghost of Mullet near his much-critiqued but rescued creation—or more happy spirits, such as President William Taft's cow, which in the early 1900s would munch on the building's lawn, or the young boys of the same era who merrily sledded in wintertime down the stone steps of the War Department's south-facing wing. But take time out, like visitors today, to enjoy the view.

Sources

DeFerrari, John. "The Eisenhower Executive Office Building, America's 'Greatest Monstrosity.'" *Streets of Washington.* http://www.streetsofwashington.com/2014/09/the-eisenhower-executive-office.html.
Elliott, Cecil D. *The American Architect from the Colonial Era to the Present.* Jefferson, NC: McFarland, 2002.
Langley, Julia. "Robert Mills and Lieutenant Colonel Thomas Lincoln Casey, Washington Monument." *Khan Academy.* https://www.khanacademy.org/humanities/art-americas/us-art-19c/us-19c-arch-sculp-photo/a/robert-mills-and-lieutenant-colonel-thomas-lincoln-casey-washington-monument.
Lee, Antoinette J. *Architects to the Nation: The Rise and Decline of the Supervising Architect's Office.* Oxford: Oxford University Press, 2000.
"The Mullett Post Office Site." *New York Times,* April 28, 1912.
U.S. Department of State. Office of the Historian. "Public Building West of the White House, May 1801–August 1814." https://history.state.gov/departmenthistory/buildings/section22.
United States Government. *The Indian Treaty Room.* 2008.
White House. "Eisenhower Executive Office Building." https://www.whitehouse.gov/about-the-white-house/eisenhower-executive-office-building/.

27

How a Personal Vendetta and Patriotic Passion Led to America's Most Honored Place

Renwick Gallery, Northeast Corner of Pennsylvania Avenue and 17th Street

Theirs was an idyll at times—rather like *Life on the Mississippi*, the reminiscence written by a Confederate soldier for a brief time and big-time author for all time, one Samuel Langhorne Clemens, aka Mark Twain. True, the two men in question, one just 21 years old and the other 30, were studious and serious. They had graduated fifth and second, respectively, in their class at West Point Military Academy.

Rivers, Domes, and Aqueducts

In 1837 they were engaged in the challenging business, as U.S. Army engineers, of trying to tame the mighty Mississippi so it would be more navigable. But they took out time for fun. They caught catfish in the river and roasted them alongside the wild fowl they'd bagged shooting from their horses. The younger man, Montgomery Cunningham Meigs, of Philadelphia by way of Georgia, much admired the older one. He labeled him "one with whom nobody ever wished or ventured to take a liberty, though kind and generous to all his subordinates, admired by all women, and respected by all men ... the model of a soldier and the beau ideal of a Christian man." For his part, the older fellow, Robert Edward Lee of Alexandria and Arlington House, Virginia, the future Confederate Army commander, was impressed by Meigs' bottomless energy and many interests, which ranged from practical invention to painting with watercolors.

In the 1850s Meigs would impress another person who would rise to rebel prominence. Since its founding, Washington City had been plagued by the absence of a safe and reliable water source. Cholera and typhoid epidemics ravaged the city. Burst water pipes frustrated local fire brigades. Owners of hotels near the Capitol fretted whether the water supplied their eminent guests was potable. Montgomery Meigs solved all that. In 1853 the Army officer and engineer presented Congress a plan of breathtaking detail to construct an aqueduct to make the ancient Romans jealous. "I trust for the next thousand years," he wrote, "to pour its healthful waters in to the capital of our union."

Supervising 1,900 engineers, craftsmen, cooks, and workmen, and starting from the

27. How a Vendetta and Patriotic Passion Led to America's Most Honored Place   135

One of the Washington area's underrated greats, Montgomery Meigs was largely responsible for Arlington National Cemetery as well as the great dome of the Capitol, and even the capital's water supply (Library of Congress).

Potomac River's Great Falls of Maryland, he built a 12-mile water channel out of millions of bricks. A crucial part was the world's longest stone arch bridge, marked on today's maps as the Cabin John Bridge. The water channel's maintenance was minimal: it had no locks like those of the Chesapeake & Ohio Canal running alongside it. Meigs' waterworks operated purely from gravity, dropping about 10 inches a mile from the rapids where it began down to the swampy lowland of Washington City. Pushing through 100 million gallons of water each day, it still supplies much of the District's water. Meigs built his aqueduct out of ambition but also for the public good. He wrote it was for the "free use of the sick & well, rich & poor, gentle & simple, old & young for generation after generation which will have come to rise up & call me blessed."

The channel's formal opening was marked by the untapping of a fountain, with a 60-foot-high spout, at the foot of the Capitol. The fountain, Meigs wrote his father, "seems to spring rejoicing in the air."

Meigs' boss—Secretary of War Jefferson Davis, the future Confederate President—admired his engineer's creation. He gave Meigs stewardship over a more renowned project: the reconstruction of the Capitol into its modern incarnation. Meigs persuaded Congress to grant the then-immense sum of $1,047,291 to refit the structure with a rotunda, a titanic dome that at its base would be 350 feet wide. Its design, by Philadelphia architect Thomas Ustick Walter, drew upon the basilicas of ancient times and the Renaissance, such as the Pantheon and St. Peter's. But instead of stone, Meigs made it out of a cheaper, yet enduring, modern material: cast iron. It was exacting work to place a nine-million-pound metal dome on top of a 288-foot-tall structure. Meigs erected a 10-story tower in the middle of the building and custom-wired the turret to a giant wooden crane. The derrick, steam-powered with burning wood scavenged from the old Capitol, hauled up 10 tons of metal or rock at a time, according to writer Robert O'Harrow. Workmen on high pieced the loads together.

The Renaissance Man in Meigs hired a Greco-Roman artist, Constantino Brumidi, an artist steeped in the Renaissance and Baroque, to paint allegories of American history on the dome's interior. Working on a scaffold, like Michelangelo at St. Peter's, Brumidi nearly fell to this death while painting William Penn. But he survived to conjure a vast canvas of General Washington rising up to heaven, accompanied by angelic figures of war, commerce, victory, and fame. It was an apotheosis, the rising up of Jesus to His heavenly Father, applied to a democratic republic's chieftain in times of war and peace. War would come again.

As he admired the aqueduct, Jefferson Davis, the Capitol's chief of architecture as well as the capital's chief of war, approved the rotunda—except for a detail. The Statue of Freedom, the dome's own Lady Liberty, was to grace its top. In a nod to the rotunda's classical roots, the original clay figure designed by Thomas Crawford sported an ancient Roman's liberty cap, worn by former slaves as a proud sign of their newfound liberty.

In 1856, as civil conflict threatened, largely over slavery, Davis, a Mississippi plantation owner, thought the symbol "inappropriate to a people who were born free and should not be enslaved." Some feared the cap could be viewed as an abolitionist symbol. Davis had Meigs and sculptor and foundry operator Clark Mills and African-American slave Philip Reid, who labored in the forge that created Miss Liberty, change the conical skull cap of a freed slave to the feathered headdress of a Native American.

The Masterful Quartermaster

War came, in April 1861, and as war does it changed everything, including Meigs' opinion of his two former superiors, Davis and Lee. He wrote of them: "No man who ever took the oath to support the Constitution as an officer of our army ... should escape without loss of all his goods & civil rights & expatriation." According to writer Robert M. Poole, Meigs continued: "[They] should be put formally out of the way if possible by sentence of death [and] executed if caught." Given the engineering and logistical skill of his work on the

To sidestep the then-pressing issue of slavery, the headdress of the Capitol's Statue of Freedom was changed from that of a freed Roman slave to one of a Native American woman (Architect of the Capitol).

27. How a Vendetta and Patriotic Passion Led to America's Most Honored Place   137

water channel and the rotunda, President Lincoln made Meigs the Quartermaster, or head of supply, for the entire Union army. Meigs set up his headquarters at the Winder Building, on 17th Street two blocks down Pennsylvania Avenue from the War and Navy Departments.

The President broke normal procedures for this appointment, promoting Meigs over hundreds of higher-ranking officers. Lincoln said of Meigs, "I do not know one who combines the qualities of masculine intellect, learning and experience of the right sort, and physical power of labor and endurance so well as he." Old Abe needed a wizard. His first Secretary of War, Simon Cameron, an industrialist and head of a Pennsylvania political machine, presided over a corrupt and wasteful supply effort. Dealers supplied horses that were lame, cannonballs that didn't explode, and uniforms so poorly made they earned the derisive term of "shoddy." Lincoln sent Cameron off to Siberia, so to speak, as Minister to Russia. He replaced him with a driven lawyer turned intense, honest administrator, Edwin McMasters Stanton of Ohio.

As Stanton's aide, Meigs procured the guns, bullets, billets, uniforms, foodstuffs, and medicines for a force that grew from under 20,000 men in 1861 to over 600,000 at its peak. In addition to provisioning soldiers and sailors, Meigs was in charge of building more than 600 vessels, procuring several hundred thousand mules and horses, and maintaining 21,000 miles of railroads, the latter the vital artery for the movement of Northern might.

Four days before Christmas 1864, after General William Tecumseh Sherman's war-winning march through rebel Georgia from a burnt Atlanta to the Atlantic shore, his men found a cornucopia of fresh supplies awaiting them at the coastal city of Savannah. Meigs had sent them, special delivery via Union ships. Sherman's weary and bedraggled troopers reveled in new boots, coats, belt buckles, even fresh underwear, according to O'Harrow. On the other hand, the Confederate troops on Sherman's periphery were scrawny, their uniforms and shoes in tatters, their rifles bereft of bullets. Meigs and his vast procurement apparatus buried the Confederacy, with its far weaker industrial economy, under a mountain of Union provisions and arms. His became a template for the American way of war, highlighted by the 20th century's global brawls. The U.S. military would overwhelm the battle-hardened, technically advanced foes of the Kaiser's Germany, Imperial Japan, and Hitler's Reich with almost endless provisions of trucks, planes, and tanks and cigarettes, chocolate, and K-rations.

It takes a driven and resourceful man to outfit a giant army, and Meigs seemed destined to be that one. His was a learned and accomplished family. His father was a nationally recognized obstetrician. His grandfather was a president of the University of Georgia and a classmate of Noah Webster, the dictionary author and advocate of a uniquely American form of English. This strong family line has reached the present. As of autumn 2019, General Meigs' great-great-great-grandnephew and namesake, Montgomery Cunningham Meigs, was a retired four-star general, who in the late 1990s led NATO forces during the war in Bosnia.

From the youngest age, Montgomery Meigs of the Civil War era was rock-tough and hard on others. His mother recalled a boy younger than seven who was "high-tempered, unyielding, tyrannical." He grew up tall, restless, and stubborn. As a father, he disciplined his son, disobedient at age 10, by tying his wrists to a clothes chest, leaving him without food for much of a day, and spanking the lad with a rope. Meigs' mother hated slavery, and her son inherited the animus. Like Lincoln in his second inaugural address, Meigs saw the war's costs as expiation for the stain of the dread institution. He wrote his father: "God does not intend to give us peace again until … the last shackle is stricken from the wrist of the black man." He wrote his brother: "God for our sins leads us to [triumph] through seas of blood." His rage against President Davis and General Lee swelled as the war's casualties reached unimaginable tolls. Things got very personal when his son, 22-year-old John Rodgers Meigs, was killed during a chance encounter with Confederate scouts.

John Rodgers Meigs was the grandson of Lafayette Square's valiant Navy Commodore, John Rogers, builder of Secretary of State William Seward's "Old Clubhouse" residence. John Rodgers Meigs served as General Philip Sheridan's aide-de camp in Virginia's Shenandoah Valley. The elder Meigs was convinced, probably wrongly, that rebel troops had shot his son in the back. Sheridan, convinced, ordered burned every home near the place of the killing and the arrest of every man of military age. Lincoln and Secretary of War Stanton joined Meigs for the son's funeral in Georgetown.

Origins of an Honored Place

Summer 1864 saw the war's bloodbath overflow, as Lee and Union Army General Ulysses S. Grant faced off in seven weeks of savage fighting, from the forested Wilderness near Fredericksburg, Virginia, to the approaches of Richmond, the Confederate capital. Casualties on both sides tallied 85,000 dead, wounded, and missing. The District's Old Soldier's Home cemetery and Alexandria's National Cemetery were full up. Another graveyard, a big one, was needed. Working in the flat landscape of downtown Washington, Meigs and others gazed across and above the Potomac to Arlington House, Lee's former estate and mansion, modeled on an ancient Greek temple. Robert E. Lee had managed the sprawling property and its 196 slaves after the 1857 death of his father-in-law, George Washington Parke Custis. Custis was the adopted son of George Washington and father of Lee's wife, Mary.

According to the terms of Custis' will, the slaves were to be freed within five years, after the finances of his various holdings were put in order. Lee had taken two years off from U.S. Army service to manage the properties, now owned by Mary Lee, who had grown up at Arlington House (see Chapter 25, "Lincoln Makes Lee an Offer He Could Refuse"). Before departing the mansion due to the war, Lee and Mary, the mother of the seven Lee children, had often walked, worked, or sat in the garden outside the manse, lulled by the honeysuckle scent of its garden.

In 1861 Federal troops occupied the Arlington estate's strategic heights on the day after Virginia declared its secession from the Union. Soldiers there built a Freedmen's Village for escaped slaves, now free and working for wages to supply crops to the Union cause while puzzling over the novel concept of paying rent. The Lees lost formal possession of the estate in 1862, after a congressional law let authorities tax and seize "insurrectionary" property. Mrs. Lee was required by law to pay a property tax of $92.07. Since she was residing in the Confederate capital of Richmond, she had Alexandria lawyer and relation Philip R. Fendall show up to pay the levy. The tax commission insisted the owner had to personally pay it. This was impossible for Mrs. Lee, and the federal government took over the estate. Montgomery Meigs couldn't think of a better choice to place a new Union cemetery. In June 1864 he wrote War Secretary Stanton: "I recommend ... the land surrounding the Arlington Mansion, now understood to be the property of the United States, be appropriated as a National Military Cemetery, to be properly enclosed, laid out and carefully preserved." Stanton immediately concurred, and 200 acres were so designated. In a deliberate slight against the former colleague he now branded a traitorous turncoat, Meigs ordered 40 deceased Union officers buried around the Lees' garden.

After Appomattox, Meigs remained as Army Quartermaster General for over 20 more years. He kept populating Arlington with deceased soldiers and memorials in order to stop the grounds from ever reverting to their former owner. He was spurred on by a visit to Arlington by Smith Lee, Robert E. Lee's brother. Smith Lee concluded the estate could be made habitable again for his family if a wall was built to screen the graves from the mansion. Word of this leaked to Meigs, who reacted strongly. In late 1865 he dispatched federal troops to collect the remains of over 2,110 soldiers, mostly from the First and Second Battles of Manassas. Their body parts—skulls, leg bones, arm bones—were separated out and placed in different niches of a circular pit near the Lees' garden. The wide, deep pit was covered with a cenotaph, a memorial marker for someone whose remains are elsewhere or whose identity is unknown ("ceno" in Greek means "empty"). The brick, concrete, and granite structure became the estate's first tomb of the unknowns—not today's famous Tomb of the Unknown Soldier to the south of Arlington House, but the Civil War Unknowns Monument.

Ironically, many of the remains were those of Confederates, found lying near their former foes in arms. Without dog tags, without DNA analysis, there was rarely any way to identify one from the other. Near the tomb, Meigs also built—due to overflow crowds for Decoration Day, the precursor to Memorial Day—a theater for memorial events, called today the Tanner Amphitheater. It's a lovely place of colonnades crowned by wisteria trellises. Finally, at the eastern entrance to the grounds, seen by most tourists entering today, he placed a sandstone McClellan gate, after the Union Army commander of the war's early years. Marked onto it is the designer's "autograph": MEIGS.

After the war, Robert E. Lee, after avoiding banishment from the United States or a trial for treason, moved to Lexington, Virginia. He became president of Washington College (later Washington and Lee University, a noted liberal arts institution). He advocated peaceful reunion with the North, was opposed to full civil rights for blacks, and stressed the need for education to uplift the South. Lee and his lawyers were dubious he could win back the estate. Mrs. Lee tried, however. In a move dispiriting to many people, she urged that Congress look into the cost of removing those buried there. Allies in Congress introduced a bill to look into her land claims. With passions from the war still raw, the Senate shot it down by vote of 54–4. In 1870 Robert E. Lee died and was buried in Lexington. In 1873 Mary Lee quietly rode a carriage through her former estate. She wrote, "My visit produced one good effect. The change is so entire that I have not the yearning to go back there & shall be more content to resign all my right in it." Meigs' changes had produced the desired effect. Later that year, Mrs. Lee passed on.

But a new chapter in the saga opened. In 1877 Reconstruction—the North's attempt to administer and reshape the South—sputtered to an end. The attitude of Congress and the courts improved for the Lee family. The Lees' eldest son, George Washington Custis Lee—Custis Lee for short—was a former Confederate general and aide-de-camp to Confederate President Davis. Custis Lee had a financial and personal stake in reclaiming the land as his inheritance, so he took the estate matter to the federal circuit court in Alexandria. The judge, appointed to the bench by President Grant, called for a jury trial. A prominent Alexandria attorney, Francis L. Smith, argued that the decision requiring Mrs. Lee to pay the tax in person had denied her due process. The jury agreed with Smith, as did the judge, who stated such rulings "would be liable to fall not only upon disloyal but upon the most loyal citizens." The Justice Department of President Rutherford B. Hayes appealed the case before the Supreme Court. In 1879 Kentucky Justice Samuel Freeman Miller, a Lincoln appointee, wrote in a 5–4 decision that the Lees had been denied their constitutional rights.

The federal government then was faced with the prospect of digging up and transferring the graves of 20,000 soldiers, banishing the Freedmen's Village, and returning the property to the leading family of the former Confederacy. Instead, it negotiated with Custis Lee, who readily agreed on a cash settlement. For $150,000, the market price, the federal government retained possession for all time the hallowed grounds of patriots in eternal rest. The formal transfer was made in 1883 with the Secretary of War, Robert Todd Lincoln, President Lincoln's son. The settlement met Meigs' main goal of keeping the place a sacred burial ground. In acknowledgment he built in the old flower garden a small Temple of Fame, with Doric Greek columns, to honor noted Americans: Lincoln, Washington, and Union generals (the Temple was taken down in 1967).

Meigs had one more major architectural task, much related to the Civil War. The largest federal agency had become the Pension Bureau, administering benefits up through the Civil War to retired soldiers or their widows and orphans. The Bureau needed a big new building for its thousands of employees paying pensions to the hundreds of thousands of Union veterans. Out of 15 million red bricks Meigs created the Pension Building, finished in 1887. Some didn't take to the giant, Lego-like box. With his earthy terseness, General

Arlington National Cemetery hosts the startlingly graphic tomb of John Rodgers Meigs—the son of Union General Montgomery Meigs—who was killed in a Civil War skirmish (Wikimedia Commons, photography by Tim1965: Own work, CC BY-SA 3.0, https://commons.wikimedia.org/w/index.php?curid=16620032).

Sherman said, "It's too bad the damn thing is fireproof." The "Scourge of Atlanta" was uncharitable. Meigs' innovative design outfitted the edifice with spacious windows and vents that afforded workers sunlight and air. Architect and German immigrant Adolph Cluss took a similar approach with the city's Eastern Market as well as his Franklin Institute and Charles Sumner School. Places of work and study were supposed to be pleasant, not prison-like, such builders believed, to benefit the employee and society at large.

The Pension Building's vast atrium, with its tiered, arched floors and supported by 75-foot columns, channels ancient Roman temples. For the exterior walls, Meigs hired a Czech immigrant sculptor, Caspar Buberl, to place on a 365-meter frieze some 1,300 figures of marching Union soldiers, sailors, and cannoneers, as well as Meigs' supply teams. The artwork recalls Roman Emperor Trajan's Column in Rome of marching legionnaires spiraling up an obelisk to conquer ancient Romania and Iraq. Today, Meigs' final masterwork fittingly houses the National Building Museum. In his sunset years, Meigs transferred the remains of his slain son, John Rodgers Meigs, to Arlington. Over the grave was built an astonishing bronze sculpture of the soldier. It depicts him lying on his back in the mud, the impressions of hooves of Confederate cavalry about his body. In Meigs' view it was another way of striking back at the rebel traitors.

In 1892 Meigs himself succumbed, to influenza. With much fanfare, a large honor guard laid him to rest at Arlington on Meigs Boulevard. The rolling hills about his graveyard, which started out with the burial of humble privates on the ground's lower slopes, had become the nation's most sacred soil, Arlington National Cemetery. In 2019 it was the resting place, from every era of American history, of 400,000 soldiers, sailors, and high-ranking government officials.

Postwar Reconciliations

In a strange way, the competition between Meigs and the Lees didn't end at Arlington. In 1889, with fanfare from retired Confederate veterans, the *Appomattox* statue of a rebel soldier lost in reflection was unveiled in Alexandria, Virginia, Robert E. Lee's hometown. The featured speaker was Virginia Governor Fitzhugh Lee, Lee's nephew and himself an ex-Confederate general. Governor Lee had recently spoken for national unity at West Point, where his uncle and Meigs had excelled in their studies. At Alexandria he stated, "Today Federal and Confederate soldiers are citizens of one country. Over their head flies one flag, and a common destiny is revealed to both … so may every section of what is now a common country, remembering the valor and the heroism of the soldiers who fought upon either side from 1861 to 1865, be able to exclaim, 'There were American soldiers, and were splendid illustrations of American prowess.' Rejoice with me that the smoke of battle has vanished and the roar of hostile guns is no longer heard." Some noted the *Appomattox* statue's sculptor. It was Caspar Buberl, the sculptor of the Union Army frieze around Meigs' Union Army Pension Building—a reconciliation of sorts between North and South afforded by a Czech immigrant who worked for both sides of the great, and then somewhat healed, national divide.

The Renwick Gallery itself represented another reconciliation of sorts. Before the Civil War, it housed the sterling, private art collection of William Corcoran. During the war, the

Union Army confiscated it and turned it into offices and a storehouse of supplies under Quartermaster Meigs. Corcoran had been, along with partner George Washington Riggs, the wealthiest banker in Washington City. After he formally retired from finance, in the 1850s he focused on investing, charity, and art collecting. He had a magnificent mansion, formerly the home of Senator Daniel Webster, redesigned by James Renwick. It was on the site of today's Chamber of Commerce Building at 1615 H Street facing Lafayette Square.

A man of superb taste, Corcoran displayed art works there for guests. The best known was a marble sculpture, *The Greek Slave*. It depicts a nude female in chain cuffs auctioned off by the Ottoman Turks. Corcoran purchased the masterpiece by artist Hiram Powers in 1851—the year after the Compromise of 1850 postponed a civil war over slavery. Some art critics believe it was a subdued commentary on involuntary servitude. The depiction of a black woman on the slave block was hardly possible in antebellum days, thus the more palatable display of an enslaved white female from a bygone era.

A Southern sympathizer reared in the Tidewater, Corcoran resided in Europe during the Civil War. When he returned, he was driven, somewhat like Meigs, by his own peculiar vision for Washington. In his case, he turned to reconciliation between North and South through philanthropy. He was major benefactor to the poor, the Washington City Orphanage Asylum, and various colleges in Virginia, Maryland, and the District, in particular Columbian College, later George Washington University. His most famous and enduring

Philanthropist and financier William Wilson Corcoran, who resided in a lavish mansion off Lafayette Square, pictured here, endowed the Renwick Gallery and the Corcoran Gallery of Art (Library of Congress).

gift was his private art house turned Quartermaster's storehouse. After regaining control of the property, he turned it over to the public as a public art gallery, one of the first in America. Known as the Renwick Gallery, it was recrafted by the great architect of the Smithsonian Castle, James Renwick, retained by Corcoran. It is famous for its collections of handicrafts and contemporary art.

Corcoran's larger and namesake museum, the Corcoran Gallery of Art, takes up a whole city block three blocks down 17th Street. It was built in 1897 in an imposing Beaux Arts style, with the names of artistic legends—Giotto, Durer, Rubens—etched in its façade. Sadly, in recent times its management failed to compete with the vast collections and free entry price of the Smithsonian galleries, and in 2014 turned its artwork over to that institution. George Washington University, the college richly endowed by William Corcoran, took over its Corcoran School of the Arts and Design.

Lastly, it might be noted that just down 17th Street from the Corcoran Gallery of Art is an edifice that also stemmed from the public duty and civic vision of a Civil War–era figure. It is the American Red Cross building, the organization founded by Civil War caregiver Clara Barton. At the end of the War Between the States, Barton took on a remarkable mission for President Lincoln: to identify the remains of tens of thousands of deceased soldiers. From her office on 7th Street, Barton took on the herculean task of such identification, and informed countless families of the fate of their lost loved ones.

In their own ways, and in strong echoes of the Civil War, Meigs, Corcoran, and Barton placed their distinctive stamps on the capital city.

Sources

Architect of the Capitol. "Frieze of American History." Updated May 30, 2017. https://www.aoc.gov/art/other-paintings-and-murals/frieze-american-history.
_____. "The Statue of Freedom." Updated May 1, 2018. https://www.aoc.gov/art/other-statues/statue-freedom.
Heidler, David Stephen, Jeanne T. Heidler and David J. Coles. *Encyclopedia of the American Civil War: A Political, Social, and Military History*. New York: W.W. Norton, 2002.
Miller, David W. *Second Only to Grant: Quartermaster General Montgomery C. Meigs*. Shippensburg, PA: White Mane, 2000.
Mitre. "General Montgomery C. Meigs, USA (Ret.)." https://www.mitre.org/about/leadership/trustee/general-montgomery-c-meigs-usa-ret.
Moser, Edward P. "Clara Barton: Angel of the Battlefield." In *A Patriot's A to Z of America*. Nashville: Turner, 2011.
Mr. Lincoln's White House. "The War Effort: The Winder Building Annex." http://www.mrlincolnswhitehouse.org/washington/the-war-effort/war-effort-winder-building-annex/.
O'Harrow, Robert, Jr. "Montgomery Meigs's Vital Influence on the Civil War—and Washington." *Washington Post Magazine*, July 1, 2011.
Poole, Robert M. "How Arlington National Cemetery Came to Be." *Smithsonian*, November 2009. https://www.smithsonianmag.com/history/how-arlington-national-cemetery-came-to-be-145147007/.
_____. *On Hallowed Ground: The Story of Arlington National Cemetery*. London: Walker, 2009.
Towns, Walter Stuart. "Ceremonial Speaking and the Reinforcing of American Nationalism in the South, 1875–1890." PhD diss., University of Florida, 1972. https://archive.org/stream/ceremonialspeaki00townrich/ceremonialspeaki00townrich_djvu.txt.
U.S. General Services Administration. "Pension Building (National Building Museum), Washington, DC." 2018. https://www.gsa.gov/historic-buildings/pension-building-national-building-museum-washington-dc.
Wheelan, Joseph. *Terrible Swift Sword: The Life of General Philip H. Sheridan*. Cambridge, MA: Da Capo, 2013.

28

The Spook Who Spied on the President and Inspired the Formation of the NSA

One-Half Block South of 17th Street and Pennsylvania Avenue, the West Side of the Street at the Entrance to the Eisenhower Executive Office Building, the Old War, Navy, and State Department Building

The 28-year-old clerk from Worthington, Indiana, was both restless and deeply curious about his work. There was a war on, the Great War, World War I. And he was working in the code room of the telegraph office in the State Department next to the White House. The office was handling the messages between President Woodrow Wilson, the head of a still-neutral nation, and the warring powers of Europe. Herbert Yardley performed an interesting variation on his work as a telegraph clerk. Without authorization, he began decoding the secret transmissions to Wilson, such as the one from the President's chief advisor, Colonel Edward House, regarding his meeting with Germany's Kaiser, Wilhelm II, about the prospects for peace.

Such tinkering came naturally to Yardley. His father had been a railroad telegraph operator, and had steeped him in the intricacies of Morse code. He was himself a superb poker player who relied on mathematical probabilities as well as hunches—an excellent background for code breaking. He quickly deciphered the confidential message to the President. He was shocked at the feeble encryption for diplomatic cables.

Building a Spook Group

Yardley knew that, unlike the United States, other powers such Germany, Britain, and France had set up formal organizations for the encoding and decoding of diplomatic and military traffic. Such agencies regularly tried breaking the codes of their rivals. In a time of war, he realized, such skills could mean the life or death of a nation. Glibly persuasive, he approached officials in the War Department, and convinced them to set up an equivalent spy organization for the U.S.—with himself as its head and with a special commission as an Army Lieutenant. He later wrote, "Why did America have no bureau for the reading of secret diplomatic code and cipher telegrams of foreign governments? Perhaps I, too, like the foreign cryptographer, could open the secrets of the capitals of the world."

For the rest of the war Yardley and his modest-sized staff ran MI-8, Military Intelligence (MI)-8, the Code Bureau. It was America's first signals intelligence agency. His boss was Colonel Ralph Van Deman, MI's founder. Van Deman tended to attract daredevils. His wife was the first American woman to fly—with the Wright brothers as her pilots. Yardley farmed out a bunch of his work to an Illinois millionaire, George Fabyan, who set up a private research facility at his 325-acre Riverbank Laboratories estate. It was a kind of early Bletchley Park, the compound where British mathematicians in the Second World War would break the encrypted messages of Germany's Enigma machine. Fabyan was an eccentric literary scholar convinced that Sir Francis Bacon had actually written Shakespeare's plays. He'd employed wordsmiths and code breakers to try to determine the true authorship of the Bard's works. One hire was a geneticist turned cryptanalyst, William F. Friedman. (In 1940 Friedman would head a team that broke Japan's PURPLE encryption codes.) In 1917, as the U.S. entered the First World War, Riverbank's literary analysis had turned into a codes and ciphers office. Fabyan offered its services to the U.S. military.

Yardley's MI-8 had success. For instance, it cracked a coded message found in the sleeve of a captured German spy, Lothar Witzke. He was probably behind the 1916 arson of the Black Tom ammunitions depot in Jersey City, New Jersey, across from New York Harbor. That act of sabotage killed at least four people. It threw shrapnel clear across the harbor that permanently damaged the torch of the Statue of Liberty. Witzke was part of the 1917 bombing of San Francisco's Mare Island Navy Yard, which killed six people. An aide to Yardley deciphered Witzke's letter. According to the U.S. Army, it read, "Strictly Secret! The bearer of this is a subject of the Empire who travels as a Russian under the name of Pablo Waberski. He is a German secret agent." Witzke was imprisoned at Fort Leavenworth. The Code Bureau had failures too, some prosaic. The Justice Department once asked Yardley to find secret messages thought hidden in the feathers of a carrier pigeon. His team found lice instead.

Overall, the Great War underlined the importance of signals intelligence. The U.S. funneled all its telegrams from Europe through a single relay station in England. Britain's own coding and decoding bureau, known as Room 40, tapped into the weakly encrypted messages and read America's electronic mail—and found a smoking gun, a message from the German Foreign Minister in Berlin, Arthur Zimmermann, to the German ambassador to Mexico. It contained a German proposal whereby Mexico would wage war on the U.S. to regain its lost territories of Texas, Arizona, and New Mexico. The publication of the "Zimmermann Telegram" pushed an enraged America toward war with Germany.

After the November 1918 armistice ending the Great War, Yardley employed his promotional skills to elicit $100,000 from the State and War Departments. With the funds he set up a peacetime snooping operation. Officially it was called the Code Bureau and unofficially the Black Chamber. To some, the name recalled the English Renaissance court, the Star Chamber, where the king's men harshly punished suspects for suspected treason. Yardley's Black Chamber targeted the communications of foreigners, but also American citizens and companies. Washington, D.C., was deemed to have too many prying eyes and ears, so the Black Chamber set up a front company on East 38th Street in Manhattan. As in a spy movie, the actual operation took place in secret rooms behind the company's walls. Yardley lived with his wife above the snoop shop.

Spying on Americans was illegal. So Yardley and General Marlboro Churchill (a distant relation of Winston Churchill, who was a direct descendant of the Duke of Marlboro), the new head of military intelligence, visited the chiefs of the main telegraph companies, including Western Union. Western Union's president, Newcomb Carlton, was wary of cooperating for fear of being prosecuted for unlawful disclosure of private information. But when the visitors "put all our cards on the table," Yardley coyly recalled, "President Carlton seemed anxious to do everything he could for us." An MI operative called on Western Union's D.C. headquarters each morning to pick up requested telegrams. To get other data, Yardley bribed telegraph company workers.

Yardley's most significant postwar feat came with the 1921–22 Washington Naval Conference. After the carnage of the Great War, and with the peaceful, prosperous Roaring Twenties underway, limits on armaments were popular. Three major naval powers, the United States, Britain, and Japan, met in D.C. to hash out ceilings on the size of their fleets. The U.S. Navy and the Royal Navy were to have the same proportion of battleships, Japan somewhat fewer. A key issue was what the Japanese proportion should be. The American negotiating team would have a big advantage if it knew what Tokyo's diplomats would settle for.

Enter Yardley and his team. They obtained Japan's coded telegrams on the conference. By guessing commonly used words in Japanese, they were able to quickly decipher the messages. They found that the Japanese, who were arguing for a proportion of 10 to 7 ships, were willing to accept a ratio of 10 to 6. A decoded Japanese telegram revealed the lower number might be "necessary to avoid any clash with Great Britain and America." That became the U.S. negotiating position, and the Japanese accepted it. "Stud poker is not a very difficult game," Yardley noted, "after you see your opponent's hole card." Pleased with the conference's outcome, the military awarded him a Distinguished Service Medal.

However, peacetime usually brings cuts in military and intelligence spending, and that happened to the 1920s War Department. During that decade the budget for Yardley's Black Chamber was slashed by two-thirds. The Twenties ended with disaster for the spook. In 1929 Henry Stimson, the Secretary of State for new President Herbert Hoover, was briefed on Yardley's work. At a meeting he was reportedly told the Black Chamber could read the Vatican's communications. The Secretary stormed out of the briefing and shut the Code Bureau down. Stimson famously remarked, "Gentlemen do not read each other's mail."

Moonlighting by a Spy

Yardley was out of work—and pocket. He and his wife now had a child and mounting expenses. Ever the card-playing gambler at heart, Yardley tried flipping houses in New Jersey, but his investments didn't play out. He even tried making money by selling the invisible inks with which spies scribble their messages. For most of the rest of his life, Yardley turned to work outside the federal intelligence agencies. Historians disagree on whether, around 1930, he sold some of his encryption secrets to the Japanese government for $7,000. He did decide to write what's become a Washington staple: a tell-all book on things no one is supposed to tell, in Yardley's case, his work as a snoop and decoder of other people's messages.

In 1931 he published *The American Black Chamber*. The book was a hit, selling over 50,000 copies. It was more popular abroad than at home, especially among the 19 nations whose supposedly secret mail Yardley had read. In Japan it sold twice as many copies as in the U.S. *The American Black Chamber* told all about the code breaking for the Washington Naval Conference. The Japanese were irate at learning their communications had been pilfered and for being snookered at the bargaining table. The anger might have helped the rise to power of the Japanese military, which accused Japan's worldly, pro–American diplomats of being incompetent or worse. Oddly, the tiff might have also helped the Japanese lose the next war. They switched to a more secure encoding system, one deemed so reliable they stuck with it all the way through the Second World War. But U.S. Navy signal analysts, led by William Friedman and Frank Rowlett, decoded it. This code busting played a big role in America's triumph over Tokyo.

After founding America's signals intelligence, Herbert Yardley turned to spy books and screen plays. He is pictured here with glamorous movie star Rosalind Russell (National Security Agency).

During the Great Depression, Yardley's blockbuster book made him a star and a friend of movie starlets. He wrote spy novels. One helped inspire the 1935 film *Rendezvous* starring Rosalind Russell. It depicted an American cryptanalyst who broke the codes of a German spy ring. During this period and others, Yardley drank heavily and had an eye for the ladies, traits that have caused many others to be denied security clearances. Yardley had hoped his book would alert the U.S. on the need for peacetime signals intelligence, but his notion backfired. Due to secrets spilled in *The American Black Chamber*, he became persona non grata at the War, Navy, and State Departments. A crusading federal attorney, Thomas Dewey, the future New York Governor and presidential candidate, seized his manuscript for a follow-up book on Japan's diplomatic codes. The government mulled prosecuting him, but decided a court case would highlight sensitive intelligence operations. Congress did change the espionage laws to punish the disclosure of secret diplomatic data. And the State Department put out "fake news" that the contents of Yardley's book were false.

The advent of the Second World War for a time revived Yardley's coding career. Starting in 1936, Japan began a brutal invasion of China. Who better to help the embattled Nationalist Chinese government, it seemed, than the man who'd broken the Japanese code? In 1938 Yardley, a free-agent spook, set up shop in Chongqing, the Nationalists' wartime capital. He helped the Chinese with their own encryption operation. He claimed he foiled a Japanese conspiracy to kidnap Chinese President Chiang Kai-Shek. He remained in China until 1940. In the months before Pearl Harbor, Yardley traveled on to Canada to help with its research on encryption. By then he'd aided at least three countries—the U.S., China, Canada, and perhaps Japan—in setting up or revamping their coding operations, truly a signal feat. But Canada's Commonwealth partner Great Britain and its de facto ally the United States did not trust Yardley, and he was obliged to leave Canada for the U.S.

In Washington, William "Wild Bill" Donovan, a First World War Medal of Honor winner and mob-busting attorney, was setting up the Office of Strategic Services, the OSS. It was a special-ops agency of analysts, commandos, and saboteurs and was the precursor of the CIA. In 1942, according to FBI records, Donovan apparently wanted to resurrect the

Black Chamber, with Yardley in charge. The notion fell through when the FBI placed under surveillance a Yardley-owned restaurant four blocks from the White House. The bistro was another one of his odd money-making schemes. It was also a suspected nest of pro–Nazi agents. Investigators staked out the place and found the allegations groundless. By then, however, Yardley's chances of working with "Wild Bill" Donovan had slipped away.

Long after his anti-climactic labors in the Second World War, Yardley finally achieved financial and personal success by returning to his first love. In 1957 he published *The Education of a Poker Player*. It sold well and is considered a classic on card playing. Yardley also became recognized as the godfather of modern signals intelligence. His Black Chamber was the forerunner of today's giant National Security Agency, with its supercomputers "surveilling" billions of e-mails and phone calls planetwide. His exposé, *The Black Chamber*, foretold Daniel Ellsberg, the leaker in 1971 of the Pentagon Papers, which revealed the U.S. government's secret decision-making during the Vietnam War. It also paved the way for Julian Assange, the WikiLeaks publisher of massive amounts of U.S. government information, notably that relating to the 2016 presidential campaign. Yardley was also a distant inspiration for Edward Snowden, who disclosed that the NSA's data gathering was much more widespread than thought.

Although shunned by U.S. military intelligence in the 1930s and 1940s, and despite being a model of sorts for Snowden, the NSA whistle blower, Yardley is celebrated today in the NSA's Hall of Honor. Further, due to his stint as an Army intelligence officer, he is buried at Arlington National Cemetery. According to an official NSA history, Yardley is "by all odds the most colorful, controversial, enigmatic figure in the history of American cryptology."

Sources

Banford, James. *The Puzzle Palace*. New York: Houghton Mifflin, 1982.

Cromwell-intl. "Herbert O. Yardley's Suspicious Restaurant." 2018. https://cromwell-intl.com/travel/usa/washington-yardley.html.

Friedersdorf, Conor. "82 Years Before Edward Snowden, There Was Herbert O. Yardley." *Atlantic*, December 4, 2013. https://www.theatlantic.com/politics/archive/2013/12/82-years-before-edward-snowden-there-was-herbert-o-yardley/282019/.

Gilbert, James L., and John P. Finnegan, ed. *U.S. Army Signals Intelligence in World War II: A Documentary History*. PDF. United States Army Center of Military History, CMH Pub 70–43. 1993.

Johnson, Thomas R. CIA. "Intelligence in Recent Public Literature." Review of *The Reader of Gentlemen's Mail: Herbert O. Yardley and the Birth of American Intelligence*. https://www.cia.gov/library/center-for-the-study-of-intelligence/csi-publications/csi-studies/studies/vol48no2/article13.html.

Kahn, David. *The Codebreakers*. New York: Macmillan, 1972.

_____. *The Reader of Gentlemen's Mail: Herbert O. Yardley and the Birth of American Codebreaking*. New Haven: Yale University Press, 2004.

King, Gilbert. "Sabotage in New York Harbor." *Smithsonian*, November 1, 2011. https://www.smithsonianmag.com/history/sabotage-in-new-york-harbor-123968672/.

Lardner, George, Jr. "Curtain Around Cryptography." *Washington Post*, May 18, 1986. https://www.washingtonpost.com/archive/politics/1986/05/18/curtain-around-cryptography/c5b25cbf-d7a9-408c-8660-f6e3443c91f6/?utm_term=.caf84a9a0181.

National Archives, "The Zimmermann Telegram." https://www.archives.gov/education/lessons/zimmermann.

U.S. Army. Lori Tagg. "February 1918: WWI Counterintelligence Agents Get Their Man." February 9, 2017. https://www.army.mil/article/182075/february_1918_wwi_counterintelligence_agents_get_their_man.

"William Friedman Dies; Broke Japanese Code; Truman Gave Cryptanalyst Highest Civilian Award; Marshall Said Work Saved Many American Lives." *New York Times*, November 2, 1969.

Witcover, Jules. *Sabotage at Black Tom: Imperial Germany's Secret War in America, 1914–1917*. Chapel Hill: Algonquin Books of Chapel Hill, 1989.

Yardley, Herbert Osborn. *The American Black Chamber*. Annapolis: Naval Institute Press, 2004 (originally published 1931).

29

The Most Criminally Inept Family in Military History

The Winder Building, 600 17th Street

The venerable structure at 600 17th Street is the Winder Building, bankrolled by William H. Winder, a member of one of the prominent Maryland families that dominated the region until the Civil War. It contrasts nicely with the concrete modern monstrosity, an example of D.C.'s Brutalist architecture, just to its north. Nowadays the Winder Building, much in the news, houses the offices of the U.S. Trade Representative, charged with handling commercial disputes with other countries. Its architect was probably the versatile Philadelphia craftsman Richard A. Gilpin, who also worked as a surveyor and railroad and aqueduct engineer. However, some sources give credit to the designer of the Treasury Building and the original architect of the Washington Monument, Robert Mills.

W.H. Winder was a businessman and real estate speculator with excellent timing. He erected the place in 1847 and 1848, during the Mexican-American War. Just yards north and east of it, from the early 1800s until the 1880s, stood the small building that housed the War Department, the Navy Department, and the State Department. In 1848 the offices of those departments were jam-packed with wartime personnel. Desperate for office space, the military agencies quickly rented out the entire Winder Building. At the time, it was the tallest building in the District and the most spacious, with 130 rooms.

It is ironic in the extreme that a building named for a Winder stands across 17th Street from the former War and Navy Departments, today's Eisenhower Executive Office Building, or EEOB. The EEOB is named after the triumphant General Dwight David Eisenhower, the Supreme Commander of the Allied forces in Europe during the Second World War, and later, as President, the Commander-in-Chief. In fact, the locale of the EEOB has always been at the center of military affairs in D.C. It still hosts military-related personnel from the National Security Council, thus providing a President his top security advisors.

It is ironic because the Winders were likely the most disgraced, incompetent military family in U.S. history.

America's Worst Soldier

On August 24, 1814, during the War of 1812, British invaders burned down the offices of the War, Navy, and State Departments. At the same time, the British immolated the White

House next door, as well as the Treasury Building on the other side of President's Park. That they were able to enter the city to create such havoc had much to do with a Winder—General William H. Winder, the uncle and namesake of the businessman W.H. Winder. General Winder was in charge of the military district responsible for defending Washington and fighting the battle of Bladensburg, Maryland, seven miles to the northeast, where on that August 24 the outnumbered British routed the ill-prepared Americans, clearing the way for their unmolested rampage through the capital.

It's an understatement that President Madison's appointment of General Winder to defend the capital was a blunder. Winder was a lawyer, not a solder. At the start of the war, while Winder was fighting in Ontario, then part of British Canada, enemy troops promptly captured him and then released him (which might have been, as things turned out, a sly strategic move). Winder essentially got his military position due to political ties. His own uncle, the Governor of Maryland, had recruited many militiamen, which Winder was anointed to lead.

At Bladensburg the 39-year-old General Winder erred in the overall strategy of confronting the advancing British. Guerrilla tactics and skirmish lines were called for, as the British were a regular armed force advancing through hostile territory. Winder determined instead to fight a conventional battle of the type where the British had much experience but where the American forces had none. Further, Winder was supposed to craft a plan of retreat in case things went badly. That he failed to do this contributed to the subsequent panicky flight of the federal soldiers and local militias. The retreat was so precipitous that some of the British played bugles, as if they were on a fox hunt or a horse track. Indeed, newspapers referred to the battle as "the Bladensburg races."

Admittedly, Winder had plenty of help in the disaster. President Madison, though a peerless constitutional lawyer—in fact, the main author of the Constitution—was a scholarly man with no military experience. He had inherited a federal military his friend and predecessor, Thomas Jefferson—another scholarly type with little military experience—had much downsized. In lieu of costly but effective warships, Jefferson had built an array of oared, single-cannon skiffs, dubbed "Jeffs," which the Royal Navy swept aside in seizing the nearby inlets of the Chesapeake Bay. Further, Madison's Secretary of War, John Armstrong, Jr., had failed to fortify Washington City after promising Madison the British would never attack Washington. Astonishingly, the Secretary of War, when the British approached the District, fled the city! Madison had him court-martialed.

At Bladensburg, General Winder's subordinate, General Tobias Stansbury, was in immediate charge of the forces. He had more troops than the British, about 7,000 to their roughly 3,000. True, about 6,000 of his men were raw militia. But Stansbury also had cannon while the quick-marching Royal Marines had none, so he had a real chance at winning. One of Stansbury's roles was to pick a site to make a stand. At first, he placed his forces atop a steep hill. That ground dominated the approaches to Washington, Baltimore, and Annapolis. For inexplicable reasons, he then moved his men off the strategic high ground and onto much flatter terrain. There his inexperienced troops would become easy pickings for the British, veterans of victories in Europe over the forces of Napoleon himself.

Winder compounded this gross error. Instead of setting up interlocking lines of defense, he positioned troops so that the guns of various units couldn't support each other. Before the battle, President Madison rode out with his staff to Bladensburg. There Madison

29. The Most Criminally Inept Family in Military History

himself erred, and was poorly served by his usually adept Secretary of State, James Monroe. The latter was made acting Secretary of War after the cowardly flight from town of War Secretary Armstrong. Monroe was a bona fide war hero who had crossed the Delaware with George Washington during the Revolution. But at Bladensburg, he and Madison moved about the troops—already exhausted in the August heat from their repositioning—with little reason or purpose.

On the day of battle, the only American unit that fought with distinction at Bladensburg were the 480 U.S. sailors and Marines under Navy Captain Joshua Barney. They repulsed the initial British assault. But when General Winder failed to direct troops to support them, and indeed called for a general retreat, they were overwhelmed. Barney himself was wounded and captured. But the British released him in respect for the valor he and his men had shown. And when they reached Washington and burned down much of the city, they spared the Marines Corps Commandant's House, down from the Navy Yard, in further homage to Barney's valor. The home still stands, an instance of chivalry in a bloody time.

After the Bladensburg debacle, the Madison Administration court-martialed General Winder. He was acquitted, but his reputation was tarred. When the British turned their sights on Baltimore, Winder's superiors dumped him in rearguard duty. He was ordered to protect the western, inland approach to Baltimore. This assured Winder would be out of the battle, as the war fleet carrying the British attackers approached the city from the Chesapeake to the city's south and east. The Battle of Baltimore yielded a much happier result than the Battle of Bladensburg. Skilled American commanders—including Maryland militia General Samuel Smith, Joshua Barney, released from British detention, and Commodore Oliver Perry—fortified the city and fought off the invaders at Hampstead Hill. They even killed the man who had led the British ground troops at Bladensburg, Major General Robert Ross. The Americans crowned things off with a stout defense of Fort McHenry before the watchful eyes of lawyer-poet Francis Scott Key.

But Bladensburg and the subsequent burning of Washington is a low light in American military history, and General William Winder, the commander of the region where the debacle occurred, deservedly gets a major share of the blame.

Commander of the Camps, and a Camp Commandant

Military disgrace continued in his family. One of General Winder's sons, John Henry Winder, was much responsible for an even greater ignominy. A West Point graduate, the junior Winder had been a highly regarded federal officer during the Mexican-American War. When the Civil War broke out in 1861, John Henry, as the scion of a prominent Tidewater family, joined the Confederacy. He was promoted to General and then made head of the Confederate agency that managed prison camps. He was in charge of the detention, provision, and health of the many Union prisoners of war confined in Georgia, far from the front lines. His bureau was responsible for a prison camp filled with 45,000 federal soldiers. Due to a lack of proper medicine, food, and sanitation, perhaps 13,000 of the men died in the encampment, nearly one of three. It was the infamous Andersonville prison, the subject of a gripping 1959 play, *The Andersonville Trial*, and the basis of a 1970 television movie (co-starring, of all persons, William Shatner).

Other members of the Winder clan were involved with Andersonville. John Winder's cousin, Captain W. Sidney Winder, picked the site of the camp. John Winder's nephew, Captain Richard B. Winder, the camp's quartermaster, supervised the prison's construction. He later admitted he committed a terrible mistake in placing the camp kitchens upstream of the prison. As a result, the inmates used polluted water from the cookhouse for washing and drinking.

The administration of Andersonville prison was generally awful. Food shortages were common, although numerous observers noted plentiful orchards and farms nearby. No dwellings were supplied for the inmates as protection against the sun and rain. Prisoners themselves built "shebangs"—rude sheds or coverings from scraps of wood and brush, even from the arms and legs of the dead. Captain Winder wrote a superior that a "train load of lumber has been waiting transportation ... for the last twelve days.... I am burying the dead without coffins.... I shall be compelled to report the matter to the authorities at Richmond."

The horrific conditions of the prisoners at Andersonville triggered outrage in the victorious North and led to one of the only two war crimes trials from the Civil War. The other was the conviction and execution of Tennessee Confederate guerrilla leader Champ

Although Confederate General John Winder may have been more responsible for thousands of deaths at the infamous Andersonville prison, camp Commandant Dr. Henry Wirz got the blame—and a hangman's noose (Library of Congress).

Ferguson. A Union Army tribunal for Andersonville was formed, led by General Lewis Wallace. General Wallace was himself under a cloud for alleged tardiness at the 1862 Battle of Shiloh. His reputation would rise after penning a bestselling novel, *Ben Hur*, which generations later was turned into motion-picture spectaculars.

The courtroom proceedings took place in the Capitol, with the accused jailed across the street at the Old Capitol Prison, the site today of the Supreme Court. Wallace and the panel of officers tried and convicted—not Confederate General John Winder—but the Andersonville's camp Commandant, Dr. Henry Wirz. The original indictment also named John Winder, as well as Robert E. Lee and Jefferson Davis and other ranking rebels, but in the end only Wirz was tried. The trial was a sensation, with front-page coverage for a nation seeking some redress for the Lincoln assassination that April and for the war's massive body count. Wirz was convicted of multiple counts of murder. On November 10, 1865, he was hanged at the Old Capitol Prison, in the shadow of the Capitol, as Union soldiers looked on in shock from atop nearby trees—in shock because during the hanging Wirz' neck didn't snap. He dangled on the noose for minutes before strangling to death.

Ever since, historians have argued whether the trial and execution were just. True, some courtroom witnesses stated Wirz beat some of the prisoners. However, a star prosecution witness was Felix de la Baume, a Frenchman who claimed ancestry from the Marquis de Lafayette. It later came out that during the trial he'd received, in a likely pay for play, a position at the Interior Department. Worse, it was shown after the fact that he had assumed a false identity and thus perjured himself. His real name was Felix Oesser, a German not a Frenchman, and a deserter from the Union Army.

An immigrant from Switzerland, Wirz had worked in business, as a plantation overseer, and as something of a quack in medicine. He settled in the South, and like most people from that region joined the Confederacy. Given his training in medicine and his foreign-language skills, Confederate President Jefferson Davis appointed Wirz as a Special Minister to ferry confidential instructions to Confederate envoys in Britain and France. As Commandant of Andersonville, he faced wartime shortages, for instance of medicine, that influenced the camp's terrible death toll. At least in part Wirz seems to have been the victim of circumstances—of the harsh conditions of the war. But he was also the victim of his superior, General John Winder. Some historians believe Winder, as the overall commander of the region's prison camps, was probably criminally negligent in getting adequate supplies to Andersonville. He supposedly said of the dire prison, "I am killing off more Yankees than twenty regiments in Lee's army." However, unlike Wirz, Winder was never charged. He died of a heart attack before war's end. Wirz may have gotten the blame, and punishment, that his superior officer Winder more fully deserved.

Given John Winder's criminal incompetence and William Winder's ineptitude at Bladensburg, it seems incredible that a prominent federal building just a block from the White House still bears their family name. Local wags say only Washington, D.C., would reward such malfeasance.

Sources

Eschner, Kate. "How the Trial and Death of Henry Wirz Shaped Post-Civil War America." *Smithsonian,* November 10, 2017. https://www.smithsonianmag.com/smart-news/how-trial-and-death-henry-wirz-shaped-post-civil-war-america-180967139/.

Levitt, Saul, and Virginia Williams. *The Andersonville Trial: A Play*. New York: Random House, 1960.
Mr. Lincoln's White House. "The War Effort: The Winder Building Annex." http://www.mrlincolnswhitehouse.org/washington/the-war-effort/war-effort-winder-building-annex/.
National Park Service. "Andersonville National Historic Site, Georgia." https://www.nps.gov/ande/index.htm.
Office of the United States Trade Representative. "History of the Winder Building, Home to USTR's Washington D.C. Headquarters." https://ustr.gov/archive/Who_We_Are/History_of_the_Winder_Building,_Home_to_USTR's_Washington_DC_Headquarters.html.
Reynolds, Brad. "The Worst Leaders in History: General William H. Winder." *WarfareHistoryNetwork*, September 18, 2018. http://warfarehistorynetwork.com/daily/military-history/the-worst-leaders-in-history-general-william-h-winder/.

30

A Peerless Singer Lays the Groundwork for "I Have a Dream"

Constitution Hall, 1776 D St, Off of 17th Street

She was a world-renowned singer, and friend of Albert Einstein and some of Europe's famed conductors and composers. Her contralto ranged over Italian arias and German song poems and American popular standards and Negro spirituals—highbrow to field holler. The problem was, they wouldn't let her sing—not the operators of Constitution Hall, a concert stage with superb acoustics. She had faced this matter before. In Philadelphia, where she'd grown up, she applied for the University of the Arts, then called the Philadelphia Music Academy. The admissions office told her, "We don't take colored."

She turned to private tutors and attained much success. But her experience was rather like that of another singing wonder, Ella Fitzgerald. Though a major star, that queen of jazz was barred from some arenas and was at times directed to a hotel's rear entrance. So, for much of the 1930s, classical stylist Marian Anderson toured in Europe. Much of the continent was more open to black performers, whether their inspirations were Basie or Beethoven. Finland's greatest maker of symphonies, Jean Sibelius, wrote or revamped songs to suit her high, clear vocals. Scandinavia liked her the most; remote villages in Europe's northland were gripped with "Mariana fever." Maestro Arturo Toscanini said a voice like Anderson's "comes around once in a hundred years."

Busting the Color Line

Marian Anderson returned to her adopted hometown of Washington an international star. Her sponsor, the mostly black institution Howard University, strove to find her major venues. Constitution Hall, with a 3,700-seat theater and often host to classical performers, seemed to beckon. It had been built in 1928 near the former home of city Mayor Thomas Carbery and his stricken sister Ann Mattingly (see Chapter 31, "The Miracle Manse").

The auditorium was at that time, and is today, owned and managed by the DAR, the Daughters of the American Revolution, a historical society of women who trace their lineage to the leaders and foot soldiers of the Spirit of '76. But the DAR and Constitution Hall had taken a dispiriting stance against racial integration. The first half of the twentieth century was a different time in the District. In the 1920s, a public beach near today's Tidal Basin had separate sections for blacks and whites. Restaurants on Pennsylvania Avenue were segregated into the 1950s. Trolley cars in the city were integrated, but when they clattered over the 14th Street Bridge into Virginia, black passengers moved to the back of the cars and whites to the front. In the roaring 1920s, black entertainers had performed at Constitution Hall. However, customers of color were confined to a portion of the balcony. When an African-American singer declined to sing at the Hall due to the Jim Crow seating, the DAR changed its policy—and forbade any black performers at all.

That's where things stood in early 1939 for the 42-year-old Marian and her agent, impresario Sol Hurok. The latter was a Russian-Jewish immigrant who managed other orchestral stars like pianist Van Cliburn, guitarist Andrés Segovia, and violinist Isaac Stern. Hurok requested that the DAR book Anderson at its Hall. The DAR declined, citing the whites-only clause in its contracts. It further noted the Hall didn't have separate bathrooms for blacks and whites, as the city's laws required.

Denied a Constitution Hall performance by the Daughters of the American Revolution, African-American singer Marian Anderson turned in 1939 to a far larger, outdoor venue: the Lincoln Memorial (Addison Scurlock/Smithsonian Institution, National Museum of American History, Archives Center).

Fortunately, Marian Anderson had powerful friends, friends who thought her treatment and her vocals might be used as instruments to advance civil rights. A key ally was the First Lady, Eleanor Roosevelt, a DAR member. When the DAR barred Anderson, Mrs. Roosevelt resigned from it. She wrote its leadership: "You had an opportunity to lead in an enlightened way, and it seems to me that your organization has failed." In tandem, black civil rights leaders such as Charles Hamilton Houston, Dean of Howard's School of Law, organized protests against the DAR. (In 1954, Houston's legal team, with an assist from paratroopers sent by President Eisenhower, would overturn public school segregation nationwide in the Little Rock, Arkansas, *Brown v. Board of Education* case.)

The head of the Interior Department of Eleanor Roosevelt's husband, President Franklin Roosevelt, was Harold L. Ickes. Secretary Ickes turned the tables on the DAR and its Hall. He granted Anderson a permit to perform at a far grander and more prestigious locale—the Lincoln Memorial.

On Easter Sunday, April 9, 1939, Anderson sang from the steps of the Great Emancipator's shrine to an audience of 75,000 whites and blacks gathered around its Reflecting Pool. Ickes introduced her with a homily: "In this great auditorium under the sky, all of us are free. Genius, like justice, is blind. Genius draws no color lines." Accompanied by her Finnish pianist, Anderson began with a patriotic anthem that the occasion turned into a protest song: "America." She altered the opening lyric slightly, to "to thee 'we' sing." Anderson intoned a composition of Schubert's. She closed with spirituals, including "Gospel Train" and "My Soul Is Anchored in the Lord."

Before a bank of eight microphones, with Lincoln's marbled image looming behind her, the granddaughter of a slave freed during Lincoln's presidency seemed regal. She wore a mink cloak over an orange velour coat with turquoise buttons and a gold, paisley-patterned trim. Indeed, on tour she hauled a sewing machine with her to make her own articles of apparel to go along with those that her enamored fans created. The radio networks relayed her concert to a national audience. She said she was frightened, but the audio from that day presents a voice that is clear. The concert garnered rave reviews.

More Musical Landmarks

By 1940 the Nazis had taken over much of Europe. The continent had become less open to persons of color and others. When the United States entered the Second World War in 1941 stars like Anderson were asked to raise money for the war effort. This reopened her battle with Constitution Hall. In October 1942 American troops were fighting in Guadalcanal in the Pacific and preparing to invade North Africa. Stung by criticism of its ban, the DAR invited Anderson to perform at a Constitution Hall show to benefit civilian victims of German and Japanese aggression. Anderson agreed to the request under the condition that the DAR end its audience segregation and its general ban on black entertainers. The DAR insisted on a single performance by her only, with no conditions. Anderson declined. The DAR relented, in part, before Christmas. It would allow her to sing before a mixed audience as part of a Red Cross benefit. Anderson agreed and performed at the Hall on January 7, 1943. The sold-out arena that night included the First Lady and Supreme Court Justices William O. Douglas and Hugo Black. The latter judge was a former member of the

Ku Klux Klan who became amenable to civil rights. Anderson donated the concert proceeds to China, then wracked by a Japanese invasion. She remarked, "When I finally walked onto the stage of Constitution Hall, I felt no different than I had in other halls. There was no sense of triumph. I felt that it was a beautiful concert hall and I was very happy to sing there."

Her performance was, as at the Lincoln Memorial, a mix of the classical and the devout, with a bit of the political. She sang Handel and Haydn and the gospel songs "My Soul's Been Anchored in the Lord" and "Ride On, King Jesus." Anderson dedicated one number to black agronomist George Washington Carver, who replaced cotton on plantations with the humble cash crop of the peanut. (In 1965, Anderson would christen the nuclear aircraft carrier the USS *George Washington Carver*.) She closed with an audience sing-along to "The Star-Spangled Banner," written by that Georgetown lyricist Francis Scott Key.

Marian went on to a yet larger, more prestigious stage: the White House. She performed for the Roosevelts there. She also sang at President Harry Truman's 1949 inaugural after his astonishing come-from-behind election win the previous autumn. Truman, whose daughter, Margaret, was a performing grand pianist, had commented on the DAR's segregationism: "One of the marks of a democracy is its willingness to respect and reward talent without regard to race or religion." Others, such as DAR member and Republican Congresswoman Clare Boothe Luce, the wife of *Time* and *Life* magazine publisher Henry Luce, pushed the organization to change its ways. Luce was miffed after Hazel Scott, the pianist wife of black Harlem Democratic Congressman Adam Clayton Powell, was blocked from playing at the Hall. In 1952 the DAR let African-American soprano Dorothy Maynor perform there. The following year, Anderson herself sang at Constitution Hall. For the first time, people of any skin color were allowed to sit where they wished. Devoutly religious, the tranquil diva harbored no rancor. "All I want to be remembered for is the voice the Lord gave me," she said, "[which] hopefully made people happy."

Marian Anderson went on to break a color line in the North as the first black person, American or foreign, to sing at the Met, New York's Metropolitan Opera. This was in 1955, a full 12 years after her first appearance at Constitution Hall. Director Rudolf Bing stealthily signed Anderson to a contract before letting the Met's board members know about the booking so they could not veto it. Her performance as a witch in a Verdi opera opened the door for the first black male singer at the Met: Robert McFerrin, father of jazz vocalist Bobby McFerrin.

On August 28, 1963, Marian Anderson reprised her performance at the Lincoln Memorial—before a far bigger audience. The size of the crowd was 500,000. As part of Dr. Martin Luther King's March on Washington, she sang right after King delivered his "I Have a Dream" speech. Her song was "He's Got the Whole World in His Hands." King's talk that day was the text behind the civil rights movement that finally brought to fruition the vision of Civil War–era emancipation. Yet it was Marian Anderson who, years before, gave voice to it—after being denied a stage at Constitution Hall.

Sources

Anderson, Marian. *My Lord, What a Morning: Autobiography of Marian Anderson*. New York: Avon, 1968.
Freedman, Russell. *The Voice That Challenged a Nation: Marian Anderson and the Struggle for Equal Rights*. Boston: Clarion, 2004.

30. A Peerless Singer Lays the Groundwork for "I Have a Dream"

Katz, Jamie. "Four Years After Marian Anderson Sang at the Lincoln Memorial, D.A.R. Finally Invited Her to Perform at Constitution Hall." *Smithsonian*, April 8, 2014. https://www.smithsonianmag.com/history/four-years-after-marian-anderson-sang-lincoln-memorial-dr-finally-allowed-her-perform-constitution-hall-180950468/.

Kiger, Patrick. "Marian Anderson Actually Did Get to Sing at Constitution Hall." WETA. *Boundary Stones*, April 9, 2014. https://blogs.weta.org/boundarystones/2014/04/09/marian-anderson-actually-did-get-sing-constitution-hall.

Righthand, Jess. "When Marian Anderson Sang at the Lincoln Memorial, Her Voice Stunned the Crowd, and Her Gold-Trimmed Jacket Dazzled." *Smithsonian*, April 8, 2014. https://www.smithsonianmag.com/smithsonian-institution/when-marian-anderson-sang-lincoln-memorial-her-voice-stunned-the-crowds-her-gold-trimmed-jacket-dazzled-180950454/.

Stamberg, Susan. "Denied a Stage, She Sang for a Nation." NPR. April 9, 2014. https://www.npr.org/2014/04/09/298760473/denied-a-stage-she-sang-for-a-nation.

31

The Miracle Manse

17th Street and C Street, West Side of Street, Near the Site of Today's Constitution Hall and the Organization of American States

The sister of Washington's Mayor lay near death on March 10, 1824, in the three-story manse on 17th and C streets. Ann Mattingly, age 39, had years before discovered an egg-sized lump below her left breast. A widow and the mother of four children, the stricken woman had moved into the large residence of her brother, the Mayor of Washington, Thomas Carbery.

Ann's cancer had steadily progressed, covering her shoulders with ulcers and paralyzing her left arm. Her parched, swollen tongue was "as hard as a nutmeg grater." Her doctors treated her with the unusual, sometimes injurious, medicines of the day: compounds of mercury, up to 400 grams daily of the opiate laudanum, and a hemlock concoction. She also wasn't helped by the nearby, trash-filled Washington Canal—Constitution Avenue today—at that time the font of cholera, typhus, and other deadly woes. "Her case is hopeless," declared one of her physicians, Dr. Alexander Williams. Another doctor sadly remarked Ann was "out of the reach of medicine."

With the suffering woman on her deathbed, the Carbery family felt it had one last card to play. They were devout Irish-Catholics in a region that, unusually so for early-19th century America, had noted Catholic institutions. Georgetown College, three miles to the northwest, had been founded in 1789 by the prominent Maryland priest John Carroll. The Carroll family owned much of what became Capitol Hill. The District's downtown St. Patrick's Church, founded in 1794, and where Mayor Carbery was a member, lay less than a mile to the northeast on 10th Street and G Street The bordering state of Maryland had been founded by the English Catholic George Calvert, Lord Baltimore. One of Ann Mattingly's aunts had been the first American nun. In Washington, Irish-Catholic immigrants made up many of the laborers and mechanics working at the Washington Canal, the Washington Navy Yard, and the city's workshops.

Trans-Continental Prayer Sessions

For years, Ann Mattingly's family and fellow parishioners had been praying for her, praying for her life. Now, with her condition terminal, they would up the ante. They would take part in a remarkable prayer ritual involving three high-powered, and controversial, clerics—including a faith healer who would pray long-distance, from clear across the

31. The Miracle Manse

Atlantic! The first of these men was Father Anthony Kohlmann, the former President of Georgetown College and founder of what became the city's prestigious Gonzaga College High School. An erudite priest typical of the church's Jesuit order, the Alsace-born Kohlman had run a college in the Netherlands and had managed a Bavarian seminary. In later years he would advise the church's College of Cardinals and would tutor Vincenzo Pecci, later known as Pope Leo XIII. In 1812, as administrator for the Bishop of New York, Kohlman set up a girls' school run by nuns from County Cork, Ireland, and founded an institute on ancient Greek and Roman literature. He supervised the start of construction of the city's first St. Patrick's Cathedral. Soon thereafter, he became embroiled in a controversy with Protestant leaders.

In New York, Kohlmann had been the priest-confessor to a man caught in a highly publicized robbery. As such, he'd listened to the felon's confession and administered to him the Roman Catholic sacrament of Penance (today called Penance and Reconciliation). The New York police, seeking the full details of the crime, demanded Kohlmann tell them what he had heard during the confession. Kohlmann refused, citing the church's ironclad rule of confidentiality for any conversation between the confessing person and priest. The issue went to court, with New York Mayor Dewitt Clinton—famous for building the Erie Canal—deciding things in Father Kohlmann's favor. The verdict stated, "Secrecy is of the essence of penance. The sinner will not confess, nor will the priest receive his confession, if the veil of secrecy is removed." Protestant writers denounced the decision, believing it violated separation of church and state, and gave Catholic teachings supremacy over secular law. But the legal precedent that was set remains in force today.

The second formidable cleric to help Ann was the assistant pastor of D.C.'s own St. Patrick's Church. Fluent in several languages, Father Étienne Larigaudelle Dubuisson was a Haitian-born Creole of an aristocratic French family. He'd served as a ranking Treasury official for King Louis XVI. Dubuisson had fled his disapproving parents to study for the priesthood in America. At Georgetown College he excelled at preaching but was a sullen instructor, so much so that in 1818 some of his own students plotted to murder him on campus before their conspiracy was unmasked. The learned but high-strung Dubuisson was later appointed Georgetown College's President.

But the key to saving Ann's life, it was thought, was a third priest: a bona fide Prince and reputed miracle worker. The offspring of German and Hungarian nobility, with a grand and long Germanic name and title—Alexander Leopold Franz Emmerich of Hohenlohe-Waldenburg-Schillingsfürst, Hohenlohe for short. Hohenlohe had a reputation of curing the sick, the blind, and the lame, most famously a paralytic and fellow member of the German nobility, Princess Mathilde von Schwarzenberg. Yet the 30-year-old cleric was controversial. Some critics asserted medical science, not prayer, was responsible for his many apparent cures. Others accused him of being a drunk and a philanderer. Authorities kicked him out of several countries, and the Pope restricted his prayer sessions to private gatherings, forbidding him from curing people in public. In German, Hohenlowe means "High and Low," a term that captured people's disparate views of the man.

Meanwhile, Hohenlowe had sent a letter to the Bishop of Baltimore, Maryland, stating that, for any unfortunate seeking his intervention, he would celebrate Mass on the tenth day of every month at exactly nine o'clock in the morning. He'd conduct the liturgy from his residence in Hamburg, Germany. Along with his own liturgy, he recommended the parish priests of the ill person stage a novena—a formal Catholic ritual involving nine days of prayer—for the stricken person's sake.

Ann's Catholic friends and prelates laid plans for a massive barrage of prayer to save her. Kohlmann wrote to Hohenlohe in Germany to seek his help. The plan was this: On March 10, 1824, the German cleric would pray for Ann in Hamburg, at 9 a.m. in central Europe. At the same time, accounting for time differences across two continents, Father Kohlmann would say a Mass for her at Georgetown's Holy Trinity Church. Reverend Dubuisson would do double duty. After holding a Mass for her at D.C.'s St. Patrick's Church, he would rush over by horse to Ann's bedside to give her a consecrated wafer of unleavened bread.

Early on the designated morning, Dubuisson said the Mass at St. Patrick's, took the Holy Communion wafer, hurried to the Carbery mansion, and entered Ann's chamber. At about 3 a.m. he found the woman, watched over by seven other witnesses, close to death. Ann took over five minutes, in between bouts of vomiting, to swallow the wafer the priest offered her. Dubuisson readied the church's Last Rites for those approaching their demise.

Ann Mattingly later recalled, "In the distressing situation, I calmly and without agitation of mind awaited the final close of my earthly miseries." She said to herself, *Lord Jesus! Thy holy will be done.* Reverend Dubuisson heard Ann sigh heavily. Then, in a stunning development, the woman sat up in bed. "Lord Jesus," she stated, "what have I done to deserve so much?" To the amazement of her onlookers, Ann put on socks and slippers and got out of her cot. Kneeling down to pray, she told those assembled the tumor was gone. So were her terrible bedsores and also, witnesses said, the stains on her clothes and sheets. She freely and painlessly moved her previously stricken arm. Ann remembered, "In the twinkling of an eye, the pain left me, my body was entirely healed." Later that morning, she devoured breakfast and cleaned her room. She was cured.

The reaction of the Catholic rank and file, and some of the Protestant faithful in the city, was ecstatic. At news of Ann's recovery, the bells of D.C.'s Catholic churches clanged in celebration. Of "Miracle Ann" a cleric enthused, "Her breath, lately so intolerably fetid and disgusting, was become very sweet." Kohlmann stated, "America is moved as Jerusalem formerly was at the arrival of the Three Wise Men. It is in a transport of religious awe." In the aftermath, 34 persons signed affidavits swearing to Ann Mattingly's otherwise unexplainable recovery. These included the cream of Washington society, many of them non–Catholics: White House architect James Hoban; Supreme Court Chief Justice John Marshall; and D.C.'s first elected Mayor, Samuel Smallwood; as well as Father Dubuisson and Father Kohlmann. Some local Protestants reportedly were so impressed by the miracle they converted to the "One True Holy Catholic and Apostolic Church."

Dampening the Spirits

Most American Protestants of the early 19th century, however, were very skeptical of the supernatural. Protestant publications cited the "Mattingly miracle" as proof that Catholics were superstitious and unscientific. A New York newspaper sarcastically referred to the matter as "the days of St. Patrick and the snakes returned." The reaction of the

Catholic hierarchy was surprisingly subdued. This reflected a fear the evident miracle would spark a reaction against Catholics, a decided minority in the nation. Church leaders told Kohlmann to temper his enthusiasm. Baltimore's bishop ordered Dubuisson to "moderate the popular emotion." One worried priest gave thanks that "such miracles didn't happen more often."

Catholic thinkers knew the United States were then going through a period of fervent nationalism that might make a "foreign" faith like Catholicism suspect. In 1824 President James Monroe and Secretary of State John Quincy Adams issued the Monroe Doctrine, proclaiming that America would no longer tolerate interference from foreign powers. Along with imperial Britain, France, and Spain, that presumably meant the Vatican as well as the priest Hohenlohe, a prince of Central Europe's Holy Roman Empire. Further, unease among native-born Americans was rising over growing Irish-Catholic immigration, which would peak during Ireland's Potato Famine of the late 1840s. This, coupled with an early wave of German migrants that included many Catholics, would ignite the nativist Know Nothing political party of the 1850s, and spark riots between nativists and the Irish in Washington and calls for a blanket ban on Catholic immigration.

In time, the hubbub over Ann Mattingly's miraculous recovery subsided. Ann lived until 1854, surviving a second serious illness affecting one of her feet. She swiftly recovered after another round of prayer.

Oddly, the story of Ann's cheating death might not have occurred as it has been told for almost two centuries. Author Nancy Lusignan Schultz recently found evidence that Prince Hohenlowe might not, in fact, have prayed for Ann. Although he issued general prayers for the sick that March 10, 1824, he probably had not been informed of Ann's particular plight. He had been traveling, and the letter Kohlmann sent him about Ann probably did not reach him in time. So perhaps it was only the prayers of Fathers Kohlmann and Dubuisson, and not Hohenlowe, that saved Ann. Or maybe it was a very unusual coincidence, or the intangible love and support the woman had long received from her many friends, relatives, priests, and fellow parishioners. In any event, each year leading up to March 10, the District's St. Patrick's Church commemorates Ann's miraculous recovery in the miracle manse with nine days of a prayerful novena.

Sources

Buckley, Cornelius Michael. *Stephen Larigaudelle Dubuisson, S.J. (1786–1864), and the Reform of the American Jesuits.* Lanham, MD: University Press of America, 2013.

Demers, Daniel. "Ann Mattingly: Hard and Rough as a Nutmeg Grater." *Catholic Standard*, October 6, 2017. http://www.catholicstand.com/rough-nutmeg-grater/.

Schultz, Nancy Lusignan. *Mrs. Mattingly's Miracle: The Prince, the Widow, and the Cure That Shocked Washington City.* New Haven: Yale University Press, 2011.

_____. "Prince Hohenlohe's Miraculous Meddlings: Transatlantic Intercessions in Washington, D.C., and Charlestown, Massachusetts, 1824–1827." *U.S. Catholic Historian* 20, no. 1 (Winter 2002). History and Gender.

Winters, Michael Sean. "The Beltway Healing." *New Republic*, June 28, 2011. https://newrepublic.com/article/86080/mrs-mattingly-miracle-nancy-schultz.

32

The Lost Barracks of the National Mall

Constitution Avenue, from the Washington Monument and West Toward the Vietnam Veterans Memorial

The northern edge of the National Mall, starting from 15th Street and Constitution Avenue, across from the Ellipse just south of the White House, makes for a scenic and informative walk. Past the 555-foot-high white obelisk of the Washington Monument, finished in 1888, there is the mysterious Jefferson Stone of 1804, planted to mark a planned new Prime Meridian of North America. Next is the Toll Keeper's House of the old Washington City Canal, a ditch buried under Constitution Avenue in the 1870s. Near it was the old White House wharf, from which workers unloaded goods from barges on the canal for the Executive Mansion. A few hundred yards to the south is the World War II Memorial. Then onward to the left is the long, evocative Reflecting Pool, leading on the right to the sublimely simple Vietnam Veterans Memorial. On the left are the Korean War Memorial's wary, sculptured soldiers on patrol. At the terminus is the grand Lincoln Memorial, bustling with patriotic pilgrims day and night.

Keeping to a Wartime Tempo

Yet, today the area is strikingly different from the way it was for most of the 20th century. From 1918, during the First World War, and all the way to 1970, it was occupied by a massive complex of three-and-four-story concrete and wooden barracks, home to tens of thousands of military and civilian employees.

In April 1917, when the United States entered the First World War, the city of Washington was a sleepy Southern city of 350,000, a city that quickly faced a housing and office crisis for the vast number of officers, civilian workers, and enlisted men and women pouring into D.C. to administer the rapidly expanding Army and Navy. The wartime Assistant Secretary of the Navy was Franklin Delano Roosevelt, later President during the Second World War. Roosevelt, who loved ships and the U.S. Navy, was the de facto Secretary of the Navy. Because the actual Secretary, Josephus Daniels, had little interest in the operations of the service (he was more interested in racial segregation), this gave FDR, a rising young politico from New York, much clout. He proposed to President Woodrow Wilson the construction of temporary barracks south of the War, Navy, State Department Building, today's Eisenhower Executive Office Building, to house a big chunk of the military's burgeoning workforce.

Woodrow Wilson asked Franklin Roosevelt exactly where he would put the barracks. Roosevelt said the Ellipse, then as now the large, oval-like park just below the White House South Lawn. Wilson queried, "Why do you select that site?" FDR replied, "Mr. President, because it would be so unsightly right here [next to] the White House, it just would have to be taken down at the end of the war." "Well," Wilson responded, "I don't think I could stand all that hammering and sawing right under my front windows. Put it down there, and we will get rid of it." Thus the barracks, dubbed the Navy Building, for FDR's Navy office workers, and the somewhat confusingly named Munitions Buildings, for the Army workers, was placed on the Mall. (No munitions were actually manufactured there, given the danger of making bombs in such a crowded space.)

Under wartime pressure, construction took a little less than half a year. Offices three stories in height stretched for 600 yards, from 17th Street all the way to 21st Street along B Street, as Constitution Avenue was then termed. The structures did not go all the way to the Lincoln Memorial, which was then a swamp next to a brewery (the Memorial was finished in 1922 after the war). The roughly 1,600,000 square feet of space hosted a mammoth workforce of about 14,000. As the buildings were supposed to be temporary, they were at first made of wood. But steel and lots of concrete were added to make them stable and fire-resistant.

The war ended in November 1918, and the "tempos," the temporary buildings, were in theory to come down. Instead they remained as government offices. This enduring, unsightly blot on what was supposed to be, in Pierre L'Enfant's design for the District, an enchanting national park, caused heartburn for Roosevelt. "I didn't think I would ever be let into the Gates of Heaven," he remarked at the start of the Second World War, "because I had been responsible for desecrating the parks of Washington."

Building Boom Redux

In that second conflict, the housing demands in the sleepy Southern city were even more dire than in the first. The Willard Hotel, for instance, limited the number of days guests could stay to force a high turnover and open up space for military officers. All about the city, residents of small apartments took in roommates. Especially swamped was the War, Navy, and State Department: three big agencies in one building, a large edifice yet tiny compared to today's Pentagon, and utterly inadequate for the personnel demands of a global conflict. Moreover, for years the State Department had been taking over most of its space, pushing out the Army and Navy personnel, who desperately required new workplaces. So the Munitions Building and Navy Building expanded. A fourth floor was dropped on top of the original three levels of the barracks. New tempos were built on the south side of the Reflecting Pool. Three small bridges were installed to let workers easily cross over its water. The Washington Monument grounds itself was studded with tempos made of beaverboard, not concrete and metal. From an airplane or the Monument's observation deck, they looked like keyboards with missing keys or a giant computer circuit board of a future era.

The temporary barracks near the Washington Monument in 1944. From above, the offices resembled giant keyboards (Naval Historical Center Photographic Section # 80-G-K-14433, Navy Department, Washington, D.C.).

The most important wartime work in the barracks might have been the Navy cryptanalysts of Operation Magic. From offices on the Mall, among other sites, they broke the secret codes of Imperial Japan's Foreign Office. This gave the U.S. critical intelligence for the pivotal maritime Battle of Midway. It informed a U.S. Army Air Force mission to shoot down the mastermind of the Pearl Harbor attack, Admiral Isoroku Yamamoto. Some code breakers worked in a "penthouse," a concrete box on the Navy Building's roof, where they practiced stealing their own radio signals so they could learn how to snatch the secret missives of a foe. Tempos were placed in other parts of town. Two were plopped diagonally across the Mall, close to today's Air and Space Museum. There were 54 temporary structures in all.

The War Department built a big, permanent complex up 23rd Street from the Lincoln Memorial, but the building didn't have enough office space. So, the Army handed it over to the State Department. Nicknamed Foggy Bottom, possibly after the area's swampy mists, it remains today the State Department headquarters. The War Department would get bigger digs. President Roosevelt ordered a logistical genius, General Leslie Groves, to build the world's largest office building right across the Potomac in Arlington, Virginia. Remarkably, though a Washington, D.C., government project, Groves built it ahead of schedule and under budget. In 1941 Secretary of War Henry Stimson, and over the next two years most of the Army barracks personnel, moved to the new Pentagon. This left the Mall a largely naval preserve—rather fitting given its origins as a tidal lake.

When the war—and its personnel demands and housing crunch—ended in 1945, the barracks stayed, despite grumbles and complaints about the ugliness. By then the tempos contrasted poorly with the improvements made in the area since their construction, namely the Lincoln Memorial, the stately Interior Department Building, and the Federal Triangle complex on the other side of the Ellipse.

In the postwar era, the Navy's "temporary" denizens were joined by employees from the State Department, the new U.S. Air Force, and the Veterans Administration. In the middle of the Eisenhower Administration, the number of barracks employees had swelled to over 65,000, more than in the war and making up over a third of all the federal workers in D.C.

Denouement and Deconstruction

Finally, the administration of President John Kennedy spun plans to take down some of the tempos. Demolition began in the administration of his successor, Lyndon Johnson. But the real barracks buster was Richard Nixon, like Kennedy and Johnson a wartime Navy officer taking aim at the Navy work spaces. After his inauguration in 1969, Nixon announced to great skepticism that the tempos would soon be kaput. Although not always one to keep his word, "Tricky Dicky" was in this case "Honest Abe." People began to suspect the President was serious when they saw moving vans taking files and office equipment out of the buildings, even more so when the last 3,000 employees departed. But they really believed it when they noticed scores of other longtime residents departing the barracks—not workers but rats, the masses of rodents that had found the crumbling, dirty structures built atop a marsh an ideal nesting place. Noted an official of the General Services Administration, "They were very old buildings, and they ... were practically impossible to clean." Local wags gibed that the rats left the Mall for newer and better quarters at the lawyer-and-lobbyist complex of K Street. The tempos were finally proven to be temporary. In 1970, when the last one was razed, some Navy brass—musicians, not admirals—gathered near and tooted out "Auld Lang Syne."

Today there is no trace of the once-huge array that sprawled from the Washington Monument to the Vietnam Wall. It takes an effort to imagine the barracks were ever there—with one exception. If you cross into D.C. from Virginia via the 14th Street Bridge, and head toward the U.S. Mint and the Holocaust Museum on the left, you'll pass a nondescript, five-building complex. Many assume it is part of the Bureau of Engraving and Printing, but it's actually something called the Bureau of the Fiscal Service, built in the First World War as the Liberty Loan annex. As in the $21 billion worth of Liberty bonds that financed the war along with steep income taxes. Long since modernized with computers and air-conditioning, it is the lone remaining relic of the National Mall's remarkable Barracks Row.

Sources

Kelly, John. "Answer Man Remembers the 'Temporary' Office Buildings That Once Blighted D.C." *Washington Post*, January 7, 2017. https://www.washingtonpost.com/local/answer-man-remembers-the-temporary-office-buildings-that-once-blighted-dc/2017/01/07/3f97674c-d2ab-11e6-945a-76f69a399dd5_story.html?utm_term=.e4fca99db913.

National Park Service. "'Temporary' War Department Buildings." https://www.nps.gov/articles/temporary-war-department-buildings.htm.

U.S. General Services Administration. "Liberty Loan Building History." 2017. https://www.gsa.gov/real-estate/gsa-properties/visiting-public-buildings/liberty-loan-federal-building/whats-inside/liberty-loan-building-history.

U.S. Navy. Naval History and Heritage Command. "Main Navy and Munitions Buildings." Accessed 2018. https://www.history.navy.mil/our-collections/photography/places/washington-dc/main-navy---munitions-buildings.html.

Wikipedia. "Main Navy and Munitions Buildings." http://en.wikipedia.org/wiki/Main_Navy_and_Munitions_Buildings.

33

George Washington, the Flinty Scot, the Powerful Mayor, and the Children's Angel

17th Street and Constitution Avenue, Site of the Organization of American States Headquarters

The federal agents could hardly believe their own eyes. They had just seven years left to fulfill their directive: Build Washington City from scratch by 1799. But the project was already behind schedule, partly because control over much of the land for the new capital was under dispute. In 1792 the visible evidence of that was clear. The land agents were near the shore of the creek—grandly named Tiber after ancient Rome's river—down the western slope of the hill where the President's House was to be built. But there were wood fences marking the farm and grazing lands of the man who for decades had owned President's House hill and the marshy expanse to its south, today's National Mall. He was irate that the government had yet to pay him for the property, so he had built fences to mark his land and to show his ire. The obstinate fellow could put the entire federal enterprise at risk! President Washington, operating from the temporary capital of Philadelphia, had tried his best. He wrote letters to David Burnes (sometimes spelled as Burns), the Scotsman who had held title to 700 acres of Tidewater lands slated to become the Chief Magistrate's mansion and part of the properties that were to house the Treasury, War, Navy, and State Departments—most of the original agencies of the federal government.

The city planner that Washington had retained, Frenchman Pierre Charles L'Enfant, had crafted a design for a grand new capital. The idea was to buy out the area's property holders, with the further enticement of giving them back about half of the land for use as private lots. With that real estate they could build homes and businesses for the new city and gain rental or sales income. The federal government would get the rest of the turf for government buildings and L'Enfant's planned boulevards, traffic circles, and memorials.

Eminent Domains

Burnes was one of the handful of large landowners whose holdings would make up the District. The others included Daniel Carroll—not the Daniel Carroll who was a major player at the 1787 Constitutional Convention in Philadelphia, which got the ball rolling for the founding of the District, nor his cousin, Charles Carroll of Carrollton, the only Catholic signer of the Declaration of Independence, and not John Carroll, a founder of Georgetown College, now Georgetown University, but John Carroll's nephew, Daniel Carroll of Duddington. Daniel Carroll of Duddington owned the forested knoll that would become Capitol Hill. There were so many Carrolls in old Maryland that an individual Carroll, such as Daniel or Charles, attached his hometown name to his last name, as in Duddington or Carrollton, to distinguish him from his other relations! The Irish-Catholic Carroll clan was a very wealthy Maryland Tidewater family—and prolific. One needed a scorecard to keep track of them.

Another major landholder was Notley Young. He was the brother-in-law of Daniel Carroll, not of Duddington but plain Daniel Carroll of the Constitutional Convention. That Daniel Carroll was one of the three Washington-appointed federal supervisors charged with surveying and laying out the boundaries of the new city, as well as laying down the law on unhappy residents like David Burnes. Another commissioner was David Stuart, a Virginia legislator and the step-father of Martha Washington's son from her first marriage (things seemed pretty incestuous at D.C.'s founding). The third commissioner was Thomas Johnson, Maryland's first Governor and later a U.S. Supreme Court Justice.

Landowner Notley Young owned the land south of Burnes' estates along the Potomac River, near where the Jefferson Memorial is today. There were more incestuous ties: Young's second wife was the daughter of Daniel Carroll, but not Daniel Carroll of Duddington nor plain old Daniel Carroll of the Constitutional Convention but another Carroll clansman: Daniel Carroll of Upper Marlboro, Maryland. He was also known as Daniel Carroll of Rock Creek, the stream that became the new city's biggest park. Clear enough? The estate of Notley Young was a classic Tidewater plantation: a mansion house, cash crops, many slaves, barns and stables, vegetable garden, a river shore, and pasture land. Young agreed to sell his land to plain old Daniel Carroll and his federal agents.

Yet another land magnate was Samuel Davidson, later the builder of the grand Evermay mansion in Georgetown. Davidson bought up 150 acres of land north of President's Hill, in today's downtown D.C. He readily agreed to sell his land to the feds and became a land speculator on the half he got back from them. However, the commissioners threatened Davidson with arrest when he mulled digging an outhouse on soil slated for a city street. Much of his acreage had been owned by the Peerce family, whose family graveyard was on what would become the southwest corner of Lafayette Square, behind today's statue of General Rochambeau. When President John Adams resided at the White House (1799–1801), and during part of President Jefferson's first term, the Peerce cemetery was still there—right in President's Park. This must have seemed an ill omen: the first Presidents residing next to tombstones. In 1804 the family remains were removed to Holmead's Burying Ground, north of today's Dupont Circle.

A Cantankerous Celt

Back to the landowner named Burnes or Burns. President Washington had made an attractive offer for his estates. GW's government offered to buy his river-bottom land at well-above-market prices. The President probably appealed to the patriotism of the man, who was a veteran of the French and Indian War under General Edward Braddock, Washington's British commander at the time, as well as a veteran officer of the American Revolution. But the 53-year-old Burnes behaved like a caricature of a Scotsman. He was a drinker of Scotch, for one thing. Burnes stayed "in a mellowed condition under frequent libations of good Scotch whiskey," according to a history of the region. He was also stubborn, irascible, and penny-pinching (allow the author, who is of partly Celtic ancestry, to indulge in generalizations about Scots). For some time Burnes refused to sell, throwing a wrench into the federal project. One might note that, in addition to his farm work, Burnes was an official for Prince Georges County, Maryland, a lower-income district across the Potomac from D.C. He seemed to embody this local expression: "You can take a man out of Prince Georges County, but you can't take Prince Georges County out of the man."

Yet the cranky Celt had a point. L'Enfant's scheme reserved a great deal of the new city for his broad boulevards and streets. And, according to the terms of the agreements between the Washington Administration and the landowners, the latter got no compensation for farm, forest, or grazing land turned into roads. Pennsylvania Avenue alone, the great conduit to run from the President's House to the Capitol, was laid out at an astonishing width of 400 feet. According to L'Enfant's original plan, the byways would account for fully 59 percent of the city's space. This land grab gave the private owners pause. However, because the administration would pay them a steep premium for the turf not slated for roads—about $65 an acre, or about 1,000 percent over the market value—the landowners still agreed to the sale—except for that stubborn Mr. Burnes.

Washington likely thought of how much easier it might have been if the government had made a capital of an existing city, namely nearby Georgetown. After all, a great swath of soil stretching from today's Arlington, Virginia, and through the center of Georgetown was owned by someone much more reasonable: himself, George Washington. The President might have thought of his colleague who had authored the Constitution, James Madison, and of his Secretary of State, Thomas Jefferson, and how they had scoped out another site for the capital. The two had hiked up wooded Shuter's Hill, in Washington's homeplace away from Mt. Vernon: Alexandria, Virginia, just eight miles from his estate. Madison and Jefferson briefly considered the hill, today's site of the George Washington Masonic Temple, as the spot to put the Senate and the House of Representatives. Jefferson, an architect himself, was helping to select the designers for the new federal buildings. But in meetings in 1791, at Suter's Tavern in Georgetown, President Washington, L'Enfant, Jefferson, Major Andrew Ellicott of Maryland, and others had decided against placing the capital in the elegant, established cities of Georgetown or Alexandria. Instead, they would plop it on a mosquito-infested flood plain—if they could nail down full ownership of it.

A frustrated Washington, the man of action, decided to act. He arranged a face-to-face meeting with Burnes. It was a disaster. The Scotsman not only turned down Washington's offer of compensation, but he also insulted the President. Referencing Washington's marriage and move up in the world with the wealthy widow Martha Custis, Burnes told him, "I suppose Mr. Washington that you assume people here are going to take every grist from you as poor grain. But what would you have been if you had not married the widow Custis?" No one spoke to Washington like this, and Washington reacted in a way that was totally out of character. The President was known for an iron control of his temper, but he stormed out of the meeting.

From the knoll that was supposed to hold the President's House, the federal land agents would shake their heads. Visible down the slope, like a thumb in their eyes, was Burnes' rude plank-wood cottage. It was located, ironically, just a few hundred yards northwest of today's Washington Monument, the memorial to the man Burnes angered like no one else, except perhaps King George III. After the meeting blowup Washington refused to meet with Burnes again and turned things back over to the federal commissioners.

But even the "obstinate Mr. Burnes," as the President called him, gave in. Sort of. He might have worried the feds would simply take his land in a kind of eminent domain. And his stubbornness had the positive effect for him of raising the government's asking price. He was, in the end, a shrewd Scottish merchant. When he did sell, he pocketed about $14 million in 2018 dollars, making him as wealthy as a Carroll. He kept, and continued to live in, his humble cottage, that thumb-in-the-eye of the government agents.

But President Washington was to hear from Burnes again. Because the government, after taking over Burnes land, was slow in paying him. The funds were supposed to come from the federal government's sale of building lots. However, demand for the lands was feeble, and for a time the former owners were left holding the bag. In 1793 the President got this scathing and grammatically suspect letter—and a threatened lawsuit—from the tart Scotsman. It references "Presidents Square," his former property and the site of the White House and Lafayette Square to come:

The humble cottage of David Burnes, who in the 1790s battled President Washington's plans for the new federal city. The lodging stood long enough to witness the completion of the Washington Monument in 1888 (Library of Congress).

33. Washington, the Flinty Scot, the Powerful Mayor, and the Children's Angel

Sir

   I Presume to Address you a second time on a Subject which materially concerns me and my family—I have applied to your Commissioners for redress to no purpose…. [If the commissioners] … had done right in my opinion they would have paid me for the Presidents Square Octr 1st 1791 when they began Occupying the above mentioned Square and I deprived of the use of the Ground. The Sales have taken place pretty generally on my Ground, I therefore expect payment Immediately, for all the appropriated ground, otherwise I must bring Suit against the Commissioners in order to make them do Justice—Mine is a peculiar case and requires Immediate redress—I possess no other Lands than those in the Center of the City All cut up and rendered useless for farming—I hope to be redressed through your interference and Procure from the Commissioners of the Federal City such assistance as the nature of the Original agreement and my exigencies render absolutely requisite. I have the Honour to be with great respect.

   Your Obt & Hble Sert
   David Burnes

In another missive, Burnes was evidently worried about landing in debtor's prison if he wasn't paid. He informed the city commissioners that "my family may starve and my person be imprisoned."

Mr. Burnes had multiple reasons to dislike the commissioners and, in his words, their "cringing meanness." When he tried building a log cabin on property of his within the new city boundaries, he got a thumbs down from the three commissioners, in an enduring style of impersonal bureaucratese. They wrote to Burnes that their "approval is necessary for the erection of any temporary building in the City of Washington. We yesterday saw one carrying on, avowedly under your authority, in which we were not consulted, and which we do not approve of, and to prevent unnecessary expense and trouble to you, we thus notify you of our sentiments."

An Early Power Couple

The fortune in payments that Burnes eventually did receive had an important impact on the city's future. David Burnes passed on in 1799, and when his wife, Anne Fleming, died in 1807 the family had but one heir. That was their only surviving child, a daughter, Marcia (some records list her name as Maria—spellings varied much in the era before spell-check). As such, Marcia, or Maria, became one of the wealthiest and most eligible women in town. Before he passed on Burnes told her, "Marcia, you have been a good daughter; you'll now be the richest girl in America." The vivacious Marcia Burnes had a lot going for her other than money. She was sent to a finishing school in Baltimore

The daughter of a Washington landowner and the wife of a congressman and general, Marcia Van Ness was heralded for her work in helping orphans and the sick (Courtesy Estate of Richard Hampton Jenrette).

where she learned to embroider, dance the minuet, and speak French—all valuable skills for attracting a gentleman.

The popularity of lovely, intelligent women like Marcia Burnes in early D.C. wasn't surprising. The populace consisted of powerful, affluent men residing far from home for their work in Congress or the federal agencies. The town had few if any theaters or other places of entertainment. It was boring, except for the soirees put on by the likes of Marcia. She had her pick of Washington's crème de la crème and settled on a distinguished-looking New York Congressman from a wealthy Dutch family of judges and diplomats: John Peter Van Ness.

Van Ness started a Washington tradition of men from old Dutch New York clans gaining great power in the capital. Examples are Theodore Roosevelt and Franklin Delano Roosevelt. President Jefferson made Van Ness a Major in the Washington, D.C., militia, and Van Ness rose to the rank of Major General. He became head of the city's largest bank, the Bank of the Metropolis, on 15th Street just down from Lafayette Square. He was part of the commission that rebuilt the city after its 1814 destruction by the invading British. A well-connected man of ability and wealth, Van Ness was elected Mayor of Washington in 1830. The Van Ness station of the D.C. Metro rail line is named for him.

His next-door neighbor was Thomas Carbery. Like Van Ness, Carbery became president of the Bank of the Commonwealth, and the Mayor. His own house was one door up 17th Street from the Van Nesses (see Chapter 31, "The Miracle Manse"). He built the "White House wharf" on the old Washington Canal just below his home, from which materials were offloaded to rebuild the White House after its torching during the War of 1812.

Peter and Marcia Van Ness built a grand mansion for themselves in 1816, at the foot of 17th Street and B Street, as Constitution Avenue was then known. Their home was on the site of today's Organization of American States headquarters in the old Pan American Union building, across from the Ellipse and the White House South Lawn. To erect their manse, the Van Nesses brought in Benjamin Latrobe, the "founder of American architecture" and a designer of the Capitol and the Decatur House. Along with the White House and the Decatur House, their home, marked by multiple chimneys and a portico, became a center of social life. Guests included James and Dolley Madison. The Van Ness mansion was adjacent to a pestilent and frequently flooding tidal marsh, today's Tidal Basin. Marcia's undying affection for her persnickety Scottish dad was a reason for its locale. Their estate encompassed the rude hut where Marcia had grown up, the David Burnes cottage the federal agents so despised. The humble 20-foot-by-24-foot dwelling with the stone chimney endured until 1894, by which time the monument to Washington, the frustrated purchaser of Burnes's land, had risen behind it.

Despite their wealth and status, the Van Nesses knew tragedy, as did so many parents in the days before antiseptics and modern obstetrics. In 1822 their only child, Ann Elbertina, wed Arthur Middleton, the South Carolinian son of a Revolutionary War patriot. In 1823, at age 20, Ann died giving birth, the infant dying as well. Tragedy could be widespread. During the War of 1812 the region witnessed battles at Bladensburg, Maryland, and Baltimore and elsewhere in the Tidewater. The war dead yielded many orphans and widows. The public-spirited Marcia Van Ness drew on her family wealth and, with friend Dolley Madison, set up the Washington City Orphan Asylum. Completed in 1828, it was located downtown on H Street between 9th and 10th streets, not far from the later Ford's Theater.

Charles Bulfinch, who designed the Capitol after the British burning, designed the facility. (New Englanders may also know him as the architect of Boston's Faneuil Hall.) Quartered in other locales today, Marcia's Orphan Asylum is now known as the Hillcrest Children and Family Center.

Marcia turned to public service again during the Great Cholera Epidemic of 1832, which had spread to the New World from Asia and Europe. The cholera organism infects the lower intestines and triggers prolonged and painful diarrhea. A victim, unable to hold down food and drink, can die rapidly from dehydration. In France during the outbreak, 13,000 Parisians fell to it. The dread bacterial infection thrived in the first decades of Washington City, which had no water or sewer systems. By 1832, B Street had become the Washington Canal, awash with muddy flood water and sewage. Indeed, two Presidents, William Henry Harrison in 1841 and Zachary Taylor in 1850, died in office due, possibly, to the city's tainted drinking water.

Putting her own life at risk, Marcia worked as a nurse to aid those stricken by the cholera plague. But 40 years before Louis Pasteur's germ theory of disease, no one was sure what caused the ailment. A prevailing view was that drinking too much alcohol brought on the malaise. People observed the incidence of cholera was highest in the poor districts, such as neighborhoods of Irish immigrants, known for a predilection for beer and whiskey. In fact, in 1832, while the epidemic raged, the city banned the sale of liquor. This early Prohibition didn't help Marcia. She succumbed to cholera, at age 50, on September 9, 1832. Due to her charitable work, the city staged its first major public acknowledgment of the life of a woman of distinction (the second was for Dolley Madison, upon her death in 1849). Congress suspended session in Marcia's honor. Poet and sculptor Horatio Greenough lauded Marcia's humility and courage with these words:

> *Mid rank and wealth and worldly pride.*
> *From every snare she turned aside.*
> *She sought the low, the humble shed.*
> *Where gaunt disease and famine tread....*

Marcia's grief-stricken husband did the poet one better. Peter Van Ness hired architect George Hadfield, designer of the Lee family's Arlington House, which has become the centerpiece of Arlington National Cemetery. He also planned the District's original, imposing City Hall, today's D.C. Court of Appeals. For Van Ness' departed spouse, Hadfield constructed a mausoleum in the style of a temple for an ancient Roman goddess. It was located downtown at 9th and G streets, N.W., near Marcia's orphanage. Peter Van Ness passed away in 1846. After his funeral, a throng watched the former Mayor's six white horses carry his coffin off to the mausoleum, here he was buried next to Marcia. Their temple and remains were later moved to Georgetown's Oak Hill Cemetery.

After the deaths of Peter and Marcia Van Ness, assorted people resided in their mansion down from the White House. In the 1860s Thomas Green, a Virginia state official, lived there. His two sons fought in the Civil War with the feared Confederate raider of northern Virginia, General John Mosby. Green's cellar, the spacious though clammy Van Ness wine cellar, might have sheltered rebel spies within a few blocks of President Lincoln's house. After Lincoln's assassination in April 1865, Union authorities jailed Mr. Green for suspicion in John Wilkes Booth's plot. He was placed without formal charges in the Old Capitol

Prison, on the grounds of today's Supreme Court, the same jail that housed the captured General Mosby. Green was let go after officials found no real evidence linking him to the conspiracy. Thereafter the grand home was variously and prosaically employed as a beer garden, a sports club, and an administrative office for the city's sanitation workers.

With the mansion going to seed by the early 1900s, George Washington University, then called Columbian College, acquired the property. But the school disliked the unhealthy marsh on the other side of Constitution Avenue. However, the State Department found the locale well sited. It was just six blocks down 17th Street from the State Department, then quartered off Lafayette Square. In 1908 State took down the crumbling Van Ness mansion and built the Pan American Union Building in its stead. With its medieval-like statue of Queen Isabella, sponsor of Christopher Columbus, the building has been a kind of homage to U.S.–Latin American relations. It dates from the period the United States was asserting itself in the Caribbean and in Central America, with the acquisition of Puerto Rico from the 1898 Spanish-American War and the start of construction of the Panama Canal in 1903. David Burnes, of the modest wood cottage and the irritating wood fences, might be impressed by it. Perhaps the canny Scotsman would demand a landlord's rent.

Sources

Arnebeck, Bob. "Samuel Davidson for Sale." *DCSwamp*, March 21, 2011. http://dcswamp.blogspot.com/2011/03/samuel-davidson-for-sale.html.

Boese, Kent. "Lost Washington: The Van Ness House." *Greater Greater Washington*, August 11, 2009. https://ggwash.org/view/2564/lost-washington-the-van-ness-house.

Columbia Historical Society, Washington, D.C. Records 22, p. 129 ff.

Malesky, Robert. "Local Lore: The Bodies in the Intersection." *Bygone Brookland*, April 13, 2016. http://bygonebrookland.com/local-lore-the-bodies-in.html.

National Archives. "To George Washington from David Burnes, 12 February 1793." *Founders*. https://founders.archives.gov/documents/Washington/05-12-02-0087.

Swain, Claudia. "The First Leading Lady of Washington: Marcia Van Ness." WETA, May 6, 2016.

34

The Near Drowning of the President in the Potomac

Just up from 15th Street and Constitution Avenue, East of the White House South Lawn and the Ellipse

On the early morning of June 13, 1825, John Quincy Adams, the sixth President of the United States, began a journey that nearly ended his life. Today's National Mall was then a swampy tidewater, down a steep hill from the White House, that reached south to the Tidal Basin of today and the Potomac River. Flowing steadily from the east, along today's Constitution Avenue, was Tiber Creek. It was formerly called Goose Creek and then whimsically renamed after the Tiber River of ancient Rome in the hope America also might grow into a vast and powerful republic.

Ill Tidings for a President

Below the President's House, the President, his steward, Antoine Michel Giusta, and Adams' son and secretary, John Adams II, gathered for exercise near a dugout canoe. The 57-year-old Chief Executive liked to swim, and he and Giusta planned to paddle out to the far shore of the Potomac, then swim the two miles back. Washington City was then startlingly rural, and outdoor endeavors appealed. The younger Adams warned his famous father, however, that the canoe was less than watertight and unfit for a long journey. The 21 year old decided to swim most of the way, and meet his dad and Giusta in the middle of the river upon their return. Giusta stripped naked, while the President retained his semi-formal clothing for the time being, and off they went. The Chief Executive had no formal guards or protectors. As was the custom of the time, he moved freely about the town and its surroundings by himself or with an aide or two.

Unfortunately, Adams' son was correct. Partway across the Potomac, the canoe began to leak. And as often happens on a warm humid summery day in Washington, a storm kicked up. "[A] breeze from the northwest blew down the river as from the nose of a bellow," Adams would recall. Soon the craft was half full of water. To his chagrin and alarm, the President realized they had brought nothing to use to bail the boat out. With the canoe foundering in the squall, both men jumped in the water. Giusta swam along easily but Adams, weighed down by his heavy clothes, nearly foundered himself. "My principal difficulty," states Adams' diary, "was in the loose sleeves of my shirt, which filled with water and hung like two fifty-six pound weights upon my arms." Only with great difficulty, and with the help of his faithful steward, did the President make it safely to shore. After a while, Adams' son swam up to his father on the riverbank. Not finding the President and Giusta on the river, the young man had swum clear across.

President Adams sent Giusta off to try to find the boat and some of his belongings he'd left on board, and to send a carriage to pick him up. It was mid-morning on a Monday, and he should head back to the office, the President's office, to start the work week. Yet the old canoe was never recovered, and Adams also lost one of his shoes. "By the mercy of God," noted a relieved President, "our lives were spared, and no injury befell our persons." Also spared, perhaps, was the republic, for if Adams had died his Vice President, John C. Calhoun of South Carolina, would have become the Chief Executive. And Calhoun would soon proclaim his doctrine of nullification and secession by the states. The Civil War might have come 35 years sooner, instigated by a President Calhoun.

The boating mishap became the talk of Washington, which was then as now rife with gossip. Adams had nearly become the first President to die in office. (That sad honor belongs to William Henry Harrison, who died in 1841 after one month as President.) Adams and his aides had already been snickered at for swimming in the nude.

A Potomac River Press Conference

According to some sources, this was not the only time Adams' affection for swimming, along with his related eccentricity of doing so naked, led to an embarrassing event. Before his watery exercise, President Adams was known to take off all his clothes and place them on a bank of the Potomac. An enterprising woman reporter, Anne Newport Royall, decided to use this unusual habit to her professional advantage. One of the first female journalists in America, Anne Royall had requested an interview with Adams. It would be the first time a woman had ever interviewed a President. However, Adams' staff had turned her down. But Royall was not one to give up easily. Early one morning, after the President had stripped down and gone into the river, Royall came along, anxious for an interview with the Chief Executive. She thought of an innovative way of bringing this about. She sat down on his clothes.

Adams returned from his swim, was stunned to see his attire occupied, and was shocked when the person doing the occupying, Anne, who had bulldog tenacity, refused to budge from the spot until the President gave her an exclusive interview. So, while standing in waist-deep river water, John Quincy Adams granted the woman a very exclusive interview indeed. It's little wonder that Royall the reporter was later nicknamed the Huntress. When the unique media session was concluded, Anne turned away from the President and his clothes, permitting the Chief Magistrate to dress without prying eyes on him. Anne Royall had successfully pulled off quite the exposé.

Sources

Cain, Áine. "The 6th US President Rose Before Dawn for His Favorite Morning Habit: Skinny-dipping." *Business Insider*, February 21, 2017. https://www.businessinsider.com/john-quincy-adams-skinny-dipping-routine-2017-2.

Jensen, K. Thor. "The First Woman to Interview a President Got Him in the Nude." *Observer*, April 24, 2017. http://

observer.com/2017/04/the-first-woman-to-interview-a-president-got-him-in-the-nude-john-quincy-adams-anne-newport-royall/.

New England Historical Society. "June 13, 1825: President John Quincy Adams Nearly Drowns in Tiber Creek." http://www.newenglandhistoricalsociety.com/june-13–1825-president-john-quincy-adams-nearly-drowns-tiber-creek/.

Seale, William. "An Essay on 'Tiber Creek: The Bathers' by Peter Waddell." https://www.whitehousehistory.org/tiber-creek-the-bathers-john-quincy-adams-takes-a-deadly-chance-1825-by-peter-waddell.

35

The Forgotten Terror Attack

City Hall, 14th Street and Pennsylvania Avenue

Early in the afternoon of Wednesday, March 9, 1977, City Council member and future longtime D.C. Mayor Marion Barry stepped into an elevator at City Hall, two blocks from the White House. Barry was heading up to the City Council offices on the fifth floor. The Mayor's office was there too. A security guard, Mack Wesley Cantrell, rushed into the elevator with Barry. He told the 41-year-old Councilman there was "some trouble" on the fifth floor. At the same time, two young journalists, Maurice Williams of WHUR radio and his friend, a newspaper reporter, stepped into an adjacent elevator with the same destination. They joked about the tedium of the Council meetings they covered.

A Citywide Series of Attacks

The four men walked out onto the fifth floor at about the same time. They saw a man down the hall facing the City Council offices. Suddenly he wheeled and fired shotgun blasts in their direction. Williams, Barry, Cantrell, and a Council aide were all hit. Reporter Williams took a shotgun blast in the chest. His friend crept over and took his pulse and found Williams was dead. The guard, Cantrell, took a bullet to the head, a mortal wound. Councilman Barry was shot in the chest, the bullet coming within an inch of his heart. Grabbing his bleeding rib cage, Barry lurched into a meeting room, saying, "I've been hit. Don't go out in that hall!"

D.C. Mayor Walter Washington heard the shots and shoved a cabinet against his locked office door. The two attackers in the building, Abdul Nuh and Abdul Murikir Do, seized six hostages. They had planned to take Mayor Washington but had blundered into the City Council offices instead. Earlier that day, at 11 a.m., a U-Haul van had pulled into the alley of the headquarters of B'nai Brith International, the Jewish services organization, at 16th Street and Rhode Island Avenue. Seven men armed with shotguns, rifles, machetes, and a crossbow entered its lobby. They seized over 100 hostages and confined them on the eighth floor. The women were ordered, in a nod to Sharia law, to cover up their legs with newsprint. Some of the male captives were beaten.

At 11:30 a.m. three men with knives and shotguns walked into the Islamic Center off Rock Creek, recognizable for its graceful mosque and tall minaret. They demanded to see its head, Dr. Muhammad Abdul Rauf. The director came down to meet them. The terrorists seized him and 10 others, binding them with cords. In all, over 130 hostages were taken.

35. The Forgotten Terror Attack

Four people wound up dead, and 18 others were wounded in the worst terrorist attack in Washington's history. The three linked incidents were the work of 54-year-old Hamaas Abdul Khaalis and his 11 collaborators. Khaalis had a terrible ax to grind.

Born Ernest McGhee, Khaalis had a history of mental illness. A former jazz drummer who'd become a Muslim, he joined the Nation of Islam, run today by Louis Farrakhan. After a falling-out, he criticized its leadership. He formed a splinter group, the Hanafi sect, which follows a form of Sunni Islam. Khaalis resided in D.C.'s Shepherd Park neighborhood in a home donated by basketball star Kareem Abdul Jabbar. In January 1973, Khaalis experienced the worst horror imaginable. At the house, he found the slain bodies of five of his children and his newly born grandson, the latter drowned in a tub. It was the worst mass slaying in the city's history until the Washington Navy Yard killings of 2013. In the related court actions, the surviving family members became the first African Americans to join the Federal Witness Protection Program. Five men linked to the Nation of Islam were arrested, convicted, and given life sentences for the crimes. To Khaalis, that was small justice for his six dead relatives. He swore revenge on what he saw as the enemies of Islam: municipal authorities, Jews, and fellow Muslims. He blamed the Jewish judge in the case for supposed leniency toward the killers. He gathered 11 other like-minded Hanafi men around him and planned and set in motion the three attacks. He personally led the operation at B'nai Brith.

On the day of reckoning, the Metropolitan Police Department rushed to surround the three besieged buildings with hundreds of cops. They were joined by dozens of FBI agents. Sharpshooters stood at the ready. The counterreaction team was led by the D.C. Police Chief, Maurice Cullinane, and Deputy Chief Robert Rabe. They decided the best strategy for saving the hostages was to wait the terrorists out. At the White House, presidential aide Hamilton Jordan informed President Jimmy Carter: "The damnedest thing has just happened." In his Georgia drawl, Carter said of the three attacks, "It's difficult for me to believe they're not connected." The White House formed a crisis team of National Security Advisor Zbigniew Brzezinski, Press Secretary Jody Powell, and other top aides. The group decided they would try to keep the President out of any negotiations with Khaalis. Officials canceled a 21-gun salute to visiting British Minister James Callaghan lest the terrorists at City Hall hear the shots and conclude they were under attack.

The 1970s made up a decade of hostage taking. Palestinian terrorists had killed Israeli hostages at the 1972 Munich Olympics. In 1979 an Iranian mob seized 52 hostages at the U.S. embassy in Tehran. In Washington, after the Hanafi attacks, the Park Service shut down the city's monuments and memorials. Israeli Prime Minister Yitzhak Rabin, fearing he might be the next target, rushed through a scheduled speech, then flew out of town. Tense hours went by. Khaalis released some of the hostages. Firemen rescued Councilman Barry after placing a ladder to the window of the office where he had taken refuge. He was rushed into surgery and rapidly recovered.

At length, Khaalis spoke by phone with a WTOP radio reporter, and stated his demands. "I want the killers of my babies," he told the reporter. "We want them right here." He also demanded the killers of Malcolm X be sent to him and a ban be placed on a movie *Mohammad, Messenger of God*, whose premier was that day. "It's a fairy tale.... It's misrepresenting the Muslim faith," said Khaalis. Further, Khaalis demanded that heavyweight boxing champ Muhammad Ali meet him. He also wanted back the $750 he was fined for interrupting court proceedings during the trial of his family's killers. "You killed my babies and shot my women!" he had cried in the court.

Ambassadors from three mostly Muslim countries—Egypt, Pakistan, and Iran, the latter still ruled by its Shah—got involved. They were Ashraf Ghorbal of Egypt, Sahabzada Yaqub-Khan of Pakistan, and Ardeshir Zahedi of Iran, the last having rushed to the crisis from Europe on the Concorde jetliner. The three spoke to Khaalis by phone. They heard him attack the Egyptian envoy for his country's willingness to make peace with Israel. During their heated discussions, Khaalis and the ambassadors traded dueling verses from the Koran. "Our task was to establish rapport with him," said Ghorbal. "To persuade him to release the hostages as a merciful action and to play to his religious sentiments to that end." The police officials also spent long hours talking and negotiating with Khaalis. "You just keep talking," later commented Police Chief Cullinane. "You keep waiting them out."

A Disaster Defused

The climax came at a showdown on Thursday. In the late afternoon Khaalis agreed to meet with the three ambassadors, the Police Chief, and the Deputy Police Chief at the B'nai Brith headquarters. All agreed to go to the meeting unarmed. In the building's lobby, Khaalis politely greeted the envoys and nodded at the police officials. The six men sat down and talked for three hours. As the negotiations seemed to be going well, Egypt's Ghorbal decided to ask for a concession. Could Khaalis release, say, 30 hostages as gesture of good will? His response—"Why don't I release them all?"—stunned his interlocutors.

Deputy Police Chief Rabe urged Khaalis and his men to give up their weapons. Khaalis agreed provided he was permitted to leave on his own recognizance, without bail, and then show up at court himself. The deadlock was broken. City and federal officials scrambled to waive the normal procedures requiring bail for a violent offender. D.C. Superior Court Judge Harold Greene rushed into the city to work out the terms. He arraigned Khaalis and told him he couldn't leave D.C. and had to show up for his hearing. Khaalis made phone calls to his other two groups of armed men. After 40 nerve-wrecking hours, the Hanafi Siege was ending. The hostage takers at B'nai Brith suddenly left the building without speaking to the hostages and were taken into custody. At the Islamic Center, Khaalis' men gave themselves up. At City Hall the two terrorists met two police officials and placed a sword, a machete, and a shotgun on the ground. They put their hands up and were taken out of the building. The following day Khaalis' men went to court. Bail was set at $50,000 or more for each, according to *Newsweek*.

"We have discovered a new syndrome," Mayor Washington later remarked. "It's a terror syndrome." Indeed, the Hanafi incident seemed to presage 9/11, when the Pentagon and Washington became the target of two jetliners hijacked by Al Qaeda terrorists. Khaalis was arraigned, tried, and sentenced to between 41 and 123 years for conspiracy and armed kidnapping. He died in a federal prison in 2003. The others in his Hanafi gang got stiff jail sentences. Marion Barry fully recovered and went on to be Mayor for 16 years. He also drew nationwide publicity himself in 1990 during an FBI and D.C. police sting that caught him smoking cocaine with an ex-girlfriend and FBI informant. Mayor Barry passed away

35. The Forgotten Terror Attack

The 1977 Hanafi terror attack on City Hall and other District buildings led to four deaths and the wounding of then-Councilman and future Mayor Marion Barry. Barry died in 2014, and was laid to rest in Congressional Cemetery (Wikimedia Commons, photograph by Lorie Shaull, 2016).

in 2014 and is buried in Congressional Cemetery. In 2018 a bronze statue of him was unveiled outside the City Hall where he'd almost lost his life.

In 2007, 30 years after the Hanafi attack, Barry commented, "It's been a long time, but some things you never forget."

Sources

Davis, Aaron C. "The Day Terrorists Took D.C. Hostage." *Washington Post*, March 10, 2017. https://www.washingtonpost.com/local/dc-politics/the-day-muslim-terrorists-took-dc-hostage—and-there-was-a-happy-ending/2017/03/10/e7cf4918–0517–11e7-ad5b-d22680e18d10_story.html?utm_term=.7389a5fb93e2.

"Muslim Terrorists Took 134 Hostages in the Name of Allah in a 1977 Guerrilla Raid." *Newsweek*, March 21, 1977. Archives. https://www.newsweek.com/muslim-terrorists-took-134-hostages-645620.

Zeman, William F. "Today in D.C. History: Hanafi Hostage Stand-Off Continues into 2nd Day." *Washington City Paper*, March 10, 2011. https://www.washingtoncitypaper.com/news/city-desk/blog/13063162/today-in-d-c-history-hanafi-hostage-stand-off-continues-into-2nd-day.

36

A President's Brush with Death After a Deadly Navy Accident

Pennsylvania Avenue and 14th Street, Northeast Corner of Today's Willard Hotel

The Chief Executive was threatened with death when his horses raged out of control along Pennsylvania Avenue, that grim Saturday in early March of 1844. The Treasury Building ahead seemed to swell in size as his carriage careened toward it. In vain, the driver for President John Tyler tried to get the team of horses under control, but they sprinted on through crowded streets. The President's son, John Tyler, Jr., desperately grabbed the reins. The horses kept galloping. Galabrun's European Hotel, the site of today's Willard Hotel, flashed up on the right. Pedestrians scampered out of the way of the onrushing animals. It seemed certain the carriage would crash or overturn, killing or maiming its passengers. Then a man in the street, an African-American fellow experienced with horses, rose to the occasion. Near the 14th Street intersection he sprinted to the carriage, jumped onto the harness, and seized the reins, managing to calm the horses to a steady trot and then a stop.

Spared a tragedy, President Tyler and his entourage continued the short distance to the White House. His lady friend, 23-year-old Julia Gardiner, had been disconsolate even before the equestrian incident, and now she took to her bed to recover.

Although the President was unhurt, he'd been shaken up by another terrifying event in what had been a horrific week. It had all started in such a festive mood, on the past Wednesday, February 28.

A Mighty Ship Emerges

Tyler, Miss Gardiner, her father, much of the Cabinet, and much of the rest of Washington's elite had gathered in mild, late-winter weather at Greenleaf Point. That locale, also called Buzzard Point, is where the Anacostia River meets the Potomac, near today's Fort McNair. There the thin, elegantly dressed President and hundreds of others boarded steam-powered launches and journeyed to Alexandria, Virginia, the port city and then part of the District, seven miles down the Potomac. At its busy docks they transferred to the Navy's new vessel, the USS *Princeton*, the most powerful and the fastest warship in the world. The guests were there to observe the first public demonstration of its unmatched powers.

36. A President's Brush with Death After a Deadly Navy Accident

Whereas vessels up to that time had been steered by rear rudders or steamboat paddles, the 164-foot *Princeton* was the first ship directed by underwater propellers powered by its steam engines. This was a more efficient mechanism, used by ships into the present day, and one that kept the propulsion system underwater and shielded from attack. In initial test voyages, the steam-driven propellers, matched with the ship's full rigging, lent the *Princeton* unparalleled speed.

Even more impressive to the guests on hand were the vessel's twin mammoth guns, the largest wrought-iron ship cannons ever built. They were an astonishing 12-inch caliber, not that far off from the 16-inch guns standard on the battleships of the Second World War. The ship had a regular complement of cannons as well, but it was the two behemoths that caught everyone's eye. One was nicknamed the Peacemaker, either ironically or to intimidate. The other was dubbed the Oregon, a nod to an ongoing border dispute with Britain over the Oregon Territory. Americans seeking to push their Northwest frontier further north clamored, "Fifty-four forty, or fight!"—a reference to the preferred line of latitude to mark the American and British Canadian border.

Earlier that month the ship's designer and captain, Robert Stockton, had briefed congressmen and journalists. He boasted of the mighty guns, stating, "It is believed that the art of gunnery for sea-service has, for the first time, been reduced to something like mathematical certainty." President Tyler was a friend and backer of Stockton, who was a Navy officer and real estate and gold mine speculator. From Princeton, New Jersey, Stockton named the U.S. warship for his hometown after, with Tyler's approval, he paid for much of the cost of its construction. This was a highly unusual

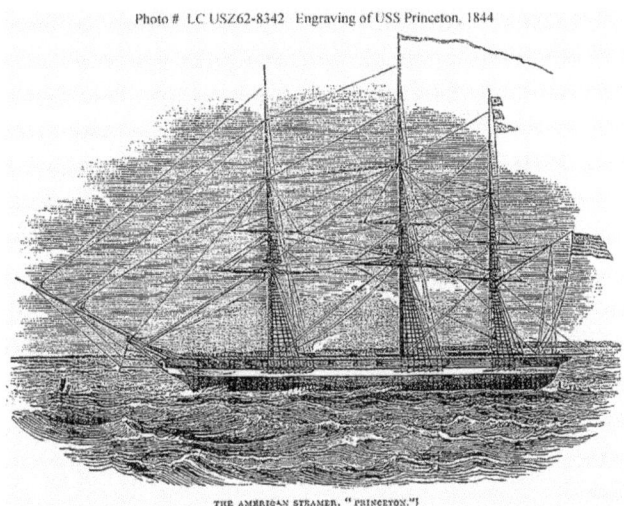

In 1844, the USS *Princeton* was the quickest and most powerful ship on earth, yet it witnessed great tragedy (Library of Congress).

The USS *Princeton*'s Captain, Robert Stockton, ignored the advice of Master Engineer John Ericsson by rushing into test firings of his ship's giant gun (Engraved portrait by H.B. Hall, from a painting on ivory by Newton, London, 1840; published by Derby & Jackson, New York City; U.S. Naval History and Heritage Command Photograph).

arrangement, but when Congress balked at fronting the entire cost of the pricey ship, the wealthy Stockton made up the difference.

Stockton could be impetuous. In the 1810s he became the first U.S. Navy commander to enforce the ban on the African slave trade that President Jefferson had signed into law. During his expedition, Stockton helped establish the country of Liberia for freed slaves—by placing a pistol to the head of a tribal chief until the man agreed to cede territory for the new nation. Robert Stockton had built his powerful vessel with the considerable help of an engineering genius, John Ericsson. An immigrant from Sweden, and an innovator in steam locomotives in England, Ericsson had invented the screw propeller and applied it to the *Princeton*. During the Civil War he would design the famed ironclad ship the USS *Monitor*. Unfortunately, the impatient Ericsson and the hard-driving Stockton did not get along. Before the Alexandria excursion Stockton appears to have downplayed the Swede's role in the *Princeton*'s design, and Ericsson was worried the ship was rushing into a live-fire demonstration with insufficient testing. He did not go on the test run.

With conflict possible with Britain over Oregon, and with Britain and Mexico over the new Republic of Texas, the *Princeton* got caught up in the politics of the day. Ex-President, and then–Congressman John Quincy Adams, glumly claimed the goal of the ship was "to fire … souls with a patriotic ardor for a naval war."

A Perfect Day for a Voyage

Packed with hundreds of guests, the warship cast off in calm, sunny weather from Alexandria's Old Town, then somewhat younger. Guests were dressed to the nines. Recalled Pennsylvania Representative George Sykes, "As the president and members of the Cabinet passed over the side of the ship on a plank … sailors and Marines in the shrouds [sails] pulled off their hats and gave three cheers while the Marine band, a full band of excellent musicians, struck up 'The Star-Spangled Banner' with a very happy effect."

Along with the President and Miss Gardiner and her father David, the high-powered guests included the Secretary of State, Abel Upshur, of Virginia; the new Secretary of the Navy, Thomas Gilmer, also from Virginia; Secretary of War William Wilkins, formerly U.S. Senator from Pennsylvania as well as Minister to Russia; Postmaster General and former Kentucky Governor Charles Wickliffe, with his daughters; Captain Beverley Kennon, chief of the Navy's construction bureau; Marylander Virgil Maxcy, formerly U.S. envoy to Belgium and the Treasury's top lawyer; and powerful Missouri Senator Philip Hart Benton, formerly the brawling foe and eventually bosom friend of retired President Andrew Jackson. On board too, distinctive in her exotic turban, was the ebullient, former First Lady, Dolley Madison, then 75. Dolley was still the social queen of the region, at the social event of the season.

The President and some of his Cabinet men had been working long hours to try to coax Texas into the Union, and they looked forward to a relaxing day on the waves. With Alexandria's wharves behind them, Captain Stockton ordered the first test firing of the Peacemaker cannon. All watched with rapt attention as a fuse was lit. With a crashing roar, the gun let loose its 200-pound projectile and hurled the shell a full two miles downriver. Guests and officers with spy glasses watched it hit the surface of the river and then, like a flat stone skipped across a pond, hurtle hundreds of yards further along the surface before sinking. A raucous cheer went out from the guests onboard.

It was noted that the Peacemaker and Oregon had a maximum range of five miles, the longest of any guns in the world. Such a mighty demonstration deserved another. Captain Stockton gave his assent. The President and his Cabinet Secretaries looked on with Dolley Madison and Julia Gardiner and all the rest. The Peacemaker boomed again. And again a cannonball was hurled several miles down the Potomac in a daunting display of America's new maritime muscle.

The USS *Princeton* reached the turnaround point of its thus far very successful trip: Mt. Vernon, the estate of George Washington. The guests went belowdecks to feast on wine and braised fowl. The ship started to steam back to Alexandria and the launches waiting to whisk the guests back to Greenleaf Point. Some of the passengers, including the President's enslaved valet, Henry Armistead, went back on deck. Captain Stockton stood next to the Peacemaker. Nearby were the Secretaries of State, War, and Navy, as well as Mr. Gardiner, a wealthy, retired lawmaker from New York. Dolley Madison was belowdecks, as was the President and Miss Gardiner.

Some guests wanted a third demonstration, but Stockton answered, "No more guns tonight." Secretary of the Navy Gilmer, with Mt. Vernon in mind, mentioned it might be fitting to fire off another round—in honor of the nation's first Commander-in-Chief. Captain Stockton may have misinterpreted the suggestion as an order. Secretary Wilkins joked, "Though Secretary of War, I do not like this firing, and believe I shall run." He walked to the other end of the ship. For a third time, the fuse was lit.

Horror on the Potomac

President Tyler had begun climbing the gangway from below. He paused for a toast and to listen to a young man singing. Then he and Dolley Madison and Julia Gardiner and everyone belowdecks were shaken by a tremendous roar from above. Then there was silence—then screams of anguish. Rushing above, the President witnessed a vision from the Inferno. The breech of the Peacemaker had split, shooting white-hot shrapnel from its heavy cannonball onto the deck and sails. Onlookers had literally been cut to pieces. Navy Secretary Gilmer and Secretary of State Upshur were dead. So were Mr. Gardiner, with all his limbs torn off, and Captain Kennon and a sailor. The President's valet, Armistead, was fatally wounded. Severed arms and legs hung from the riggings. Attorney Maxcy was killed, his blown-off arm having knocked off a woman's bonnet and spewed blood onto her dress. One woman, unhurt, was flung into the rigging. One of Postmaster General Wickcliffe's daughters was wounded (that same year, Wickcliffe was stabbed by a lunatic on a steamboat, and late in life he was crippled in a carriage accident). Senator Benton had been thrown onto his back unconscious. Others among the ladies on deck wailed uncontrollably.

Captain Stockton lay next to the shattered gun. Powder burns covered his face, and the hair on his head had been blown off. Otherwise, miraculously, he had no serious wounds. In shock, he cried out, "My God! Would that I were dead too!" It was one of the worst peacetime accidents in U.S. naval history and the worst to ever strike a presidential Cabinet. Virginia Senator and writer William Cabell Rives, who was there, commented:

"Never in the mysterious ordinance of God has a day on earth been marked in its progress by such startling and astounding contrasts—opening and advancing with hilarity and joy, mutual congratulation and patriotic pride, and closing in scenes of death, and disaster, of lamentation and unutterable woe."

The wounded and the dead were carried belowdecks and the *Princeton*, part of its bulwark shredded, staggered back to Alexandria. There the President carried a distraught Miss Gardiner down the ship's hurricane ramp to the dock. She later recalled, "I fainted and did not revive until someone was carrying me off the boat and I struggled so that I almost knocked us both off the gangplank. I did not know at the time, but I learned later it was the President whose life I almost consigned to the water." The steam launches took the stunned passengers back to Washington. Word of the tragedy quickly spread throughout the town and the nation.

On the night of the disaster Dolley Madison was met by anxious friends and relatives at her home on Madison Place. Mary Cutts, her niece, remembered the following: "She came in quietly, with her usual grace, spoke scarcely a word—smiled benignly—but those who knew her perceived her faltering voice and inability to stand without support. Of the horrible scene she dared not trust herself to speak, nor did she ever hear it referred to without a shudder."

A shocked President Tyler returned to a White House wrapped in gloom. The bodies of Upshur, Gilmer, Maxcy, Kennon, and Gardiner were laid in state in the East Room. Thousands of citizens paid their respects there. The deceased would receive mahogany coffins for their burials. The slave, Armistead, would be buried separately in a cherrywood casket.

Funerals and Fallout

On Friday, two days after the disaster, President Tyler presided over a day of mourning. Funeral services were held for Gilmer, Upshur, Gardiner, and Kennon at St. John's Church at the northeast end of Lafayette Square. On Saturday morning, as military cannons boomed from outside St. John's, a funeral train of five hearses led by gleaming white horses left a White House draped in black crepe. Hordes of mourners poured into the city to watch the procession. The President, members of Congress, surviving Cabinet members, Supreme Court justices, and other officials rode with the hearses to the Capitol, then to the Washington Navy Yard, and then to the Congressional Burying Ground, today's Congressional Cemetery several miles southeast of the Capitol. After the burials, a preoccupied President Tyler journeyed in his carriage back toward the White House along Pennsylvania Avenue and almost met his own doom from the runaway horses.

Later, Tyler described the incident to Congress as "one of the casualties which, to a greater or lesser degree, attend upon every service, and which are invariably incident to the temporal affairs of mankind." A formal inquiry absolved Stockton, though he was seemingly culpable, of any blame.

Devastated by the sudden loss of her father, Julia Gardiner fell, perhaps, for a father figure. "After I lost my father," she later recalled, "I felt differently towards the President. He seemed to fill the place and to be more agreeable in every way than any younger man

36. A President's Brush with Death After a Deadly Navy Accident

ever was or could be." On June 26, just four months after the ship disaster, 53-year-old President Tyler married 23-year-old Julia Gardiner in New York. They would have seven children, adding to the eight Tyler had fathered with his first wife.

President Tyler had taken office by accident. He had been the Vice President, from the opposing party, of President William Henry Harrison. In 1841, Tyler became Chief Executive after Harrison died in office. After the *Princeton* calamity and the near disaster with his horses, the nickname of "His Accidency" stuck to him. He failed to win renomination for another presidential term. When the Civil War erupted, Tyler, the owner of Sherwood Forest Plantation in southern Virginia—still owned today by his descendants—briefly served as a congressman in the Confederate Congress. He was the only ex-President to hold such a position.

Amid legal wrangling, Captain Stockton prevented Ericsson from obtaining patents or full compensation for his work

The death of her father in a naval disaster directly pushed the youthful Julia Gardiner into the arms of her future husband, President John Tyler (**Library of Congress**).

on the *Princeton*. In time, Ericsson received his due as an engineer without equal. Stockton went on to serve ably in California during the Mexican-American War as head of the Pacific Fleet. (On several occasions he was senior officer to a noted Decatur House resident, Edward Fitzgerald Beale—see Chapter 19, "The King of the Camel Corps"). The town of Stockton, California, is named for him. A naval reformer, Stockton banned the flogging of sailors. He was elected a U.S. Senator from New Jersey.

As for the ill-fated *Princeton*, after extensive service in the Mexican-American War, it was rendered into scrap at the Boston Navy Yard. Except for its Peacemaker, which was salvaged and in time placed on the grounds of the Naval Academy in Annapolis, as a warning perhaps that overweening pride, on the sea or land, leads to dramatic falls. There is another postscript. Although Stockton had run the *Princeton* project, the head of the Navy's Bureau of Construction and Hydrography was a Commodore William Crane. He was the grandson of a Revolutionary War congressman bayonetted to death by Hessian mercenaries. (He was the great-grandfather of Civil War novelist Stephen Crane—noted for *Red Badge of Courage* with its blood-soaked battle scenes.) The *Princeton* affair might have weighed on Commodore Crane, a highly emotional man known for harshness toward his crews. On March 18, 1846, he was found dead in his locked office in the State, War, and Navy Department Building. Despondent for weeks, he had slit his own throat from ear to Adam's apple. He may have been another, if belated, high-profile tragedy associated with the nightmare excursion of the USS *Princeton*.

Sources

Blackman, Ann. *Wild Rose: Rose O'Neale Greenhow, Civil War Spy*. New York: Random House, 2005.

Bytesofhistory. "William Crane." 2015. http://bytesofhistory.org/Cemeteries/DC_Congressional/Obits/C/C_PDF/Crane_William.pdf.

Encyclopedia.com. "John Ericsson." *Dictionary of American History*, 2004.

Heywood, Toussaint. Slaves. "From a Runaway Carriage to a Runaway Slave." *Homestead,* August 3, 2015.

Hollmuller, Anne. "A 'Most Awful and Most Lamentable Catastrophe': The Explosion on the USS *Princeton*." WETA. *Boundary Stones*, April 25, 2018. https://blogs.weta.org/boundarystones/2018/04/25/most-awful-and-most-lamentable-catastrophe-explosion-uss-princeton.

Kelly, John. "From Peacemaker to Widowmaker." *Washington Post*, October 25, 2014. https://www.washingtonpost.com/local/from-peacemaker-to-widowmaker-remembering-the-uss-princeton-disaster/2014/10/25/2587af18-592e-11e4-bd61-346aee66ba29_story.html.

Library of Congress. *National Intelligencer*, March 4, 1844. Article on President Tyler's runaway carriage.

Merry, Robert W. *A Country of Vast Designs: James K. Polk, the Mexican War, and the Conquest of the American Continent*. New York: Simon & Schuster, 2009.

Sioussat, St. George L., ed. "The Accident Aboard the USS *Princeton*, February 28, 1844: A Contemporary Newsletter." *Pennsylvania History* (July 1937).

Walters, Kerry. *Explosion on the Potomac: The 1844 Calamity Aboard the* USS *"Princeton."* Charleston, SC: History Press Library, 2013.

37

The Poetess Behind America's Most Inspiring Song

The Willard Hotel, 1401 Pennsylvania Avenue

There was death and despair in town but also an enduring determination. From the Willard Hotel across from the Treasury Building onlookers could take in a garish advertisement. An undertaker company was hawking its practiced skill at preparing the bodies of dead Union soldiers for shipment to hometown burials. Just four months before, the Union Army had lost the First Battle of Manassas, or Bull Run, located just 36 miles west of Washington. Things hadn't gone well since then. From the hotel entrance, 42-year-old Julia Ward Howe could gaze at soldiers with missing limbs trudging along the grit of a still-unpaved Pennsylvania Avenue.

The Blood of Patriots

Julia Ward Howe and her husband, Samuel Gridley Howe, from Boston, Massachusetts, had patriotism and public service in their veins. Julia, an outspoken abolitionist, was kin to Francis Marion, the "Swamp Fox," whose guerrilla tactics bedeviled the more conventional British forces during the American Revolution (Marion Park southeast of Capitol Hill is named for him). Her financier father had helped found, with Treasury Secretary Albert Gallatin, what became New York University. Julia's father also set up an early society, fueled by Christian concern for alcohol-addicted immigrants, for the prohibition of liquor.

Samuel Howe was the son of a Revolutionary War officer who, with Ben Franklin and a then-patriotic Benedict Arnold, had tried in 1775 to capture Quebec, in British Canada. In his youth, Howe had himself soldiered abroad to liberate Greece from the Ottoman Turks. He was arrested in Berlin for trying to free the Poles from the yoke of the Russian Czar. In 1833 he'd founded the Perkins School for the Blind, with donations from a tradesman in opium and slaves. There Howe sponsored seven-year-old Laura Bridgman, a blind-and-deaf girl who learned to read tactile text a half century before the institution's Anne Sullivan aided Helen Keller.

New England royalty, the Howes decided to journey to Washington to see how the war for Union and abolition was going. President Lincoln welcomed them at the White House. Old Abe seemed mostly exhausted, they thought, failing to mask the war's mounting toll on himself and the nation. One of the President's woes was that he had yet to find a

The Willard Hotel in the decade before writer Julia Ward Howe's stay there during the Civil War (Library of Congress).

"fighting general" to command his army. But he had found a disciplinarian, a role essential in the war's early stage, for molding the raw recruits rushing to the Union banner. This mercurial martinet was General George McClellan of New Jersey. McClellan placed his in-town quarters in Lafayette Square at the Dolley Madison House.

Once, when the President called on him there, McClellan kept his Commander-in-Chief in the parlor waiting, impatiently fingering his stovepipe hat. McClellan had insulting views of his boss. "The President is no more than a well-meaning baboon," he stated, channeling Charles Darwin, whose *Origin of the Species* had been published two years before the Civil War's outbreak. "I went to the White House … where I found the Original Gorilla, about as intelligent as ever. What a specimen," he groused, "to be at the head of our affairs now." Not surprisingly, Lincoln would fire McClellan in 1862. In 1864 McClellan would run for President against Lincoln. But for now, Lincoln welcomed his genius for instilling martial discipline.

On November 18, 1861, Julia Howe and her husband, Samuel, went by carriage the nine miles out to Bailey's Crossroads, today a knot of suburban Virginia highways and high rises and even then a busy crossroads. They were accompanied by a minister of the Unitarian Church, a transcendentalist (think *Walden* by Henry David Thoreau) named the Rev. James Freeman Clarke. At Upton's Hill they witnessed a grand review of troops General McClellan had prepped in march, maneuver, and marksmanship. Then came a report that a large Confederate force was approaching. Around dusk, the troops of "Little Napoleon," as McClellan was dubbed, rushed off for possible battle. Julia and the others headed back to Washington.

During the journey, on a road clogged with soldiers and illuminated by army bonfires, some troopers began singing a folk song turned popular ditty. Its genesis had been with the Massachusetts Second Battalion, with a common soldier there who had the very common name of John Brown. But it was a renowned name from the time of the 1859 raid by abolitionist John Brown on the federal arsenal at Harpers Ferry in today's West Virginia. That assault had been a primer cord for the war unfolding. Brown's fellow soldiers made fun of his name, jokingly wondering if he would free the slaves and sardonically noting the famous John Brown, hanged for his trouble, was now "a-mouldering in the grave." Over time, the soldiers made up lyrics and created the celebrated song "John Brown's Body":

Poetess Julia Ward Howe overcame the objections of her husband to write the enduring anthem "Battle Hymn of the Republic" (National Portrait Gallery, Smithsonian American Art Museum; gift of Maud Howe Elliott to the Smithsonian Institution; portrait by John Elliott, finished by William Henry Cotton—begun c. 1910, finished c. 1925).

> John Brown's body lies a-mouldering in the grave,
> His soul's marching on....
> He's gone to be a soldier in the army of the Lord,
> His soul's marching on....

The melody originally came from a church revival song, "Say Brothers." The new tune became an informal anthem for Union soldiers. Julia listened intently to the troopers singing it. A woman of many talents, she was a published author and a trained singer as well. And she was not shy. Joining in with the men, her fine soprano trilled a high harmony for the song. "Good for you!" the troopers shouted with delight. Reverend Clarke suggested to Julia the tune would be even better if she outfitted it with refined lyrics. After a long and wearying trip, she got back to the Willard Hotel and slept soundly that night.

The Genesis of a Stirring Song

Before sunrise, Julia awakened. She recalled, "I awoke in the gray of the morning twilight; and as I lay waiting for the dawn, the long lines of the desired poem began to twine themselves in my mind. Having thought out all the stanzas, I said to myself, 'I must get up and write these verses down, lest I fall asleep again and forget them.'" She grasped the stump of a pencil and wrote quickly, barely seeing the words. Then she set the scrawled text to the tune of "John Brown's Body." Her poem was about the Union Army and the reasons why it fought. Reflecting the Calvinist upbringing her father had given her, and the King James Bible in which she was steeped, she imbued the lyrics with startling religious imagery:

> Mine eyes have seen the glory of the coming of the Lord;
> He is trampling out the vintage where the grapes of wrath are stored;
> He hath loosed the fateful lightning of His terrible swift sword:
> His truth is marching on.

The first stanza alone coined two phrases that would become famous: "the grapes of wrath," which John Steinbeck would take for the title of his novel on the Great Depression exodus of impoverished Okies to California vineyards, and "terrible swift sword," the Biblical title of Bruce Catton's classic centennial study of the Civil War (and today the name of many video and board games with military themes). The chorus was indelibly catchy, its first three lines matching the old Roman word glory with the Hebrew phrase, Praise ye, Lord:

> Glory, Glory, hallelujah!
> Glory, glory, hallelujah!
> Glory, glory, hallelujah!
> His truth is marching on....

In the dimness of her hotel suite, Julia went on. Daringly, she placed Jesus Christ within the Union encampments:

> I have seen Him in the watch-fires of a hundred circling camps,
> They have builded Him an altar in the evening dews and damps;
> I can read His righteous sentence by the dim and flaring lamps:
> His day is marching on.
> Glory, glory, hallelujah!
> Glory, glory, hallelujah!
> Glory, glory, hallelujah!
> His day is marching on.

The lyrics streamed on like a vision from Heaven. With a graceful but strong cadence that quickened at the end of each line, echoing the beat of drums for soldiers on the march, their pace fastest just before entering battle:

> I have read a fiery gospel writ in burnished rows of steel:
> As ye deal with my contemners, so with you my grace shall deal;
> Let the Hero, born of woman, crush the serpent with his heel,
> Since God is marching on....

To Julia Howe, the war was righteous. First crush the serpent of sedition and then its wicked proponents, destined to fall before the reckoning of Judgement Day:

> He has sounded forth the trumpet that shall never call retreat;
> He is sifting out the hearts of men before His judgment-seat;
> Oh, be swift, my soul, to answer Him! Be jubilant, my feet!
> Our God is marching on....

In the final stanza, Julia Howe made an astonishing and lovely analogy between the Christ sacrifice to free men from sin to the sacrifice of the Union dead to end slavery:

> In the beauty of the lilies Christ was born across the sea,
> With a glory in His bosom that transfigures you and me.
> As He died to make men holy, let us live to make men free,
> While God is marching on....

Julia Ward Howe sent the lyrics to the editor of Boston's *Atlantic Monthly*. Her note to him asked, "Do you want this?" He did (the magazine paid her $5). Published the following February, the "Battle Hymn of the Republic" became a sensation, as popular with Northern troops as "Dixie" was with Southern—and Northern—troopers.

A House Divided

With her literary talent, Julia Ward Howe helped inspire the Union Army. But long before, she was fighting her own personal civil war—with her husband. For Samuel Howe forbade his wife, and mother to their six children, to publish her own work. His suppression of her writing skill caused painful loneliness. In a note to herself, Julia stated, "I am forced to make to myself an imaginary public. I have seen and heard only myself, talked with myself, eaten and drunk with myself ... and condoled with myself that I was about to be left to myself for another day. Oh cursed self. How I hate the very sight of you!" Yet, given her prowess and passion for words written or sung, her husband's edict was like trying to dam a river on porous soil. The fertile stream merely goes underground, to emerge in another place.

Julia went ahead and published reviews of the German Romantic poets Schiller and Goethe and secretly published a collection of her own poems. For the latter, her husband, appearing as a character who tries to stifle a lady's talents, was sometimes the thinly veiled theme. Samuel found out about his wife the anonymous poet. He was apoplectic. "The book ... was a blow to him," she noted. "He has been in a very dangerous state, I think, very near insanity." Samuel Howe went on, unsuccessfully, to demand a divorce and custody over their children. The marital brawls went on for years. "I make no opposition of will or of temper," Julia wrote her spouse, "because it would be useless, I cannot struggle with so fierce an opponent." At the end of the Civil War, while elated at the Union's triumph, she grieved over their personal disunion: "I have been married twenty two years today. In the course of this time I have never known my husband to approve any act of mine.... Books, poems, plays, everything has been contemptible ... in his eyes." Due to the internecine warfare, they separated for a time before the war. Yet Julia's determination proved too much for Samuel to overcome. By 1868 he had given up opposing his spouse's literary output. By then her reformist impulse had turned to another cause, as she became the head of the American Women Suffrage Association.

Few remember Julia Ward Howe for her work in voting rights or for her other poems and books. But the "Battle Hymn of the Republic" is immortal. When she died in 1910,

49 years after its authorship, it was sung at her funeral. Much later it was sung at Winston Churchill's funeral and the burials of many of the 9/11 victims and for many other occasions since.

It's apt that Julia Ward Howe penned her masterpiece in the Willard Hotel, for the place is linked to her older brother and to the uniquely Washington enterprise for which he and the Willard became famous.

Lobbying's Prime Practitioner

His notoriety came in the Civil War's aftermath and the election as President of the "fighting general" who'd taken McClellan's place. While waiting to assume office at the White House, Ulysses S. Grant lived at the Willard Hotel. After becoming President, he'd still spend time there, relaxing in its sumptuous lobby in an upholstered chair while drawing on a fine cigar. Swarms of people seeking federal favors would approach him. Some of them would become infamous in the scandals of the Grant Administration. Thus, the lobby of the Willard became synonymous with—lobbyists. The term "lobbyist" had been coined before, but with Grant and the Willard it became a household term.

The best-known Washington lobbyist of the postwar Gilded Age of money and politics was Julia Ward Howe's brother: Samuel "Sam" Cutler Ward. For a time, it seemed Sam Ward would never lack money. He helped run a Wall Street bank. In 1838 he wed Emily Astor, the granddaughter of perhaps America's richest man ever, John Jacob Astor, Sr. (Emily Astor's maternal grandfather, by the way, was John Armstrong, the cowardly, court-martialed Secretary of War who fled Washington during the British invasion of 1814). Tragically, Sam Ward's wife Emily and their son died in 1841 while Emily was giving birth to him. Then, in 1847, Sam Ward's financial enterprise went belly-up. So, in 1849, he joined the 49ers chasing California gold and grew rich in San Francisco real estate—until a fire destroyed his holdings. Drifting south into Latin America, he mysteriously rebuilt his wealth and returned to Washington to be the lobbyist for, of all places, Paraguay. Then the Civil War intervened.

Unlike his sister, Sam Ward had Southern sympathies and was for gradual, not immediate, abolition. But like his sister and brother-in-law, he was staunchly pro–Union. So he became a spy of sorts. Traveling through the South, he sent letters containing confidential information on the Confederate military to Secretary of State William Seward. After the war, in the 1870s, he found his calling—as the capital's lobbyist par excellence. He didn't pocket favors; he put on banquets. Representing the triumphant Northern industries—railroads, insurance firms, miners and manufacturers—he held sumptuous dinners where he placed corporate chiefs with the heads of congressional committees on commerce and finance. Once plied with champagne and wine and lobster and steak, the guests would start the deal making.

A sign that Sam Ward didn't do pay for play was that he went broke again. A friend he'd helped succeed back in his 49er days gave him a six-figure gift of appreciation. Sam squandered the funds in a failed New York speculation. To escape his creditors, he had to abandon Washington's opulent lobbies and flee to Europe. In 1884 he died penniless in Italy but not before he invented a cooling libation—of French liqueur and lemon smothered in ice—for high-powered guests sweltering in a Washington summer.

Sources

Evers, Donna. "The Willard: Birthplace of 'Battle Hymn.'" *Georgetowner*, June 18, 2013. https://georgetowner.com/articles/2013/06/18/willard-birthplace-battle-hymn/.

"A Famous Lobbyist Dead; Sam Ward Dies in Italy in His Seventy-First Year. A Man Who Enjoyed Himself in Making Others Happy—Prince of Good Fellows and Friend of Great Men" *New York Times*, May 20, 1884.

HistoryNet.com. "War Watchers at Bull Run During America's Civil War." June 6, 2006. http://www.historynet.com/war-watchers-at-bull-run-during-americas-civil-war.htm

Howe, Julia Ward. *Reminiscences: 1819–1899*. New York: Houghton, Mifflin. 1899.

Jacob, Kathryn Allamong. *King of the Lobby, the Life and Times of Sam Ward*. Baltimore: The Johns Hopkins University Press, 2010.

Kimball, George. "Origin of the John Brown Song." *New England Magazine*, 374. 1890.

Moore, Frank, ed. *The Rebellion Record: A Diary of American Events, Volume 3*. New York: G.P. Putnam, 1864.

Ruane, Michael E. "How Julia Ward Howe Wrote 'Battle Hymn of the Republic'—Despite Her Husband." *Washington Post*, November 18, 2011. https://www.washingtonpost.com/local/how-julia-ward-howe-wrote-battle-hymn-of-the-republic—despite-her-husband/2011/11/15/gIQAnQRaYN_story.html.

Showalter, Elaine. *The Civil Wars of Julia Ward Howe*. New York: Simon & Schuster, 2016.

Stauffer, John, and Benjamin Soskis. *Battle Hymn of the Republic: A Biography of the Song That Marches On*. Oxford: Oxford University Press, 2013.

38

Hamilton! The Tour!!
A White House Area Itinerary

The Corner of Pennsylvania Avenue and 15th Street, West Side of 15th Street

The popularity of the Broadway and Kennedy Center musical *Hamilton* has ignited interest in the thrilling life of the Founding Father and Treasury Department founder. It is easy to take an informative tour on the war hero of the American Revolution and "right-hand man" of President Washington's first term from the Treasury Department he brought into being and into adjacent Lafayette Square. Although the Revolution ended seven years before D.C.'s founding in 1790, and Hamilton concluded his command of the Treasury Department just five years after that, there are a surprising number of local sites relating to the colleagues, rivals, and issues of the immigrant orphan turned high-powered New York politician and statesman. A select itinerary for a self-guided Hamilton tour of the White House environs follows (such a tour costs far less than the price of a ticket to the play). Start at the corner of Pennsylvania Avenue and 15th Street.

The Hamilton Statue

The statue stands in front of the main Treasury Building, headquarters of Hamilton's powerful Treasury Department. After experiencing the great difficulties of Washington's revolutionary army in funding soldiers' provisions and providing pay, Hamilton pushed for a stronger federal government with a robust financial system. After the new central-government was set up, he established a U.S. currency based on gold and silver, one that held its original value until the Depression of the 1930s. He divided the dollar into 200 units, half pennies, so that everyone, including the poor, would use it and so increase its circulation.

It is fitting that Mr. Hamilton's image is not far from the statue of General John J. Pershing, just to the east off Pennsylvania Avenue. Pershing was the commander of the American army in France during the First World War. In Paris, Pershing aide Charles Stanton, the nephew of President Lincoln's War Secretary, uttered the famous expression, "Lafayette, we are here!" referencing the French ally and friend of Hamilton from the American Revolution.

The Hotel Washington, 515 15th Street

The Hotel affords a good view across 15th Street of the massive Treasury Building, designed by Robert Mills, also architect of the memorial to Hamilton's boss, the Washington Monument, which is prominently in view on the National Mall to the south. It's a good spot to ruminate over "the room where it happened," in the *Hamilton* play's phrase. "It" was the 1790 New York City dinner between Hamilton, Secretary of State Thomas Jefferson and, perhaps, then-Congressman James Madison, when the location of the permanent U.S. capital was decided. In exchange for agreeing to Hamilton's "debt assumption" plan, whereby the federal government picked up the Revolutionary War debt owed by the states—thus increasing the central government's financial heft—the Virginians Jefferson and Madison (and Washington) got the capital moved to their backyard, namely the Southern Tidewater surrounding the soon-to-be-built city of Washington. That's why this tour of Hamilton is in the District, and not the Big Apple or the other temporary federal capital of Philadelphia.

Metropolitan Square, 15th Street and F Street

This former site of the Bank of the Metropolis was, in the early 1800s, the city's biggest bank, as well as its voting place, and a tavern. (Wags say the combination of voting and a bar is why Washington politics has often been such a muddle.) In August 1814, during the War of 1812, invading British Marines prepared to burn the place, along with ransacking and burning the Treasury and White House. They were met by the bank's washerwoman, Irish immigrant Sarah Sweeney. She implored British Major General Robert Ross to spare the place lest its owner/resident, an elderly woman like herself, she claimed, would be put out on the street. The General chivalrously granted Sweeney's request. The actual owner was a wealthy man, the city Mayor—but the Irish woman's "blarney" saved her workplace (see Chapter 41, "A Humble Cleaning Lady Gulls a Mighty Invader"). It is thus an appropriate place to mull over the issue of immigration, a burning one then as now. Some of Hamilton's supporters, worried about social stability from a big influx of Irish and French migrants, generally favored smaller numbers of immigrants. Some of Hamilton's opponents, like Jefferson and the Clinton family of New York (George and DeWitt, not Bill and Hillary), generally favored larger-scale immigration, in part to shepherd more voters to their side.

New York Mayor DeWitt Clinton came up with a compromise: vet the newcomers in lower Manhattan's Castle Island, the old Dutch fort on the Battery and precursor to Ellis Island out in the harbor. (His Uncle George Clinton—the politician, not the head of Parliament-Funkadelic—was the Vice-Presidential successor to Aaron Burr, Hamilton's killer).

The Treasury Building, Corner of 15th Street and G Street, Treasury Side

A look at the Treasury Building's aircraft-carrier size is afforded here. According to local lore its height results from a controversy over one of Hamilton's creations, the Bank of the United States, a kind of early Federal Reserve. In the 1830s President Andrew Jackson, who was no admirer of Hamilton and advocated states' rights, deemed the bank a font of corruption and shut it down. An irate Congress reacted by censuring Jackson, the only President the legislature has ever formally denounced. A possibly apocryphal story holds that Jackson, during Robert Mills' construction of the Treasury Building, ordered the architect to build it high enough so that whenever the President turned his gaze toward the Capitol he wouldn't be able to see the workplace of his hated congressional foes. In 1913 President Woodrow Wilson revived Hamilton's bank idea, in a different form, as the Federal Reserve. It largely sets the interest rates on your mortgages and certificates of deposit.

Gallatin Statue, Treasury Building's North Side

Many tourists mistake the statue of the fellow in caped, early-Federal garb as Hamilton. It's actually one of his successors, Albert Gallatin, a French-speaking Swiss immigrant who was Treasury Secretary for Hamilton's rivals Presidents Jefferson and Madison. Gallatin was a financial wizard like Hamilton: he was able to cut taxes and federal spending while still financing the 1803 Louisiana Purchase. But his most intriguing role was in 1794, after Treasury Secretary Hamilton put in place the first taxes to fund the new government. Most revenues came from Hamilton's tariff on imports, but other revenue raisers included a very unpopular one that caused thousands of farmers on the frontier, particularly in western Pennsylvania, to revolt. That was the excise on whiskey, the farmer's moonshine. Thus the resulting Whiskey Rebellion (see Chapter 44, "The Financial Wizard Who Helped Stave Off a Civil War"). Federal tax collectors in the region were threatened, even tarred and feathered.

President Washington and his de facto chief-of-staff Hamilton, at the head of over 12,000 federalized militia, rode out toward Pittsburgh to restore order. Rebel leaders were arrested, convicted of treason, and sentenced to be hanged.

Gallatin, then the Congressman for the region, and an anti–Federalist sympathetic to the rebels, got involved. He helped persuade Washington to show magnanimity, and the President pardoned those slated for the gallows. The U.S. thus sidestepped a possible civil conflict during its very first federal administration. Washington directed Hamilton to stop collecting the whiskey impost that had caused so much trouble. It remained uncollected until the War of 1812, when it raised money for the war courtesy of the Treasury Secretary—Albert Gallatin!

This depiction of Alexander Hamilton reveals a tough-minded man of finance and military affairs (Library of Congress).

Freedmen's Bank, Corner of Madison Place and Pennsylvania Avenue, the Southeast Side of the Square

The bank's name refers to the former slaves, the "free men and women of color," of the Civil War era. Thousands of African Americans, many of them former slaves, placed their savings in the Bank that operated here—and lost part or all of their savings when the Bank went under after one of the Grant Administration scandals (see Chapter 45, "The Crooked Bank for the Former Slaves").

This raises the matter of slavery, and where Hamilton stood on it. He gets a more than passing grade. He was a founding member of the New York Manumission Society, which pushed for emancipation (Aaron Burr also belonged). Hamilton's colleague and fellow Federalist, New York Governor John Jay, signed a law that gradually abolished slavery in the Empire State. And Hamilton's close friends John Laurens and the Marquis de Lafayette were abolitionists.

Like most Founding Fathers, however, Hamilton's record wasn't spotless. He was slow to recognize the civil rights of free men and, as a prominent New York attorney, he sometimes represented clients whose businesses profited from the slave plantations of the Caribbean and the American South.

Lafayette Statue, Southwest Corner of the Square

Hamilton and Major General the Marquis de Lafayette—Gilbert du Motier—formed a deep friendship as aides to General Washington. Lafayette was the key man in America's alliance with its crucial Revolutionary War ally of France. After the American Revolution, the Marquis returned to France and, as head of France's National Guard, supported the French Revolution. He would send one of the keys to the infamous Bastille prison—stormed on July 14, 1789, by rebellious Parisians—to President Washington. As the French Revolution turned bloody, however, consigning thousands to the guillotine, Lafayette was branded a counterrevolutionary. He was forced to flee France, even as his wife, Adrienne, was clamped into a Parisian jail to await execution. The U.S. Minister to France, future President James Monroe, a political foe of Hamilton's, and Hamilton's friend Gouvernor Morris, the former U.S. Minister to France, both helped free Adrienne. Lafayette's son, George Washington Lafayette, fled France for America and stayed for a time with Hamilton. In the meantime, the Marquis, after crossing the French border, was arrested and imprisoned by Austrian troops (Austria was then at war with France). Incredibly, Hamilton's sister-in-law, Angelica Schuyler Church, the sister of his wife, Elizabeth Schuyler Hamilton, hatched a daring plot to free Lafayette from jail. Sadly, the scheme failed. However, Hamilton helped support Lafayette's family financially during his time in prison.

Three decades later, in 1824, a 67-year-old Lafayette made a grand "reunion" tour through all of America's 24 states. He began his journey in Hamilton's hometown of New York City, where veterans of the Revolution cried out the names of battles he had fought with Hamilton: "Brandywine!" "Yorktown!" In Washington, D.C., he was feted as a guest of honor by President James Monroe, who renamed the President's Park Lafayette Square. (Interestingly Monroe, for a long time a Hamilton antagonist, came around to his views on a permanent standing military and a powerful Bank of the United States). The Marquis also visited Quincy, Massachusetts, and his old friend and Hamilton's former rival for influence in Washington's Cabinet, the 88-year-old John Adams. He laid the cornerstone for the new Bunker Hill Monument, which commemorated an opening battle of the Revolution. Lafayette took soil from Bunker Hill back to France with him. At his 1834 funeral in Paris his son and George Washington's godson, George Washington Lafayette, poured the soil of the nation he'd help liberate on top of his coffin. The Marquis thus lies in eternal rest beneath the soil of a free people he and Hamilton helped free.

The White House, 1600 Pennsylvania Avenue

It's probable that if the ghost of Hamilton had appeared here in 1804, the year of his death, he would have shuddered. True, he had much to do with creating the strong office of the presidency represented by this place. But in 1804 his chief antagonist, Jefferson, would have occupied the residence. President Jefferson was often visited by another Virginia antagonist, James Madison, then the Secretary of State, who'd accused Hamilton of pretensions to monarchy and military rule. He was also occasionally visited by the Vice President, Aaron Burr, Hamilton's executioner. And then there was the previous, and first, occupant of the White House, John Adams, who angrily dismissed all of Hamilton's supporters from his Cabinet, partly due to their rigid pro–British stance and loyalty to his New York rival. No, unlike most visitors to the Executive Mansion, a ghostly Hamilton, soon after his demise, would not have enjoyed his stay.

Rochambeau Statue, Southwest Corner of the Square

The Marshal Comte (Count) de Rochambeau was commander of the French forces at the key Battle of Yorktown. For much of the Revolution Hamilton, as Washington's aide-de-camp, was a key confidante, writing out the General Washington's orders and helping plot strategy. Yet he was always pestering Washington for a battlefield command as opposed to a staff job. At Yorktown he got his wish. With Lafayette, he led a daring nighttime bayonet attack against British redoubts. Their capture helped seal the fate of General Charles Cornwallis' army, leading to his surrender that shook an empire and turned the world upside down.

Eisenhower Executive Office Building (EEOB), Pennsylvania Avenue and 17th Street

The large ornate edifice, finished in 1888, occupies the locale that from the early 1800s was the main quarters for the War and Navy Departments, and today hosts the National Security Council. Renamed for the Supreme Allied Commander of the Second World War's European Theater, the place serves as a tribute of sorts for Hamilton, the early apostle of American military strength.

In the early 1800s its predecessor building, on the same site, contained the offices of the U.S. Army and as such was the formal headquarters of the Commander of the U.S. Army, General James Wilkinson. Wilkinson was a senior member of the conspiracy of Aaron Burr, Hamilton's killer, to set up his own nation in Mexico and the West of the United States. This "artist in treason" was also a paid secret agent for the Spanish Empire.

The Winder Building, 600 17th Street

This elegant structure, with its New Orleans–style wrought-iron balcony, was constructed in 1848 by a prominent Maryland merchant. It provided space for military officers administering the Mexican-American War. Today it hosts the U.S. Trade Representative, an official responsible for trade negotiations with foreign nations. The position took on much significance with the Trump Administration given its emphasis on tariffs as an instrument of pressure vis-à-vis China, the European Union, and others.

Hamilton was the original proponent of an excise tax on foreign imports, both to fund the new federal government and to nurture and protect nascent American industries from foreign competition. The Treasury Secretary also called for subsidies to American industries. In Hamilton's time, critics said the tariffs hurt the U.S. by raising prices on businesses and on the purchasers of goods. Over two centuries later, the American people are still having the same debate.

The Blair-Lee House, 1651–1653 Pennsylvania Avenue

This spacious townhouse, now the residence of foreign dignitaries visiting the President, is where Abraham Lincoln, in the Civil War's early days, offered a high command in the Union Army to future Confederate General Robert E. Lee (see Chapter 25, "Lincoln Makes Lee an Offer He Could Refuse").

It raises a "what if" of history: If Hamilton had lived during that period, which side would he have taken, North or South? The answer seems clear that the New Yorker who had done much to bolster Northern industry and to craft a strong central government and who helped found an anti-slavery society would have come down firmly on the side of the Union and abolition. Supporting evidence of this is that several of Hamilton's grandsons were Union Army officers during the Civil War.

Another "what if" is whether Hamilton would have supported the War of 1812, the conflict that resulted in the burning of the White House, which was located just down the Avenue. Hamilton died eight years before its outbreak. Most of his Federalist Party allies opposed the war, in large part because the conflict disrupted the trade relations between New York and New England merchants with Britain, their main trading partner. It was partly for this reason that Hamilton had persuaded President Washington to take a mostly pro–British, anti–French, stance during his administration. During the 1812 war some Federalists at a Hartford, Connecticut, assembly even discussed secession—of New England from the Union! Yet indications of how Hamilton would have reacted to this event comes from his sons. The trio of them in the federal army continued to serve against Britain during the war. It's likely Hamilton would have opposed the War of 1812, but would have remained loyal to the still-new government and military he'd striven so hard to create. (Hamilton had eight children, all of whom reached adulthood. It might be said that he, and not George Washington, as Washington was often called, was the true "Father of His Country"!)

712 Jackson Place

In 1859 this stately residence was the home of Congressman Dan Sickles and his passionate wife, Teresa. When Sickles, a notorious womanizer, found that Teresa was conducting her own affair—with District Attorney Philip Barton Key, the son of Francis Scott Key—he lost control. Spotting Key in the Square, he bounded down the steps of his townhouse with three loaded pistols and shot his amorous rival dead.

Since its creation, the federal government has seen sexual misbehavior by powerful men. Even Hamilton—although seemingly in an ideal marriage with the spirited, educated Elizabeth "Eliza" Schuyler Hamilton of wealthy old Dutch New York lineage—was seduced into an affair. With blonde bombshell Maria Reynolds (portrayed in *Hamilton* by a beguiling African-American actress, Jasmine Cephas Jones). Maria and her husband, James, a counterfeiter, blackmailed the Treasury Secretary for $1,300, a whopping sum in the 1790s. After the matter ended, word leaked out. Political foes such as Monroe confronted Hamilton on suspicion he siphoned off Treasury funds as hush money. To clear his name, Hamilton published a hundred-page document that admitted fault and contained the "love letters" between him and Mrs. Reynolds. Later, Monroe traded insults with Hamilton over French policy, and the two men agreed to a duel—"I am ready get your pistols"—wrote the future President to Hamilton. The duel was on until Monroe was dissuaded from the gunfight—by Aaron Burr! Mrs. Hamilton, angered at her public humiliation by the extramarital affair, left her husband for a time to live with her Schuyler family. A strong and forgiving woman, she eventually reconciled with him. After Hamilton's death, she moved to Washington and became the chief proponent of his legacy, ensuring publication of his official correspondence and his biography.

748 Jackson Place, the Decatur House

On March 22, 1820, Navy hero Commodore Stephen Decatur, after being fatally wounded in a duel with a fellow Commodore, expired in agony in the first-floor living room of his house (see Chapter 17, "The Violent End of America's Bravest Sailor"). Duels were common in the early Federal period. President Andrew Jackson, who shut down the Hamilton-inspired Second Bank of the United States, took part in over 100 "affairs of honor," usually as a "second," or helper, of a duelist. Secretary of State Henry Clay, who also resided at the Decatur House—and who advocated a Hamilton-like "American System" of tariffs and road building—had a bloodless duel with eccentric Virginia Representative John Randolph. Hamilton himself took part in over 10 duels, and his eldest son, Philip, was killed in 1801 in a duel with George Eacker—an ally of Aaron Burr's.

Along with the death of Hamilton's firstborn, Hamilton and Burr had long-standing grievances. Hamilton had denied Burr the presidency in 1800 during a series of deadlocked votes in the Electoral College by throwing his support to his arch-rival, Jefferson, so much did he despise Burr. The anti–Federalist Burr and the Federalist Hamilton, both from New York, vied for political supremacy over the Empire State. Finally, letters of Hamilton's that attacked Vice President Burr in personal terms led the latter to issue a deadly challenge. On July 11, 1804, the two men, their seconds, and others met at Weehawken, New Jersey, below the rugged Palisades overlooking Manhattan. It was the same dueling ground where Philip Hamilton had lost his life.

At a duel it wasn't uncommon for a man to "throw away his fire," to deliberately miss his opponent after proving his courage by showing up. We know that Aaron Burr aimed to shoot to kill Hamilton, because he did. We don't for sure know Hamilton's intent, because despite the crowd that gathered for the fight there were no eyewitnesses. That was because dueling was illegal in New Jersey, and anyone observing a duel could be arrested as an accessory. So as the countdown was given to fire, the spectators turned their backs to Hamilton and Burr. Hamilton was fatally wounded.

Afterwards friends of the deceased returned to Weehawken and inspected the dueling grounds. They found that Hamilton had fired his pistol: its bullet was lodged in a tree above where Burr had been standing. Did Hamilton throw away his fire? Did he fire at Burr but miss? Did Burr's bullet hit him first, causing him to shoot errantly? Due to conflicting accounts and the lack of eyewitnesses, we'll likely never know for sure. It remains one of the enduring mysteries in American history. However, the last letter Alexander wrote to Eliza, on the Fourth of July 1804, suggests he thought he would die in the upcoming duel, perhaps by deliberately not shooting at his enemy—perhaps to show he was a better man than Burr. Whatever the case, the husband-to-wife "farewell" is heartrending:

> This letter, my very dear Eliza, will not be delivered to you, unless I shall first have terminated my earthly career; to begin, as I humbly hope from redeeming grace and divine mercy, a happy immortality.
> If it had been possible for me to have avoided the interview [duel], my love for you and my precious children would have been alone a decisive motive. But it was not possible, without sacrifices which would have rendered me unworthy of your esteem. I need not tell you of the pangs I feel, from the idea of quitting you and exposing you to the anguish which I know you would feel. Nor could I dwell on the topic lest it should unman me [lose courage for the duel].
> The consolations of Religion, my beloved, can alone support you.... Fly to the bosom of your God and be comforted. With my last idea; I shall cherish the sweet hope of meeting you in a better world.
> Adieu best of wives and best of Women.
> Embrace all my darling Children for me.
> Ever yours
> AH

Baron von Steuben Statue, Lafayette Square's Northwest Corner

During the frigid winter of 1777–78 at Valley Forge, Pennsylvania, Hamilton met and befriended Baron von Steuben, who had joined Washington's army as its drillmaster. This German-speaking, former Prussian military captain taught Washington's men how to maneuver and fight like professional European soldiers, allowing the Americans to hold their own with the British in pitched battles (see Chapter 16, "The Backstory of the American Revolution's Martinet"). Brought to America on the recommendation of the U.S. envoy to France, Ben Franklin, von Steuben agreed to an unusual work agreement: he wouldn't be paid for his military services unless the Americans won their revolution.

Hamilton was a close friend of von Steuben's private secretary, John W. Mulligan, the son of Hercules Mulligan. When Hamilton, as the American Revolution was breaking out, moved from the British Caribbean to New York to pursue studies at King's College (now Columbia University), he lodged with Hercules. Hamilton was at first sympathetic to the British view; it was Hercules Mulligan who persuaded the young immigrant to rally to the patriot cause.

The elder Mulligan, featured in the play *Hamilton*, was a critical member of the New York spy ring that funneled vital intel to General Washington and that foiled British plots to kidnap him (Mulligan's work is detailed in the bestselling book *Washington's Spies* and in the TV series *Turn*).

Andrew Jackson Statue, Center of the Square

Although Andrew Jackson came to national prominence after Hamilton's death—his statue depicts Jackson's triumph over the British at the 1815 Battle of New Orleans—he prominently opposed several issues linked to Hamilton. As mentioned, President Jackson undid Hamilton's Bank of the United States. Further, historians call his presidency the era of "Jacksonian democracy," in which suffrage was much extended, to almost all white males. This put Jackson, a supporter of expanded voting rights, at odds with Hamilton's Federalists, who generally believed voting should be restricted to men of property and education. This belief, which not surprisingly was unpopular, was a major factor in the decline and ultimate demise of the political party Hamilton founded. Another factor was the Federalists' opposition to the War of 1812, a war personified by the Jackson statue. Many viewed such opposition, rooted in the Hamiltonian desire to keep prosperous trade relations with the old mother country, as unpatriotic.

Kościuszko Statue, Northeast Portion of the Square

Tadeusz Kościuszko is the fourth of the statues in Lafayette Square honoring European military officers who helped the U.S. win its independence. Below the figure of Kościuszko is a stirring image of a Polish peasant directing his scythe toward a foreign invader, probably the Russian Czar. Hailing from Poland and Lithuania, Kościuszko was an engineer known for fortifying West Point, a key bastion in the Hudson River near where Hamilton and General Washington were stationed, at the time of Benedict Arnold's treason, and later the site of the United States Military Academy.

Kościuszko was friends with Hamilton's best friend and fellow and youthful aide-de-camp to Washington (as well as character in the *Hamilton* play): Lt. Colonel John Laurens. As General Washington observed, Laurens was possessed with an almost reckless courage. At the Pennsylvania Battle of Germantown, Laurens single-handedly attacked a fortified enemy stone house, lighting fire to it with one hand while holding off the British with his sword. Tragically, he died near the war's end. Disobeying instructions to not assault a large British force and instead wait for reinforcements, he was killed during the battle because, a fellow officer observed, he lusted for the glory of a difficult fight.

Although a South Carolinian whose father, Henry, made a fortune buying and selling slaves, Laurens, like Hamilton, held abolitionist views. He proposed, and the Continental Congress approved, a startling plan to arm 3,000 slaves from Carolina to fight in the Revolution in exchange for their freedom. South Carolina politicians blocked the plan three times. Kościuszko shared Laurens' opinion on the matter. In his will, the impoverished Polish hero pledged his remaining funds for the freeing of American slaves.

James and Dolley Madison House, aka Cutts-Madison House, 1520 H Street

This stately corner home was the residence of President James and First Lady Dolley Madison after their departure from the Executive Mansion. James Madison was both a close colleague and bitter rival of Hamilton: a colleague in coauthoring with Hamilton and John Jay *The Federalist Papers*, the chief justification for the stronger federal authority established in 1789; a rival in cofounding with Jefferson the Anti-Federalist Party, a counter to Hamilton's Federalists. A wary Madison noted Hamilton had at times called for electing a President and Congress for life and for the federal government, not the state legislatures or the people, to select the governors of the states.

It was Madison as much as anyone who reconciled Hamilton's desire for a very strong central government with Jefferson's penchant for power spun off to the states, localities, and individuals. He did this through his famous system of "checks and balances." The federal authority was granted a powerful President and, à la Hamilton, a powerful Treasury. Further, President Madison, as the Commander-in-Chief during the War of 1812, came around to Hamilton's view of a robust and permanent military. But in the Constitution, Madison carefully enumerated the federal powers, with major roles reserved to the states—for instance the election of federal Senators—and the people, through the election of congressmen. Madison shepherded the Bill of Rights, envisioned as a firewall against federal overreach, through the first Congress.

The final word on the Constitution to which Hamilton and Madison gave birth goes not to Madison, its principal author, but to Hamilton's friend Gouverneur Morris. It was he who wrote the document's most famous passage, highlighting the aims demonstrated in the play *Hamilton!*:

> We the People of the United States, in Order to form a more perfect Union, establish Justice, insure domestic Tranquility, provide for the common defense, promote the general Welfare, and secure the Blessings of Liberty to ourselves and our Posterity, do ordain and establish this Constitution for the United States of America.

Sources

Auricchio, Laura. *The Marquis: Lafayette Reconsidered*. New York: Knopf, 2014.
Bailey, Ronald. "Hail, Lafayette." *American History*, December 3, 2010. http://www.historynet.com/hail-lafayette.htm.
Ball, Ankeet. "Ambition and Bondage: An Inquiry on Alexander Hamilton and Slavery." Columbia University in the City of New York. https://columbiaandslavery.columbia.edu/content/ambition-bondage-inquiry-.

Chernow, Ron. *Alexander Hamilton*. New York: Penguin, 2004.

———. *Washington: A Life*. New York: Penguin, 2010.

Ellis, Joseph J. *Founding Brothers*. New York: Knopf, 2000.

Encyclopedia.com. "'Lafayette, We Are Here.'" *Dictionary of American History*, September 10, 2010.

Fitzpatrick, Siobhan. "John Laurens." George Washington's Mount Vernon. https://www.mountvernon.org/library/digitalhistory/digital-encyclopedia/article/john-laurens/.

Hoover, Michael. "The Whiskey Rebellion." U.S. Department of the Treasury. Alcohol and Tobacco Tax and Trade Bureau, August 21, 2014. https://www.ttb.gov/public_info/whisky_rebellion.shtml.

Moser, Edward P. "Hamilton and Jefferson: Differing Visions." In *A Patriot's A to Z of America: Things Every Good American Should Know*. Nashville: Turner, 2011.

National Archives. "From Alexander Hamilton to Elizabeth Hamilton, 4 July 1804." Hamilton Papers, Library of Congress. Copy, Rare Book and Manuscript Library, Columbia University in the City of New York. https://founders.archives.gov/documents/Hamilton/01-26-02-0001-0248.

Office of the United States Trade Representative. "History of the Winder Building, Home to USTR's Washington D.C. Headquarters." https://ustr.gov/archive/Who_We_Are/History_of_the_Winder_Building,_Home_to_USTR's_Washington_DC_Headquarters.html.

Oubre, Claude F. *Forty Acres and a Mule: The Freedmen's Bureau and Black Land Ownership*. Baton Rouge: Louisiana State University Press, 1978.

Pitch, Anthony. *The Burning of Washington: The British Invasion of 1814*. 3rd ed. Annapolis: Naval Institute Press, 1998.

Remini, Robert V. *The Life of Andrew Jackson*. New York: HarperPerennial, 1988.

Selig, Robert A. *The Washington–Rochambeau Revolutionary Route in the State of New York, 1781–1782: An Historical and Architectural Survey*. Hudsonrivervalley.org., 2001. http://www.hudsonrivervalley.org/themes/pdfs/rochambeau_revolutionary_route.pdf.

Sheppard, Nicholas. "The Gay Man Who Saved The American Revolution." *Huffington Post*, July 23, 2016, updated. Digital. https://www.huffingtonpost.com/nicholas-sheppard/the-gay-man-who-saved-the_b_7838506.html.

Stewart, David O. *Madison's Gift: Five Partnerships That Built America*. New York: Simon & Schuster, 2015.

"That Treasure, the Treasury." *Washington Post*, May 4, 1988. https://www.washingtonpost.com/archive/lifestyle/1988/03/04/that-treasure-the-treasury/4lf6e76a-19e7-44f9-9090-f42bc934b88b/.

Unger, Harlow Giles. *The Last Founding Father: James Monroe and a Nation's Call to Greatness*. Boston: Da Capo, 2009.

39

Murder Bay and Hooker's Division

The Old Ebbitt Grill, 675 15th Street, Southeast Corner of G Street

Other than hotel bars and some fast-food joints, the closest restaurant to Lafayette Square is the Old Ebbitt Grill. The sprawling tavern with a soaring rear atrium started up in 1856, but at a different location. It was originally in the city's Chinatown, on the east side of downtown. In the early 1900s, it moved one block east of its current address to the top of the 14th Street hill up from Pennsylvania Avenue.

A Barrio of Bars and Brothels

Next door to Old Ebbitt Grill was a gambling den—and a house of ill repute. These establishments marked the start of Washington's notorious red-light district, the aptly named Murder Bay. Murder Bay was huge. It sprawled from east of the Treasury Building and along, and south of, Pennsylvania Avenue, then all the way to 6th Street, near today's National Archives. The bordellos and bars then jumped the National Mall and picked up again at an even racier section, "Louse Alley," at the foot of Capitol Hill. During its roughly 80 years of operation, Murder Bay had at times upwards of 100 houses of prostitution and thousands of prostitutes. Clients would frequent many a cathouse, such as the Devil's Own and the Bake Oven, according to the book *City of Mud*.

As the oldest profession was then legal in Washington, most of the working madams practiced their trade within the law, although some purveyors of flesh crossed the line. One harlot and her daughters would gyrate and undress for bystanders as a monkey grinder played musical accompaniment. They were all hauled into court, chimp included. The under-the-covers trade spun off supporting commerce. Murder Bay had hundreds of bars, both legal and unlicensed, serving both top-shelf and rotgut spirits. Those so inclined could find smut shops. The district also included many places of wholesome, or at least palatable, entertainment: opera houses, music halls, and sports events, including boxing. The city's newspapers were strategically located on its Pennsylvania Avenue spine between the President's House and the Capitol. The joke was that the denizens of the latter were often "in congress."

The sheer volume of vice attracted countless crooks: pickpockets, housebreakers, confidence men, violent thieves, and murderers. Corpses were found dumped under garbage

This image from 1855 depicts Murder Bay extending south of Pennsylvania Avenue and across from the Smithsonian Castle on the National Mall (Smithsonian Institution Archives, Image #MAH-18603).

heaps or floating in the Washington Canal. Sexually transmitted diseases were common, as were widespread communicable diseases like tuberculosis. Purveyors of patent medicines did a brisk trade, leading to addictions in then-legal painkillers derived from the coca plant. For much of Washington's history, Murder Bay was its late-night, early-morning center of action.

The neighborhood had sprung up before the Civil War in the streets south of Pennsylvania Avenue along the fetid canal, buried today under Constitution Avenue. Few but the poor, the rootless, and the criminal would dwell in a place washed by the dark smelly muck of the waterway, which overflowed during storms and stranded barges during low tide. The locality was endemic with cholera, malaria, and typhus. Its population swelled with the War Between the States. "Contraband" blacks fleeing slave plantations huddled in shacks and hovels behind the main streets. For generations the city was known for such alley-filled slums. Moreover, the fight between North and South brought into the capital hundreds of thousands of Union soldiers and thousands of federal administrators. Most of them were hundreds of miles away from their wives and girlfriends, and were eager for entertainment. Murder Bay supplied it.

One ranking officer anxious about the rampant sex traffic between trooper and temptress was Major General Thomas Hooker, from prim Massachusetts. Although a brave and, usually, able man, General Hooker was on the receiving end of the South's two biggest victories, Fredericksburg and Chancellorsville. In Washington City, Hooker reasoned that concentrating the prostitutes and his men's misbehaviors in one place would help regulate and dampen the liaisons. Instead, his imprimatur gave Murder Bay's denizens carte blanche to expand their operations. Commented the *Evening Star* newspaper in 1863, "There are at present, more houses of [prostitution], by ten times, in the city than have ever existed here before, and loose characters can now be counted by the thousands."

General Hooker's authorized neighborhood of bawdy houses and bars was dubbed Hooker's Division. Inevitably, the sex workers of his division were called hookers. The term had been coined before, but Hooker's Division made it a common and enduring euphemism. The locale ran mostly south of Pennsylvania Avenue, from 14th Street near today's Department of Commerce, and along the canal to around today's National Gallery of Art at 6th Street. In response to its popularity, wartime authorities dreamed up a novel way of cleaning up the division some, while also boosting the war effort. They permitted over 500 criminal denizens there, and scores of ladies of the evening, to skip jail by slipping into Confederate territory, there to lay low the foe.

Princess of the Prostitutes

Early in the division's life, prostitutes operated as sole proprietorships. A hooker could make about $175 a month, about five times more than a factory worker. Over time, the harlots organized themselves into houses where sharp business girls ran the red-lit abodes. The queen of the madams resided not in Hooker Land but on the Mall's far side, in Louse Alley. The Smithsonian discovered this in 1997 when it dug up the site for its new Museum of the American Indian. Archaeologists at the excavation puzzled at a long-buried trove of luxury items. They found shards and chunks of porcelain, marbled wall clocks, and Belgian carpets. They sifted through the discarded foods of the One Percent: lobster claws, Brazil nuts, turtle shells from turtle soup, and corks from Piper-Heidsieck champagne. But the vanished house in question had been in Louse Alley, the very worst part of town, which made Hooker's Division seem almost gentrified. The place couldn't have been the home of a wealthy merchant or a congressman on the take. A look through the real estate archives revealed the place as the abode of Mary Ann Hall, her sister Lizzy, and their fellow 15 "substitutes," as the

The queens of old Washington's red-light districts were madams Elizabeth and Mary Ann Hall, on the left and right, respectively. The seductive sisters operated the town's largest house of ill repute (Wikimedia Commons, photograph by "Smallbones," 2012).

U.S. Census termed them. Mary Ann ran the biggest and most lucrative leaping house in all of Washington. The pricey relics were from the well-upholstered rooms of her house, and from the sumptuous banquets given her well-heeled Johns.

Prostitution was legal but running a cathouse was not. The police once busted Madam Mary Ann for disturbing the peace. The wealthy businesswoman hired the best legal talent, the barrister, Frederick Aiken, who ably defended Lincoln conspirator John Surrat. Hall got off with a stiff fine. She and sister Lizzy retained enough of their licit and illicit

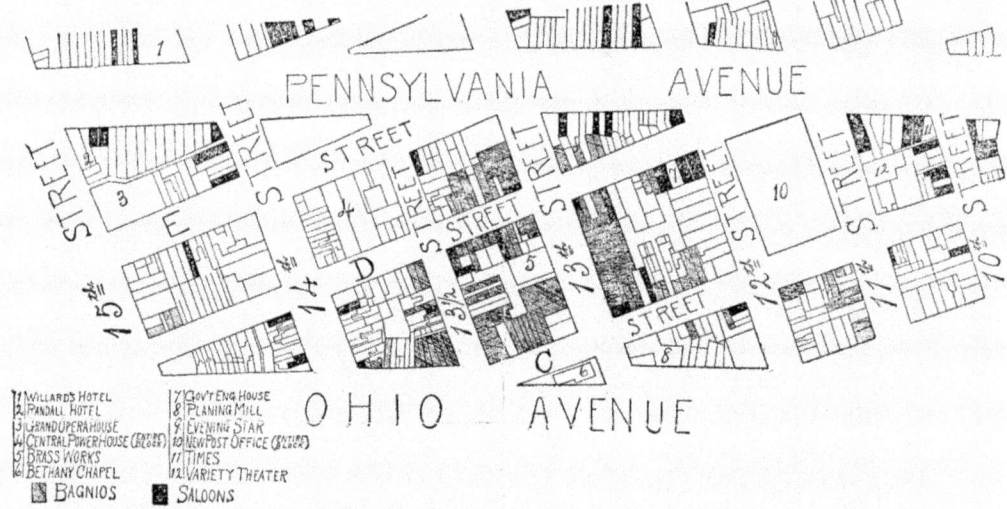

A newspaper map from the late 19th century reveals that the city's neighborhood of streetwalkers and street toughs—Hooker's Division—began within a stone's throw of the Executive Mansion (Library of Congress; originally from the *Evening Star*).

gains to afford, on Mary Ann's death in 1886, lavish funeral sculptures. Their busts grace Congressional Cemetery, where the two ladies of the evening lay sleeping forever next to some of their former clientele. Alas, Mary Ann's demise ended one of the futile efforts to reform the bawdy-house districts. The Women's Christian Association had set up a health clinic for streetwalkers, but the infirmary shut its doors with the demise of its landlady, the enterprising Madam Hall.

After the Civil War, the masses of soldiers went home, but Hooker's Division stayed and prospered in the wild booms and busts of the late-1800s Gilded Age. An article from the *Evening Star*, published from its printing plant in Hooker's Division, offered a detailed exposé, and map, of its environs. The newspaper counted 61 licensed "bawdy-houses" and 48 unlawful ones, plus 50 saloons in partnership with the brothels. The *Star* stated that President "Grover Cleveland can sit in his bedroom window at the White House and survey this entire territory. He is within sight and gunshot of each of these ... dens which defy the laws." That seemed apt, as Cleveland's 1884 presidential bid had almost been derailed by a sex scandal in which he may have fathered an out-of-wedlock child. Grover owned up to the affair, and paid child support, even as opponents cried out a campaign slogan of: "Ma, ma, where's my Pa?!"

Cleaning Up Sin City

At least the malodorous and disease-ridden Washington Canal had been filled in during this time, by Mayor Alexander "Boss" Shepherd. A downside, though, was that his costly public works for the public good wrecked the city's finances. Hooker's Division, aka Murder Bay, roared all the way into the 1910s. Then it fell victim to the Progressive Era and the same do-good politics that gave us civil service reform, Prohibition, women's suffrage, and the income tax. In 1914, the year after the IRS was set up, the city made prostitution illegal in the wake of critical hearings in a Senate whose galleries were sprinkled with the lawmakers' madams. (Three years later, in another Southern city famous for vice, the U.S. Navy, as a wartime prophylactic, closed Storyville, the anything-goes part of New Orleans. The move had unin-

The Temperance Statue is a reminder of the network of legal and illegal bars that ran east of the Treasury Building. Its fountain encouraged pub crawlers to quench their thirst with water (Wikimedia Commons; photograph by "Smash the Iron Cage," 2015).

tended consequences. Many of the musicians playing the dance halls and houses of the rising suns headed up the Mississippi and founded jazz scenes from Memphis to Chicago.) By then in decline, Hooker's Division came to a full stop in the 1930s. During the New Deal, an outgrowth of the Progressive Era, the old neighborhood was condemned and demolished. Louse Alley was also torn down in the Depression-ridden '30s. The Division's gambling dens and cathouses were ousted, but, over time, the legitimate neighborhood businesses also departed—the vaudeville theaters and German restaurants and a chunk of old Chinatown. The vacuum was filled by the Federal Triangle, containing impressive but staid structures like the William Jefferson Clinton environmental protection building and the Old Post Office turned Trump International Hotel. Today the neighborhood has lost its tawdriness but also some of its vibrancy, its sense of city. It has instead taken on the forced feel of a mausoleum, a tribute to things long gone.

One token remains of the wild times past as an admonition against them. On 7th Street off of Pennsylvania Avenue is a strange statue of a crane, its long thin legs standing atop a water fountain. It's the Temperance Statue, built at the urging of Victorian Era ladies of temperance and propriety—an attempted antidote to the unwashed hordes who partook of the taverns and trysting lounges of Hooker's Division in murderous Murder Bay.

Sources

Blitz, Matt. "Meet the Madam on the Mall." *Smithsonian*, February 20, 2015. http://www.smithsonianmag.com/history/meet-madam-mall-180954371/.

Dickey, J.D. *Empire of Mud: The Secret History of Washington, D.C.* Guilford, CT: Lyons, 2014. https://erenow.com/common/empire-of-mud-the-secret-history-of-washington-dc/8.html.

Ghosts of DC. "Rough-and-Tumble Lost Neighborhood of Murder Bay." https://ghostsofdc.org/2012/03/29/washingtons-rough-and-tumble-lost-neighborhood-of-murder-bay/.

Press, Donald E. "South of the Avenue: From Murder Bay to the Federal Triangle." *Records of the Columbia Historical Society* 51 (1984), Washington, D.C. https://www.jstor.org/stable/40067844?seq=1#page_scan_tab_contents.

Seifert, Donna. "Within Site of the White House: The Archeology of Working Women." *Historical Archeology* (1991).

Swain, Claudia. WETA. "The Oldest Profession in Washington." *Boundary Stones*, June 3, 2015.

40

A Wartime Tavern Keeper's Unwanted Guests

Southeast Corner of 15th Street and F Street

During the British sacking and burning of Washington on August 24, 1814, during the War of 1812, their invading force of Royal Marines marched from the Capitol, which they'd set afire, down Pennsylvania Avenue to the Treasury Building and the White House, which they would also set on fire. They strode past MacLeod's Washington Hotel on the site of today's Hotel Washington and Willard Hotel. Marching up toward the Treasury Building, they encountered a long, low, brick structure. It was just up the hill from 15th Street and Pennsylvania Avenue. The Marines were led by the expedition's overall commander, Rear Admiral George Cockburn, and by the head of its land forces, Major General Robert Ross.

General Ross had escaped death that day. Earlier, when approaching the Capitol Building, a Maryland militiaman had shot his horse out from under him, almost killing him. Enraged, the General had his men burn the house of Treasury Secretary Albert Gallatin, from where the shooter had fired. (Today the site is the Sewall-Belmont House and Museum, which honors suffragettes.)

Unwelcome Clientele

Hours later, as evening neared, Ross was dirty, hungry, and thirsty. Since dawn on a hot and humid day he'd been riding and marching, issuing orders and fighting. He came up to the squat building in question, which doubled as a tavern and an inn. A widow named Barbara Suter ran it. She was related to the Suter innkeepers of Georgetown. There, in Suter's Tavern, Washington, Pierre L'Enfant, and others had thrashed out plans to build the new capital city the British were then destroying. Hotel management was in Barbara Suter's blood. She had run her boardinghouse business across the street, at the Rhodes Tavern, before moving the enterprise to the current location (see Chapter 41, "A Humble Cleaning Lady Gulls a Mighty Invader").

Earlier that terrible day Barbara had endured an emotional parting from her son. He was a soldier in one of the American militias, and she had met him when his unit was retreating through the city. With strong roots in the region and a son in the military, Barbara Suter was a patriot. She didn't like her unwelcome guest, but General Ross hardly cared. "Madam," he told her cavalierly, "I have come to sup with you." He directed Suter to prepare a dinner for him and his men—to be consumed that evening, after they had looted and burned the Treasury across the street and the Executive Mansion around the corner. Suter tried to fob the General off to MacLeod's Hotel, according to historian Anthony Pitch. It had a bigger menu, after all, and better accommodations. Ross replied sarcastically that he preferred the view of the Treasury from the hilltop of her place. Then he shocked the widow by telling her a spy from his force, when scouting out the city earlier in the week, had stopped by her tavern. With a start, Suter recalled a beggar with a British accent, a ragged fellow presumed to be a deserter from the British Army. Taking pity, the widow had fed him. He had been Ross' man!

Suter had scant choice but to accept the General's dining request. She and her servant went to the tavern's backyard and wrung the necks of some chickens. Then they prepared a dinner. True to their word, Ross and his entourage returned to Suter's that night after burning the White House, and the Treasury right across the way. Among the group of 10 diners was the British spy Suter had fed. But Barbara Suter was shaken as much by the weird entrance into her inn of Ross's superior, Admiral Cockburn, who showed off his sardonic sense of humor. Having mounted a pack mule outside, he mockingly entered her tavern atop it. Some of Cockburn's men were in a less jocular mood. They had hoped to find a fortune in gold and cash in the Treasury Building, but all they found were burnt journals and outdated documents. That shouldn't have been surprising, as the U.S. government was nearly bankrupt from the war.

The Admiral, the General, and their entourage sat down to the chicken and bread dinner Suter and her servant had prepared. Then Cockburn did something else that was highly unusual. Although the meal was about to begin and it was growing dark outside, he snuffed out the candles to their room. Suter wondered why. Cockburn replied in words to this effect: "Why Madam, so that we can dine in light cast by the glowing embers of your President's House and his Treasury!" Barbara Suter would recall that time of "great trouble, hardly sleeping at night, and all the day spent in fright."

Admiral George Cockburn—commander of the British force that sacked Washington in 1814—is portrayed preening in front of the city he destroyed (Library of Congress, http://www.loc.gov/pictures/item/2012645261/).

A Hero of the Hour

Still, a bright spot during that otherwise baleful period was the brave action of a prominent Washingtonian. As one of the original architects of the Capitol, Dr. William Thornton had been devastated to see its immolation. He was then Commissioner of the Patent Office and feared the building housing it would share the same fate. The Patent Office, a warehouse for early Yankee ingenuity, held the models of many inventions, including a musical instrument of the multitalented Thornton's own devising. This office was then housed in the former Blodgett Hotel, across town on 7th Street and F Street. Mr. Blodgett had built a "hotel," in the French sense of a mansion, as a prize for the winner of the city's first lottery, held to defray the costs of the new city's construction. When the lottery failed, the federal government took over the hotel and, rooting about for a purpose, made it the place of patents.

Over in Georgetown, Thornton heard the British were readying to add the Patent Office to their burn list. He rushed over and found two columns of troops with ignitables moving toward it. Thornton faced up to the British commander, a Major Waters. The records are skimpy, but he made an impassioned plea along these lines:

> Are you and your soldiers men, or are they savages? Are they like the Huns who toppled old Rome? Akin to the Vandals who carried off the fruits of a sagely and venerable civilization? Are they not civilized men? Or are they like the Turks who, like barbarians, set fire to the Library of Alexandria, Egypt, immolating the learning of centuries, and earning the censure of the civilized world?
>
> The repository behind you belongs not to any one nation or people, but is the treasure chest of innovations that belong to the entire world! Are you not civilized men?

Thornton added that the patents were the submissions of private individuals to the government and not the product of the U.S. government, which was the true object of British ire. He slyly suggested any offending items be brought outside and burned, instead of setting the entire building and all its patents ablaze.

Dr. Thornton's oratory had its effect. Major Waters hesitated. He decided to check with his superior, a Colonel Jones. He and Thornton found him a few blocks away, at the *National Intelligencer* newspaper, whose offices British troops were wrecking. Colonel Jones thought things over and agreed the Patent Office should be spared. Thornton had lost his Capitol Building, but his Patent Office was safe—at least from the British. But mass looting, by Americans, had broken out in a city devoid of federal troops, state militia, and local police. Thieves descended on the old Blodgett Hotel, as they did on the White House and the Navy Yard. Among his many roles, which included a physician's practice, Dr. Thornton was also an officer of the law. He gathered and stationed armed volunteers to keep watch over the Patent Office as well as remnants of the Capital Building, Navy Yard, and other structures. He even tried enlisting British stragglers as guards, and later took grief for such a putatively traitorous act. But more than anyone else, Thornton was able to salvage a chunk of original Washington from the rampaging British.

Sources

Bank of America. "Rebuilding Our Nation's Capital." Retrieved 2018.
Pitch, Anthony. *The Burning of Washington: The British Invasion of 1814*. 3rd ed. Naval Institute Press, 1998.
Pohl, Robert S. *Urban Legends and Historic Lore of Washington*. Mt. Pleasant, SC: History Press Library, 2013.
Wheeler, Linda. "The Night 'the City Was Light.'" *Washington Post*, August 29, 1999. https://www.washingtonpost.com/archive/local/1999/08/24/the-night-the-city-was-light/19c8cc92-48ee-473c-b2c3-f1d40973c43f/.

41

A Humble Cleaning Lady Gulls a Mighty Invader

15th Street and F Street, Metropolitan Square, Site of the Former Bank of the Metropolis/Rhodes Tavern

Various days contend for the worst in Washington, D.C.'s history:

- April 14, 1865—The night of President Lincoln's assassination and the attempted assassination of Secretary of State Seward;
- April 4, 1968—The day of Martin Luther King's assassination, which set off four days of bloody and destructive rioting in the District;
- September 11, 2001—The day on which terrorists crashed a jetliner into the Pentagon across the Potomac from Washington, killing 125 people in the Defense Department headquarters as well as 59 passengers and crew (another set of terrorists flew a hijacked jet, United Airlines Flight 93, toward either the Capitol or the White House before the doomed jet crashed in Pennsylvania);
- July 19, 1919—The day in which a race riot, largely between white, off-duty U.S. military personnel and black civilians, erupted. The disturbances lasted four days, and resulted in as many as 30 deaths.

Day of Rage

Still, many peg August 24, 1814, as the worst day in the capital's 220-plus years. That was the date an invading British Army during the War of 1812 conquered the city and set much of it ablaze. Early that fateful day, British Marines, led by Admiral George Cockburn and Major General Robert Ross, crushed an American army in nearby Bladensburg, Maryland. That afternoon, they marched into a defenseless capital from the northeast. Late that afternoon, if you had gazed eastward toward the Capitol from this area, you would have been shocked. The Capitol Building was on fire, its interior gutted by flames. The blaze also consumed the Supreme Court chamber and the Library of Congress, which were then both located inside the legislators' home. Gazing to the southeast, you would see smoke from the Washington Navy Yard, set ablaze by its Commandant, Thomas Tingey, to deny the British naval stores, ammunition, and a spanking-new 74-gun warship. Most disturbing of all, you would see several hundred Royal Marines striding down Pennsylvania Avenue,

41. A Humble Cleaning Lady Gulls a Mighty Invader

The Rhodes Tavern/Bank of Metropolis was both the city's largest bank and, formerly, a pub and lodging house. This view dates from 1979, five years before it was demolished (Library of Congress).

unopposed, toward their next targets, the Treasury Building, the White House, and the War and Navy Departments. A bit later, if you had stood halfway up the steep slope of 15th Street and looked down the hill, you would see British soldiers near the corner at Pennsylvania Avenue marching up to the intersection of 15th and F streets. You would also see, at the northeast corner of the street, an unusual business locale and an unusual woman. There stood the Bank of the Metropolis, the largest bank in the city. But Washingtonians thought of it as much more. It had long and previously been a boardinghouse and pub called the Rhodes Tavern. And, during elections, it had been a voting place. In fact, the earliest municipal elections were held there in 1802.

It seems strange that elections were held in a pub. But at the time, the town was essentially a small federal village encased in forest, swamp, and farmland. Its few buildings served multiple roles. A tavern could be a "public house" in every sense of the term (in Georgetown, town meetings were held at the City Tavern on M Street near Wisconsin Avenue).

A Bit of Balderdash

The unusual woman in this unusual place was the Bank's cleaning lady and caretaker. She was an Irish lady with the very Irish name of Sarah Sweeney. Sarah was charged with keeping the place tidy, and the marauding British Marines threatened to make quite a mess. Sarah Sweeney was all by herself. The other bank employees had fled. The cashier had left with the cash, safeguarding it in the hills of western Maryland. And the mighty British commander leading the invasion, Admiral Cockburn, and his sidekick General Ross, were in the vicinity. Locals pronounced Cockburn's name, normally uttered as "co-burn," as "cock burn," a reference to a disease his sailors sometimes caught. They called him this because for 18 months before he destroyed Washington his men had rampaged up and down the Chesapeake Bay, ransacking and burning coastal villages, assaulting women, and imprisoning Americans. During this time, Washington's leading newspaper, the *National Intelligencer*, vilified Cockburn in its stories and editorials.

But earlier that day, Cockburn had gotten revenge. He came across the newspaper's offices and printing press on Pennsylvania Avenue, and ordered his Marines to burn the place down. However, a brave lady living nearby approached the fearsome Cockburn. She beseeched him to spare the newspaper building lest sparks from the fire ignite private homes in the vicinity. Cockburn, who had a kinder, gentler side, chivalrously countermanded his order. But then he sternly directed his men to wreck the *Intelligencer*'s offices and dismantle its printing press piece by piece—paying special heed to the "c" letters of the press that had begun the many insults to Cockburn's name.

Now, Cockburn and Ross neared the Bank of the Metropolis. It was thought the structure—tavern and boardinghouse turned voting place turned countinghouse—might make the next good place to loot and burn. Ross was strolling over from Barbara Suter's tavern just across the street, where he had just arranged a victory supper (see the preceding chapter, "A Wartime Tavern Keeper's Unwanted Guests"). Ross had asked Suter whether the bank was privately owned, in which case the British were supposed to spare it, or whether it was a public endeavor, in which case they were ordered to destroy it. Their marching orders were to target government properties only, not the private holdings of individuals. Suter replied she thought it was a private bank. Almost for sure she lied, because the Bank of the Metropolis, like any public bank, paid its investors dividends. Suter, who had previously run the tavern there for seven years, must have known how it operated.

In any case, Ross and other British soldiers went over to the Bank to see for themselves. There they ran into Sarah Sweeney. Sweeney, perhaps because she was Irish, had the gift of gab, what some call malarkey. (The author, whose Irish grandmother came through Ellis Island, is allowed to trade in Celtic stereotyping.) She told the all-powerful General that if his men torched her place of work they'd be putting her boss out of work and out onto the street. The owner and resident of the bank, said Sarah, was an elderly widow. Needless to say, Sweeney would also be out of work and perhaps cast out onto the street if her own place of employment went up in smoke. Her story was blarney, as the Bank's actual president was businessman and future city Mayor John Peter Van Ness. The War of 1812, like most wars, was brutal. But it had traces of noblesse oblige. The General considered Sarah's plea—and ordered the men to leave the Bank of the Metropolis untouched. Might the fact that Ross was Irish himself—from Trinity College, Dublin, by way of County Down—have factored into the decision?

In any event, after the British departed Washington, the grateful shareholders of the Bank of the Metropolis rewarded Sarah Sweeney and her white lie. They gave her $100, a sizeable sum in those days, for her quick thinking to save their enterprise. Moreover, the Bank granted the federal government a loan of $100,000, a princely sum in 1814, to help rebuild the city.

There is a postscript. The Bank of the Metropolis building could have used Sarah Sweeney in 1984. The venerable structure remained intact until that year. But then, despite the pleas of preservationists to retain such a historic spot, developers demolished most of the building. Its Irish custodian was long gone, unable to save it the second time around.

Sources

Bank of America. "Custodian Who Saved Capital." Retrieved 2018. https://about.bankofamerica.com/en-us/our-story/custodian-who-saved-capital-hill.html.

———. "Rebuilding Our Nation's Capital." Retrieved 2018. https://about.bankofamerica.com/en-us/our-story/custodian-who-saved-capital-hill.html#fbid=8K141E0dcip.

Bryan, W.B. "Hotels of Washington DC Prior to 1814." *American History and Genealogy Project (AHGP)*. Speech originally read on March 9, 1903. https://doc.genealogyvillage.com/hotels_of_washington_dc_prior_1814.html.

Holmes, Oliver W. "The Colonial Taverns of Georgetown." Columbia Historical Society, Washington, D.C., 1951.

Jones, Mark. "Red Summer Race Riot in Washington, 1919." *Washington Post*, April 18, 2017. https://www.washingtonpost.com/wp-srv/local/2000/raceriot0301.htm.

Pitch, Anthony. *The Burning of Washington: The British Invasion of 1814*. 3rd ed. Naval Institute Press, 1998.

42

The Entrepreneur and the Ingénue
A Match Made in Heaven Gone to Hell

Treasury Building, 15th Street and F Street

She was a ray of light in the bloodiest time. In 1863 tens of thousands of Americans were falling in the battlefields of the Civil War. The Union war effort was financed from the Treasury Department on 15th Street down from Pennsylvania Avenue. The overworked Treasury Secretary, Salmon Chase of Ohio, was under fire for bankrolling the military with a steep income tax, the first in American history, and for inflating the currency with "greenbacks," the country's first uniform paper currency. Chase was normally rigid and calculating, but a smile broke over his fatherly visage when he thought of his 23-year-old daughter, Katherine "Kate" Chase. Whether she was in the neighborhood of the Treasury or elsewhere in town the lovely Kate turned heads.

Bachelorette and Bachelor

Soldier-statesman Carl Schurz recalled her as a teenager before the war: "She was … tall and slender and exceedingly well formed … vivacious hazel eyes, shaded by long dark lashes and arched over by proud eyebrows. The fine forehead was framed in waving, gold-brown hair. She had something imperial in the pose of the head, and all her movements possessed an exquisite natural charm. No wonder that she came to be admired as a great beauty and broke many hearts."

Kate provided succor for her father, who had suffered great tragedies in his marital and parental life. Salmon Chase was widowed three times, and four of his children had died by 1854. But Kate had reached adulthood lovely and learned, the product of years at finishing school.

Chase knew that Kate was perhaps the most eligible woman in Washington and its social queen. Partly by default, he knew. The natural leader of Washington society was the First Lady: Mary Todd Lincoln, the wife of Chase's boss, colleague, and political rival, residing at the White House one door down from Chase's Treasury office. But Mrs. Lincoln detested the capital's social scene. Kate, in contrast, reveled in it.

42. The Entrepreneur and the Ingénue

Chase had built an imposing townhouse at 6th and E streets, near today's Judiciary Square. There Kate, as hostess for her widowed dad, had wowed the city's elite with her lively receptions. She also toured the battlefronts and befriended Union officers, peppering them with her irreverent opinions on the conduct of the war. The ingénue soon caught the eye of one of the town's most eligible bachelors, the brave and industrious Governor of Rhode Island, William Sprague IV. As the nephew of a Governor and a U.S. Senator, the 33-year-old Governor Sprague was assured of a life in politics. But he got involved in much more. An industrial innovator, Sprague devised a machine for the manufacture of horseshoes, critical to the era's chief means of transport. He improved on calico printing, on plain cotton cloth from the fruit of Southern plantations, a chief product of the ongoing Industrial Revolution. Owner of five textile mills in New England, Sprague was among America's wealthiest men. In 1860 Sprague IV was elected Governor, at age 29, a self-described "boy Governor." With the war's outbreak he was made an officer. He then proved his valor if not his luck. He accompanied the First Rhode Island Regiment into Washington, where he was chief aide to a fellow Rhode Islander, Ambrose Burnside.

It was Sprague's ill fortune to fall in with a commander who would be part of some of the worst Union defeats in the war (however much Burnside's "sideburns" influenced manly style). In 1862 Burnside would lead the Union Army at the disastrous Battle of Fredericksburg, Virginia, marked by its "Pickett's Charge in reverse." A year earlier, in the war's first major fight, at Bull Run, in Manassas, Virginia, a thumping Confederate win, then-Colonel Burnside and Sprague were forced to scurry back to the capital with the remnants of their battered brigade. Yet, earlier that day Sprague had helped lead a successful federal assault, despite having two horses shot from under him. For the youthful politician, soldier, and entrepreneur, the future seemed without limits. Some thought the White House might be in his future. Along with his commercial and military exploits, Sprague lusted for romantic conquest. He wooed the capital's alluring jeune fille, Kate Chase. It is believed Kate and her father, in addition to Sprague's virile qualities, prized his pocketbook—for Salmon Chase deeply desired the presidency. Although the Treasury chief had his fingers on a budget of billions, he himself lacked the requisite funds for a White House bid. That could change with his daughter's marriage to a magnate.

A Mathew Brady photograph of the city's 1860s power couple: Rhode Island Governor William Sprague IV and Kate Chase, the daughter of Lincoln's Treasury Secretary Salmon Chase (National Archives).

In the meantime Kate Chase, who dreamed of being the First Lady she thought Mary Todd Lincoln should be, seemed willing to match her ambition to her father's. In 1863 she agreed to a political marriage of convenience. For their nuptials that November Sprague presented Kate with a Tiffany diamond-and-pearl wedding crown. The marriage took place at Secretary Chase's E Street home. In a lavish ceremony, the U.S. Marine Corps Band not only performed there but also played a song written for her, "The Kate Chase March." Given the dead soldiers piling up on battlefields, some chided such ostentation. The couple would eventually welcome four children into their family: a son, William V, and three daughters: Ethel, Catherine, and Portia. But almost from the start, things fractured for the seemingly perfect couple, for, along with being a canny businessmen and a courageous soldier, Sprague had a wandering eye. Despite a bride lovely and intelligent, he took up with mistresses.

Matrimonial Malaise

Sprague had a second vice as well: drinking, which worsened the first. Moreover, his commercial investments went south. The textile tycoon illicitly traded in wartime Southern cotton, the Confederacy's cash crop, and lost money on it. He and Kate bickered over the family's declining finances and expensive tastes. The once-dashing military man became disheveled and put on weight. His extramarital affairs were an open secret, mortifying his wife and father-in-law alike. Kate expressed her distress to her father, who counseled patience—until patience became impossible. Distracted at home, Kate Chase Sprague turned her focus to politics. In a highly unusual move for a woman of the time, she became a political advisor to her powerful dad.

In 1864 Chase bungled a try to unseat President Lincoln in a contest for the Republican Party nomination. Lincoln, partly to rid himself of a rival, made him Chief Justice of the Supreme Court. In 1868 Chase failed to wrest the Republican nomination from Ulysses S. Grant, so he switched to the Democratic Party. For the party's presidential nominating convention that year, held in the exclusively male, smoke-filled room of New York City's Tammany Hall, Kate worked out of a posh Manhattan hotel as her father's campaign chief. Still, the nomination went to New York Governor Horatio Seymour. Kate blamed her father's loss on powerful New York politico Samuel Tilden. (In 1876, she would play a role in denying Tilden the presidency, in the Electoral College, after he won the popular vote.)

While she was engaged in politicking, her marriage worsened as Sprague's finances fell apart. In 1873 a Wall Street panic turned into the Long Depression. Banks seized control of Sprague's factories and demoted their owner to a mere salaried employee. The same year, Salmon Chase died of a heart attack, his hopes of the presidency long since faded. Although Kate's finances were now much reduced, she kept trying to live as a Washington society queen, holding parties at her husband's grand Edgewood estate on the city's northern edge. She impressed guests with her expert knowledge of politics. But she and her sister quarreled bitterly over their deceased father's will, even bickering over his furniture.

During this troubled time, while at a lavish masquerade ball, Kate fell for a Washington figure far more influential than her fallen spouse, a man who was in fact a body builder and a boxer and had served as bodyguard for a firebrand abolitionist, Thaddeus Stevens of Pennsylvania, when Stevens was threatened with violence by slavery's defenders. Yet, this man dressed elegantly and had an orator's golden voice of persuasion. He was a cunning man who became the political boss of New York State and a three-time Empire State Senator. He also became a leading advocate of the freed slaves, helping push through the 14th Amendment mandating due process for all under federal law, and befriended Mississippi's Blanche Kelso Bruce, one of the first two African-American Senators. Yet he was accused of selling out blacks in the Compromise of 1877, which withdrew federal troops enforcing equal justice in the Southern states. He also was a mainstay of the Republican "Stalwarts" of New York's corrupt political machine and its financial font, the Manhattan Customs House, overseer of a chief revenue source, the tariff, collected at the country's largest port. Where he and his political ally Chester Alan Arthur, the future President, filled the offices with men who sent back a slice of their salaries to those who hired them. Finally, the man obstructed fellow Republican President Rutherford B. Hayes' effort to clean up Customs through Civil Service reform.

The man was Roscoe Conkling, a legend of the anything-goes politics of the time. And he was an "eligible" man because his wife, Gov. Seymour's daughter, shunned Washington, residing in faraway Utica, New York. Roscoe Conkling also had a wandering eye. At the masquerade, replete with symbolism on their faux public roles, Conkling and Kate swooned for each other. Soon they were lovers. He and she, the married woman of a former Governor and lauded Union officer, were often seen in public together, Conkling serving as her "escort." A new form of public discourse, the gossip column, targeted them. Later on it was said that someone other than Sprague was the father of several of Kate's children. It was probably true, for the person making this assertion was Sprague himself.

A Cuckold's Confrontation

Things came to an explosive head on August 9, 1879. Kate was vacationing that summer with her four children in the Spragues' summer home in Narragansett, Rhode Island. Mr. Sprague was away. Then he suddenly, unexpectedly, returned. Reports soon emerged that he, armed with his rifle from the Civil War, had chased a man out of his home and through the streets of Narragansett. A story was put out that the fleeing man was the tutor of Kate's children, a professor from Germany, named George Linck—until Herr Linck, perhaps disdaining the money he had been offered for a cover-up and embarrassed by wall-to-wall press attention, announced he had not been the man hunted about town by Kate Sprague's husband. The newspapers pieced together what happened. Conkling, who had been vacationing nearby, had spent the night at the Sprague estate. An inebriated William Sprague had surprised him there the next morning while Conkling was still in his sleeping clothes—with the Sprague children in the house—his wife's lover discovered! Conkling had been forced to hastily leave after Sprague told the other houseguests that a murder might soon be committed in the house—by him. In the meantime, Kate had been locked in her room, then fled through a window, then escaped to a hotel. Later, she sought shelter at the mansion of a wealthy cousin, Austin Corbin (a railroad tycoon who cheated the Montaukett Indians out of their Montauk, Long Island, lands). It was Conkling, not the German teacher, who had been chased—but certainly not chaste—across the Rhode Island cobblestones by the cuckolded Sprague. Commenting on the sordid mess, a Midwestern newspaper spoofed a children's tune:

Sing a song of Shot Gun/Belly full of rye/Two loyal Senators making mud pie/
When the pie was opened/The public got a smell/And Sprague said to Conkling/
Now you go to H-ll!

The scandal ended Conkling's own dreams of becoming President and terminated the Spragues' long-troubled marriage. The following year, 1880, they filed for divorce. The proceedings were nasty. Sprague accused Kate of adultery. He lamented, "I could not control my domestic affairs. That was a great mortification.... I found Conkling in possession of my household at Washington." Kate accused Sprague of adultery and cruelty. She said he once set her bedclothes on fire and tried throwing her out of a window. In the end, the couple withdrew the most spiteful allegations. They divorced and divided up the children. Kate got the three girls.

Sprague got the son, young Willie, after the lad was accused of trying to kill Kate's trustee.

The rest of their lives mostly followed a track of sorrow. Their wayward son killed himself in 1890 when living destitute in a Seattle, Washington, flat.

Sprague remarried—a West Virginian, Dora Inez Clavert. In Narragansett in 1883, as if reliving the Conkling incident, he chased the brother of his new wife off the premises with a shotgun after mistaking the sibling for an unwanted suitor. In 1909 the couple's Narragansett mansion and valuables went up in flames. They spent their final years in France on a grace note: they turned their rooms into a hospice for wounded First World War soldiers. After her son took his life, a devastated Kate, once the "Northern belle" of Washington, became a virtual shut-in. She sold off property she had gained in the divorce settlement and lapsed into poverty. She traipsed daily from a suburban farm into Washington to sell a few dollars' worth of eggs. Afflicted by severe kidney disease, she died at age 58 in 1899.

Kate Chase and William Sprague's heaven-sent match, once the talk of Lafayette Square and the stuff of the grandest ambitions, had long before turned to rust. They and Conkling were players in a great and tragic array of Washington scandal.

Sources

Columbia Historical Society, Washington, D.C., *Records* 22.
Conkling. A.R., ed. *The Life and Letters of Roscoe Conkling: Orator, Statesman, Advocate*. Cornell: Cornell University Library, 2009 (originally published in 1889).
HistoryNet. "War Watchers at Bull Run During America's Civil War." June 6, 2006. http://www.historynet.com/war-watchers-at-bull-run-during-americas-civil-war.htm.
Malesky, Robert. "The Rise and Fall of Kate Chase." *Bygone Brookland*, March 9, 2017. http://bygonebrookland.com/the-rise-and-fall-of-kate.html.
Oman, Anne H. "Passion on the Potomac." *Washington Post*, February 12, 1982. https://www.washingtonpost.com/archive/lifestyle/1982/02/12/passion-on-the-potomac/8a940021-2754-4723-aec6-249b8a554243/?utm_term=.210b50962e45.
Paxson, Frederic Logan, Allen Johnson and Dumas Malone, ed. *Dictionary of American Biography: Conkling, Roscoe*. New York: Charles Scribner's Sons, 1930.
Presidential History Blog. "Kate Sprague and Roscoe Conkling: Beauty and the Boss." June 8, 2015. https://featherfoster.wordpress.com/2015/06/08/kate-sprague-and-roscoe-conkling-beauty-and-the-boss/.

43

The Black Businessman Whose Workplace Birthed Jim Crow

Union Trust Company Building, 740 15th Street, Southwest Corner of 15th Street and H Street, Formerly the Site of 1500 H Street, the James Wormley Hotel

On a clear night in downtown Washington, starry-skied with the moon waxing, a dozen or so of the most powerful men in the nation stepped out of their horse-drawn carriages. On February 26, 1877, they slipped into a luxurious hotel just down H Street from the venerable Cutts-Madison House, where James and Dolley Madison had lived. Despite the glow from the moon and stars, the thoroughfare was darker than on most nights. In the aftermath of a recession the city government was trying to save money, so workers hadn't filled the streetlights with lamp oil.

An Uncivil Election

The Republican and Democratic power brokers moved into the smoke-filled, spittoon-studded rooms of the James Wormley Hotel. The secret conclave grappled with a constitutional crisis and a country on the verge of another civil war just 12 years after its inconclusive conclusion. The crisis stemmed from the previous November's presidential election. The Democratic candidate, New York Governor Samuel Jones Tilden, had taken the popular vote 51 percent to 48 percent over the Republican nominee, Ohio Governor Rutherford B. Hayes. Tilden also had the edge in the Electoral College, 184 to 165. But that margin fell one ballot short of victory because in three southern states—Louisiana, South Carolina, and Florida—the election results were in dispute because of massive fraud and vote rigging by both parties.

Since the end of the Civil War, federal troops had occupied much of the region and had enforced the new voting rights and other civic privileges for the recently freed slaves. But now, a dozen strife-filled years into Reconstruction—the federal effort to usher the southern states back into the union with civil liberties for all—northern resolve was flagging. In the South in 1876 Democrats had attacked and disenfranchised many blacks and white Republicans. Now it was but six days before the end of the presidency of the former Union Army commander, President Ulysses S. Grant. Yet the country didn't have an elected President. And it still might not have one on March 4, Inauguration Day. The New Yorker Tilden, with strong southern support, had campaigned on withdrawing federal troops from the South, in effect ending Reconstruction. Some people in both the North and the South, including General William Sherman, predicted that if Tilden were not awarded the White House the former Confederacy would again rise up in bloody revolt. And, without a Commander-in-Chief in the Executive Mansion, there would be no one to stop it.

The locale of the hush-hush gathering to deal with the crisis was ironic in the extreme. It was the hotel of James Wormley, the son of a former slave and one of the nation's leading African-American businessmen.

An Unusual Ascent

The hotelier's father, the enslaved Lynch Wormley, from east-central Virginia, had moved to the District as the War of 1812 drew to a close. He had retained one of the region's most skilled lawyers, one Francis Scott Key, the author of that war's "The Star-Spangled Banner," to sue his owner. Key obtained Wormley's certificate of freedom.

Washington, D.C., was then relatively better than other places for African Americans to make a living. When President Washington and Secretary of State Jefferson fell behind schedule in building the new federal city, they turned to the region's plentiful slave labor. Some of the blacks who helped erect the new Capitol, White House, and other federal structures were compensated with wages, and some were able to keep enough of their pay to buy their own liberty. Further, many of the area's slaves had been manumitted, or freed, by cash-rich planters like Washington and his wealthy friend Thomas Fairfax. Moreover, at the time of the American Revolution and the early republic, the Tidewater's main plantation crop, tobacco, was unprofitable. This led to a number of tobacco planters freeing their slaves. Thus the District from its founding had a sizeable community of free men and women of color.

In adjacent Virginia and Maryland, then as now, was horse country, that surrounded a fledgling capital city requiring many horse-drawn hacks as well as delivery and messenger services. Lynch Wormley and his sons were among the many blacks going to work as stablers, carriage drivers, and horse breeders. In his youth, James Wormley was a jockey at the city's racetracks. One concourse was on the edge of Lafayette Square, and stretched from the Decatur House west to near 17th Street, then down the hill to near today's Washington Monument. Another circuit, on land later purchased by James Wormley, was in the city's Tenleytown district, close to what became the Civil War–era Fort Reno. (After the civil rights movement it became an unfashionable stereotype to place the figurine of a black jockey on one's front lawn, but there was a historical basis to the image.)

Wormley graduated from horse rider to a horse-and-cab driver, his father's occupation. In that role he took many of the city's powerful men about town and became the confidante of some of them. These connections aided the Wormley family in 1831 when, in the wake of the failed and bloody Nat Turner slave rebellion west of Norfolk, Virginia, the Washington region placed tight restrictions on the work and movements of African Americans. Because the Wormleys were employed in a transport trade essential to the functioning of the capital city and its key players, they were exempt from the rules.

James Wormley must have liked transportation of all kinds, for he went on to work aboard steamboats and oceangoing ships. In 1841 he married Anna Thompson of Norfolk.

The couple would have four children. On ships of steam and sail Wormley was introduced to the food trade and became a steward for the onboard restaurants. From this he got deeper into the food business, where he flourished. He catered to the elite of Washington's antebellum era. He went on to own lodging and restaurant properties along I Street, two blocks from Lafayette Square and the White House. Among Wormley's customers were:

- Mississippi Senator, Secretary of War, Architect of the Capitol, and later Confederate President Jefferson Davis, who lived with his wife, Varina, nearby at 17th and I streets;
- Massachusetts Senator Daniel Webster, who resided two blocks away at H Street and Connecticut Avenue;
- Secretary of War, Secretary of State, Vice President, and South Carolina Senator John C. Calhoun, who lived a block away on Pennsylvania Avenue;
- Kentucky Senator, House Speaker, Secretary of State, and presidential candidate Henry Clay, who resided at the Decatur House.

Wormley seemed to know everyone, North and South and from abolitionists to slavery's proponents.

In 1854 a U.S. Navy fleet under Commodore Matthew Perry ended the isolation of the island nation of Japan. When, six years later, Japan sent its first legation to the United States, Wormley won the prestigious and lucrative right to offer catering services to the travelers. He supplied them during their long journey by boat from Norfolk, Virginia, to Washington and on to Philadelphia. For a subsequent visit, his neighbor William Seward—Secretary of State for Presidents Lincoln and Andrew Johnson—arranged for Wormley to lodge and feed the Japanese delegation at Wormley's I Street holdings. British novelist Anthony Trollope, after lodging there, noted, "I found myself put up at the house of one Wormley, a colored man.... I conceived myself to be greatly in luck."

After the Civil War broke out in 1861, Wormley's catering business took on Union clientele. When President Lincoln held late-night strategy sessions, Wormley's proffered snacks to Lincoln's Cabinet. When Secretary of War Stanton jailed rebel spies and soldiers at the Old Capitol Prison, on the site of today's Supreme Court, Wormley provisioned the prisoners. As a noted black businessman he befriended the ranking black leader of the time, Lincoln's advisor Frederick Douglass. As Douglass's sons had done, Wormley's sons joined the Union military, serving in the Navy. When Massachusetts Senator Charles Sumner successfully coaxed Lincoln into passing the 13th Amendment abolishing slavery, Sumner gave Wormley his personal copy of the amendment. After the war, Wormley took his business abroad. In 1868, when Senator Reverdy Johnson of Maryland was appointed ambassador to Great Britain, he invited Wormley to join him as his steward. The pairing seemed odd. A noted attorney, Johnson had helped trigger the Civil War by arguing the side of the slave owner in the infamous Dred Scott case, in which the Supreme Court ruled that slaves had no citizenship rights in federal courts. At war's end, he was defense attorney for Mary Surratt, in whose boardinghouse the John Wilkes Booth conspirators had met. During Reconstruction Johnson also defended members of the Ku Klux Klan (during the Civil War, Johnson had come down forcefully for the Union and for slavery's abolition). For their weeks-long voyage to Britain, Wormley insisted to a skeptical Johnson on taking along regional delicacies such as Chesapeake Bay crabs and Maryland terrapin turtles. Among London's smart set, his recipe for terrapin turtle soup proved a sensation.

In the era that would see books by Horatio Alger and the founding of Tuskegee Institute by Booker T. Washington, Wormley seemed to personify hustle and uplift. In 1869 he obtained financial backing from a business partner, Massachusetts Representative Samuel Hooper, chairman of the Ways and Means Committee. With this he took over a property at 15th and H streets and transformed it into the Wormley Hotel. Although smaller than the Willard Hotel three blocks to the south, his place grew into the city's finest "boutique hotel," renowned for its victuals and conveniences.

As noteworthy as Wormley's rise in a world of slavery and segregation was his apparent pedigree. According to some researchers, James Wormley was the grandson of prominent Virginia plantation and slave owner Ralph Wormley V, who supposedly had an out-of-wedlock son with a woman of African descent, a son who supposedly was none other than Lynch Wormley, James Wormley's father. That would be remarkable, as the Wormleys of Virginia were among the best-connected families of the Old Dominion's aristocracy. They intermarried with the Lees of American Revolutionary and Confederate military fame; the Armisteads, one of whom ordered the creation of the Star-Spangled Banner flag at Fort McHenry and another of whom led the spear point of Pickett's Charge at the Battle of Gettysburg; and the Beales, cofounders of nearby Georgetown. Further, the Wormleys intermarried with the aristocratic Tayloe and Ogle families who built the Tayloe residence on Lafayette Square next door to the Cutts-Madison House. Thus came about the alleged descendant of slaves and slaveholding planters running a hotel that hosted a meeting to determine the treatment of the nation's blacks for generations to come! That would be quite the twist to the tale. However, recent DNA evidence suggests that the aristocrat Ralph Wormley V was not the father of Lynch Wormley, and thus not the grandfather of James Wormley.

Reconstruction's Deconstruction

We return to the deadlocked presidential contest of 1877. Democrat Tilden, though moving to just one Electoral College vote shy of victory, had squandered his advantage postelection. He wasted his time writing a detailed legal treatise explaining why he should be awarded the presidency. His Republican rival Hayes was more practical and effective. With his party in control of the White House and the Senate, Hayes and his political team pressured Congress to appoint an Electoral Commission to decide the presidential winner. It was made up of 15 members, seven of them Democrats, and eight of them Republicans. Most observers figured the commissioners would vote along party lines, and the Republicans would win. Fearful Southern Democrats began a protracted filibuster in the Capitol to block this. Political passions got heated, as did fears of another civil war.

Earlier that February 26, the night of the Wormley Hotel meeting, a leader of the southern forces, Edward Burke of Louisiana, had visited President Grant at the White House. An advocate of "intelligent, white rule," Burke was hoping for a resolution of the crisis and deliverance for his South from the man who had conquered it in battle. In his first term, Grant had strenuously enforced Reconstruction, sending in federal troops and legions of Justice Department lawyers to suppress the vigilante group the Ku Klux Klan, which mounted violent assaults on freed men and women and Republican officials. (Although the South deservedly gets much blame for the trouble, the northern-controlled government during this time stripped voting rights from thousands of former rank-and-file Confederate soldiers, even as former slaves were granted voting privileges. Moreover, many parts of the North continued to deny voting rights and other privileges to blacks). In his second term, starting in 1873, even the stubborn, stout-hearted Grant, the Defender of the Republic, had grown weary of his task. Resistance to Reconstruction had been unrelenting, with pitched, bloody battles between Democrats and Republicans in the cities of New Orleans and Memphis. In South Carolina violent backers of the 1876 Democratic gubernatorial candidate, former Confederate General Wade Hampton III, had intimidated blacks and Republicans at the voting booth. Moreover, Grant's administration had been weakened by endless rounds of scandal. The country had also become preoccupied with a severe economic downturn.

Reflecting all this, Hayes, the Republican candidate, was willing to withdraw federal troops from the South in return for the presidency. Like some others, he had been more concerned with preserving the Union and ending slavery than in promoting full rights for former slaves. But he balked at making an explicit quid pro quo, and being seen as gaining high office from a corrupt bargain. He hoped President Grant, who was still threatening to crush any new insurrection down South, would instead quietly signal his support for a deal. Grant could take the blame—or credit—and Hayes could take the White House.

At his meeting with Louisiana's Burke, a tired Grant informed him he was willing to withdraw the troops as long as this wouldn't undermine Hayes. Grant wrote out a document indicating his support for a return to Democratic Party rule in the Bayou State. This was the break Burke had been angling for. He rushed back to the Capitol, where he met with ranking aides to Hayes and with Senator John Sherman, the brother of the Confederacy's great foe, General Sherman. Senator Sherman, a supporter of black rights, was dubious of Burke's arrangement but agreed with the other men to get together again that night. Wormley's Hotel was chosen as the place to confer. At the hostelry, the men from North and South assembled in the suite of former Attorney General William Evarts, soon to be the Secretary of State for a new President. Puffing on cigars and sipping whiskey, the politicos settled on an accord. The northerners received pledges from the southerners that Reconstruction would continue and that they would stop their filibuster against Hayes' election. The southerners received a pledge from Hayes' men that a President Hayes would stop "the occupation by bayonet."

On March 4, 1877, Rutherford B. Hayes was sworn into office on the Capitol steps. Keeping the promise his aides had agreed to, he subsequently withdrew federal troops from Louisiana, Florida, and South Carolina. But the southern states did not hold to their pledge, nor did the northern states force them to keep it. Over several decades the system of Jim Crow for blacks would take hold—restrictions on voting rights, freedom to work, and separate-but-quite-unequal facilities in education and train stations, schools, and even public restrooms.

Wormley was unaware of the fateful meeting, and if he had known of it he would have been aghast given the effect it had on the fortunes of blacks. Afterwards, he was disappointed at Frederick Douglass's sanguine reaction to the gathering and its result. Some black leaders of the time, such as Douglass and Booker T. Washington, with some logic, thought further progress on civil rights had become politically impossible in both the South and the North. It was time for a "time out," they felt, for a period of personal uplift and public education. In any event, after the "Wormley Conference of 1877," the Wormley Hotel's owner continued his close relationships with the city's potentates.

In 1881, President and former Union Army General James Garfield was severely wounded by assassin Charles Guiteau at the old 6th Street train station near today's National Gallery of Art. Wormley's kitchen supplied a palliative of its own creation: beef broth from porterhouse steak and tea. But it was to no avail, as after two months of suffering Garfield succumbed to his bullet wound.

The Wormley Hotel closed in the decade after its founder's death in 1884. Today it is the locale of the Union Trust Bank building. In Georgetown, an imposing local building imprinted with the black entrepreneur's name is the Wormley School. Today, like so many historic buildings in the capital region, it is a high-priced condominium. Wormley had the red-bricked structure built at the end of his life as an elementary school for blacks, and set it in the heart of Georgetown's poshest district, far from its students' mosquito-infested black neighborhood near Rock Creek.

But the saga of the old hotel itself is today marked by a simple plaque on the Union Trust structure, as if the city—and the nation—wished to forget the dubious deal, which helped put off civil rights for a century, at the workplace of a leading advocate for, and exemplar of, civil rights and the will to succeed.

Sources

DeFerrari, John. "The Talented Mr. James Wormley." *Streets of Washington*. http://www.streetsofwashington.com/2012/09/the-talented-mr-james-wormley.html.

Encyclopedia.jrank. "Wormley, James (1819–1884)–Entrepreneur, Chronology, Opens Elegant Hotel." http://encyclopedia.jrank.org/articles/pages/4526/Wormley-James-1819-1884.html.

Foner, Eric. *A Short History of Reconstruction, 1863–1877*. New York: HarperPerennial, 1990.

Gelderman, Carol. *A Free Man of Color and His Hotel*. Lincoln, NB: Potomac, 2012.

Geni. "Lynch Wormley." https://www.geni.com/people/Lynch-Wormley/6000000013763633618.

Graves, Donet D. "Wormley Hotel." White House Historical Association. http://www.whitehousehistory.org/presentations/the-half-had-not-been-told-me/wormley-hotel.html.

Moser, Edward P. "Frederick Douglass: Ride to Freedom." In *A Patriot's A to Z of America*. Nashville: Turner, 2011.

Shroder, Tom, and Mary Kay Ricks. "Out of the Mud." December 8, 2002. https://www.washingtonpost.com/archive/lifestyle/magazine/2002/12/08/out-of-the-mud/39250520-9dd7-4f92-b351-ef3c5de129da/.

Wormley Family History. "Notes on the American Wormleys: Wealthy Landowners and Slaves." http://www.wormleyfamilyhistory.com/. Retrieved 2018.

44

The Financial Wizard Who Helped Stave Off a Civil War

Albert Gallatin Statue, North Entrance of the Treasury Building, 1500 Pennsylvania Avenue

Given the popularity of a recent Broadway star, many tourists misidentify the statue of the fellow in caped, early-Federal garb in the front of the Treasury Building. They peg the figure as Alexander Hamilton. In fact, the image is of an illustrious successor, Albert Gallatin, a French-speaking Swiss immigrant who headed the Treasury Department for Hamilton's rivals Presidents Jefferson and Madison. (Surely capes, like Hamilton, should come back into style. They allow the wearer to strike a stylish and arresting pose, as befitting a Broadway sensation.) Like Hamilton, Albert Gallatin was a financial genius. As Treasury chief, he financed the $15 million Louisiana Purchase—while simultaneously slashing federal taxes and spending and cutting the national debt by over a third (contrary to a recent Capital One ad, the Purchase was not purchased via a cell phone). Yet another intriguing role for Gallatin took place in 1794, during the federal government's first presidency under George Washington—and it had a lot to do with Hamilton.

A Spirited Rebellion

The new United States government, like any government, had expenses, such as funding the new Treasury Department and the State and War Departments, setting up the Coast Guard and the Patent Office (Mr. Hamilton and Mr. Jefferson, respectively), and paying the salaries of Cabinet members and Congressmen. Also like any government, it needed revenue—tax revenue. So the first and founding Treasury Secretary, Hamilton, put in place the first federal taxes. Most monies came from his tariff on imports. However, there were other revenue generators, including a very unpopular one that led thousands of farmers who lived out toward the frontier, particularly in western Pennsylvania, to resist. This was a tax on the most prized commodity of their region, more prized than land or slaves or tobacco—especially among the fiercely independent Scotch-Irish who largely peopled the place. It was, of course, a tax on their moonshine, the federal excise on whiskey and other distilled spirits made from corn, barley, and rye. Thus came the Whiskey Rebellion.

Beginning in 1791 and continuing into 1794, farmers, distillers, and other frontier folk rose up against the hated tax. The revolt extended from Appalachian Georgia up to the

A particularly brutal punishment in the American Revolution and the Whiskey Rebellion, for either pro–British Tories or federal tax collectors, was to cover a man with hot tar and feathers (Library of Congress).

western fringes of the northern states. In far-off Kentucky, later the land of bourbon, the tax proved completely uncollectible. But the focus of the turmoil was in four southwestern Pennsylvania counties: Westmoreland, Washington, Fayette, and Allegheny. There the rebels tarred and feathered federal tax collectors, burned down the barns of tax supporters, and threatened to march on Pittsburgh.

The West still had a barter economy, and whiskey was the commodity with which a fellow bartered. And the tax, irritating in itself, had to be paid in cash. Further, the excise was a direct tax, which hit the pocketbook right away, unlike an indirect tax like a tariff. The liquor levy was particularly felt by people with little income. The American Revolution had been in large part a revolt over taxes. Many of the whiskey rebels were themselves veterans of the Revolution. In fact, they were so exercised over the excise they formed committees of correspondence and raised up liberty poles. It was like 1776 all over again.

Naturally, the new federal government was mighty displeased with the insurgency. A frustrated President Washington is said to have cried something like, "But the people now have taxation WITH representation! And they're revolting against ME—George Washington! Who do they think I am: King George?!" Washington and his de facto chief-of-staff Hamilton refused to swallow this threat from frontier rabble to their fledging authority, which they had fought a bloody Revolution and painstakingly pushed through a Constitution to establish. What to do?

A Forceful Response

First the Administration tried negotiation. A federal commission composed of Pennsylvanians was sent to parley with the rebels. This move met with some success: many of the rebels agreed to stop the violence and obey federal law. But Washington, and especially Hamilton, believed a show of force was required to fully cow the insurgents and to underscore federal power, especially when the rebellion reached its peak in the summer of 1794. South of Pittsburgh a clash between 600 rebels and a squad of Army troops led to several deaths. To Washington's shock, 7,000 insurgent sympathizers, many of them dirt poor, gathered at Braddock's Field. There, 39 years earlier, a British colonial soldier named Washington had saved the remnants of British General Edward Braddock's defeated army at the start of the French and Indian War!

Foreign events factored into the Administration's thinking. That very summer, the Reign of Terror gripped the French Revolution. Some at Braddock's Field, echoing the mayhem abroad, demanded the guillotine for backers of the whiskey tax. Some Federalists, who loathed French-speaking immigrant "radicals" like Albert Gallatin, feared a bloody revolution breaking out on American soil.

In September, Washington and Hamilton brushed off their old uniforms from their own Revolution. From Pennsylvania, New Jersey, Maryland, and Virginia they gathered some 12,950 federalized militia. It was the largest army assembled up to that time in North America—larger than any single force on any side in the American Revolution or the French and Indian War.

It was so large that conscription was necessary to fill out the ranks. For the first time, a U.S. military draft was held. For the first time, protests against a military draft erupted.

The army was led by Washington, Hamilton, and two noted ex-Revolutionary War Generals: Henry "Harry" Light Horse Lee, and Daniel Morgan of Virginia. (Lee was the father of that fellow from the Civil War. Daniel Morgan, a possible descendant of buccaneer Henry Morgan, was mimicked by Mel Gibson in the film *The Patriot*.)

The militias mustered and left from Carlisle, Pennsylvania. That town was 30 miles north of a future domestic clash: Gettysburg, involving that latter-day Lee. The overweening show of force then marched out to the western reaches of the Keystone State. To some people, America seemed to verge on civil war even as America herself was just getting started—and some 60-plus years before the actual Civil War! But Albert Gallatin had a role to play. The learned, articulate man from Geneva, Switzerland, had arrived in the U.S. during its Revolution. A merchant at heart, in Boston he sold non–British tea to Americans whose tea party protests had destroyed chests of the hated, taxed British variety.

Gallatin had settled in Pennsylvania, south of Pittsburgh, in what would be the epicenter of the Whiskey Rebellion. In 1793 he was elected to the U.S. Senate as an Anti-Federalist skeptical of centralized power. However, Federalist Senators ousted him in a precedent-setting Senate debate, one that took place not behind closed doors but in open session. Gallatin was found, wrongly, to lack the requisite length of U.S. residence for a Senator. He returned to a western Pennsylvania in upheaval.

A Crisis Defused

When the revolt broke out, Gallatin opposed the violent actions of the rebels yet was sympathetic to their complaints. He stated the liquor tax "will bear hard upon the honest and industrious citizens whilst the wealthy and conniving parts of the community will avoid payments by stratagems" (which sounds like hiring accountants to lower one's taxes today). Gallatin spoke at length to the insurgents, gained their confidence, and helped persuade their leaders to put away their weapons. His actions would help convince Washington to show magnanimity toward the insurrectionists.

In the meantime, Washington and Hamilton and their minions didn't fool around. In autumn 1794 the federalized militia reached the Alleghany region. The insurgency, which had looked so strong that summer, melted away. Rebel leaders were arrested and convicted of treason. Two rebels were sentenced to be hanged. With things well in hand, President Washington had gone back to the then-federal capital of Philadelphia, leaving others in charge. Following the advice of Gallatin's westerners, Washington pardoned those slated for the gallows. Others who had been arrested for lesser offenses never did jail time. Less merciful than the President was Hamilton, who blamed Gallatin, incorrectly, for plotting the revolt. Under political pressure from westerners like Gallatin, Washington directed his Treasury Secretary to reduce the whiskey tax. Congress later suspended it entirely, and it remained uncollected until the War of 1812. Then it was put back in place to raise money for the war—by the Treasury Secretary at that time: Albert Gallatin!

With the liquor rebellion over, the federal soldiers went back to their homes, the farmers returned to their stills, and the United States sidestepped a potential civil war during its very first federal administration. Still, the political impact of the Whiskey Rebellion was large. Although most Americans believed in taxation with representation, many thought the federal government, by calling out a massive army against a local tax uprising, had overreacted. This fueled support for those wary of the strong new federal entity, the so-called Anti-Federalists of Thomas Jefferson, James Madison—and Albert Gallatin. The political appeal of these three men would grow in the ensuing years and culminate in the election of Presidents Jefferson and Madison, with the tax-averse Gallatin as their Treasury Department chief.

More than a moneyman and mediator, Albert Gallatin was, like Jefferson and Ben Franklin, a Renaissance man. A linguist, he published dictionaries. An educator, he cofounded New York University. After acting as the longest-serving Treasury Secretary in U.S. history, he became Minister to France and Minister to Great Britain and also served as an envoy to Russia. He was part of the diplomatic team that included John Quincy Adams and Henry Clay and negotiated an end to the War of 1812—and a second end to the whiskey tax. All this gave him a resume suitable for the presidency but, being foreign-born, he was ineligible. In 1824 he did receive, against his will, his Democrat-Republican Party's nomination for Vice President before withdrawing under fire.

Further—unusually so for his era,

A daguerreotype is employed to capture this image of an aged Albert Gallatin, a sympathizer of the Whiskey Rebellion insurgents and later an influential Secretary of the Treasury (Photograph from the studio of Mathew Brady).

a time of incessant warfare between Indian tribes and Gallatin's frontier supporters—he had an abiding interest in the Native American and co-founded something called the American Ethnological Society, one of the first organizations to study the languages and cultures of the American Indian. His research led to the insight that the Indians of North and South America are descended from Asian peoples. It seems fitting, therefore, that the creator of the Gallatin statue in front of the Treasury Building also designed the most famous image of the Native American: the statuette *The End of the Trail*. James Earle Fraser's masterwork shows an Indian warrior slumped over his horse after an exhausting buffalo hunt. Thus it is also fitting Fraser designed the Buffalo Nickel. For a quarter century the striking visage of an Indian brave and bison graced the five-cent piece, until its replacement by the images of Gallatin's boss and friend, Jefferson, and his Monticello home. (Fraser's interest in and sympathy for Indians stemmed from his youth in Minnesota and South Dakota in the late 1880s, as the federal government consigned to reservations the once free-roaming tribes of the Great Plains.) By the way, that statue of Hamilton on the other side of the Treasury Building? Fraser sculpted it too. Talk about playing both sides of the fence!

Albert Gallatin died in 1849 at age 88 and lies in Manhattan's Trinity Church graveyard, not far from his famed predecessor at Treasury, Mr. Hamilton. Gallatin lived longer than anyone else closely associated with the Founding Fathers. Indeed, he is, as a biography attests, the forgotten Founding Father. He survived until the invention of the daguerreotype and that image shows a realistic portrait of an elderly, avuncular gentleman. He poses for the picture with a twinkle in his eye, as if he's just sipped from a mason jar of rye whiskey.

Sources

Adams, Henry. *The Life of Albert Gallatin*. Philadelphia: J.B. Lippincott, 1879. Vol. 3. Reprint. New York: Chelsea House, 1983.
Chernow, Ron. *Alexander Hamilton*. New York: Penguin, 2004.
_____. *Washington: A Life*. New York: Penguin, 2010.
Dungan, Nicholas. *Gallatin: America's Swiss Founding Father*. New York: New York University Press, 2010.
Hogeland, William. *The Whiskey Rebellion: George Washington, Alexander Hamilton, and the Frontier Rebels Who Challenged America's Newfound Sovereignty*. New York: Scribner, 2006.
Hoover, Michael. "The Whiskey Rebellion." U.S. Department of the Treasury, Alcohol and Tobacco Tax and Trade Bureau. August 21, 2014. https://www.ttb.gov/public_info/whisky_rebellion.shtml.
Lafayette Square Tour of Scandal, Assassination, and Spies. https://www.tripadvisor.com/Attraction_Review-g28970-d12791843-Reviews-Lafayette_Square_Tour_of_Scandal_Assassination_Intrigue-Washington_DC_District_of.html.
Slaughter, Thomas P. *The Whiskey Rebellion: Frontier Epilogue to the American Revolution*. Oxford: Oxford University Press, 1986.

45

The Crooked Bank for the Former Slaves

Freedmen's Bank Site: Corner of Madison Place and Pennsylvania Avenue, Southeast Corner of the Square

In early 1874 Frederick Douglass approached the Freedmen's Savings and Trust Company building a worried man. He had learned at his home in Rochester, New York, that the Bank was in bad financial shape and some of its trustees were likely crooks.

A Freedom Fighter's Daunting Mission

As its name attests, the Freedmen's Bank had been set up near the end of the Civil War as part of the Freedmen's Bureau. This was the federal agency aimed at aiding the education, work skills, and finances of the millions of newly emancipated slaves, as well as the basic needs of shelter and food. President Lincoln himself, on March 3, 1865, six weeks before his assassination, signed the Freedmen's Bank into existence. At the time, Douglass had hoped the Bank would afford blacks the "lessons of sobriety, wisdom, and economy, and to show them how to rise in the world." It had been a long road, Douglass knew: Centuries of slavery then finally freedom born out of the terrible, bloody war. Then there was the first taste of life as liberated men and women. And now came increasing resistance to full civil rights for blacks, in both the South and the North. It had been a long road for Douglass as well. Born a slave, possibly the son of his owner, on the Wye Plantation on Maryland's Eastern Shore, he was beaten bloody for his refusal to bow to an overseer and then punching back.

Leased out as a Baltimore dockworker, and saving almost enough of his share of the wages to buy his own freedom, he had impatiently lit out on his own to the free states of the North. Disguised as a sailor during his escape from Baltimore to New Jersey, he fretted every moment along the journey that he would be recognized and returned to the backbreaking toil of the plantation. He worked at the dockyards of New England, where he was astonished at how much harder the men labored there as they worked for themselves and not a master. Then he went to Rochester, where he set up a site on the Underground Railroad helping other escaped slaves headed north. Self-educated, he lectured and wrote and published a world-famous autobiography. Yes, it had been a hard road, although with much success. But now in 1874 there was growing resistance to the formerly enslaved, and even

Douglass's seemingly indomitable spirit was glum. But as he arrived at the Freedmen's Bank, his attitude shifted. Gazing up at the fine, five-story structure, canopies neatly placed above the windows, he would recall, "The whole thing was beautiful.... I had indeed been solicited to become one of its trustees, and had reluctantly consented to do so: but when ... I saw its magnificent brown stone front, its towering height, its perfect appointments ... I felt like the Queen of Sheba when she saw the riches of Solomon, that 'half had not been told me.'" In this passage, Douglass used a phrase that describes the often-ignored history of African Americans: the "half had not been told."

The Bank's new headquarters was directly across Pennsylvania Avenue from the Treasury Department and the White House of President Grant, the former Union Army commander. Surely the Bank could be turned around, with a location so close to those centers of power. Yet as Douglass took over and soon afterward became the Bank's president, he realized its situation was dire indeed.

Built to Fail

There was trouble from the start, in 1865, from the way the Bank was set up. It had been established in New York by high-minded men with the best of intentions. The driving force was the Reverend John W. Alvord, an abolitionist worried about the financial state of the newly emancipated. The South's economy was a wreck from the war. Plantations were confiscated or burned, the few factory towns like Atlanta and Richmond were in ashes, and the Confederate currency was worthless. Much of the South's workforce had been killed or maimed in battle, as in the case of whites, or were displaced and destitute, as in the case of blacks. Most former slaves were illiterate, with few skills outside of physical labor. Most had little money and no knowledge of finance. Reverend Alvord was particularly worried about the blacks who did have some savings, namely the thousands who had served in the Union Army or worked as freed, wage laborers during the Union Army campaigns. More than a few were squandering their savings, and con artists preyed upon others.

What was required, Alvord believed, was a savings bank expressly aimed at the freed men and women where they could safely deposit their money and learn the rudiments of personal finance. In Virginia, for example, Union General Benjamin Butler, the scourge of "Yankee occupied" New Orleans, had established such a repository. Another Union commander set up a freedmen's bank in Beaufort, South Carolina. In New York, Alvord got many of New York's elite, including inventor and reformer Peter Cooper, to sign off on his plan (Lincoln had launched his presidential campaign at his Cooper Union College). Industrialists promised to serve on the Freedmen Bank's board of trustees. Massachusetts Senator and abolitionist Charles Sumner introduced legislation to establish the Bank. Lincoln signed it into law. The Freedmen's Bank was to accept deposits "by or on behalf of persons heretofore held in slavery in the United States, or their descendants."

But right away the enterprise faced obstacles. Many of the experienced businessmen who were supposed to be on the Bank's board turned out to be mere window dressing to get the establishing legislation through Congress. Seven board members resigned soon afterward. The Bank would be in time be run, along with the remaining trustees, by a secretive committee of three men, men who lacked financial acumen and worked without congressional oversight. Although Congress had intended to restrict the Bank's operations to the city of Washington, a mistake in the legislation allowed branches outside the capital. The idealistic Alvord, although lacking any banking expertise, took that ball and ran with it. As Bank president he quickly formed 37 branches in 17 states. The locations read like an urban geography of the South. Banks were placed in such cities as Charleston, South Carolina; New Orleans, Louisiana; Vicksburg, Mississippi; Savannah, Georgia; Richmond, Virginia; and Houston, Texas. The large number of branches meant that from the beginning the Bank's financial assets and human resources were stretched paper thin. Unlike most financial institutions, the Freedmen's Bank raised no capital, subsisting only on the money of its depositors. Congress provided no funding. Bank assets peaked at around $60 million. It had many depositors, 70,000 of them, but most were very small holders with accounts worth between $5 and $50. Moreover, administering the cost of a small account was the same as administering a large one. Since the Bank had many small depositors, its relative administrative costs were very high. Such expenses amounted to more than 5 percent of the bank's assets. Since most of its investments were in Treasury bonds, which paid about 6 percent, there was a perilously low profit margin of under 1 percent.

Despite the shaky finances, Alvord and other managers marketed the bank as if it were a monetary Promised Land. Images of "Father Abraham" Lincoln and Union General Oliver Otis Howard, the founder of the African-American college Howard University, were inscribed on marketing materials. These promotions falsely implied the Bank's deposits were secured by the federal government. Bank officials marketed to black churches, schools, and mutual aid societies. In addition to ex-Union soldiers, pitches were made to barbers, shoemakers, seamstresses, farmers, porters, carpenters, and cooks. Disturbingly, given how things turned out, a special effort was made to have children set up small accounts. For instance, about one-quarter of the depositors in the Augusta, Georgia, branch were children. Depositors' bankbooks were inscribed with the phrase "temperance, frugality, economy, chastity, the virtues of thrift & savings." The Bank trained African Americans to operate the branch bank in D.C. and, over time, almost all of the other branches. But financial literacy among most freedmen at the time was limited; some employees were incompetent.

As the postwar economic boom lost steam, Congress, with scant opposition, changed the Bank's charter to allow it to make investments in real estate, stocks, and even unsecured loans. It was like a presage of the 1980s savings and loans crisis or the 2007 mortgage banking bust, with unchecked overinvestment heading toward a financial cliff. The lone voice in the wilderness was Pennsylvania Republican Senator Simon Cameron, who warned, "Depend upon it, the moment you allow them to put their money ... in real estate, that moment you weaken the credit of the institution and its stability." Another dubious move was to erect the Freedmen's Bank building itself, at its new headquarters in Lafayette Square. The structure, as Douglass noted, was impressive. But its cost, $260,000, put added pressure on the bank's shaky bottom line. The Freedmen Bank's low margins and scarce capital meant that it had to be honestly run and that it couldn't make bad investments. This proved presumptuous. One shady trustee was a railroad executive who borrowed $175,000 of the Bank's limited funds for "junk bonds." And he did this when the railroad industry was in a speculative bubble.

One Too Many Cookes

A bank manager who did great harm was Henry David Cooke, a whiskered Ohioan in his late forties. Cooke was a wild speculator who (unlike Garth Brooks) had friends in very high places. Around the time of the California Gold Rush, Cooke dreamed up the idea of a steamship line from New York to San Francisco by way of Panama's land passage. It was a success, but a business partner pilfered his assets. Returning to his native Ohio, Cooke headed up a failed newspaper. Its pro–Republican Party editorials led to warm relations between Cooke and his brother, Philadelphia banker Jay Cooke, with powerful G.O.P. politicians from Ohio. These included Treasury Secretary Salmon Chase; Senator John Sherman, the brother of General Sherman; and Ohio-born General and later President Ulysses S. Grant.

During the Civil War, Jay Cooke financed much of the Union effort, selling government bond issues in 1862 and 1865 worth, respectively, $511 million and $830 million (roughly $150 billion in 2018 dollars). In a marketing campaign that presaged the sale of Liberty bonds during the world wars, he hired 2,500 agents to hawk the securities from big-city streets to remote mining camps. The monies raised were a major factor in the North's financial and industrial muscle overwhelming the South. However, after raising the funds—on which he earned a commission of a bit over 0.375 percent, about $5 million—Jay Cooke would delay placing them in the Union war coffers. This let him make more money in the interim. Some in Congress accused him of war profiteering.

Jay Cooke put his brother Henry in charge of his Washington, D.C., office. Senator Sherman, from his perch on the Finance Committee, assisted Henry in becoming head of the Washington and Georgetown trolley system. In 1865, when the Freedmen's Bank was set up, Henry Cooke became one of its trustees. In the meantime, Henry formed his own firm, the Seneca Sandstone Company. Its quarry, located just 22 miles north of Washington, had long supplied much of the stone for the capital's public buildings, notably the red sandstone for the magnificent Smithsonian Castle, designed by James Renwick, architect of the Renwick Gallery. Seneca Sandstone's quarry was originally established by John Parke Custis Peter. He was the great-grandson of Martha Washington, the grandson of Georgetown's first mayor, Robert Peter, and the son of Thomas Peter, builder of Georgetown's grand Tudor Place mansion.

John Parke Custis Peter made a fortune off the quarry. He was able to underbid rivals for government contracts for at least three reasons. He was a competent businessman. The quarry was close to Washington, so his transportation costs were low. And, his labor costs were very low because slaves worked the quarry. When Henry Cooke took over this business, in which Irish laborers mingled with now-free black workers, he decided to cut deals with his friends in high places. He sold shares of the company, at half price, to influential officials, including President Grant. When the Grant discount was revealed critics cried bribery, and the President sold off his holdings. In 1871 Grant appointed Cooke to be Washington's first "Territorial Governor," essentially its mayor, of the capital as well as Georgetown, which previously had its own governing body. Cooke got the job despite having no experience in city administration. Critics cried quid pro quo.

Henry Cooke focused on his business interests. He left the job of running the city to others such as Alexander "Boss" Shepherd. The latter, by paving the streets of "the city of mud" and by providing safe water and sewer systems, transformed Washington, formerly a sleepy backwater, into a modern city. But he so overspent he bankrupted the place. However, there was another silver lining: Cooke, Shepherd, and especially future Mayor Sayles Bowen were Radical Republicans and, as such, were staunch supporters of civil rights. Before Jim Crow took over Washington—as it did elsewhere in the South and some of the North—the city's African Americans profited from full voting privileges as well as a building boom in municipal schools.

In 1873, as President Grant began his second term, there came a nationwide financial collapse. This was the aptly named Panic of 1873, leading to the aptly named Long Depression, which lasted through most of the 1870s. It was a classic bursting bubble, brought on by overspeculation in railroads, the nation's largest industry after the toppling of King Cotton and, as in the Great Recession of 2007, by overinvestment in real estate. The real estate plunge hurt companies like Seneca Sandstone, which supplied materials for the developers of Washington real estate. Henry Cooke's firm was already underfinanced from having sold its stock at half price to his political pals. Now he used his position as Freedmen's Bank honcho to try to save his company. He had his firm take out large unsecured loans from the Bank. This was not only a conflict of interest, it was also against the law. You couldn't be an officer of a bank that gave a loan to your own company. Predictably, the loans went south. Seneca Sandstone went out of business. And the unpaid loans were the final straw that broke the teetering Freedmen's Bank.

Frederick Douglass, as Bank president, soon realized the institution was past repair. He felt he was "married to a corpse." (In this he presaged the 1879 remark of German Chancellor Otto von Bismarck, in opposing Kaiser Wilhelm's alliance to the tottering empire of Austria-Hungary: "Mein Kaiser, you have married us to a corpse!") Douglass asked Congress for a bailout, but Congress refused. Depositors, knowing the Bank was in trouble, made panicky withdrawals. Despite putting $10,000 of his own money into the place, Douglass agreed in June 1874, just months after taking over, to shut it down. On July 2 the institution closed. The immediate effect of the Seneca Sandstone disaster and the closure of the Freedmen's Bank was that $3 million went "poof." In time, about 30,000 depositors, almost all of them African American, would lose their life's savings. In Washington City itself 3,000 depositors saw their money disappear.

The Treasury Department took over the Bank's remaining capital. Over many years it made interest payments to the remaining holders—if a depositor could prove his identity and mail to the Department his bankbook of deposits and accumulated interest. Over time, the government paid back about half of the depositors about three-fifths of their money. Eventually all the depositors died off. The program was shut down early in the 20th century.

The implosion of the Freedmen's Bank soured many in the post–Civil War black community on money matters just as they could have been learning more about, and profiting from, such things. Congress held hearings. Lawmakers were astounded at the testimony of the Bank's inspector, Anson Sperry, a Union Army paymaster as well as Bank cofounder. Sperry had certified the books of many of the bank's branches with the notation "E&OE." He explained that meant "Errors and Omissions *Excepted*." In other words, Sperry knew the books were cooked but out of sympathy for the freemen let them pass. "I should have known more and had less enthusiasm," he lamented. Some in Congress called for Henry

Cooke's indictment, but despite his unlawful conflict of interest with Seneca Sandstone he was never tried. After his own financial hard times, he got back on his feet by working as the executor of the estate of a friend in a high place: the Supreme Court's Chief Justice and former Treasury Secretary, Salmon Chase.

Due to the lack of justice meted out to the guilty and the crushed financial hopes of so many former slaves, the Freedmen's Bank affair ranks among the most disturbing scandals in Lafayette Square's long history.

A Scene of Civil Rights

Still, much later, the bank's location became a touchstone of the civil rights movement. After the demolition in 1895 of the bank building, a six-story Lafayette Square Opera House took its place. In 1906 the 1,500-seat-plus structure became the home of the Belasco Theater Company. Enrico Caruso, Sarah Bernhardt, and Ethel Barrymore performed there. The Lee, Sam, and Jacob Shubert brothers of New York owned the Belasco; the Shubert Organization owned the National Theatre at 1321 Pennsylvania Avenue, some two blocks east of

The Freedmen's Bank at the corner of Madison Place and Constitution Avenue was replaced by an opera house and the Belasco Theater. The emporium was one of Washington's first integrated public places (Library of Congress; originally from the *Washington (DC) Morning Times*, 1895).

the Willard Hotel. The Belasco Theater struck a blow for civic equality in 1932 after the New York Metropolitan Opera House, the Met, blocked America's first professional black opera singer, Lillian Evanti, from performing there. Evanti, hailing from D.C., had attended the Howard University School of Music. The Belasco, where she had performed since the 1920s, let her sing on its concert stage instead. Several years later she performed at the White House, according to the White House Historical Association. First Lady Eleanor Roosevelt, Evanti said, "made me feel right at home." Mrs. Roosevelt went on to support the 1939 Easter Sunday performance of black recital singer Marian Anderson at the Lincoln Memorial—after the Daughters of the American Revolution barred her concert at their Constitution Hall (see Chapter 30, "A Peerless Singer Lays the Groundwork for 'I Have a Dream'").

In 1942, during the Second World War, the Theater became a "stage door canteen," a center of arts and entertainment for enlisted men. And it again battered old Jim Crow. Allied soldiers, including "colored" ones, from places as far away as British India and French colonial Africa, were welcomed inside contrary to the segregation in most of the District's other houses of entertainment. During the Korean War, which began in 1950, the United Services Organizations (USO) managed the space as a place of recreation for GIs. During that conflict Americans, black and white, served for the first time in fully integrated units under President Harry Truman's desegregation order. Frederick Douglass, who recruited his own sons to serve in the Union Army, no doubt rolled over in his grave—with a smile on his face.

In 1964, the elegant theater complex was razed, to be replaced by the sterile red-brick and metal grating of the U.S. Court of Federal Claims. Jacqueline Kennedy and friends had been able to save many historic buildings of Lafayette Square, but the venerable Belasco and the star-crossed Freedmen's Bank vanished into history.

If only such places could reappear. What a tale they'd have to tell. Of two centuries of crime, scandal, triumph, and intrigue, of the wild saga in and around Lafayette Square.

Sources

Douglass, Frederick. *Narrative of the Life of Frederick Douglass, an American Slave*. Chapel Hill: University of North Carolina Press, 1999. First published in 1845. https://docsouth.unc.edu/neh/douglass/douglass.html.
Encyclopaedia Britannica. "Freedmen's Bank." https://www.britannica.com/topic/Freedmens-Bank#ref1223106.
Freedmansbank. "Freedmen's Savings Bank." http://freedmansbank.org/.
Gordon, John Steele. "The Freedman's Bank." *American Heritage* 44, no. 8 (December 1993). https://www.americanheritage.com/content/freedman%E2%80%99s-bank.
Jones, Mark. "The Seneca Stone Ring Scandal." WETA. *Boundary Stones*, February 19, 2013. https://blogs.weta.org/boundarystones/2013/02/19/seneca-stone-ring-scandal.
Moser, Edward P. "Brave Man, Bad Advisors." Grant Administration. In *The Two-Term Jinx: How Most Second-Term Presidents Stumble and Why Some Succeed*. Book 1. CreateSpace/Amazon (self-published), 2016.
_____. "Frederick Douglass: Ride to Freedom." In *A Patriot's A to Z of America*. Nashville: Turner, 2011.
Oubre, Claude F. *Forty Acres and a Mule: The Freedmen's Bureau and Black Land Ownership*. Baton Rouge: Louisiana State University Press, 1978.
Stiller, Jesse. U.S. Department of the Treasury, Comptroller of the Currency, History. "The Freedman's Savings Bank: Good Intentions Were Not Enough; A Noble Experiment Goes Awry." Retrieved 2018. https://www.occ.treas.gov/about/what-we-do/history/freedman-savings-bank.html.
Washington, Reginald. "The Freedman's Savings and Trust Company and African American Genealogical Research." *Prologue* 29, no. 2 (Summer 1997). Federal Records and African American History. https://www.archives.gov/publications/prologue/1997/summer/freedmans-savings-and-trust.html.
White House Historical Association. "Lillian Evanti." https://www.whitehousehistory.org/lillian-evanti.
_____. "Rodgers House and Belasco Theater." https://www.whitehousehistory.org/rodgers-house-belasco-theater.
Wikipedia. "Henry Cooke." https://en.wikipedia.org/wiki/Henry_D._Cooke.

Index

Numbers in *bold* italics indicate pages with illustrations

Adams, Abigail 57, 77, 78
Adams, Charles 77, 78
Adams, Charles Francis 57–58
Adams, Henry 57, **58**, 59–60, 62, 64, 65, 66, 129
Adams, John 7, 15, 26, 48, 49, 50, 57, 77, 80, 170, 202
Adams, John, II 177–78
Adams, John Quincy 15, 17, 19, 23, 48, 57, 89, 100, 163, 186, 236; nearly drowned 177–78
Adams, Marian Hooper "Clover" 58–60
Alexandria, Virginia 23–24, 101, 102, 141, 171, 184–88
Ali, Hadji "Hi Jolly" 95, 96
Ali, Muhammad 181
Alston, Willis 89
Alvord, John 239–40
Ambler, Betsy 114
Amendment, 13th 229
The American Black Chamber 146–47
American Colonization Society 100
American Philosophical Society 27
Amistad 23
Anaconda Plan 120, 125
Anderson, Marian 155–58, 244
Andersonville prison 151–53
Antietam, Battle of 69, 107
Anti-Federalist Party 26, 49, 207, 235
Appomattox statue 141
Arlington House 121, 122, 124–125, 138–140, 175
Arlington National Cemetery 119, 148
Armistead, Henry 187, 188
Armstrong, John 40, 150, 196
Army, U.S. 38, 93–96, 166–67
Arnold, Philip 63
Arthur, Chester A. 225
assassinations: Lincoln 107–109; Seward attempt 3–6; Truman attempt 117–119
Astor, Emily 196
Atlantic Monthly 31, 195
Atzerodt, George 5

Bailey, Gamaliel 23, 24
Bainbridge, William 81, 85–86
Baltimore, Battle of 151
Bank of the Metropolis 174, 199, **219**, 220–21
Bank of the United States 199–200, 206
Baptists 26
Barbary Pirates Wars 28, 80, **81**, 82
Barker, Jacob 41
Barney, Joshua 151
Barnum, P.T. 33, 93
barracks, military 164–168
Barron, James 83, **84**, 85–87, 89
Barry, Marion 180, 182, **183**

Barton, Clara 143
Battle Hymn of the Republic 194–195
Beale, Edward "Ned" Fitzgerald 91–93, **94**, 96–97; Camel Corps 93–96; Mexican-American War 92–93
Beale, Mary 93
Beale, Truxtun 93, 96–97
Beales 230
Beaumarchais, Pierre 76
Beauregard, P.G.T. 69
Beecher, Henry Ward 24
Belasco Theater **243**, 244
Bell, Daniel 22
Bell, William 4
Benjamin Ogle Tayloe House 66, 105, 230
Benton, Jesse 45–46
Benton, Philip Hart 24, 45–46, 186, 187
Bill of Rights 41–42, 207
Birdzell, Donald 117–119
Black Butte 63
Bladensburg, Battle of 150–51
Bladensburg, Maryland 40, 89–90; Battle of 150–51; Decatur-Barron duel 83–87
Blaine, James G. 97
Blair, Elizabeth 122
Blair, Francis Preston 121–22, 124
Blair, Montgomery 122
Blair-Lee House (Blair House) 117–119, 127, 204
Blodgett's Hotel 117
B'nai Brith 180, 182
Bollman, Justus 14
Bonaparte, Jerome 82
Bonaparte, Napoleon 14, 35–36
Booth, John Wilkes 5, 31, 108, 229
Braddock, Edward 170–71, 235
Brady, Matthew 69, 236
Brandywine, Battle of 10
Bristow, Benjamin 131
Brooks, Noah 31–32, 107
Bruin and Hill slave traders 23
Brown, John 22, 123, 193
Brown v. Board of Education 8–9, 157
Brumidi, Constantino 136
Buberl, Caspar 141
The Buccaneer move 38
Buchanan, James 68, 92, 123
Buchignani, Anthony Gabriele 56
Buffon, Comte de 27
Bull Run (Manassas), Battle of 69, 191, 223
Bullfinch, Charles 175
Bunker Hill 15, 202
Bureau of the Fiscal Service 167
Burke, Edward 230–31

245

Burnes, David 169–71, *172*, 173, 176
Burning of Washington City 215–221
Burnside, Ambrose 223
Burr, Aaron 45, 49, 82, 86, 201, 203, 204

Calhoun, Floride Bonneau 54
Calhoun, John C. 19, 54, 55–56, 68, 121, 178, 229
Camel Corps 93–96
Cameron, James Donald 66
Cameron, Simon 120, 121, 124, 137, 240
Canada 147
Cantrell, Mack 180
Capitol Building 8, 135–136, 217, 218
Capitol Hill 170
Carbery, Thomas 155, 160, 174
Carroll, Major Charles 40–41
Carroll, Daniel (Constitutional Convention) 169, 170
Carroll, John (priest) 160
Carroll, William 45
Carroll of Carrollton, Charles 170
Carroll of Duddington, Daniel 170
Carroll of Rock Creek, Daniel 170
Carson, Kit 91, 92
Carter, Jimmy 119, 181
Carver, George Washington 158
Casey, Thomas Lincoln 131
Cash, Johnny 47
Catalano, Salvador 81
Catholicism 160–163
Center Market 7
Chain Bridge, Virginia 42, 90
Chamber of Commerce Building 142
Chaplain, William 22
Chase, Katherine "Kate" 222, *223*, 224–26
Chase, Salmon 131, 222, 223, 224, 241, 243
Cheese, Mammoth 26–29
USS *Chesapeake* 83–84, 112
Chesapeake Bay 220
Cheshire County 26
China 147
Choctaw Indians 37
cholera 175
Church, Angelica Schuyler *13*, 14, 201
Church, John Barker 14
Churchill, Winston 43, 145, 196
City Hall 180, 181, 183
City of Mud 209
Civil War 24–25, 34, 120–125, 203–4, 210–13, 222–24, 229, 239, 241; Greenough, Rose O'Neale 68–72; Howe, Julia Ward 191–96; Lincoln, Mary Todd and seances 30–33; Meigs, Montgomery 136–141; Rathbone, Henry 107–8; Seward assassination attempt 3–6; Winders 149, 151–53
Civil War spies 68–72
Claiborne, William 37, 38
Clarke, James Freeman 192–93
Clavert, Dora Inez 226
Clay, Henry 54, 55, 82, 91, **99**, 204, 229, 236; duel with John Randolph 88–90, 204; Dupuy, Charlotte 98–102
Clay, Lucretia 101
Cleveland, Grover 213
Clinton, Dewitt 161, 199
Clinton, George 199
Cluss, Adolph 141
Cockburn, Admiral George 3, 36, 42, 215, **216**, 218–20
Code Bureau 145–46
Cody, William "Buffalo Bill" 91, 96
Coffee, John 38, 45
Coffelt, Leslie 118–119

Colchester, Lord 31–32
Collazo, Oscar 118–119
Columbian College 142, 143, 176
Commerce Department 211
Compromise of 1820 98
Compromise of 1850 23–24, 98, 101
Condon, John 99, 100
Congress 15, 50, 88–89, 153, 200, 207, 213, 240, 242–43
USS *Congress* 91–92
Congressional Cemetery 5, 183, 188
Conkling, Roscoe 224–26
Conrad and McMunn's Hotel 50
Constitution 41–42, 207, 229
Constitution Hall 155–58, 244
Cook, John, Sr. 8
Cooke, Henry 241–43
Cooke, Jay 241
Cooper, Peter 239
Corcoran, William 58, 141–43
Corcoran Gallery of Art 143
Corcoran mansion **142**
Cornwallis, Charles 75, 111, 202
Court of Appeals, D.C. (Old City Hall) 175
Craik, James 10
Crane, William 189
Creek Indians 46
Crosman, George H. 93
Cullinane, Maurice 181, 182
currency, U.S. 198
Custis, George Washington Parke 121, 122–23, 138
Cutts, Mary 188
Cutts-Madison House *see* Dolley Madison House

Daisy Miller 59
Dana, James Dwight 62
Daughters of the American Revolution (DAR) 155–58, 244
Davidson, Samuel 170
Davis, Jefferson 69, 71, 93, 100, 133, 135, 136–37, 138, 153, 229
DC Emancipation Act 102
Deane, Silas 76
debt assumption 199
Decatur, Stephen, Jr. 80–88, 90, 91, 127, 204; Barbary Pirates Wars 80–82; *Chesapeake* incident 83–84; duel with James Barron 83–87
Decatur, Stephen, Sr. 85
Decatur, Susan Wheeler 80, 82, 86–87
Decatur House 80, 83, 91, 96–97, 98–99, 127, 204
Declaration of the Rights of Man 11
Democracy: An American Novel 59
Democrat-Republican Party 236
d'Estaing, Comte 11
Dewey, Thomas 147
Dickinson, Charles 46–48
Diggs, Judson 23, 24
Dodge, Francis, Jr. 23
Dolley Madison House 21, 58–59, 62, 186, 188, 192, 207
Donelson, Andrew Jackson 54
Donelson, Emily 54
Donovan, William "Wild Bill" 147–48
double standard 105
Douglas, Stephen 57, 68
Douglass, Frederick 231, 238–39, 242, 244
Downs, Joseph 119
Drayton, Daniel 22, 23
Dubuisson, Étienne Larigaudelle 161, 162, 164
dueling 46–48, 84–86, 88, 89–90, 204–205

Dunbar, Paul Lawrence 8
Du Ponceau, Pierre-Étienne 76, 77
Duportail, Louis 11
Dupuy, Aaron 100, 101
Dupuy, Charlotte 91, 98–102
Duvall, Betty 69
Duvall, Robert 69

East Room of White House 26, 28, 33–34
Eastern Market 7
Eaton, John 53–55
Eaton, Peggy O'Neale 52, *53*, 54–55, 56
Edmonson, Daniel 22
Edmonson, Emily 23, *24*
Edmonson, Mary *24*
Edmonson, Paul 24
The Education of a Poker Player 148
The Education of Henry Adams 58
Egypt 182
Eisenhower, Dwight 157
Eisenhower Administration 167
Eisenhower Executive Office Building (EEOB) *see* State, War, and Navy Department Building
election of 1800 49–50
Electoral College 49, 227
Ellicott, Andrew 171
Elliott, Jesse Duncan 85, 86
Ellis Island 199
Emancipation Proclamation 32
The End of the Trail 237
USS *Enterprise* 80, 112
Ericsson, John 185–86, 189
espionage 68–72, 144–148
Evanti, Lillian 244
Evening Star 132, 210–11, 213

Fabyan, George 145
Falguière, Alexandre 11
Federal Bureau of Investigation (FBI) 181, 182
Federal Reserve 200
Federal Triangle 167, 214
The Federalist Papers 207
Federalist Party 18, 26, 207, 235
Fendall, Philip Richard II 100, 101, 138
Fillmore, Millard 23
First Colored Presbyterian Church 8
Foote, Henry 21, 23–24
Ford's Theater 5, 107–108
Forester, C.S. 84
Fort McNair 184
Fort Sumter 120
Fox sisters 30
Franklin, Ben 76, 191, 206, 236
Fraser, James Earl 237
Frederick the Great 73, 75
Free Soil Party 100
Freedmen's Bank 201, 238–243
Freedmen's Bureau 238
French Army, attitudes of 113
French Guiana 10
French Revolution 11–13, 201, 235
Friedman, William F. 145, 147
Fugitive Slave Act 24, 98

Gadsby, John 19, 101
Gadsby's Tavern 19
Gallatin, Albert 28, 84, 191, 200, 215, 233–35, **236**; statue 200

Gardiner, David 185, 186, 187, 188
Gardiner, Julia 184, 186–88, **189**
Gardner, Alexander **5**, 69
Garfield, James 232
George Washington University *see* Columbian College
Georgetown 170, 171
Georgetown College (University) 87, 160, 161, 162
Germany 78
Gettysburg, Battle of 105–106, 235
Ghorbal, Ashraf 182
Gilmer, Thomas 112, 186, 187, 188
Giusta, Antoine Michel 19, 177
Glory 60
Gold Rush 91, 92–93, 196
Grant, Julia 107
Grant, Ulysses S. 91, 93, 96, 106, 107, 125, 131, 138, 196, 201, 224, 231, 239, 241, 242
Grasse, Comte de 11, 111
Great Britain 35–36, 39
Great Diamond Hoax 63–64
Great Falls, Virginia 90
The Greek Slave 142
Greeley, Horace 63
Green, Thomas 175
Greenleaf Point 184, 187
Greenough, Horatio 175
Greenough, "Little Rose" 70, **71**
Greenough, Rose O'Neale 68–72; Pinkerton, Allan 69–71
Grief statue **60**
Groves, Leslie 166–67

Hadfield, George 175
Haiti 37
Hall, Elizabeth "Lizzy" 211–13
Hall, Mary Ann **211**, 212–13
Hamilton (play) 199, 204
Hamilton, Alexander 10, 11, 12, 13, 26, 49, 50, 75, 77, 85, 89, **200**, 237; statue 198; tour 198–207; Whiskey Rebellion 233–36
Hamilton, Elizabeth Schuyler 204, 205
Hamilton, Philip 204–205
Hanafi Siege 180–82
Hancock, Winfield Scott 95
Hanover, Germany 109–110
Harpers Ferry 22, 123, 193
Harris, Ira 107, 109
Harris, Dr. Thomas 44, 46
Harrison, William Henry 85, 175, 178, 189
Hay, Clara Louise Stone 59, 65–66
Hay, John 57, 59, 62, 64, 65
Hay-Adams Hotel 61
Hay-Adams mansion 62
Hayes, Rutherford B. 140, 227, 230–31
Heath, John 85
Henry, Joseph 31
Herold, David 5
Hoban, James 43, 162
Hohenlohe, Prince Alexander 161–62, 164
Hohenzollern-Hechingen 75
Holmead's Burying Ground 170
homosexuality 76–78
Hooker, Thomas 210
Hooker's Division 209–211, **212**, 213–14
Hooper, Ellen Sturgis 58
horse country 228
Horseshoe Bend, Battle of 46

Hotel Washington 199
Houston, Charles Hamilton 8-9, 157
Houston, Sam 100
Howard, Oliver Otis 8, 240
Howard University 8, 155, 240, 244
Howe, Julia Ward 191-92, *193*, 194-96
Howe, Samuel Gridley 191-92, 195, 196
Huger, Francis 14
Hume, David (newspaper critic) 117
Humphreys, Salusbury Pryce 83
Hurok, Sol 156

Ickes, Harold L. 157
immigration 199
impressing of sailors 83-84
inaugurations 17-19, 50-51
Indian Treaty Room 129, *130*
Indians, American 37, 46, 237
Ingram, Samuel 55
Iran 182
Irish 175, 199, 219, 220
Islamic Center 180, 182

Jabbar, Kareem Abdul 181
Jackson, Andrew 11, 15, *18*, 28, *47*, 49, 89, 91, 100, 121, 200, 204, 206; big cheese 28-29; Dickinson duel 46-48; Eaton, Peggy 52-56; inauguration 17-19; Nashville brawl 44-46; New Orleans, Battle of 35-39, 44, 52; statue 35, 52, 206
Jackson, Rachel Donelson 44, 46, 54
Jackson, Thomas "Stonewall" 35, 69
Jackson Place, 712 *see* Rathbone, Henry 107-110
Jackson Place, 722 *see* Sickles, Daniel 103-106
Jackson Place, 748 *see* Decatur House
Jacksonian democracy 206
Jaegers, Albert 78
James, Henry 59
Japan 146-47, 166, 229
Jay, John 13, 201, 207
Jefferson, Thomas 7, 11, 12, 13, 15, 36, 42, 43, 48, *51*, 80-81, 84, 88, 114, 151, 170, 174, 199, 202, 228, 233, 236, 237; Election of 1800 49-50; inaugurations 50-51; mammoth cheese 26-29; Pennsylvania Avenue and President's Park 49, 50-51
Jefferson Day dinner 55, 98
Jennings, Paul 21-22, 24-25, 40-41
Jesus Christ 194-95
Jim Crow 231, 242
John Brown's Body 193, 194
Johnson, Andrew 5, 229
Johnson, Lyndon 167
Johnson, Reverdy 229
Jones, Colonel 217
Jones, Jasmine Cephas 204
Jones, Thomas Catesby 92
Jordan, Hamilton 181
Judiciary Square 23

Kearny, Stephen W. 92
Kennedy, Jacqueline Bouvier 133, 244
Kennedy, John F. 119
Kennon, Beverley 186, 187, 188
Key, Francis Scott 100, 103, 125, 151, 158, 228
Key, Philip Barton II 23, 103-105, 127, 204
Khaalis, Hamaas Abdul 181-82
King, Ada Copeland 64-65, 66
King, Clarence 59, 62-66; Great Diamond Hoax 63-64
King, Martin Luther, Jr. 158, 218

Know-Nothing Party 163
Kohlman, Anthony 161-63
Korean War 244
Kościuszko, Tadeusz 206-7; statue 206-7
Ku Klux Klan 229, 230

Lady Liberty 136
Lafayette, Adrienne de 12-13, 14
Lafayette, George Washington 12, 14, 15, 201, 202
Lafayette, Marquis de 10, *11*, 73, 75, 199, 201-2; French Revolution and imprisonment 11-14; statue 11, 201-2; tour of U.S. 14-15, 201-2
Lafayette Square, creation of 49, 50-51
Lafitte, Jean *37*, 38
Lake Erie, Battle of 85
Lamon, Ward Hill 33-34
Latrobe, Benjamin 83, 174
Lauberdière, Comte de 111-113, *114*, 115
Laurens, John 10, 201, 206-7
Laurie, Margaret 31
Lee, Fitzhugh 141
Lee, George Washington Custis 139-40
Lee, Henry "Harry" Light Horse Lee 235
Lee, Mary Anna 121, 124, 131, 139
Lee, Robert E. 69, 95-96, 100, 106, *121*, 133, 136-37, 138, 153, 203; Lincoln, Abraham 120-22, 124-25
Lee, Samuel Phillips 122, 124
Lee, Smith 139
Lee, Sydney Smith 124, 125
Leland, John 26-27
L'Enfant, Pierre Charles 165, 169, 171, 215
HMS *Leopard* 83-84, 112
Lewis, Charles Lee 82
Liberia 100
Library of Congress 131, 218
Linck, George 225
Lincoln, Abraham 3, 5, 6, 23, 69, *70*, 102, 105, 137, 138, 157, 191-92, 203, 218, 229, 238, 239, 240; assassination 3-6, 107-109, 218; Lee, Robert E. 120-22, 124-25; Rathbone, Henry 107-109; seances and dreams 30-34
Lincoln, Mary Todd 30, *31*, 32-33, 107-108, 125, 222; seances 30-33
Lincoln, Robert Todd 33, 107, 140
Lincoln, Willie 30-32
Lincoln-Douglas debates 57
Lincoln Memorial *156*, 157, 158, 164, 165; concerts 157, 158
Livingstone, Edward 36, 38
lobbyists 196
Lodge, Henry Cabot 65
Lodge, Nanny Mills Davis 65
Lord Baltimore 121, 160
Louis Napoleon III 71
Louis XVI 11-12, 14
Louis XVIII 14
Louisiana Purchase 200, 233
Louse Alley 209, 211, 214
Louvre 128
Luce, Claire Booth 158

HMS *Macedonian* 82
Madison, Dolley 21-22, 40-43, 44, 68, 174, 175, 207
Madison, James 15, 22, 24-25, 35-36, 40-43, 48, 80, 102, 150-51, 171, 199, 202, 207, 233, 236
Mammoth 27
Mann, Horace 23
Marines, Royal 150-51, 199, 218-20

Marines, U.S. 81–82, 103, 151, 224
Marion, Francis 191
Marshall, Humphrey 89
Marshall, James 13
Marshall, John 7, 13, 44, 162
Marshall, Thurgood 9
Marszalek, John 52
Mason, James 58, 59
Mattingly, Ann 155, 160–63
Maxcy, Virgil 186, 187, 188
McClellan, George 63, 125, 192–93
McKim, Charles Follen 132
McKinley, William 57, 111
McLane, Louis 53–54
McNair, Fort 5
Meacham, Jon 28
Meacham, Thomas S. 28
Meade, George 106, 125
"Mechanics" 51, 160
Meigs, John Rodgers 138, *140*, 141
Meigs, Montgomery 134, *135*, 143; Arlington National Cemetery 138–41; Capitol Building 135–136; Pension Building 140–41; Quartermaster 136–38, 142; Washington Aqueduct 134–35
Mellon, Andrew 132–33
Melville, Herman 92
Mercié, Antonin 11
Metropolitan African Methodist Episcopal (AME) Church 8
Metropolitan Opera 158
Metropolitan Square 199
Mexican-American War 92–93, 149, 151
Military Intelligence (MI)-8 144–45
Miller, Belle 32
Mills, Clark 35
Mills, Robert 131, 149, 199, 200
Mohammad, Messenger of God 181
Monmouth Courthouse, Battle of 75, 77
Monroe, Elizabeth Kortwright 12
Monroe, James 10, 12–13, 15, 41, 48, 82, 86, 151, 163, 201–2, 204
Monroe Doctrine 163
Mont Saint Michel and Chartres 58
Monticello 7, 237
Monty Python 50
Morgan, Daniel 235
Morris, Gouverneur 12, 13, 201, 207
Mount Vernon 12, 15, 171, 187
Mt. Whitney 62
Mountaineering in the Sierra Nevada 62
Mroz, Vincent 118
Mullet, Alfred 127–33
Mullet, Thomas 132
Mulligan, Hercules 76–77, 206
Mulligan, John, Jr. 76–77, 206
Mumler, William 33
Munitions Building 165–66
Murder Bay 209, *210*, 211–14
Museum, National, of the American Indian 211
My Imprisonment and the First Year of Abolition Rule in Washington book 71

Narragansett, Rhode Island 225, 226
Nashville 44–46
Nashville City Hotel 45–46
Nat Turner rebellion 228
Nation of Islam 181
National Archives 41

National Gallery of Art 211
National Hotel 19
National Intelligencer 217, 220
National Mall 164
National Portrait Gallery 41
National Security Agency (NSA) 148
National Trust for Historic Preservation 97
Native Americans *see* Indians, American
Nautilus 112
Naval Academy 91–92, 124, 125
Navy Building 165–66
Navy, U.S. 3, 80–87, 93–96, 112, 114, 164, 166, 184–89, 213–14
Nelson, Horatio Admiral 82
New Era newspaper 23
New Orleans, Battle of 35–39
New Orleans, battle song 35
New York 199
New York City Hall, Post Office and Courthouse 128, 131–32
New York Manumission Society 201
New York University 191, 236
Newseum 100
Nicolay, John 57
Nixon, Richard 167
North, William 77
nullification 55–56

Oak Hill Cemetery 175
Oesser, Felix 153
Office of Strategic Services (OSS) 147
O'Harrow, Robert 135
Ohio 241
Oklahoma City bombing 117
Old Capitol Prison 70, 153, 175–176, 229
Old Ebbitt Grill 209
Old Soldier's Home 31, 138
Olmstead, Frederick Law 58
Opera House, Lafayette Square 243
Operation Magic 166
Oregon Territory 92, 185
Organization of American States (OAS) headquarters 174
Orphan (Orphanage) Asylum, Washington City 142, 174
O'Toole, Patricia 64
Oval Office 43

Pakenham, General Edward 36, 38, 39
Pakistan 182
Pan American Building *see* Organization of American States (OAS)
Panic of 1873 224, 242
Parallel Survey, 40th 62
Patent Office 217
Peacemaker cannon 185, 186, 187
Peale, Charles Wilson 27
Pearl slave escape 21–25
Peerce family 170
Pennsylvania 200, 233–236
Pension Building 140–41
Pentagon 128, 166–67
Perkins, Tom 12
Perkins School for the Blind 191
Perry, Matthew 229
Perry, Oliver Hazard 85, 151
Pershing, John J. 199
Peter, John Parke Custis 241
Petticoat affair sex scandal 52–56
Peyster, Robert 41

Philadelphia 199, 236
USS *Philadelphia* 81–82
Philadelphia Music Academy 155
photography, spirit 32–33
Physick, Dr. Philip 44
Pierce, Franklin 93
Pinkerton, Allan 69–71
pirates, French 37
Pitch, Anthony 43, 216
Pittsburgh 234–35
Pleasanton, Stephen 41, *42*
police, D.C. 117–119, 181–82
Polk, James K. 23, 92
Poole, Robert M. 136
Pope, John Russell 132
Populist politics 49–51
Porter, David 85, 86
Porter, David Dixon 85
Powell, Lewis 4–6, 109
Powers, Hiram 142
Preparatory School for Colored Youth 8
President's Park 49, 50–51
Prince George's County 171
USS *Princeton* 91–92, 112, 127, 184, ***185***, 186–189
Progressive Era 213–14
prostitution 209–14
Protestantism 161, 162–63
Prussia, King of 13
Pryor, Elizabeth Brown 124
Puerto Rican nationalists 117–119
Pullman porters 64
PURPLE codes 145

Queen Victoria 71

Rabe, Robert 181, 182
race riot of 1919 218
Ralston, William 63
Randolph, John 204; duel with Henry Clay 88–90
Rathbone, Basil 110
Rathbone, Clara Harris 107–110
Rathbone, Henry 107, ***108***, 109–110
Rathbone, Henry Riggs 110
Reconstruction 139, 227–28, 230–32
Red Cross building 143
Red Room of the White House 32
religion, freedom of 26–28
Remini, Robert 37
Renwick, James 142, 241
Renwick Gallery 141–43, 241
Reynolds, Maria 204
Rhode Island 113
Rhodes Tavern *see* Bank of the Metropolis
Richardson, Henry Hobson 59
Ricks, Mary Kay 23
Riggs, George Washington 142
Rives, Cabell 187–88
Robinson, George 4
Rochambeau, Comte de 11, 111, 114–115
Rochambeau, Vicomte 113–115
Rochambeau statue 111, 202
Rodgers, John 3, 85, 91, 104
Rogers, Isiah 127
"room where it happened" 199
Roosevelt, Eleanor 157, 164–65, 244
Roosevelt, Franklin 42, 157, 164–65, 174
Roosevelt, Theodore 57, 111, 117, 174
Ross, General Robert 42, 151, 199, 215–16, 218–20

Royall, Anne 178
Russell, Rosalind ***147***

Saint-Gaudens, Augustus 60, 78
St. John's Church 48
St. Patrick's Church (D.C.) 161, 162, 163
St. Regis Washington hotel 68
San Francisco Mint 128
Sayres, Edward 22
Schultz, Nancy Lusignan 163
Scott, Dred 229
Scott, Lieutenant James 42
Scott, Winfield 120, 124
seances 30–33
Secret Service 18, 117–119
Secretary of War Suite 131
segregation 156, 157
Selig, Robert A. 113
Seneca quarry 131, 241
Seneca Sandstone Company 241, 242
separation of church and state 28
September 11 218
Seward, Augustus 4
Seward, Frances "Fanny" 4, 5
Seward, Frederick 4
Seward, William 3–6, 104, 109, 138, 196, 218, 229
Seward, William, Jr. 4
Seymour, Horatio 224
Shepherd, Alexander Robey "Boss" 213, 241–42
Sheridan, Philip 138
Sherman, Elizabeth "Lizzy" 66
Sherman, John 66, 231, 241
Sherman, William Tecumseh 63, 137, 140–41, 228, 241
Shuberts family 243–4
Shurz, Carl 222
Sickles, Daniel ***104***, 204; Gettysburg, Battle of 105–106; killing of Key II, Philip Barton 103–105
Sickles, Teresa Bagioli 103–106, 204
Sioussat, Pierre 40–41
Slack, John 63
slavery 7–9, 10, 64, 88, 91, 122–23, 186, 201, 207; Dupuy, Charlotte 98–102; *Pearl* slave escape 21–25
Slidell, John 58, 59
Smith, Gerrit 22
Smith, Jim 41
Smith, Margaret Bayard 19
Smith, Mildred 114
Smithsonian Castle 241
Smithsonian Institution 27, 31
Smithsonian magazine 27
Snowden, Edward 148
South Lawn of the White House 43
Spanish-American War 57, 111
Sperry, Anson 242
Sprague, William IV ***223***, 224–26
Sprague, William "Willie" V 224, 226
Stansbury, Tobias 150
Stanton, Charles 198
Stanton, Edwin 96, 105, 137, 138, 139, 229
State, War, and Navy Department Building 68, 112, 127–128, ***129***, 130–33, 144, 149, 164–65, 202–203
Statue of Freedom ***136***
Stevens, Thaddeus 224
Stimson, Henry 146, 167
Stockton, Robert 91–92, ***185***; USS *Princeton* 186–87, 189
Story, Joseph 18
Stowe, Harriet Beecher 24
Stuart, Gilbert ***41***

suffrage 49–50
Sumner, Charles 229, 239
Supreme Court 70, 140, 157, 218
Surratt, Mary 5, 212, 229
Suter, Barbara 215–16, 220
Suter's Tavern 215, 220
Sweeney, Sarah 199, 219–21
Sykes, George 186

Taft, William Howard 111, 117, 133
Tammany Hall 224
Taney, Roger 103
Tanner, Alethia Browning 7–9
tar and feathering **234**
"Tariff of Abominations" 56
tariffs 56, 203, 233
taxes 56, 200, 203
Taylor, Zachary 120, 175
Tejon Ranch 96
temperance statue *213*, 214
temporary insanity plea 105
"Tempos" 164–168
Tennessee militia 37, 38
terrorism 180–182
Texas 123, 186
Thornton, William 83, 216–17
Tiber Creek 169, 177
Tilden, Samuel 224, 227–28, 230–31
Timberlake, John 53
Tingey, Thomas 86, 218
Toronto, burning 42
Torresola, Griselio 118–119
Treasury Building 199–200, 216
Treasury Department 127–128, 233, 242
Treaty of Ghent 39
Tripoli 80–82
Trollope, Anthony 229
Truman, Harry 117, *118*, 119, 127, 132, 158, 244; assassination attempt 117–119
Truman, Margaret 117
Trump Administration 203
Turn television series 206
Twain, Mark 132, 134
Tyler, John 112, 184–89
Tyler, John, Jr. 184

Uncle Tom's Cabin 24
Upshur, Abel 186, 187, 188
USS *United States* 82–83]
U.S. Geological Survey 64
U.S. Trade Representative 203

Valley Forge 74–75, 77, 205
Van Buren, Martin 28, 54–55, 91, 100, 101
Van Deman, Ralph 144
Van Ness, John Peter 173–75, 220
Van Ness, Marcia Burnes *173*, 174–75
Van Ness mansion 174
Van Ness mausoleum 175
Virginians 113, 125
von Ezdorf, Richard 129
von Steuben, Baron 73, **74**, 79, 205–6; personal life and alleged scandal 75–78; statue 78, 205–6; Valley Forge 74–75

Walker, Benjamin 77, 78
Wallace, Lewis 153
Walter, Thomas 128, 135

Ward, Samuel Cutler 196
War of 1812 52, 82–83, 112, 149–151, 200, 203, 206, 216–17, 236; New Orleans, Battle of 35–39; Suter, Barbara 215–216; Sweeney, Sarah 218–21; White House, burning of 40–43
Warrington, Camilla 113–114, 115
Warrington, Lewis 112–114, **115**
Warrington, Rachel 113–115
Washington, Booker T. 230, 231
Washington, George 10, 12, 13, 15, 48, 50, 73–74, 76, 111, 113, 125, 171–73, 200, 201, 204, 206, 215, 228; Burnes, David 169–173; portrait 41; Whiskey Rebellion 233–36
Washington, Martha Custis 113, 121, 170, 241
Washington, Walter 180, 182
Washington Aqueduct 134–35
Washington Canal 160, 175, 210, 213
Washington, D.C., founding 169–173
Washington Monument 68, 128, 164, 165, **166**, 172, 199
Washington Navy Conference 146
Washington Navy Yard 188, 218
Washington Riot of 1848 23
Washington's Spies 206
Waters, Major 217
Wayne, Henry 93–94
Webster, Daniel 15, 21–22, 24, 89, 142, 229
Weehawken 85
West Point 121, 134, 141, 206
Western Union 146
Whig Party 99
Whiskey Rebellion 121, 200, 233–36
Whiskey Ring 131
White, Stanford 60
White House 8, 26, 28, 32–34, 43, 129, 202, 216; burning 40–43, 216
White House Historical Association 97, 244
White House wharf 174
Whitney, Helen Hay 65
Wickliffe, Charles 186, 187
Wilhelm, Kaiser II 144
Wilkes, Charles 59, 62
Wilkins, William 186, 187
Wilkinson, James 203
Willard Hotel 165, 184, 191, **192**, 193, 194–195, 196
Williams, Maurice 180
Wilson, Henry 69
Wilson, Woodrow 144, 164–65, 200
Winder, John Henry 151, 153
Winder, Richard B. 152
Winder, W. Sidney 152
Winder, William H. 149, 150–51, 153
Winder Building 137, 149, 203
Wirz, Henry **152**, 153
Witzke, Lothar 145
World War I 144–45, 164–65
World War II 165–67, 244
Wormley, James 228–32
Wormley, Lynch 228
Wormley, Ralph V 230
Wormley Conference of 1877 227, 230, 231, 232
Wormley Hotel 227, 230, 231
Wormley School 232
WTOP 181

Yardley, Herbert 144–148
Yorktown 11, 111
Young, Notley 170

Zimmermann Telegram 145

www.ingramcontent.com/pod-product-compliance
Ingram Content Group UK Ltd.
Pitfield, Milton Keynes, MK11 3LW, UK
UKHW050536150426
5217IPUK00026B/1962